Praise for *Business Modeling*

"This book is that rare combination of clear, informative and usable knowledge packaged within an extremely amusing and readable text. The authors have created a work that makes modeling accessible and understandable to the beginner while engaging and expanding the insights of even the seasoned practitioner. I predict that it will be a great success and I look forward to purchasing the book for my own library and recommending it to my colleagues, as soon as it hits the stands."

— **Dr. Susan E. Martin**, Senior Technology Strategist

"Business modeling is the key to unraveling the interdependencies of complex problems and generating the understanding needed to design and sell effective systems. Bridgeland and Zahavi have written a primer on business modeling that should be required reading for business developers, operations managers, and engineers in the systems integration business. They not only make business modeling understandable and practical, but interesting and engaging."

— **Brian C. Seagrave**, Vice President of Homeland Security, Raytheon Company

"I will use this book in my advanced integration classes in the Information Sciences and Technology degree program. I've used various books, but I think this is the best one I've reviewed to date."

— **Bill Cantor**, P.E., Instructor, Information Sciences and Technology, The Pennsylvania State University, York Campus

"Bridgeland and Zahavi bring into focus the necessity of models for coping with complexity and supporting collaboration in the design and management of today's enterprises. In addition, they provide organizational techniques, insights into human factors and illustrative examples to describe how to use models for timely and effective analysis, planning and decision-making."

— **Fred Cummins**, EDS Fellow

"This book is well written and will be of great interest to the business community. The authors have taken complex material and simplified it. This makes it possible to reach a far greater number of readers from a variety of disciplines."

— **Dr. Randy Gimblett**, Chair, Landscape Assessment and Analysis Program & Professor School of Natural Resources, The University of Arizona

"I can tell you that I will not only recommend this book to my colleagues and staff, but also my bosses and business constituents. I will purchase this book for others, and use it to develop various aspects of my professional engagements - absolutely."

— **George Thomas**, Enterprise Chief Architect, Office of the Chief Information Officer, General Services Administration

Morgan Kaufmann OMG Press

Morgan Kaufmann Publishers and the Object Management Group™ (OMG) have joined forces to publish a line of books addressing business and technical topics related to OMG's large suite of software standards.

OMG is an international, open membership, not-for-profit computer industry consortium that was founded in 1989. The OMG creates standards for software used in government and corporate environments to enable interoperability and to forge common development environments that encourage the adoption and evolution of new technology. OMG members and its board of directors consist of representatives from a majority of the organizations that shape enterprise and Internet computing today.

OMG's modeling standards, including the Unified Modeling Language™ (UML®) and Model Driven Architecture® (MDA), enable powerful visual design, execution and maintenance of software, and other processes—for example, IT Systems Modeling and Business Process Management. The middleware standards and profiles of the Object Management Group are based on the Common Object Request Broker Architecture® (CORBA) and support a wide variety of industries.

More information about OMG can be found at *http://www.omg.org/*.

Morgan Kaufmann OMG Press Titles

Database Archiving: How to Keep Lots of Data for a Very Long Time
Jack Olson

Master Data Management
David Loshin

Building the Agile Enterprise: With SOA, BPM and MBM
Fred Cummins

Business Modeling: A Practical Guide to Realizing Business Value
David M. Bridgeland and Ron Zahavi

A Practical Guide SysML: The Systems Model Language
Sanford Friedenthal, Alan Moore, Rick Steiner

Systems Engineering with SysML/UML: Modeling, Analysis, Design
Tim Weilkiens

UML 2 Certification Guide: Fundamental and Intermediate Exams
Tim Weilkiens and Bernd Oestereich

Real-Life MDA: Solving Business Problems with Model Driven Architecture
Michael Guttman and John Parodi

Business Modeling
A Practical Guide to
Realizing Business Value

David M. Bridgeland

Ron Zahavi

ELSEVIER

AMSTERDAM • BOSTON • HEIDELBERG • LONDON
NEW YORK • OXFORD • PARIS • SAN DIEGO
SAN FRANCISCO • SINGAPORE • SYDNEY • TOKYO
Morgan Kaufmann Publishers is an imprint of Elsevier

MORGAN KAUFMANN

Morgan Kaufmann Publishers is an imprint of Elsevier
30 Corporate Drive, Suite 400, Burlington, MA 01803, USA

Library of Congress Cataloging-in-Publication Data
Application submitted.

ISBN: 978-0-12-374151-6

For information on all Morgan Kaufmann publications,
visit our website at: *www.mkp.com* or *www.books.elsevier.com*

Printed in the United States of America
08   09   10   11   12   13   5   4   3   2   1

To my daughters: Miranda, Isabel, and Alexandra.
—David Bridgeland

To my mother, Dahlia Zahavi, and to the memory of my father, Dr. Yacov Zahavi.
—Ron Zahavi

Contents

Preface

This book is about *business models*. What is a business model? A *business model* is a model of a business—a simple representation of the complex reality of a particular organization. Business models are useful for understanding how a business is organized, who interacts with whom, what goals and strategies are being pursued, what work the business performs, and how it performs that work. We create business models to realize these understandings. We also create business models to communicate these understanding to others. Business models are often graphical, making the communication easier and more natural.

This book is also about *business modeling*—about how to create a business model that represents the reality of a business. We explain how to create business models that are useful for solving problems, for helping organizations transform, for convincing customers to purchase, and for communicating aspects of a business to others.

Business modeling is sometimes confused with software modeling. Software engineers create models of the systems they build—models of software components and the ways those components interact and communicate over time. Software models are different from business models because they are models of different things. A *software model* is a model of software—applications and databases and other information technology artifacts. A business model is a model of a business, a model of what people do and how they interact. Different techniques are used for software modeling and business modeling. Different modeling elements are appropriate. Different tools are needed.

Yet the confusion between business modeling and software modeling is understandable. Business modeling and software modeling are related activities; both are modeling. Both aspire to capture the essence of a messy complex thing—either a business or an application—in a simple rigorous model. Furthermore, we have found that many of the best business modelers come from software engineering, computer science, or other related disciplines. People who create software models sometimes cross over to business modeling. There is a technical rigor involved in business modeling that is comfortable to people with software engineering and other similar backgrounds.

Business modeling has become more popular in recent years. With the popularity has come a wide variance in the quality and usefulness of the models that are created. In our day-to-day work with business modeling, we see a lot of models. Some are good, but many are bad. Most business models simply do not achieve their intended results.

The problem is that just like any other specialization, business modeling is a complex skill. Many people expect that they can create a good business model the first time they try, the first day a business modeling application is installed on their computer. It does not work that way, any more than someone can learn to manage a profit center in one day or learn to create a marketing program for a new product in one day. Creating a good business model is a complex skill, and like any complex skill, it requires time, knowledge, practice, and patience to learn.

One of the reasons business modeling is complex is that there are four distinct business modeling disciplines. *Business process models*—the most well-understood of the four disciplines—capture how a business performs its work, the step-by-step activities that are performed. *Business motivation models* capture the goals and strategies of a business—what a business is attempting to do and how those attempts fit into its changing environment. *Business organization models* capture who performs the work in an organization and who they interact with, both inside the organization and outside. And *business rule models* capture the constraints on a business—the external constraints from regulations and laws, and the internal constraints from policies, rules, and other guidance.

Surprisingly few business modeling practitioners today know all four disciplines. Some people create business process models and ignore the relationship of processes to strategies and other motivations. Other people create motivation models but ignore how those strategies are implemented in processes and policies.

This book is intended as a guide for practical business modeling. We explain what business modeling is, what the business modeling disciplines are, how to create good business models, and how to apply models once they are built.

Good business models often include more than one of the four modeling disciplines. A business process is useful, but it is more useful when accompanied by details about the goals of the business, the organizations that participate in the process, and the rules and policies that guide the process. To be more effective, business modelers need to understand all four disciplines. They need to create models that include multiple disciplines. This book describes all four disciplines.

Standards are important in business modeling. A model created by one group of people should be understandable by others. Others should be able to update the model when business circumstances change. Models created in one modeling tool should be readable and changeable by other tools. All this happens only when standards are used. The models in this book use standards where the relevant standards exist. We also describe the state of the standardization efforts for each of the four disciplines.

Our outline for the book is focused from beginning to end on practicality. We begin with why you would want to create a business model. Next we describe the four modeling disciplines. Then we focus on practical concerns that cross all four disciplines: best practices for creating models and working with subject matter experts. We end with a discussion of the way that business models can be analyzed, simulated, and deployed.

Chapters 1 and 2 focus on the "why" and "what" of business modeling. Chapter 1 focuses on the first challenge business modelers face: explaining to others why business modeling is important and justifying it. In this chapter we explain what a business model is, the state of business modeling, and the various uses for business modeling. In Chapter 2 we explain some modeling fundamentals and introduce the four business modeling disciplines. We also cover the state of standards and tools.

Chapters 3, 4, 5, and 6 explain the four disciplines. Each chapter covers one discipline, detailing what the discipline is, how it is used, what standards are applicable, and how it relates to the other models in the other disciplines. These chapters cover the most important elements of these models, the ones we find most useful in day-to-day business modeling. We provide many examples of models within each discipline.

Then we shift to the creation of models and modeling pragmatics. Chapters 7, 8, and 9 provide advice on how to create good models and the best methods to use. Chapter 7 describes some best practices and common mistakes to avoid. Chapters 8 and 9 explain model-based workshops, the most practical method of creating models with subject matter experts. Chapter 8 describes what a model-based workshop is and some common variations on the model-based workshop theme. Chapter 9 explains how to run a model-based workshop.

We conclude the book by examining the results of a model once it is built, describing how to analyze a model, how to simulate one, and how to deploy one. Chapter 10 explains how to analyze a model and covers several different methods of analysis. Chapter 11 describes model simulations. Chapter 12 covers the deployment of business models to help run a business.

Throughout the book we present real case studies based on our own business experiences. These case studies illustrate how we have used business modeling to achieve business goals. In addition to the case studies, this book has many example models that we created to illustrate the various model elements. Many of these examples concern Mykonos Dining Corporation, a Chicago-based company that owns and runs over 100 high-end restaurants throughout the United States. Mykonos is of course fictional; no such company exists. But it is convenient both for us and for you to have a single running illustration, so we don't have to explain the background behind an automotive example in one chapter, an insurance example in another chapter, and so on. Since all of us have some experience with good restaurants, we hope you find the Mykonos examples natural and intuitive. And if, like many people, you have fantasized about opening your own restaurant, we encourage you to indulge that fantasy as you learn about business modeling.

Acknowledgments

Writing this book took a long time and required much effort. We could not have done it without the help and support of our family, friends, and colleagues. First we must recognize the patient understanding and support from our wives, Rose Ijaz and Susan Zahavi, and from our children, Miranda, Isabel, and Alexandra Bridgeland and David, Claire, and Benjamin Zahavi.

Many people reviewed this book in various stages of disorder. Jacques Rollet, Ben Corlett, Paul Harmon, Marshall Bigelow, Patrick McGovern, Don Baisley, Randy Gimblett, Susan Martin, Donald Chapin, Laura McQuade, and Al Carvalho all provided comments and insights on individual chapters. These comments and insights improved both the ideas and their exposition. George Townshend, George Thomas, and Bill Cantor read the book in its entirety and provided a wealth of thoughtful suggestions and improvements. John Butler, Ralph Welborn, Vince Kasten, Derek Miers, and Alan Leong helped us early on with the concept for the book.

Over the years we have modeled many businesses with many colleagues. These collaborative experiences influenced the approaches and techniques described here. We would like to thank Ralph Welborn, Vince Kasten, Brian Seagrave, John Butler, Jeff Pappin, Peter Bricknell, ToniAnn Thomas, Jeff Silver, Fred Dillman, Venkatapathi Puvvada, Steve Vinsik, Tom Conaway, Mike Glaser, Ken Hickok, Varun Panchapakesan, Hari Chaturvedi, Doug Humphreys, Cathy vonUnwerth, Vadim Pevzner, Vitaly Khusidman, Marc Shapiro, Ashima Munjal, Turab Mehdi, Imrana Umar, Senthil Natchimuthu, Forrest Snowden, Brian Otis, Nadine Carroll, Sonu Aggarwal, Sandy Snyder, Isaac Levy, Stephen A. White, Dorothy Yu, Henrik Sandell, Ron Strout, Andy Hoskinson, Neelam Kadam, Walcelio Melo, Michael Bean, Will Glass, and Helen Ojha.

We want to acknowledge the generous support from industry vendors Powersim Corporation, Powersim Solutions, Forio, Mega International, Artisan Software, KnowGravity, and KAISHA-Tec. And we must acknowledge the help of Terry Otsubo and Bill Bridgeland in providing a bit of realism around the restaurant business examples.

We would also like to thank Bob Costello, Kimberly Schwartz, Pat Morrin, Diane Moura, Naren Patel, Laura McQuade, Michael Hunt, Peter Archer, Brian Goebel, and Josh Kussman, who worked with us on some of the case studies described throughout the book.

We would like to thank our publisher, Morgan Kaufmann, and the Object Management Group, in particular Richard Soley, Denise Penrose, and Mary James.

About the Authors

David M. Bridgeland is chief business architect at Unisys Corporation. He has performed business modeling for more than 20 years, creating models for many clients, including Charles Schwab, AT&T, UBS, Sony, Chevron, and New York State. Prior to Unisys, he held consulting positions at KPMG and at Coopers & Lybrand Consulting as well as executive positions at two venture-backed startups, including Powersim Corporation, a vendor of business modeling tools. Currently he focuses on applying business modeling to large sales opportunities. Dave holds a BA in computer science from the University of Michigan and an MA in computer science from the University of Texas at Austin. He lives in suburban Washington, DC.

Ron Zahavi is chief business architect at Unisys Corporation. He has over 25 years of experience in all aspects of technology management and solution delivery. Prior to joining Unisys, Ron held positions as CTO and CIO, managing technology across several companies and performing due diligence of potential acquisitions. His breadth of experience includes work with startups, large companies, the commercial and public sectors, federal government, and private equity firms. Ron has served on the OMG Architecture Board, is a member of the BPM Think Tank program committee, and is a member of several regional and national CIO and CTO councils. He is author of *Enterprise Application Integration with CORBA* and co-authored the bestseller *The Essential CORBA*. Ron holds a BSEE from the University of Maryland and an MS in computer science from Johns Hopkins University.

Why Business Modeling?

1

A business model is a simple representation of the complex reality of a business. The primary purpose of a business model is to communicate something about the business to other people: employees, customers, partners, or suppliers. This chapter answers the two questions modelers face most often: what is a business model and why create one?

What is a model? A model is a simple representation of a complex reality that serves a particular purpose. We use many models in our day-to-day life: street maps, television schedules, 12-step programs, and furniture assembly instructions. We use models all the time without thinking about them.

Consider an example. You and a colleague fly to Washington, DC, to visit a restaurant. You aren't there to eat; instead your employer is considering buying the restaurant—and the four others owned by the same company, Cora Group—and your job is to evaluate the place and offer a recommendation. The restaurant is called Portia, and it is downtown. Since neither you nor your colleague know Washington, you pick up a map as you rent your car. As your colleague drives, you interpret the map and guide her, telling her when to exit the highway and where to turn on the streets and thoroughfares.

Your map is a model. It is a simple representation of the complex reality of the city. It omits the smaller roads, the sidewalks and bike paths, the streams and electrical lines, the houses and shopping malls, the gas stations and office towers. It has just the few things you need to find your destination: the highways and major streets.

This model is built for a purpose: to find a destination while driving. If you were bicycling, you would use a different map, a model that showed the bike paths and bicycle-friendly streets. You would use a different map if you were taking mass transit, one that showed the train stations and bus routes. And if you were digging up the street to lay fiber optic cable, you would carry yet a different map, a model with the locations of the gas and power lines, existing communication cables, water and sewer pipes, and everything else you might find underground. For the same territory, different purposes require different models.

Perhaps your rental car includes a navigation system. Inside the navigation system is the same kind of model of the city's road network, functionally similar to the printed street map. But instead of you reading the model and deciding where to go, the software interprets the model as your colleague drives, telling her when to turn right and how far you are from your destination. Models can be interpreted by people or they can be interpreted by software. Often a single model is built for interpretation by both people and software.

Just as a street map is a model of the far more complex reality of a city, a business model is a simple representation of the always far more complex business. A *business process model* is a business model, showing who does what work and in what sequence. *A business organization model* is a business model, showing how different people and organizations interact with each other.

The art of building these business models is called *business modeling*. This book is about that art, about how to create business models and how to solve problems using business models.

But first we must disambiguate. Sometimes when people talk about the business model of an enterprise, they are talking about something different from what we mean in this book. When they say "business model" they mean what the business sells. For example, "the business model of Google is selling advertising" means that Google makes its money by selling ads, not by selling automobiles or long distance telephony.

We mean something different. In this book the term "business model" is not just shorthand for what a company sells. Instead when we say "business model" we mean a model that describes the details of a business: its goals, organizations, business processes, or business rules.

THE RISE OF BUSINESS MODELING

Engineers use engineering models and have done so for many years. Every bridge, car, aircraft, and integrated circuit is created using models. Models are created to communicate with customers, to show how the product will look. Models are used to communicate with the engineer's managers to illustrate issues that need management attention. Models are used to communicate between engineers with different responsibilities—for example, to plan how the electronics in an aircraft are to be powered. In engineering, models are ubiquitous.

Software engineering is a newer engineering discipline, and the use of modeling in software is more recent. Starting in the 1980s, some visionaries realized the value of software modeling. Many different modeling languages and methods were developed. Some of these languages and methods had followings, but none had mass usage. In the 1990s market demand increased, and Rational Software

Corporation initiated the development of the *Unified Modeling Language* (UML), an attempt to unify the various modeling languages and methods. In 1997, Object Management Group adopted UML as a standard. UML is now widely used to design applications and systems. The use of UML is a mainstream practice for software engineers today.

Historically, business modeling has seen much more limited use. Of course, organizational charts and accounting models have been used since antiquity, but other than these two exceptions, business modeling has been rare until recent years. Until recently, businesspeople communicated using words, spreadsheets, and presentations, not business models.

Now this is changing. Businesspeople are increasingly using models to communicate. Over the last fifteen years, increasing numbers of people have built business models: models of the business processes of their organization, the goals and strategies, or the policies and rules.

We are seeing a progression from proprietary models and tools to new standards, the same kind of progression that occurred in software modeling in the 1990s. Business modeling is still a niche, but it is growing rapidly. In ten years, we expect business modeling to be mainstream, to be the natural and ordinary way for businesspeople to communicate, much as software modeling is mainstream today for software engineers.

How does a technology such as business modeling become mainstream? What steps does it go through on its path to widespread use? Geoffrey Moore [Moore 1991] describes a technology adoption lifecycle, a depiction of how technologies progress from their inception to wide adoption and use. The technology adoption lifecycle describes who adopts a new technology as the technology develops. Initially a new technology is promising but rough around the edges. It is only adopted by innovators—people who experiment with new technologies, shape them, and improve them. As the technology improves, it is adopted by early adopters, who use a new technology to achieve a competitive advantage before the technology is solid or complete. Once a technology is mature enough, it is adopted by the early majority, a large group of people who welcome new technology once it is mature. After the early majority comes the late majority, who will only use a technology after it is widely adopted by others. Finally there are the laggards who are skeptical and only adopt a technology when they feel the large costs of being left behind.

The technology adoption lifecycle is a good framework for understanding the rise of business modeling, just as it was a good framework for the rise of software modeling in the 1990s. As shown in Figure 1.1, software modeling has penetrated much of the market now and is well into the early majority stage. The market penetration of business modeling is still early. Business modeling will go from a rapidly growing niche activity to a rapidly growing mainstream activity.

What's driving the growth of business modeling? Why is it changing from a small niche activity into an increasingly mainstream technology? There are several

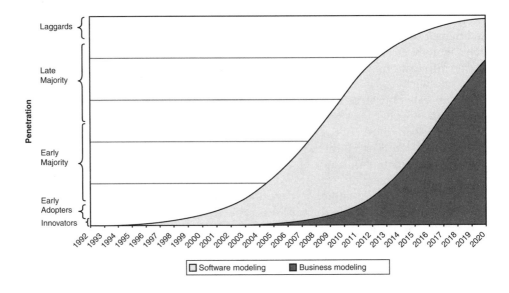

FIGURE 1.1 The rise of software modeling and business modeling

drivers for the growth of business modeling. One driver is the changing economics of corporate information technology. As information technology (IT) budgets decline, IT organizations are using business models to align IT initiatives with business needs.

BUSINESS MODELING AND IT ALIGNMENT

In the late 1990s money flowed freely to corporate IT organizations. Companies raced to develop new applications, to integrate their existing applications and make them available on the Web, and to prepare their legacy applications against the risks of Y2K.[1] Businesses competed in terms of how much they spent for IT, believing that every dollar spent would lead to competitive advantage and increased productivity. Wall Street analysts cheered them on, reporting the latest IT progress of the companies they covered.

Those days of exuberance have long passed. Since 2000, IT organizations have suffered declining budgets. Businesses now compete in terms of how little they

---

[1]Y2K was the effort to correct software problems with date calculations beyond December 31, 1999.

spend for IT, preferring to direct their dollars other purposes: new business development, acquisitions, or stock dividends. Every IT expenditure must be carefully justified with the business benefit created by the expenditure.

Since 2001, we have helped corporate IT organizations use business modeling as a way to justify their IT expenditures. Using business models, they have connected the details of their desired IT spending with their business goals, business processes, and business rules. They have used business models to communicate the value of their IT plans. They have used business models to ensure alignment of those plans with their business needs.

BUSINESS MODELING AND BUSINESS TRANSFORMATION

Outside the cubicle farms of IT is the larger business that IT supports. During the last ten years, businessees have employed business modeling independent of the IT organization, for their own reasons. One reason is business transformation. Business transformations have become more common since 1995. Business models make those business transformations easier to manage.

Forty years ago, most businesses changed slowly. Martin Mayer [Mayer 1997] tells a story from the early 1970s of a retiring banker who was asked to name the most important business change he had seen in his career. His answer? Air conditioning. From today's perspective, this story seems quaint, a picture of another, simpler (albeit sweatier) time.

Today, business transformations are common. Business transformations include changes of control: mergers, acquisitions, divestitures, and leveraged buyouts. Business transformations include changes of sourcing: outsourcing, offshoring, and many varieties of corporate teaming. Business transformations include changes in strategy and business process. And many businesses reorganize their reporting relationships and organizational responsibilities once or twice each year.

Business transformations are notoriously hard to manage. As a result, many transformations fail. For example, several banks merge, but many mistakes are made in the merger integration. Even years later the resulting bank is not a seamless whole but a motley collection of organizations glued together from the original legacy banks. As another example, a consumer product company offshores its customer support process to save money but suffers quality problems in the transition and alienates some customers. As a third example, an energy services company implements a software package, but the employees reject the new business process that the software package supports, trying to use their existing process with the new software. (This last example is explored in a case study at the end of this chapter.)

Business transformations are difficult because they always involve people. Technology challenges are easy compared to people challenges: ensuring that employees are ready for the change, that they understand what it means to them, and that they accept it. Most failed transformation projects fail for people reasons rather than for technology reasons.

Business modeling helps business transformations succeed. Why modeling? Models help with the implementation of change. If nothing changes, you don't need models, just as you don't need a street map if you never travel anywhere. If nothing changes, everyone in the organization already understands the organization's goals and strategies because they have been elaborated endlessly by senior management year after year. Everyone already understands the business processes because they have worked within these processes for years. Everyone already knows the policies because everyone remembers when each policy was violated, who violated it, and the consequences of the violation.

But when things are changing, business models are useful. With a model, an employee can see the rest of the larger process in which he plays a small part, the rest of the process that he was only dimly aware of and that he now needs to understand well. With a model, he can understand the new business processes he will use. He can understand the new business rules he will follow. He can understand the new goals and strategies. Models help an organization move from today's world to a future world, to implement a transformation. Business modeling has become more popular because business transformations have become more common.

BUSINESS MODELING AND MANAGING CHANGE

Business transformations are under your organization's control. You decide to make a change in the organization structure or in a business process or in the partners you work with. You decide when to change and how. You are in control.

But change also happens due to external reasons, circumstances outside your control, in situations when you are not transforming yourself. For example, a key supplier is purchased by a competitor and you must react. A new technology threatens to displace one of your key products, and you must do something. Washington, DC, introduces tough smoking regulations, and Cora Group—the restaurant company we introduced at the beginning of the chapter—must adapt. Every day you must manage change, even when you do not intend to transform your business.

Ad hoc changes are rarely managed well. Things happen and people react as best as they can under the constraints of budget and time. Change is difficult.

Change would be easier if each change was finished before the next one started. But that kind of clean separation of changes never happens. Organizations are always dealing with many changes, all at once, in different stages of adaptation. Usually organizations struggle with these multiple simultaneous changes. For example, your company—Mykonos Dining Corporation—is considering the acquisition of the Cora Group. This acquisition is a big change for Portia and the other Cora restaurants. It will also change some things at Mykonos. There are new Cora Group employees to interact with and a different corporate culture. In addition, both Cora Group and Mykonos are already dealing with other changes within their own organizations. Cora Group is adapting to the recent ban on smoking in Washington. Mykonos is digesting other acquisitions and understanding how to react to changing customer demand.

Today change is mostly managed in isolation. A single change is applied independently to every organization within the business. Each organization handles the change within its own structure and applies the change to its own processes. Little coordination is performed across the business or with business partners.

Business models are useful for managing change. Some business models help us understand the motivation and reason for the change. A business model can explain to Cora Group why Mykonos is interested in the acquisition. To a Cora Group employee, the Mykonos motivation matters. Is Cora Group being acquired to increase revenue? To expand into a new market? As a defensive move to respond to a competitive pressure by another company? To open one of the Cora Group's unique restaurants in another city? A model helps make the acquisition successful by ensuring everyone has the same understanding, and by dispelling myths and misinformation.

Business models also help us see the changes that result from the change. What will the new reporting structure be? Will Cora Group be completely consumed or will it maintain its own reporting under Mykonos? Where will new restaurants be opened and who will be responsible for them?

With a business model, we can see how the goals will be met. For example, today Cora Group outsources its human resources function to a third-party restaurant HR company. With a business model, we can see how a centralized Mykonos human resources function will operate and support the restaurant staff.

Business models also show what is affected by a change: what processes change and which roles change. Employees in both Cora Group and Mykonos can compare how they perform work today against how they will perform that work in the future, to better understand how their everyday lives will change.

Models are maintainable, making them a natural tool for managing change. Static artifacts such as PowerPoint™ presentations and Word™ documents have a short shelf life; they become out-of-date quickly. Modifying a static document with each change takes time and effort. Models are easier to keep up-to-date within a modeling tool because a single model change updates many diagrams at once. Models also support change because they support analysis techniques that show the consequence of a change. Chapter 10 describes model analysis.

BUSINESS MODELING AND MANAGING COMPLEXITY

Business transformation and managing change are two important drivers of the increasing interest in business modeling in recent years. But there's another important driver: the need to manage increasing complexity. Businesses have become more complex. Twenty years ago, businesses were easier to understand. There were fewer business processes, fewer products and services, less data stored in databases, fewer business partners, and fewer lines of business. Now things are more complex. There are more of everything: more business processes, more products and services, more data, more partners, and more lines of business. Businesses require multiple specialists—subject matter experts in different domains—to understand all aspects of their work.

Complexity is the key problem in business today. Decisions are harder now because there is more to consider. A company might not understand how its business partner accomplishes its work internally. This lack of understanding can cause poor decisions for the supply chain as a whole.

For example, when a medication is prescribed to a patient, four trading partners are involved. A pharmaceutical manufacturer (e.g., Merck, Pfizer) actually makes the medications. A health care provider (e.g., the Cleveland Clinic) purchases medications on behalf of its patients. A distributor (e.g., Cardinal Health, Amerisource-Bergen) purchases the medications and sells them to the providers. A group purchasing organization (e.g., Novation, Premier) negotiates prices on behalf of the providers for the medications it purchases. So when a physician at the Cleveland Clinic prescribes Singulair—a Merck medication for treating asthma—to a patient, the Cleveland Clinic has purchased Singulair through a distributor. The purchase is based on a contract between the Cleveland Clinic and Merck negotiated by a group purchasing organization, a GPO. GPOs represent hospitals and other healthcare organizations, pooling their purchases for improved pricing. The price negotiated applies to that medication only on the specific contract. Other providers will pay different negotiated prices for Singular.

The distributor has purchased Singulair from Merck based on a single standard acquisition price. The providers are all eligible for different prices based on the contracts they have. The distributor must understand the different prices each provider will back for each medication, to apply the right discounts. For example, when the distributor provides Singulair to the Cleveland Clinic, the hospital will claim it is eligible for its discounted price. The distributor then applies to Merck for a "chargeback" fee, the difference between its acquisition price and the hospital's discount.

So what happens when Merck changes prices for its medications? To Merck, this might seem like a simple internal decision, a new price for one of its products. But to the distributor, this simple price change can be difficult to implement. The distributor must figure out how the price change affects the contract (negotiated by the GPO) between the Cleveland Clinic and Merck. If the distributor makes a mistake and provides the medication to Cleveland Clinic at the wrong price, the distributor might later lose money because their chargeback is rejected.

The price change is made more complex by the numbers the distributor faces. The Cleveland Clinic is only one hospital of the many on the same contract and only one contract out of thousands that the distributor tracks.

And the problem is not just with pricing. The Cleveland Clinic may become ineligible on a contract, perhaps because it changed its group purchasing organization affiliation. Instead of one GPO, it negotiates a deal with another.

The distributor now charges the wrong price to the Cleveland Clinic until it becomes aware of the new affiliation.

Merck also adds new medications and discontinues existing medications. When the four trading partners have any differences in their understanding of medication, pricing, and eligibility, they have problems doing the right thing. A change by one trading partner impacts everyone else, in unforeseen ways.

The pharmaceutical supply chain is certainly complex, but we see similarly complex situations in other industries.

Why does complexity matter? In this pharmaceutical situation, there is a large cost incurred by all four trading partners to synchronize information and to repair information divergence. Each trading partner employs specialized departments whose sole job is to synchronize and repair. Across the United States, roughly $1 billion is spent each year in the pharmaceutical supply chain on information synchronization and repair.

Complexity is a driver of the rise of business modeling. With business modeling, each party can understand the impact of its decisions on its trading partners. With business modeling, each party can make less risky decisions. Today, no one understands the whole picture, and without understanding no one can make good decisions for the benefit of the whole. Instead people make decisions based on their own limited local understanding, without understanding the impact on others.

Dynamic Complexity and Detail Complexity

Peter Senge refers to the complexity that results from making local decisions as *dynamic complexity.* "When an action has one set of consequences locally and a very different set of consequences in another part of the system, there is dynamic complexity. When obvious interventions produce nonobvious consequences, there is dynamic complexity." [Senge 1990] Senge contrasts dynamic complexity with *detail complexity.* Senge's colleague John Sterman describes detail complexity as "the number of components in a system or the number of combinations one must consider in making a decision. . . . [The] complexity lies in finding the best solution out of an astronomical number of possibilities." [Sterman 2000]

Business models help manage detail complexity. Business models are simpler than the world they model. Only some of the detail complexity of the world is present in a model, a limited view of what is most important.

Even though they are simpler than the world they model, business models can still have a lot of detail, too much for anyone to understand all at once. Good business models are carefully designed to show only some of that detail in any one diagram, allowing you to explore the detail you want to consider now and ignore the rest, the detail that is not important for your current task.

A good business model supports different views of the same underlying knowledge. Each subject matter expert can see what they need to see, for their own purposes. Each can ignore the detail needed for other subject matter experts. For example, a strategist can look at an organization's goals, strategies, and tactics, ignoring the business processes and interactions. A sales specialist can examine the business processes supporting sales, ignoring the processes supporting operations and maintenance.

Business models also support dynamic complexity. They show the relationships between organizations, showing who interacts with whom and how they interact. The interactions expose the dependencies and show the impact of a change. Business models show the cause and effect relationships between organization's strategies and the influencers in the organization's environment, influencers such as competitor behaviors, customer purchases, and supplier innovations.

THE BUSINESS VALUE OF BUSINESS MODELS

Many people question the business value of business models. They ask why is it worth spending the time to create a model. This is a valid business question. As you build models, you will find that you often have to justify your modeling efforts with the economic value you expect to create.

Indeed, business modeling does take time, effort, and special skills. In our experience, business models create value, often significant value. They can more than earn their keep.

In our experience, business models generate value in eight ways. Business models support:

- *Communication* between people
- *Training and learning*
- *Persuasion and selling*
- *Analysis* of a business situation
- *Compliance management*
- *Development of software requirements*
- *Direct execution* in software engines
- *Knowledge management and reuse*

These eight ways of generating business value are not mutually exclusive. A single business model can be used for both communication and analysis, or for both compliance checking and for later knowledge management. Once built, a model provides many kinds of business value. We explore how to manage the value of a business model in Chapter 2, and we will return to these eight ways of generating value many times in the following chapters.

Communication

Business is a communication-intensive activity. Businesspeople give presentations about company performance. Businesspeople talk to their clients and their suppliers about new products and services. Business colleagues talk to each other about the changing competitive environment. Much of business is communication.

Some of that communication is complex. For example, business policies change. When a new policy is introduced, businesspeople discuss the dozens of business rules that need to be changed to implement the new policy.

Today most people use words, on-the-spot drawings, and PowerPoint presentations to communicate on these complex topics. These ad hoc solutions work, more or less, but they have some problems. Misunderstandings happen. People interpret the same words differently. People also interpret the same PowerPoint slides differently. Today, complex business communications leak knowledge. The words and ad hoc drawings fail to convey the rich content that is intended.

Business models are better for conveying complex business information. Business models don't replace the words or the presentations. Instead they compliment the communication by providing something rigorous and concrete to point to. The words and the slides are enhanced by the models.

Different people in a business need different detail. For example, when you return to your company—Mykonos Corp.—to report on your evaluation of Cora Group for acquisition, you will make several presentations. To Mykonos marketing, you will describe how well the Cora Group restaurants fit the Mykonos portfolio, whether they are similar enough to the restaurants you already own to fit the Mykonos brand and strategy. Marketing needs to understand the customers, locations, and competitors. To Mykonos operations, you will describe your assessment of how well the Cora restaurants are run. They need to understand the organization, processes, and policies. To the executive team, you will describe how the business is performing. They want to understand finances and strategy.

Business models support the presentation of different details to different audiences. To operations, you show a detailed model of the Cora business processes of procuring fresh fish. To marketing, a high-level model of the same process is sufficient, so they are aware of the commitment to fish freshness.

Business models are effective for communication because most models are visual. We humans are visual beings; we have sophisticated visual processing engines built into our brains. Most business models are shown as visual diagrams to take advantage of this visual processing. Diagrams make a model easier to understand and faster to communicate.

Business models facilitate a common understanding of a business situation. When two businesspeople create an on-the-spot drawing of a business process, they might think they agree on the process, but they can actually disagree because each interprets the drawing differently. Does Joe's diagram box mean the same thing as Sharon's? With a model, the modeling elements are rigorously defined. The same model means the same thing to anyone who sees it. (Or at least the modeling elements are intended to be rigorously defined, with the same meaning for everyone. In practice, the rigor is a matter of degree. But relying on business models certainly leads to much less accidental misunderstanding than relying on informal drawings.)

Why is rigor important? Communication is all about finding common ground. In some languages (e.g., Hebrew) the same word is used for hello and goodbye. The meaning is determined from the context. If you begin a telephone conversation with someone and you do not agree on the form of communication, when you say hello the other person might hang up. Modeling is similar. The model and its *semantics*—the meaning of each model element—is an agreement that allows for information to be conveyed in a consistent manner. As long as those who create the model and those who read it have the same understanding, the model can be interpreted to have the same meaning.

People with different backgrounds can use models to communicate, as long as they agree on the meaning of the modeling elements. Someone purchasing a home might not be skilled in reading the builder's plumbing or electrical diagrams. However, a floorplan can be used as a common model among the purchaser, the plumber, and the electrician. The floorplan is a baseline framework for common understanding. The floorplan includes modeling elements that are familiar to all: stairways, walls, closets, and doors.

Business models are used for communicating *project scope*. The scope of a project is its extent or range, what is included in the project, and, by implication, what is not included. Every project has a scope. Every corporate reorganization has a scope, as does every business process outsourcing, every application implementation, and every asset sale. When working on a project, businesspeople must communicate about the scope. Business models are useful for that communication. For example, a business process model can be used to communicate which processes are to be outsourced and which are not. As another example, an organization model can be used to communicate about who will use a new software application.

Business models are useful for communicating changes. For example, in your evaluation of the Cora Group for acquisition, you discover that the company outsources its human resource function to a specialized company that handles employee benefits, wages processing, hiring agreements, and the like. Your company, Mykonos, has a centralized HR function to provide HR in a consistent way across all restaurants. Instead of duplicating the HR functions, one centralized group handles everything. When you have acquired restaurants in the past, you have displaced internal HR personnel. For Cora Group, there is no one to displace; Cora Group has no internal HR today, so no existing HR employees are affected by the acquisition. But the HR processes will change for all Cora Group employees. There are processes for scheduling shifts, for hiring, and for payroll and benefits. If in fact you acquire Cora, you can use business models to explain the change to the Cora Group employees. You show simple, easy-to-understand models of how they will interact with HR and what they need to do.

Training and Learning

People learn in two ways. They learn from their own experience, via trial and error, and they learn from other people's experiences, via conversations, books, or classroom material. Learning from other people's experiences is of course cheaper, faster, and less risky. We allow others to make mistakes instead of making our own.

Business models are one way of learning from other people's experience. First, a model is built of the expert's knowledge of the business rules or the business process. Then many novices can study the model to learn what the expert knows.

Business models are surprisingly useful in training. Business models are rigorously defined, so all novices learning the model are more likely to learn the same thing. There are fewer differences in interpretation among the novices learning the modeled material.

There is another reason business models are useful in training situations. Business models communicate a different kind of knowledge, how-to knowledge that is hard to communicate in other ways. A business process model naturally communicates the task-by-task detail of how a job is performed.

Persuasion and Selling

In business, persuasion is ubiquitous. When we sell a customer on a product, we are persuading. When we pitch a new initiative to our management, we are persuading. When we convince employees to embrace a business process change, we are persuading. Persuasion is communication, of course, but it is communication in service of a goal: convincing someone to take action favorable to us, to our organization, or to themselves.

Business models are useful for persuasion. When you use a business model in a pitch, you look like an expert. You might actually be an expert in the topic and so deserve that recognition. Or perhaps the model was created by a colleague, and the model helps you convey your company's expertise. In either case, the business model bestows credibility on you and credibility to the people you are trying to persuade.

The people you are persuading have problems. Business models demonstrate your depth of understanding of their problems. Suppose you are proposing to the Cora Group that it increase its sales by offering outdoor seating in the warmer months at Cora Group restaurants, expanding its capacity during the seven months that it is pleasant to be outside in DC. You create a business model of the sales challenges the company currently faces, how the limited capacity affects its revenue goals. The model shows Cora Group you understand its issues.

Business models also demonstrate your understanding of solutions. To Cora Group, you show a model that compares three scenarios: adding outdoor seating, changing the menu, and hosting live music. Your model demonstrates the rigor of your approach. You are showing more than words. You are showing you have been thorough in your analysis and selection of the solution. The model helps you back up your claims.

Analysis

Insight is power. The business with better insight into a customer problem is more competitive. The business with better insight into how to use resources efficiently makes more money. The business with better insight into the customer touchpoints has more satisfied customers. The business with better insight into the impact of a new regulatory policy can adapt faster.

Analyzing business models provides insight. For example, if you acquire Cora Group, you will inherit Cora Group's existing supplier relationships, relationships with the companies that provide the company with fish, wine, spices, kitchen equipment, and the other sundries that a restaurant needs. Many of those Cora Group suppliers compete with existing Mykonos suppliers. As part of the acquisition, you need to decide which Cora Group suppliers to keep and which to discontinue. Analyzing a business model of the interactions with Cora Group suppliers and Mykonos suppliers can help you figure out what suppliers you want.

Analyzing a business model is particularly useful when you have a decision to make. The different alternative scenarios can be modeled and the models then analyzed and compared. For example, you may compare different business process scenarios to see which is the lowest cost. That low-cost scenario can be compared to today's business process so that you can understand what activities need to change, what new activities need to be performed, what activities should be automated, and what skills you will need to learn.

Compliance Management

Businesses must comply with law, government regulations, and other guidance. They must comply with terms of contractual agreements with their lenders, suppliers, and customers. Corporate employees must comply with corporate policies. Compliance often impacts financial results. Sometimes the impact is larger than money; noncompliance can lead to jail.

Businesses need to manage their compliance. They need to check it, to ensure that they are adhering to regulations and policies. If the business is not compliant, it needs to understand how far from compliance it is. It needs to design processes to ensure compliance. And when regulations change, it needs to understand the impact of the new regulations on its business.

Business models help with compliance management. An organization can model a new business process that complies with a new law. The existing process can be compared to determine the differences and what must be done to achieve compliance. A project plan can then be created to close the compliance gap.

The new process can also be used in compliance training. By including the new process in the training, all employees will understand the desired state in the same way. Employees can learn what they must do to ensure company compliance.

Requirements for Software Development

Requirements provide a description of what a proposed software application should do. In developing software, requirements are critical. Without requirements, software developers get lost in the details of code. Without detailed requirements, application development projects fail.

Historically, a requirements document was a dry line-by-line listing of the various things an application must do. For example, "*the application shall support 50 concurrent users*" is a typical line in a requirements document. Requirements documents explained what functionality the application needed, but rarely did they capture the real needs from the end user's perspective.

End users hate requirements documents because they have a difficult time relating to the details the documents describe. End users do relate well to descriptions of the essence of what they do. What activities do they perform to accomplish their work? What goals does their work meet? What metrics can be created to measure their performance and how well they are doing in achieving the goals? Who do they interact with in performing their work?

Business models capture this detail in a way that is understandable to both the business users and the software developers. Business users do not need to understand how the system will be created; they need to understand how it will support their need. Business models are a better form of requirements for end users.

Direct Execution in Software Engines

At the beginning of this chapter, we described using a map to navigate through Washington, DC, and compared that to the maps embedded in automobile navigation systems. A map can be used by people to make decision or by software to make decisions. Business models can also work like that. A business model can be used by people to make decisions, as in the examples we have explored so far. Or a business model can be used by software to make decisions.

Later in the book, we will examine an expense reimbursement process, a process in which employees are reimbursed for expenses they incur on behalf of their employer. This process can be directly executed (by an appropriate software engine) so when an employee claims an expense, the expense is automatically routed to the right individuals for approval and ultimately for payment. The advantage of direct execution is that the process can be changed—for example, to route expenses for greater than $1000 to a senior vice president for an additional approval. The change is then automatically executed by the engine. No software needs to be changed; only business models.

Knowledge Management and Reuse

Knowledge management is the practice of systematically capturing knowledge from some people in an organization so that the knowledge can be used by others elsewhere in the organization. Knowledge management aims to turn the everyday documents people create and use into a source of economic value for other people.

Today, the typical knowledge management approach is to collect documents, index them, store them, and make them accessible to others. Later, people can search for keywords and find relevant documents, discovering what others have done before them. Once captured, a document is no longer something personally available only to a few; instead it is now an organizational asset, available to many. People coming later do not have to reinvent the hard-won knowledge. They can learn what was done and repurpose it.

But knowledge management practices today capture only half the relevant knowledge. Typical knowledge management practices capture the *explicit knowledge* found in existing documents but not the *tacit knowledge* found in people's heads. Tacit knowledge includes what people do and how they do it. Tacit knowledge includes when each document is used and why.

For example, Crystal is a server at Adelina, one of the Cora Group restaurants. Crystal is quite good at upselling wines. She can recognize the right situation to suggest a more expensive wine, and she is successful at convincing her customers to try something new. She understands the different wines on the Adelina wine-list and which wine is appropriate for which meal, which occasions, and which tastes. Crystal's knowledge of wine upselling is not found in any Adelina document. It is tacit knowledge, not explicit knowledge.

Business modeling converts tacit knowledge to explicit knowledge. The details of business rules, the activities in a business process, and the goals and tactics are all captured and made explicit when they are turned into business models. In Crystal's case, the knowledge of wine upselling was captured in a collection of business rules that could be taught to others. These rules could be adapted for the winelists of the other Cora Group restaurants and so lead to higher wine sales across the board.

When business modeling is practiced, knowledge management becomes more useful. The tacit knowledge can now be managed along with the explicit knowledge. The other half of the knowledge can be captured.

THE RIGOR OF BUSINESS MODELING

As we discussed earlier, engineers have long used models in designing all manner of engineered objects. The engineering models bring rigor to the design process. We can feel safe driving over a bridge, because we know engineers created a model of that bridge and carefully analyzed cars driving over it.

Business modeling aims to bring the same rigor to business. Business models address the motivation of the business, the business processes, the organization, and the policies.

Rigor is critical. Would you invest in a business that had sloppy business processes? Would you acquire a business that was not organized to achieve its mission? Would you work for a business whose policies doom it to failure? Models provide the rigor needed to improve your business. Businesses that use modeling are better businesses.

Case Study

Enterprise resource planning systems—usually called *ERP systems*—are packaged applications that attempt to support all the basic functions of a business. ERP vendors implement features that they believe to be common to many organizations. When a company purchases an ERP, it can either adapt its business to the software or customize the software to its business. In the 1970s and 1980s, most large companies developed their own systems to support their needs. Nowadays, most large companies use ERP systems to support human resources, accounting, inventory, and other basic functions.

A few years ago a large energy company decided to replace its legacy systems with a new implementation of an ERP package. The company evaluated several ERP packages from different vendors and selected one that had domain-specific modules to support the energy market. The company then embarked on an implementation of the ERP package it purchased and budgeted several million dollars for that implementation, a typical expenditure for implementing ERP.

The company performed no business modeling. Its managers didn't understand how their business processes fit with the business processes supported by their ERP system. They didn't understand how their policies differed from the policies supported by the ERP system. They didn't even realize that there were big differences.

As they began their implementation, end users discovered some of the differences. The differences resulted in customization requests to make the software fit the business. Then more differences were discovered, and more customization was performed. The original costs and schedule budgeted for the ERP implementation did not include customizations. Overruns happened.

Without a common way to understand the problem, there was miscommunication among IT staff, the ERP vendor, and corporate management. Corporate management thought that with an additional $2 million the customizations would be finished and the result would be an operational system that matched the company's business processes. The ERP vendor understood that with over 1000 customizations, the application had become too different from its baseline. The vendor could no longer support the application. Corporate IT realized that the 1000 customizations would have to be ported to the next version of the ERP platform, and the next

Continued

Case Study—continued

one after that. Each port would be a completely new deployment. Each would cost between $6 million and $8 million.

When the parties finally understood the situation, heads rolled and the parties were forced to resolve their differences. Everyone suffered.

The company could have avoided this mess by using business models. If the company's managers had developed business models of their business and what the ERP package supported, they could have realized the magnitude of the gap. Knowing the gap, they might have selected a different package, one that fit their business better. Or perhaps none of the ERP packages were close enough to their business, and they could have developed a new custom application to support their business, using the business models to drive their requirements.

If they did select an ERP package, they could have adapted their business to the package rather than customizing the software. Business models would have helped them identify exactly what they needed to change in their business and helped them manage the change as it unfolded. Business models would have helped train the employees in the new processes and policies. Business models would also have helped in communication through the ERP deployment, providing a consistent picture to corporate management, the ERP vendor, IT, and the employees. Business models would have saved this company millions of dollars and saved the jobs of the senior managers.

A business model is a model that describes the details of a business: its goals, organizations, business processes, or business rules.

Business models are created because they produce business value. They make it easier for people to communicate, learn, and persuade. They support analysis of complex situations, and they support compliance with laws and policies. They serve as requirements for software development and can be executed directly in special-purpose software engines. And they capture knowledge for others to use later.

Chapter 2 explains the four different business modeling disciplines and what each discipline attempts to model.

Modeling Fundamentals

2

Models are always wrong in some ways, and they are always incomplete, missing part of the messy human complexity of the real world. But models can be useful for communication, analysis, and other purposes. This chapter explains how models are wrong and why they are useful and introduces the four business model disciplines that are explained in more detail in subsequent chapters.

There are many models described in this book, and every one of them is wrong. Every model we have ever created is wrong, as is every model you will ever build. Being wrong is part of the nature of a model. The world that we model is much richer, much more complex, and much stranger than the models that we build of it. If you are the kind of person who always wants to be right and who never wants to be wrong, you should close this book and continue with some other endeavor. Modeling is not for you.

The pioneering statistician George E. P. Box said it best: *"All models are wrong. Some models are useful."*[1] Sometimes people discuss whether a model is right or wrong, but that discussion is pointless since all models are wrong. Instead people should discuss whether the model is useful.

MODEL FIDELITY

The *fidelity* of a model is a measure of how closely the model approximates the real world. Fidelity is an inverse measure of wrongness: a high-fidelity model is less wrong than a low-fidelity model. Your drive through Metro DC, introduced in Chapter 1, provides a good illustration. The model inside your car's navigation system is similar to the paper roadmap, but it has some additional detail. The navigation system model

---

[1]Box was not referring specifically to business models. His work was in the application of statistics to the design of chemical experimentation. But his keen observation about the nature of modeling resonates with all of us who create models.

includes the typical traveling speeds of the roads and highways, so it can calculate the quickest path from where you are to where you want to go. It also knows that in Alexandria, 112 N. St. Asaph Street is on the west side of the street, between King and Cameron, that the traffic on Prince Street is one way, and that you cannot turn left from northbound Royal onto King Street but must instead turn right and go around the block. Both the paper street map and the model in the navigation system approximate the real world of Metro DC streets, but because the navigation system has additional details, it has higher fidelity.

Fidelity decays over time as the world being modeled changes. The fidelity of both the street map and the navigation system model will decline as new roads are built and old roads are closed, as overpasses are constructed and new addresses assigned. The world changes, and models must be updated to keep up with the changing world. New editions of paper street maps are published annually, and car navigation systems are regularly updated with new models on DVD.

You might think that a higher-fidelity model is better than a lower-fidelity model, and sometimes you would be right. Higher-fidelity models are more accurate—not as wrong—as lower-fidelity models. But higher-fidelity is sometimes worse than lower-fidelity. Higher-fidelity models take longer for people to understand all the extra detail. They are more expensive to build because extra detail must be created and extra time spent to check that the model is right. As the world changes, models must be maintained, to keep them up-to-date with the world they model. Higher-fidelity models are more expensive to maintain: there is more detail that must be kept aligned with the changing world. As the comic Steven Wright says, "I have a full-size map of the world. I hardly ever unroll it." Lower-fidelity models are always easier to unroll.

Modeling is always an economic tradeoff between the value that the model provides and the cost of building it. Sometimes a high-fidelity model is better, since the extra expense of the fidelity is justified by the value it delivers. Sometimes a low-fidelity model is better, since little additional value can be wrung from more fidelity.

Novice modelers sometimes try to create models that are as accurate as they can make them, as high fidelity as they can build. This is a laudable effort, but it's misguided: a rookie mistake. Modeling is not like developing software, where fewer bugs means better code. Instead modeling is more like recording music, where there are limits to how well the ears can hear, and hence limits to how perfect the sound must be. We have more to say about the economics of fidelity and how to manage the fidelity of a modeling effort in Chapter 7.

MODEL VALIDITY

Fidelity is one kind of measure of how wrong a model is. Validity is another very different kind of measure of model wrongness. A model is *valid* if it meets all the constraints, and it is invalid otherwise. Org charts are a simple and familiar type of business model. An org chart that has a circular reporting relationship—Patricia reporting to Michael and then Michael reporting back to Patricia—is invalid. An org chart that shows Michael reporting to himself is also invalid. Org charts require reporting relationships to go in one direction, without circular paths.

Validity is true or false. Either a model meets the constraints or it doesn't. There is no middle ground. Validity is very different from fidelity in this respect. Fidelity is all about shades of gray. A model can be a sort of accurate reflection of reality (for its purpose), and another higher-fidelity model can be more accurate.

Validity is a property of the model itself. Does the model meet the constraints? Then it is a valid model. Fidelity is about how the model relates to the world being modeled. Is the model an accurate reflection of the real world? Then it is high fidelity. All models have these two qualities: validity and fidelity.

CLASSIC BUSINESS MODELS

In Chapter 1, you were considering the acquisition of the Cora Group. Let's now return to that story.

When you arrive at the restaurant for your meeting, Sam Coates greets you. Sam built the restaurant group and is now eager to sell. He wants to show all the good things about it. Your job is to analyze it, to understand it well so that you can recommend whether it should be acquired. You need to weigh how much it is worth and consider the difficulties of replicating its success in other cities.

Sam starts your tour of the Cora Group by showing you an org chart, showing who reports to whom. In the org chart, shown in Figure 2.1, there are five general

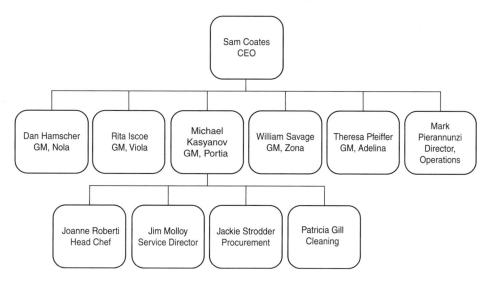

FIGURE 2.1 An organization chart

managers, one for each of the five restaurants, and a director of operations who oversees some services shared among the five. A few diagrams show all the names, the positions, and the reporting relationships. The org chart he shows is a kind of business model, a model of his business. It is certainly a simple representation; you can understand it all in a few minutes.

Sam then explains the plans for new menus. The team working on that project includes the five head chefs, one of the general managers, and the director of operations. But this cross-restaurant team is not shown anywhere in the org chart, and the members of the team report to different parts of his organization. The underlying reality of even this small business is much more complex than that shown in the org chart model, since the org chart includes permanent reporting relationships, not cross-functional teams assembled for ad hoc projects.

Sam next shows you financial statements. He presents a balance sheet and an income statement for each of the last few years, showing how his business has grown and how profitable it could be as part of your company.

Sam's income statement is shown in Figure 2.2 in dollars. It shows the revenue of his company, the expenses to achieve that revenue, and the resulting income. Income statements are always over some time period, a year, a quarter, even a month. In Figure 2.2, Sam shows annual revenue, expenses, and income for each of the last three years.

The financial statements Sam shows you are a different business model of the same business. The org chart focuses on the employees and the reporting relationships. The financial statements focus on how much money the restaurants are earning and what financial assets and liabilities they have. The two business models serve different purposes, and they are complementary.

Financial statements and org charts are classic business models. Financial statements have existed since the development of modern accounting in Renaissance Italy 500 years ago. In all likelihood, org charts date even earlier, to the first large armies and governing bureaucracies in ancient Egypt, China, or Persia.

But some questions about the business cannot be answered with these classic business models. For example: *What are Cora Group's non–financial goals for this year, and how are you trying to achieve them?* Neither the accounting models nor the org structure help with an assessment of the goals and strategies. The classic business models do not provide a complete picture of the business. We need different business models to answer those questions.

FOUR MODEL DISCIPLINES

Recently four newer business models have become important, models that complement the classic models. These new models do not displace financial statements and org charts. Income statements are not going away, not in our lifetime. Instead the four new models focus on some different parts of the

	Three years ago	Two years ago	Last year
Revenue			
Portia	1,175,811	1,579,116	2,246,780
Nola	691,061	1,293,099	2,141,021
Viola		817,218	1,274,524
Zona		720,760	1,923,590
Adelina	231,039	671,789	1,447,909
Total revenue	2,097,912	5,081,982	9,033,825
Less			
Gratuities	293,708	660,658	1,517,683
Net revenue	1,804,204	4,421,324	7,516,142
Expenses			
Personnel	920,144	2,210,662	3,833,233
Food	360,841	840,052	1,352,906
Beverages	72,168	221,066	300,646
Pastries and desserts	144,336	265,279	450,969
Premises	205,000	425,000	420,000
Depreciation	72,168	132,640	150,323
Insurance	61,000	92,100	104,000
Telecommunications	4,200	3,291	2,919
Marketing	15,922	25,929	18,299
Other expenses	8,299	3,999	5,999
Total operating expenses	1,864,078	4,220,018	6,639,292
Net income before taxes	−59,874	201,306	876,850
Income taxes	0	60,392	263,055
Net income	−59,874	140,914	613,795

FIGURE 2.2 An income statement

complex reality of business. Just as a financial statement and an org chart can show two views of the same business, these new models open up some new views of business—new views for new purposes.

The four new models are business motivation models, business organization models, business process models, and business rule models. *Business motivation* models describe business goals and the means to accomplish those goals. What are we trying to achieve at Cora Group? What strategies are we using to achieve those goals? *Business organization* models describe what groups exist and who interacts with whom to get the work done. Who at Portia interacts with the third-party bakeries? *Business process* models show the step-by-step tasks to accomplish the work. How does our waitstaff serve the customers through a dinner?

How do we hire a new assistant chef? And *business rule* models describe the laws, policies, and other guidance that constrain the work. What health rules do we enforce? What guidance do we give our waitstaff on how to satisfy unhappy customers? Together these four kinds of models describe much that is important about Portia, or about any business.

Each of these four kinds of models is a *model discipline*. A model discipline includes a set of constraints for determining whether a model is valid. The constraints are different from one model discipline to another. For example, the constraints for business process models are different from the constraints for business motivation models. A valid business process model of hiring a new assistant chef at Portia is not a valid business motivation model of anything.

We describe each of the four model disciplines in Chapters 3–6, with one chapter on each discipline. Some of our description is about the validity constraints for the discipline. For example, Chapter 3 describes business motivation models, and some of Chapter 3 is about explaining what makes a valid motivation model and when a model is invalid. The rest of Chapter 3 is devoted to explaining how to build a business motivation model and how to interpret a motivation model once one is built.

Each model discipline has a different focus, different questions that it can answer, and different analyses that it supports. When modeling a business, you usually build models in several different model disciplines, to look at the business from different angles. Recall that you examined both financial statements and org charts for Cora Group acquisition: models from two classic disciplines.

The four new business model disciplines complement each other. With a business motivation model of Cora Group, we can look carefully at the goals and influences that have led to the company's success. With a business rule model of the same restaurants, we can examine the particular policies they use to guide menu creation and customer service, and how those policies lead to a good customer experience. The two models provide different perspectives on the same business.

The four model disciplines also complement the classic accounting and organizational disciplines. Some people believe that everything important about a business is reflected in the accounting—in the dollars and cents of the income statements and balance sheets. That is true, if you wait long enough. Everything important eventually shows up in the accounting, but sometimes not until it is too late to fix. For example, a restaurant can have good books this year but be slow to seat and serve guests. This will lead to customer dissatisfaction and lower demand. Accounting will show this next year, as the revenues decline. A business process model of how people are seated and served will illuminate the problem today.

Maturity and the Model Disciplines

The four model disciplines are powerful—particularly in combination, describing a business using all of them—but all four are still evolving. In this book we describe a snapshot of current best practices, but we expect best practices to continue to improve over the coming years.

By contrast, accounting is the gold standard of business model disciplines. Accounting is mature, with a long history and hundreds of thousands of professional practitioners around the world, accountants who focus their efforts on creating and interpreting accounting models. Over its history, accountants have developed *Generally Accepted Accounting Principles (GAAP),* a framework for how to create accounting models for different real-world situations. GAAP is a standard for accounting fidelity, for judging when an accounting model is an accurate enough reflection of the company modeled. GAAP is a kind of threshold for fidelity; if a financial statement complies with GAAP, it is high enough fidelity for professional accountants to put their seal of approval on it.

Perhaps each of our four model discipline should have thousands of professionals and its own GAAP. There should be a business process GAAP that governs whether a particular business process model is an accurate enough reflection of a business process as practiced by a specific organization. Such a business process GAAP might include guidance—for example, that an unusual situation that occurs 0.1% of the time need not be modeled, but if the situation occurs 5 percent of the time, it must be modeled.

No such business process GAAP exists. Business process modeling is not mature enough yet. Until then, we must content ourselves with degrees of fidelity, without any professional consensus about how much fidelity is enough. Until consensus is achieved we must rely on our own judgments.

WRONG BUT USEFUL

At the beginning of this chapter, we introduced George Box's dictum, "All models are wrong. Some models are useful." We discussed why all models are wrong, but we ignored the second half of the quote—that some models are useful. Now it's time to examine model usefulness. In particular, we will look at some model shortcomings that make an otherwise useful model less useful or sometimes not useful at all.

To be useful, a model must have enough fidelity for the intended purpose. But fidelity alone is not sufficient. Models are read and interpreted by people, sometimes by the same people who built the model, and usually by others as well. As we described in Chapter 1, models can be useful for eight purposes:

1. Communication
2. Training and learning
3. Persuasion and selling
4. Analysis
5. Managing compliance
6. As requirements for developing software
7. Executing directly as software
8. Knowledge management and reuse

All eight require human interpretation. (Direct execution also involves computer interpretation.) And to be interpreted by people, a model must be understandable.

Some model disciplines are inherently difficult to understand. For example, the US Department of Defense uses the IDEF family of languages for both business modeling and data modeling. Most people find IDEF diagrams difficult to read and understand. IDEF requires much training, not just to create the diagrams but to interpret a diagram created by others. As a result, IDEF is not widely used outside the US military and its contractor community. In contrast, the four model disciplines described in this book have been engineered for easy understanding, so people can read a model created by others with little or no training.

Too Big to Understand

An overly large model is not useful: it cannot be comprehended, and so the purpose of the model will not be achieved. Consider Figure 2.3, a diagram that shows strategy alternatives for Adelina—one of the Cora Group's restaurants—and the consequences of the different alternatives. This Adelina strategy example will be explored more thoroughly in Chapter 3, but for now, notice the size and complexity of the model. There are 14 model elements in Figure 2.3 and 18 associations among these model elements. Parts of the model are understandable on their own, but the whole is too complex to understand all at once.

If a model is too big to be understood, it will be ignored. If you hope to train some people with the model, they will fail to learn what you are teaching. If the model is to be analyzed to transform your business, the analysts will ignore the model and rely on their own judgments and biases. If the model is to serve as requirements for software development or implementation, the resulting systems will not match the business need. An overly large model is a bad model: It cannot be comprehended, and so the purpose of the model will not be achieved.

Large models like Figure 2.3 are common; in fact we have seen many models that are much bigger and more complicated, some with over 100 model elements in a single diagram. Beginning modelers often build models that are too big and too complex; they often ignore the limits of human comprehension.

How big is too big? A useful rule of thumb is that a model should have no more than nine elements. Nine is about how many things a typical person can keep in her head on a good day [Miller, 1956]. Beyond nine, people often get confused. And if the model you built confuses the people who read it, the fault is yours, not theirs. Your model is not easy to understand.

Of course the world is more complex than can be shown with nine elements. Adelina does have three alternative strategies, each with its own consequences. In fact there are more. There are other consequences of these three not shown in Figure 2.3 and other strategy alternatives not depicted. There is always a tension between complexity and comprehension, between the great complexity of the world and the human limits of comprehension. In Chapter 7 we describe three solutions to this problem, three approaches to resolving this tension.

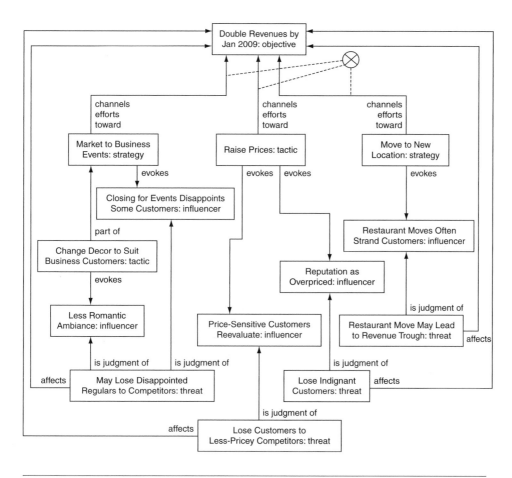

FIGURE 2.3 A motivation model with too many elements

The Appeal of Attractive Models

Model aesthetics matter. Attractive models are easier to understand and more readily accepted than ugly models. Attractive models are therefore more useful.

Consider the business process model shown in Figure 2.4. This is a valid business process model, and it is simple enough, but it is ugly. The process shows the activities performed by a server, a bartender, and a cook in taking drink and dinner orders in a restaurant, preparing them, and serving them. Figure 2.5 shows the same business process model after a makeover; it has the same modeling elements and flows, but they are arranged in a manner that is visually appealing.

Why care about the attractiveness of a model? The people who read and interpret the business process model aren't going to care if it looks good. They just want to read it to do their job: understand the new process, analyze the old

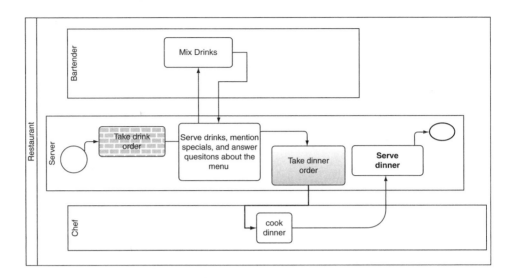

FIGURE 2.4 An ugly business process model

one, or check compliance that the work performed in the organization actually matches the activities in the model. So why does model attractiveness matter?

Model attractiveness matters because people will have emotional responses to the model they see. Their emotional responses will affect their ability to understand the model and will influence their acceptance of it. In our experience, attractive models are much easier for people to understand and accept than ugly models.[2] Attractive models are therefore more useful.

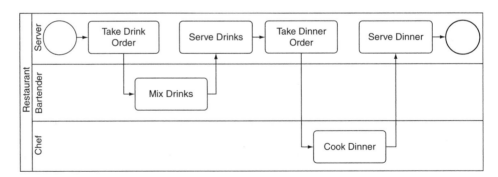

FIGURE 2.5 An attractive business process model

[2]To some extent, attractiveness is culture-dependent. An appealing model in Norway might or might not look good in Japan. But even if the particulars of what makes a model look good vary, the importance of model aesthetics seems to be universal.

This should not be surprising. Don Norman describes a similar phenomenon with user interfaces of software applications—that people find attractive user interfaces easier to understand [Norman 2004]. Model diagrams are visual. In a sense, the diagrams are the user interface to the mathematics behind the model. So, just as attractive user interfaces are easier to understand and are more effective, attractive model diagrams are easier to understand and accept.

The unconscious emotional response to an attractive model has another effect: It makes the model more persuasive. As described in Chapter 1, models are not just used for communication. They are also used for persuasion.

You don't have to be a graphic artist—or hire one—to make a model attractive. Some simple care with the size and placement of model elements, and with consistency in labeling will accomplish most of what you need. Many modelers today pay little attention to aesthetics, so some attention to graphics will make your models much better than most.

MODELING TOOLS

Most business models today are created using software applications. Some models use special-purpose modeling tools that exist just for creating business models. Other modelers use general-purpose diagram drawing tools (such as Microsoft Visio™) that are used both for creating business models and for many other diagramming uses. Either approach can work. Both the special-purpose modeling tools and the general-purpose diagramming tools support the creation of models and the saving of those models to disk. Both provide functionality to make models attractive: fonts, colors, and model element layout.

But the general-purpose drawing tools have some serious shortcomings for modeling. When you draw a business process model in Visio (for example), the activities in the model are just rectangles. Visio will allow you to make one rectangle red or make another one smaller, but Visio offers no special support for recording the typical duration of an activity or for noting the subprocess behind an activity. Visio understands the activity as a rectangle in a drawing, not as an activity in a business process.[3]

The special-purpose modeling tools are better for business modeling. These tools understand business activities as activities, not as rectangles. Durations of activities are supported, as are subprocesses behind an activity. If you use one of these business modeling tools, you will find it quicker and easier to build, maintain, and analyze your models. Models built with a special-purpose modeling tool are more useful.

---

[3]Out of the box, Visio is a drawing tool, but it can be augmented to become a specialized business modeling tool. In fact some business modeling tools have been created as Microsoft Visio add-ins. These tools do support activity durations and the subprocesses behind activities.

Special-purpose modeling tools also make it easier to build valid models. Because the drawing tools understand your business process as just a collection of rectangles and lines, they don't complain when you do something wrong—for example, when you connect a strategy to an activity with a sequence flow. Visio won't warn you that your model is invalid. But the special-purpose business modeling tools understand activities as activities. Some will warn you when you create an invalid model, like spell checking in a word processor. Other business modeling tools will prevent you from making an invalid model, in the way that a spreadsheet will prevent you from creating a circular reference.

For business process models, the special-purpose tools offer even more. Many tools support business process simulation, allowing you to experiment with prospective business processes to see what happens. Some tools support direct execution in a business process engine, allowing you to turn your business process model into executable workflow. Some tools show the status of a business process by monitoring external applications.

Using a drawing tool to construct your business process models is a bit like using a shoe to drive in nails. It works better than your fist, but you will be happier with the result if you use a hammer.

The Landscape of Business Modeling Tools

There are many special-purpose business modeling tools, and the modeling tool marketplace changes quickly, with new vendors, new products, and new releases of existing products every quarter. We don't describe the vendors and products here because the marketplace will change between the time we write these words and the time you read them. (See our companion site *bridgelandzahavi.com* for some reviews on modeling tool products.) Instead of describing the vendors and products here, we describe some of the features of these tools. Today, none of the modeling products have all the features we describe, but we expect this to change; in the future the features described here will be common to all the special-purpose business modeling tools.

Aesthetics, Multiple Disciplines, and Validity Checking

We earlier discussed the curious power of attractive models and the importance of tapping that power by making your models look good. Most of the tools support making attractive models. They have the usual palettes of drawing functionality: color and shading, inclusion of image files, alignment and distribution, and so on. They are not professional graphics applications—there is no need to recreate the complex functionality of Adobe Illustrator in a business modeling tool—but they have the basic functionality. Some of the tools can also rearrange a model to make it more attractive—for example, making business processes flow from left to right and top to bottom.

Some of the existing tools support a single modeling discipline. For example, there are numerous tools that support only business process modeling and not the other three disciplines. Some tools support multiple disciplines. These discipline-crossers have the right primitives to create models from two business model disciplines, three disciplines, or even all four, allowing you to create a business process model, a business motivation model, a business organization model, and a business rule model.

Most of the tools check for model validity. Validity checking can be done by highlighting invalid parts of a model either as it is built or as a command that can be run to find all the invalid parts. Some modeling tools actually prevent modelers from creating invalid models at all.

Publication and Application Program Interfaces

Business modelers work with a modeling tool to create models and analyze the models they create. But every model built by a modeler will be consumed by others, probably a great many others: business analysts who analyze the models, managers who use the models to make decisions, and trainees who read the models to understand the business. These consumers of business models do not have any modeling tools loaded on their desktops, and even if a tool is installed, they do not know how to use it.

To make models accessible to this wider audience, many of the business modeling tools have publication functionality. A model can be published to a variety of accessible formats: to HTML for inclusion on a website, to PDF so it can be read in Adobe Acrobat™, to Microsoft Help™ files, or to Microsoft Word™ so it can be part of a larger written document. Some tools also support publication to XML, so a model can be transformed into other formats.

Sometimes a business model is embedded inside a larger software application. For example, a business process simulation can be accessible on a website, allowing users to try different scenarios and see the simulated results. Some business modeling tools support this kind of mash-up of business modeling with other functionality by providing a runtime application program interface, an application programming interface (API) that allows other software to access the functionality of the model.

MODEL ANALYSIS

Business models are often analyzed to learn about the model and (more important) to learn about the business being modeled. Let's consider one kind of analysis: examining business rules that neither support any goals nor are formulated based on any strategies. (We introduce goals and strategies in Chapter 3 and business rules in Chapter 6. For this example analysis, consider goals to be what the business is trying to achieve, strategies as how the business is trying to achieve its goals, and business rules as individual business directives.) Any business rule that has no connection to goals or strategies deserves a second look. Does it need to exist, or could it be repealed? Are there goals or strategies that have not been modeled that would justify this rule?

For example, one of Portia's[4] business rules is: *It is prohibited that a reservation is taken more than 7 days in advance.* Our analysis discovers that this rule is not justified by any of Portia's goals or strategies. Now we should investigate whether this rule makes sense. Is there an unarticulated reason for this rule—perhaps there aren't enough people to answer the reservation phone calls and so we want to reduce the number of calls? Or perhaps Portia staff enforces this restriction for no good reason, simply because they always have done so, and we should now repeal it.

Questioning unjustified business rules is just one analysis method— one of many. Just as a socket wrench set has sockets of many sizes, business modeling tools often have built-in support for many analysis methods. Some tools even allow a modeler to create her own analysis method, to aggregate the model elements in new ways to derive new kinds of metrics, or to search for model elements with particular characteristics. Model analysis is described in Chapter 10.

SIMULATION

Sometimes it is difficult to understand the implications of a business model, particularly complex business models and models that have many interacting elements. *Simulation* is a technique for running a model to get a deeper understanding. Many business modeling tools support simulation. A model that simulates is more useful than one that does not.

Twenty years ago computer simulation was an arcane topic, understood and experienced by only a few specialists. Things have changed. The emergence of mass-market simulation video games like SimCity™, The Sims™, Zoo Tycoon™, and many others has transformed the public understanding of simulation, taken it from the arcane to the commonplace. Every teenager—and every parent of a teenager—has tried his hand at being mayor of a simulated city, at managing a simulated family, or at creating and managing a simulated zoo. Simulation is entertaining, and simulation games are a growing part of the modern entertainment industry.

The objective of SimCity is to create a city. A player can create roads and rails, place police stations, build a power grid, and zone real estate as residential, commercial, or industrial. As a result of his actions, the city prospers or declines, crime rises or falls, simulated people live, shop, commute, and work, and so on.

Thanks to simulation games, many people are familiar with simulation. But what is simulation, really? First, simulations are based on models. Within SimCity is a *model of a city:* houses, neighborhoods, roads, rail, parks, and malls and the

---

[4]As you may recall, Portia is one of the Cora Group restaurants.

interactions of people who live in those houses, travel on those roads and trains, play in those parks, and shop in those malls.

Second, a simulation shows how a model behaves over time. Things happen in SimCity over time: houses are built, existing roads become congested, crimes are committed, and neighborhoods improve or slide in disrepute. These changes are not scripted; the decline of a neighborhood in SimCity is not preordained by the application. Rather, things happen the way they do because of the gradual interaction of all the elements of the city model over time. A nearby district fills in and people start commuting through the neighborhood, leading to more traffic on the streets. The neighborhood becomes less desirable because of all the new traffic. Some crimes occur, and the local police station is a bit too far away to respond. Then more crimes are committed.

SimCity is a *playable* simulation. As a mayor, you manage the city. You open new police stations, rezone neighborhoods, create parks, and change tax rates. Depending on your actions over time, a range of behaviors can be produced: crime can rise or plummet, the citizenry can be prosperous or destitute, and they may drive cars or ride subways.

Some business simulations are also playable, like SimCity. A player can steer her business over time, changing prices, improving product design, or developing new products. Typically these simulations are played either as part of a corporate training course or to give the player some insight into a new strategic environment.

But most business simulations are not playable. They are simulated purely for understanding behavioral results of a new process or strategic environment. Simulation becomes another method of analysis. Usually many different simulation runs will be made of a nonplayable simulation, to explore a space of possibilities, and the results will be summarized in graphs or statistics.

For example, you might create a business process model of how Portia customers experience the restaurant. A customer arrives, perhaps waits for a table, is seated, orders a meal, pays, and departs. Of course, the customer's quality of experience will be affected by the food, but it will also be affected by delays and customer service. Simulating the process model will reveal where delays are present and allow us to experiment with alternative techniques—more servers, fewer reservations, etc.—to reduce those delays.

No one is playing this Portia simulation. Rather, this nonplayable simulation allows us to better analyze and understand the process.

Chapter 11 describes how to build business model simulations and how to use the simulations once they are built.

TRACEABILITY

In examining a model, it's always useful to ask about the purpose of individual model elements. *Why do we enforce this rule? Why do we perform this business process task?* The answers to the questions of purpose are usually model elements in other models. We enforce this rule because of a particular strategy we are working.

Traceability is connecting model elements between models, explaining a model element in one model by referring to a model element in another. Traceability answers "why" questions—questions about rationale, purpose, and intent. Some business modeling tools support traceability.

Consider again the business process model shown in Figure 2.5, the process that shows how the waitstaff at Portia takes a dinner order. Why does the server take the drink order first, rather than asking about drinks and dinner at the same time? At fast-food restaurants, takeout restaurants, and many other places, food and beverages are ordered together. Why do the servers at our restaurant work first on the drinks and only then on the food?

There could be many reasons for sequencing beverages first. One reason is that customers will drink more if they are served drinks first, and drinks are high-margin items for the restaurant. Another reason is that Portia aspires to be the kind of upscale place where customers stay for hours. At more sophisticated restaurants, taking the drink order and dinner order at the same time is considered to be rushing the customer and is inconsistent with a high-end image.[5]

Figure 2.6 shows part of the restaurant's *motivation model*—the goals Sam and his staff are trying to achieve at Portia and how they are trying to achieve those goals. Asking for drink orders first is a tactic, a short-term course of action that is meant to channel effort toward objectives or goals. Other tactics are also shown in Figure 2.6: describing wines that suit the food the customer orders as well as offering wine samples.

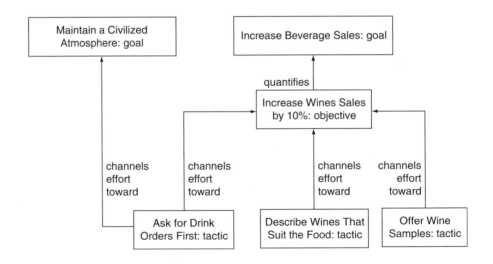

FIGURE 2.6 Part of Portia's motivation model

[5]Outside the United States, the norms of a civilized atmosphere are different. In France, for example, wine is ordered only after dinner selections have been made.

All three tactics channel efforts toward the objective of increasing wine sales by 10%. The tactic **Ask for Drink Orders First**[6] also channels efforts toward the goal of maintaining a civilized atmosphere.

Of course, this is only a small example. A more complete motivation model for our restaurant would include many more tactics, objectives, and goals as well as other motivation model elements such as influencers and threats. Business motivation models are described in Chapter 3.

The activities of Figure 2.5 are connected to the tactics, objectives, and goals of Figure 2.6 through *tracelinks*. Figure 2.7 shows the activity **Take Drink Order** (from Figure 2.5) tracelinked to the tactic **Ask for Drink Orders First** (from Figure 2.6). That tracelink explains why servers at Portia take drink orders first: It is a tactic of the restaurant, a tactic that channels effort toward both the goal of maintaining a civilized atmosphere and the objective of increasing drink orders by 10%.

Note that tracelinks are not relationships between whole models. We are not tracing the whole business process model to the whole business motivation model. Rather, we are tracing two individual elements of the business process model to a single element in the motivation model. We are not answering broad questions about the purpose of the business process model. Instead we are answering narrow questions about the purpose of serving drinks first.

Traceability is useful for understanding the impact of a change. *If we change this tactic, what activities must be changed?* By examining the tracelinks that point from activities to the tactic, we can determine which ones are affected. With the right tracelinks in place, we can continue our traceability walk, looking at which systems support the activities that are affected by the changed tactic.

Traceability is a bit like the index to a book. You can look up "Frederick the Great" in the index of a history of Prussia (for example) and find all the references to him in the book. In a similar way you can examine the tracelinks to a model element and find all the other model elements that are dependent on it.

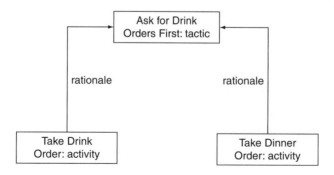

FIGURE 2.7 Tracing two activities to their motivation

---

[6]In this book all model elements are shown in bold.

Models change over time to reflect changing ideas of strategy, business processes, organization, and policy. For example, a goal might initially be active, as the organization works to achieve it. After the goal is achieved, it is no longer an active goal for the organization. But the goal wants to be retained rather than removed from the model. If it is removed, you have lost the knowledge that it ever was a goal as well as the fact that it was achieved. Some modeling tools support model version control so that you can keep track of what model elements are active today.

Traceability is explored further in this book, in Chapters 4–6. For example, Chapter 6 is about business rules and describes how rules trace to business process elements, business organization elements, and business motivation elements.

MODEL DEPLOYMENT

Business models are sometimes used to drive software development. For example, an insurance company might model its claims approval business process as a first step to writing an application that supports that business process. Of course, that is a rather slow method of assuring alignment between the model and application: Software development takes at least months to complete and can take much longer. Much can change in the claims approval business process between the time that process is modeled and the time the application is ready for use.

There is a faster alternative way for our insurance company to use its business process model to drive its software; it can *deploy* the model. When a model is deployed, it is directly executed as software. For example, a business process model can be deployed as workflow. Users of the software are not even aware that they are working with a deployed business model. To them it feels like any other application.

Of course, the business model by itself is not enough. To deploy a business model, we need a special-purpose deployment engine, an application whose sole job is to execute business models (of a particular discipline) and turn them into functioning software.

Let's consider an example. When an insurance claim completes an activity in the claim process, the deployment engine uses the claims business process model to figure out what to do next. If the next step is approval of a repair estimate to be performed by a claims adjuster (for example), the deployment engine queues up the work for the claims adjuster. Her approval will cause the next activity in the process to be queued up for the next person in the process. To the claims adjuster the business process model no longer looks like a model. Instead it looks like part of the software application she is working in.

Business rules can also be deployed. A business rules engine will notice when a travel expense policy rule is violated, will log the name of the employee who violated the policy, and will ask the individual to explain why she violated the policy.

To the woman who violated the corporate expense policy, the business rule model no longer looks like a model. It looks like part of the expense documentation application she is using to record her expenses.

Model deployment is a new and radical use of business models. It is described in more detail in Chapter 12.

BUSINESS MODELING STANDARDS

Several business modeling standards have emerged in the last few years. But what is a standard? A *standard* is a technical agreement by many people and many software applications. For example, HTML is a standard. Thousands of people agree on what the various tags in HTML mean, and thousands of software applications have knowledge of those tags embedded within them.

Business modeling is becoming standardized. Standards are useful because they provide a degree of independence between customers of business modeling technology and vendors of that technology. Without standards, a customer is vulnerable to *vendor lock-in*: their existing modeling tools vendors can raise prices freely and even reduce quality. The customer can do little but accept the worse state of affairs. Changing vendors is too painful. All of their existing models won't work in the new vendor's technology.

Standards change the nature of the game between customers and vendors. When multiple vendors support the same standard, it is easier for a customer to switch to a new vendor. When customers have the ability to switch, modeling vendors must keep prices reasonable and raise the quality of their software and service. The power of vendor lock-in is reduced.

Standards allow different modeling tools to communicate. For example, consider the deployment of a business process. A modeler can add some activities to a business process model using the modeling editor on his laptop. When this newly changed process is ready for deployment, it must be uploaded to the business process execution engine, a different application, running on a server somewhere. But how is the model communicated from the modeling editor to the execution engine? How do the two applications communicate about the model? A standard business process modeling language is the best means of communication between these two applications.

Standards also make communication easier between people. When a modeler explains a business motivation model she built to a modeler colleague, that communication is easier if they already agree on what an objective is, what a tactic is, and how tactics and objectives relate to each other. The communication can focus on the details of particular objectives and tactics rather than on what they mean. They can focus on the content rather than the form. A standard for business motivation models is a good route to that common knowledge; the two modelers can learn the right standard and then communicate with anyone else who also knows the standard.

The State of Business Modeling Standards

In the 1980s and 1990s, there were few business modeling standards, and the standards that did exist were not widely used. But in the last few years, good standards have been created and are becoming widely adopted.

Each business modeling discipline has a somewhat different standards situation. Business process modeling is the most mature of the four. There have been several proposed standards in the past. Business Process Modeling Notation (BPMN) and Business Process Definition Metamodel (BPDM), are two industry standards that are further discussed in Chapter 5.

The standard for business motivation models is the Business Motivation Model (BMM). BMM is a new standard describing an important space that has seen little attention from tool vendors until now. BMM is described in Chapter 3.

The standard for business rules is Semantics of Business Vocabulary and Business Rules (SBVR). SBVR is described in Chapter 6.

The newest of the four disciplines is business organization models. There are no adopted standards yet for business organization models. Organization models are described in Chapter 4.

Many useful business modeling practices are not yet standardized. For example, BPDM does not yet support business process simulation. Similarly, BMM does not support strategy simulation. Every year new modeling practices are created. A new practice must prove itself and become widely adopted before the standards bodies are interested in incorporating it. In Chapters 3–6 we point out what aspects of business modeling practice are not yet part of the standards.

BUSINESS MODELING AND ENTERPRISE ARCHITECTURE

An *enterprise architecture* is a description of an organization's entire information technology systems and the processes, people, and strategy that accompany those systems. In recent years, many organizations have embarked on enterprise architecture efforts. Since 2001 (or according to some observers, since 1996) the US Federal government has been developing an enterprise architecture of the entire business of the Federal government. Considering the size of the Federal government, that enterprise architecture is an enormous endeavor.

Enterprise architecture—often abbreviated EA—is different from the business modeling we explain in this book, but there are some overlapping concerns and techniques. And many of the same vendors of business modeling tools also sell enterprise architecture tools, sometimes effectively targeting the same applications at the two different markets.

Enterprise architecture has a much broader scope than business modeling. EA is concerned with the whole enterprise, capturing all the business processes, all the applications, all the data, and all the IT infrastructure in an enterprise. EA is about creating an inventory that includes everything, something comparable to an asset inventory but focused on IT assets and the business processes they support rather than physical assets such as furniture and buildings.

In contrast, the scope of business modeling is tightly focused on a particular business problem. For example, a business modeling effort might look at why it takes so long to purchase new equipment and how that procurement process could be shortened. To tackle that problem, business modelers would model only the procurement process, not the personnel recruiting process or the expense reporting process. A motivation model might be built, but only for the motivations that are relevant to procuring new equipment.

Sometimes business models are created for deployment. For example, a business process model might be deployed in an execution engine. But not every business process in the enterprise is modeled and deployed, at least not all at once. Typically the processes whose execution will generate the most value are deployed first.

Because business models are focused on a particular problem, they are much smaller than enterprise architecture models. They are also much more detailed, with all the nitty-gritty that is important for solving the problem at hand. Because enterprise architecture models endeavor to span the enterprise, they have much less detail about any business process. They can't afford much detail if they are to cover everything.

The broad inventory scope of enterprise architecture supports asking questions about overlap and redundancy, Why do we need three different financial management applications? Can we migrate to a single application and lower our costs? Why do we have different processes for recruiting nurses, recruiting physicians, and recruiting staff? Can we combine the processes and simplify our work?

In addition to eliminating existing redundancy, enterprise architecture models can help to avoid creating the redundancy, or at least avoid adding to the problem. For example, the US Federal budgeting process requires that agencies justify their IT spending. The justification needs to include how the spending helps the agency's mission and how the spending fits in the existing enterprise architecture. Central budgeting authorities use these justifications to see where a proposed new system is redundant with another system in another agency. They turn down budget requests that would create redundant systems.

Sometimes enterprise architectures are used to provide a long-term picture of where an organization should be headed: to socialize a roadmap. An enterprise architecture can provide many stakeholders with a common picture about the business processes the enterprise will use and the technology that will be adopted to support those business processes.

Enterprise architecture always includes technology, inventories of the applications and infrastructure owned and used by the enterprise. Often these applications and infrastructure are traced to the business processes they support. Business models by contrast are sometimes traced to technology models and sometimes they are not. Sometimes business models stand by themselves, without reference to any technology. It all depends on the focus problem: why the business model is being built.

Because enterprise architectures are cross-enterprise inventories, they are built to last. An EA model is intended to be updated every quarter or every year as things change. Business models are sometimes updated with the business, and sometimes they serve their purpose and are discarded. Again, it depends on the focus problem.

Business models are different from enterprise architecture models, but the two kinds of models play well together. In particular, existing business models can serve as components of a newly created enterprise architecture model. Most enterprise architecture modeling exercises include business process models. Instead of creating new business process models for just this purpose, you can reuse existing business process models originally created for other purposes. A similar situation exists for motivation models. Some enterprise architecture efforts include modeling the goals and strategies. If an existing motivation model already exists, the existing goals and strategies can be reused for the enterprise architecture.

In organizations that have created an enterprise architecture, it is useful to tie new business models to the existing enterprise architecture. Model elements in a business model are traced to model elements in an EA model to show how the focused business model fits in the larger enterprise whole.

The business modeling techniques described in this book are largely applicable to enterprise architecture as well. For example, the techniques in Chapter 5 of creating detailed business process models for analysis also apply to the high-level business process models that are part of an EA. The techniques described in Chapter 7 of keeping models simple and understandable also apply to enterprise architecture.

A business model is a map of a business, a simple representation of the complex reality. A business model can be valid or not, depending on whether it adheres to the rules of its modeling discipline. A business model can be of high or low fidelity, depending on how accurately it models the business.

To make business models more useful, we use specialized tools for creating them. These tools support us in building useful models—models that are valid, simple, attractive, and of high fidelity. We usually analyze the business models we have built. Often we simulate them. Sometimes we deploy them into an execution engine.

There are four business modeling disciplines: process modeling, motivation modeling, rules modeling, and organization modeling. Each discipline has its own standards describing what valid models are and what they mean. Chapters 3–6 explain the four modeling disciplines in detail, starting with business motivation models in Chapter 3, models of what the business is trying to achieve and why.

Business Motivation Models

3

Business motivation is the first of the four business modeling disciplines we describe in this book. A business motivation model describes what a business is trying to accomplish—the goals and objectives of the business. A motivation model is also concerned with how the business intends to go about accomplishing the goals—the strategy of the business. A motivation model includes what is happening in the world that may represent an opportunity or a threat to the business and what is happening in the business itself that may be a strength or weakness. This chapter explains business motivation models.

After some consideration, your company, Mykonos Dining Corp., does acquire Cora Group, striking a cash and stock deal with the owner. Now the general manager of Cora's flagship restaurant, Portia, has come to you with a problem. He is considering making a change to the menu. Portia's entire menu is prepared fresh on the premises. Even the breads and desserts are prepared in-house, and the general manager thinks that this in-house practice has limited the variety of the breads and desserts that are offered. He would like to procure some breads and desserts from local bakeries.

The head chef is opposed. She argues that Portia is a different kind of restaurant, that its mission is about cooking meals fresh, not serving food that others have prepared. Her argument is compelling, and the general manager has been puzzling it back and forth for several weeks as he attends to the daily demands of the restaurant. Now he seeks your advice.

This dilemma is not about the business processes of the restaurant. It is about something larger: why the restaurant exists, the goals it is trying to achieve, and the means it uses to achieve those ends. It is about the *business motivation* of Portia.

The head chef's opposition to the procurement of breads and desserts is not just a difference of opinion about the most profitable direction for Portia. She cares about the restaurant. She invests her time and energy in creating the best food she can because the restaurant has personal meaning for her. Some businesses spend a lot of time and attention figuring out what they should be doing and why. Some businesses prefer to focus instead on operational matters. But employees always care about motivation. Work is always as much about creating meaning for the people performing it as about earning a living. Business motivation matters.

We build business motivation models—models of what a business is trying to do. Business motivation is the first of the four modeling disciplines we cover in this book. Business motivation models include *goals*—what the organization is trying to do. A motivation model for Portia might include a goal like **Prepare Comfort Food for Urbane Customers**.

Business motivation models include *strategies*—how the organization is trying to achieve its goals. A motivation model for Portia might include the strategy **Extend Dessert Menu with Cakes from Local Bakeries**.

Business motivation models also include *influencers*—justifications of the goals and strategies in terms of what is happening in the organization or out in the larger world. For example, Portia's business motivation model might include the influencer **Restaurant Customers Demanding More Variety.** This is a trend about the market Portia is serving, a trend that has an effect on whether Portia's goals and strategies will be successful.

WHY MODEL BUSINESS MOTIVATION?

Why do we care about modeling business motivation? As you will recall from Chapter 1, business models in general are used for eight purposes. Six apply to business motivation modeling: communication, persuasion and selling, training and learning, analysis, managing compliance, and knowledge management and reuse.

Some businesses build motivation models of their strategy and then use those models to *communicate* their strategy across their organization and to stakeholders outside. Sometimes that communication involves *persuasion* of reluctant parties: for example, employees who are skeptical of the new strategy, or suppliers who are concerned about what the new strategy means for them. Sometimes the models are used to *train* new employees in the business strategy.

Motivation models are often *analyzed*. One potential strategy is compared with others, to see which is best. (In fact, motivation models should be analyzed more often than they are today. It is difficult to envision a situation in which a motivation model is built and no analysis is needed.) Sometimes this analysis involves simulation, to understand the implications of a strategy in the evolving business environment. Motivation model simulation is covered in Chapter 11.

Motivation models are essential for *managing compliance* against policy. The policies themselves are part of the business rule model, described in Chapter 6. But the policies can be traced to business motivations, the strategies and tactics that the policies govern, and to the goals and objectives that they support.

In some organizations, knowledge about an initiative today is carefully captured for the benefit of other initiatives in the future. This *knowledge management* sometimes includes business motivations, explaining the purpose of the initiative and the strategies that were followed. When someone else finds the details of this captured initiative, they can study the motivation model and understand why the initiative was executed the way it was.

MOTIVATION MODELING AND STRATEGY CREATION

Business motivation modeling can play a role in creating a new strategy, although the details depend on how the business works with strategy in general. Different businesses use different techniques to create strategy.[1] Some businesses see strategy as something to be periodically designed, and they convene the leadership team annually in offsite workshops to create multi-year plans that are intended to be implemented by the rest of the organization. Models can be created in these workshops; capturing the strategy as models directly in the workshops supports a different kind of offsite conversation. The leadership team can discuss alternatives by pointing to alternative models. They can see the impact of the choices they are making. Model-based workshops are described in Chapters 8 and 9.

Other businesses approach strategy very differently—as something that is *learned* as the result of ongoing conversations throughout the organization during the day-to-day work. These businesses don't design their strategy so much as incrementally refine it in response to what they are seeing in their environment. For these incrementally learning organizations, business models can be created as needed as part of the communication process, e.g., whenever someone recognizes a new trend and wants to explain to his or her colleagues how that new trend can be exploited as a new opportunity.

In creating strategy, modeling serves to legitimize differences of opinion around what the organization should do. It is a curious but widespread fact of organizational life that differences of opinion about operational matters—such as business processes—are considered to be harmless, but differences of opinion about strategic matters—such as goals—are forbidden. "Don't say that—it's against the company strategy," they warn, or "We all need to march in the same direction."

By modeling alternative strategies, the content of the opinion can be separated from the authority of the person who said it. The alternative strategies can be analyzed, maybe even simulated, and the results compared objectively.

---

[1]Mintzberg et al. [Mintzberg 1998] surveys a broad spectrum of strategy practice, all the different ways that companies create and maintain strategy.

Motivation modeling is useful in creating strategy, but model-based strategy creation is still pretty rare, in our experience. Usually strategy is created using some other, older processes that do not involve modeling. Modeling is then used to capture the strategy once it is created. When strategy is created first and modeled later, it doesn't matter how the strategy was created; the modeling simply focuses on what the strategy is. While a strategy first model later approach is not as good as using modeling to create a strategy, it is still valuable to capture what others created.

GOALS

Motivation modeling is about the achievement of goals. Organizations have goals. For example, Apple tries to create consumer electronics products that are beautiful and easy to use. Nike tries to create the best shoes for both serious and occasional athletes. Closer to home, Portia tries to serve innovative and satisfying food.

So what is a goal? A goal is simply something an organization is trying to achieve. For example, the employees of Portia are working on increasing the variety of the food offered. We could model this as the goal **Expand Menu Variety.**

A goal is an *end result*, something an organization is trying to achieve for its own sake, rather than a means to some other end. For example, Portia is trying to achieve greater menu variety by offering daily specials. **Expand Menu Variety** is a goal, whereas **Offer Daily Specials** is not a goal since Portia does not care about offering daily specials except to the extent that they expand the menu variety. **Offer Daily Specials** is a *strategy*. Strategies are attempted to achieve goals, not for their own sake. Strategies are described later in this chapter.

Goals and Organizations

A goal is defined by the organization that is trying to achieve the goal. For example, the restaurant Portia defines the goal **Expand Menu Variety**. Portia's sister restaurants have different goals. Nola—a Cora Group restaurant that just opened—defines the goal **Establish Regular Customers**. Establishing regular customers was once a goal for Portia, when it had just opened, but that goal has long since been achieved and is no longer a goal for the restaurant. Figure 3.1 shows the relationship between Portia and the goal it defines, and between Nola and the goal it defines.

Figure 3.1 also shows a goal for Cora Group and Mykonos. Cora Group—Sam's company that you acquired that includes Portia and all its sister restaurants—defines the goal **Bring Innovative Food to More People.** Mykonos Dining Corp. as a whole defines the goal **Expand Presence in Mid-Atlantic**.

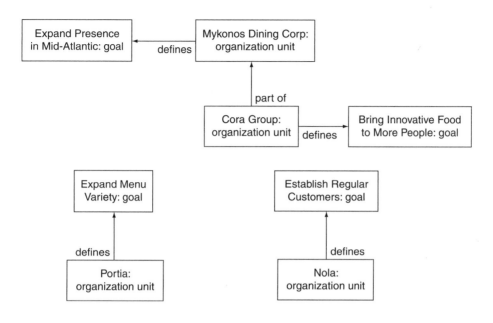

FIGURE 3.1 Organization and goals

Saying that an organization unit "defines" a goal is a bit confusing.[2] In practice an organization may set a goal for one of its constituent organizations. For example, Portia is one of the restaurants in the Cora Group, and Cora may set the goal **Expand Menu Variety** for Portia. So although expanding menu variety is a goal for Portia, it was in some sense "defined" for it by its parent organization. But the **defines** association does not work that way. When we say that an organization defines a goal, we are using a kind of convenient shorthand. We mean that the people who make up the organization are committed to achieving the goal. The employees who are part of Portia are focusing their time and attention on expanding the variety of the menu.

Goal Hierarchies

Larger goals are often decomposed into *subgoals*—smaller goals that when achieved will collectively result in the larger goal. The result is a *goal hierarchy* showing many goals and their relationships. For example, consider the Cora Group's goal hierarchy, shown in Figure 3.2. At the top of the hierarchy is **Bring Innovative Food to More People**. That lofty goal is composed of five subgoals:

---

[2]The "defines" terminology comes from the Business Motivation Model standard, commonly called BMM. BMM is described later in this chapter.

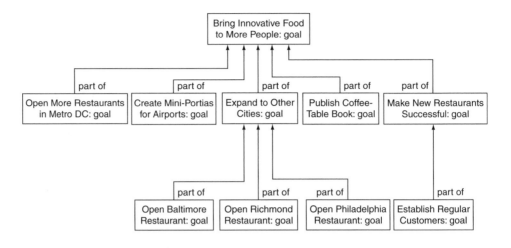

FIGURE 3.2 A goal hierarchy

- **Open More Restaurants in Metro DC**
- **Create Mini-Portias for Airports**
- **Expand to Other Cities**
- **Publish Coffee-Table Book**
- **Make New Restaurants Successful**

Each of these subgoals is a significant desired end result; each is a goal. **Expand to Other Cities** has its own subgoals: **Open Baltimore Restaurant**, **Open Richmond Restaurant**, and **Open Philadelphia Restaurant**.

The subgoal **Expand to Other Cities** is related to **Bring Innovative Food to More People** via the association **part of**. The **part of** association is what defines **Expand to Other Cities** as a subgoal. The **part of** association means that something smaller is a piece of something larger: The smaller subgoal is a piece of the larger goal. As we will see, **part of** is a useful association—useful not just for subgoals and goals but also for other things that have parts.

Goals change, typically at a pace of years or decades. Once the Cora Group opens a restaurant in Baltimore, **Open Baltimore Restaurant** will no longer be a goal. Another goal will take its place.

OBJECTIVES

Goals are not enough by themselves. Goals are vague about timing, about when a goal should be achieved. Consider the Cora Group goal **Expand to Other Cities**. Are they opening restaurants in other cities this month, next year, or within the next 10 years? Goals are also vague about measurement. At what point has

Cora Group succeeded in expanding to other cities—When they open one restaurant outside metro DC? Three restaurants? 20?

Goals are complemented by *objectives*. Objectives are desired end results like goals, but they are specific about both timing and measurement. The goal **Expand to Other Cities** is complemented by an objective to open restaurants in three cities outside of Metro DC by the end of the year. This **3 City Openings** objective *quantifies* the goal **Expand to Other Cities**: It specifies a measurement—three cities outside metro DC—and a timing—by the end of the year.

A single goal can be quantified by more than one objective. For example, **Expand to Other Cities** is quantified by both the **3 City Openings** objective and by a subsequent **7 City Openings** objective, to open restaurants in seven cities outside of metro DC by the end of next year. Both objectives quantify the same goal.

Descriptions

You might have noticed that **3 City Openings** and **7 City Openings** are named using a different style: the details of **3 City Openings** are not embedded in the name. The name of the model element does not reveal that the objective is about opening restaurants outside of metro DC. Nor does the name reveal that the objective is to be accomplished by the end of the year. **3 City Openings** has a description that provides the details. Any motivation model element can have a description. Descriptions allow names to be short, so model elements can be easily referenced. Short names are a modeling best practice, described with other best practices in Chapter 7.

For example, a description for **3 City Openings** states:

Open three restaurants outside of metro DC by the end of the year.

Objectives change faster than goals. Suppose Cora Group encounters some financing difficulties and only succeeds in opening two restaurants outside metro DC by the end of this year. The **3 City Openings** objective is no longer a current goal because the year has come and gone. Cora Group may scale back the objective for the following year, focusing on opening four restaurants by the end of the year instead of seven. The goal remains the same—**Expand to Other Cities**—but the objectives have changed.

Measuring Objectives

Objectives must be measurable. For **3 City Openings**, measuring is easy: One just counts the number of restaurants that are opened outside the Washington, DC, metropolitan area. But measuring is not always so easy. How does one measure the Portia goal **Expand Menu Variety**? What yardstick do you use to measure menu variety?

One approach to measuring menu variety is to count the number of items on the menu: 8 entrees, 11 appetizers, 4 salads, etc. But the number of menu items is a flawed measure. Fast-food hamburger chains often have a large menu but little real variety: the hamburger, cheeseburger, double hamburger, and deluxe hamburger are all very similar.

Portia might choose to measure the menu variety with a survey of their customers, asking them whether they like the variety of the menu. With the survey approach, the objective **Improve Customer Variety Perception** quantifies the goal **Expand Menu Variety**. **Improve Customer Variety Perception** is described as raising the customer variety survey results from a 3.5 to a 3.9 by June.

Another approach to measuring menu variety is to hire an expert restaurant consultant to evaluate the menu and rate it on her own variety scale. The goal is quantified by the objective **Improve Expert Variety**, described as raising the consultant's variety rating from a B+ to an A− by September.

Portia can pursue both objectives; neither objective is a perfect measure of the goal, but together they are a pretty good quantification. Figure 3.3 shows the resulting goal, objectives, and the organization unit **Portia**. Note that Portia defines the goal **Expand Menu Variety** and also defines the two objectives that quantify that goal. This is a typical relationship: Usually the organization that defines the goal will also define the quantifying objectives.

Some goals are easy to measure conceptually but difficult in practice. Consider Nola, the new restaurant with the goal of establishing regular customers. In theory, Nola could measure the percentage of customers who have returned within 90 days. But in practice, there is no good way of knowing if a customer returns. An information technology (IT) system could track the customers, perhaps using credit cards as identification. But that approach has its own shortcomings: People use different credit cards, some people pay cash, and when two people meet for

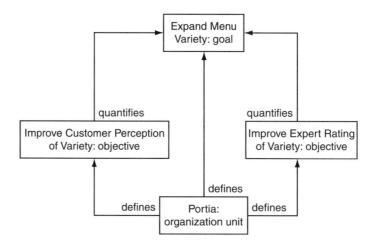

FIGURE 3.3 A goal and the objectives that quantify it

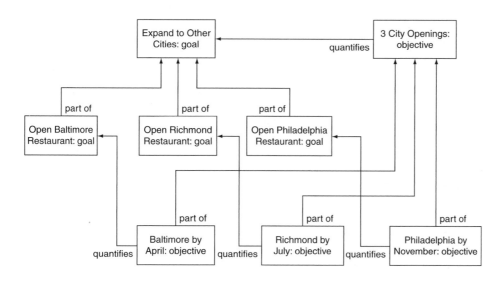

FIGURE 3.4 An objective hierarchy and a goal hierarchy

business, sometimes one pays and sometimes the other does. At best Nola is going to have an imperfect measure of repeat customers.

These difficulties with measurement are common. An objective is created with one eye on the goal it quantifies and the other eye on what can be actually measured. Goals can be lofty statements of direction, but objectives are always grounded in the constraints of measurability.

Objective Hierarchies

Like goals, objectives can be organized into a hierarchy using a **part of** association. Figure 3.4 shows the goal **Expand to Other Cities**, the objective **3 City Openings** that **quantifies** that goal, and three sub-objectives that are part of opening in three cities outside metro DC. The sub-objective **Baltimore by April** also quantifies its own goal, **Open Baltimore Restaurant**, and the other sub-objectives do the same. This kind of parallel hierarchy of goals and objectives is common.

DESIRED RESULTS AND COURSES OF ACTION

Objectives and goals are similar in that they are both *desired results*. A desired result is something an organization is trying to do for its own sake, not as a means to some other end. For example, suppose the restaurant Nola adds two goat dishes to the menu. If the head chef does this because he always wanted to serve goat, then **Add Goat Dishes** is a desired result. But suppose he added the goat dishes in an effort to attract press attention, to have some new newspaper articles written about Nola. Then **Add Goat Dishes** is a means to a larger end, the goal **Increase Media Coverage**. In that case, **Add Goat Dishes** is not a desired result and not a goal. It is instead a *course of action*.

Courses of action are similar to desired results (goals and objectives) in that both courses of action and desired results are things the organization is trying to accomplish. But courses of action are the means to other ends. They are the ways that organizations achieve their goals and objectives, the stepping stones to the success instead of the success itself. The difference between courses of action and desired results is the difference between journeys and destinations. A course of action is a journey, and a desired result is a destination.

In practice, how can you tell if an attempted thing is a desired result or a course of action? The key question is: What happens if it doesn't work? Suppose Nola's head chef is unable to secure a reliable supply of good goat meat and so cannot introduce goat dishes on the menu. If **Add Goat Dishes** is a desired result, then the failure to get goat meat is the end of the story. Nola pursues other goals. But if **Add Goat Dishes** is a means to achieving the goal **Increase Media Coverage**, then failure to secure supplies of goat will lead to a search for other ways of getting media coverage.

In practice, things can get messy. The head chef might have personally always wanted to serve goat, and **Add Goat Dishes** might have been his personal goal. But to achieve this goal, he had to convince his general manager. In selling the idea, he stressed the advantages of increased media coverage and demoted his goal to a course of action to achieve the newly minted goal of increasing the media coverage. Once he fails to secure supplies of goat, he is left with a commitment to a goal he doesn't want, and he must search for another course of action to attain that goal.

STRATEGIES AND TACTICS

Courses of action come in two varieties: *strategies* and *tactics*. The difference between the two is a matter of size and commitment. Strategies are larger and harder to change. Tactics are smaller and easier to change.

Consider Nola's goal of establishing regular customers. One approach to that goal is to establish seasonal menus—to introduce a winter menu in December, a spring menu in April, and so on. The idea is that someone who enjoyed a dinner in February might be tempted to return in the spring to see what new dishes are offered, and then return again in the summer. The strategy **Offer Seasonal Menus** is one way of achieving the goal **Establish Regular Customers**.

Another approach to the same goal is to give a discount coupon to customers as they settle their bills. The coupon, discounting a future visit to Nola, will induce some customers to return. The tactic **Offer Discount Coupon** also attempts to achieve the goal **Establish Regular Customers**.

The two approaches are quite different in size. The strategy of launching a new menu every season requires hundreds of hours of effort. The tactic of creating a discount coupon is much less work. The two approaches also represent different levels of commitment. Once a seasonal menu is established, customers will come to expect it. If the restaurant decides to drop the seasonal menu plan, some customers could be disappointed. By contrast the restaurant has made no commitments by implementing a one-time discount coupon—no commitment beyond the financial one of honoring the coupon for some limited duration.

Strategies **channel efforts toward** desired results. Figure 3.5 shows the strategy **Offer Seasonal Menus** channeling effort toward the goal **Establish Regular Customers**. Channeling effort toward a goal means that the strategy or tactic is attempting to achieve the goal, but it also means more. The whole purpose of the strategy is the goal on the other side of the **channels effort toward** link. Once the goal is accomplished, the strategy should be reexamined.

But strategies are hard to change. Once the restaurant has regular customers, it might want to retain the strategy of offering seasonal menus, channeling effort now toward other goals, such as keeping the regular customers or earning praise from restaurant critics.

Tactics also channel efforts toward goals. Figure 3.5 shows the tactic **Offer Discount Coupon** channeling effort toward establishing regular customers. And certainly once Nola has a base of regular customers, it should look closely at whether discount coupons are still useful.

Organization units *establish* strategies and tactics, just as they define goals or objectives. Figure 3.5 shows Nola establishing both the strategy **Offer Seasonal Menus** and the tactic **Offer Discount Coupon**.

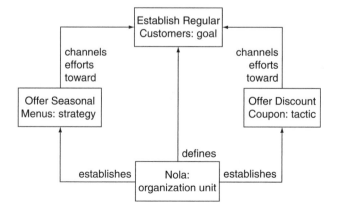

FIGURE 3.5 A strategy and a tactic

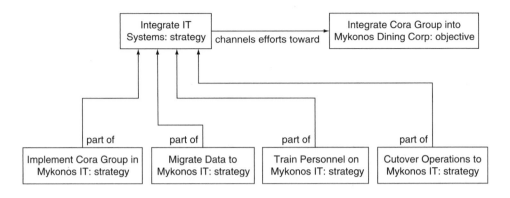

FIGURE 3.6 A hierarchy of strategies

Strategy Hierarchies and Tactic Hierarchies

Just as goals can be decomposed into subgoals and objectives decomposed into sub-objectives, strategies can be decomposed into sub-strategies. For example, consider what must be done after the Cora Group is acquired to integrate it into Mykonos Dining Corp. Part of that post-merger integration involves integrating the IT systems. Figure 3.6 shows the objective **Integrate Cora Group into Mykonos Dining Corp** and the strategy **Integrate IT Systems**. This strategy has four sub-strategies; each is a **part of** the IT integration.

Tactics can also have sub-tactics in the same way. Hierarchies of tactics are less common than hierarchies of strategies, since tactics are usually small enough to be implemented on their own without any such division.

INFLUENCERS

In everyday business language, people speak of *trends*—things that are happening in the environment of a business that might have an impact. For example, Cora Group derives more than half its revenue from business spending: entertaining clients, dinners while on travel to DC, company parties, and other events that cause businesspeople to spend company money for food and drink at good restaurants like Portia. Suppose companies started cutting expense account budgets and applying more scrutiny to the business value of expense account expenses. This is a trend, and this trend would have an impact on the Cora Group.

In business motivation modeling, trends are modeled as *influencers*. Some examples of influencers for Portia are:

- The increasing interest of Washingtonians in comfort food
- Declining readership of newspapers and declining influence of newspaper restaurant reviews

- The emergence of diner restaurant reviews on the Internet
- The declining economy in metro Philadelphia
- Rising public consumption of ethnic fare
- Public concern about food-born bacteria

Influencers also include some things that are not trends, including competitors, assets, and company habits. An influencer is anything that can have an effect on an organization, anything that can potentially hinder it or assist it. Some examples of influencers that are not trends include:

- Portia's reputation for interesting food
- Nola's nearby competitor
- Adelina's nightly review process, evaluating what went well and what should be improved
- The enactment of a local smoking ban

The category of influences is huge and astonishingly inclusive. Every business will have hundreds of potential influencers. There will always be too many influencers to model. Some kind of criterion is needed to determine what to model and what to ignore.

In practice we model the influencers that affect our strategies and tactics. If Portia's competitor introduces a radically expanded menu, the new menu will affect Portia's strategies about what to do with its own menu. The competitor is important enough to model. The declining readership of newspaper restaurant reviews will affect Portia's strategy to get good newspaper reviews, so this influencer is also important enough to model.

We also model the influencers that affect the achievement of our goals and objectives. If the economy of metropolitan Philadelphia continues to decline, that will affect Cora Group's objective of opening a restaurant there by November.

OPPORTUNITIES

An *opportunity* is a favorable situation to a business for achieving its goals. Often someone will judge that an influencer presents an opportunity. For example, the shortage of innovative restaurants in the western suburbs of DC presents an opportunity—an opportunity to open a new restaurant there to fill the need. Figure 3.7 shows the relationship between the opportunity and the influencer. The opportunity **Western Portia Branch Would Be Successful** is said to "judge" the influencer **Innovative Restaurant Shortage in Western Suburbs,** using the association **judges**. The influencer is a simple statement of the situation: that there is a shortage of innovative restaurants there. The opportunity is a claim that the situation can be exploited by the Cora Group for business advantage. The influencer is neither good nor bad by itself; it does

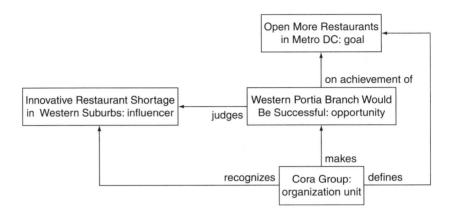

FIGURE 3.7 An influencer and an opportunity

not judge the situation. It only becomes a potential for good when it is judged to be an opportunity.

Who does the judging? As shown in Figure 3.7, Cora Group recognizes the influencer and makes an assessment that the influencer presents an opportunity. And Cora Group only recognizes it as presenting an opportunity because the opportunity affects the achievement of one of the Cora Group's goals, **Open More Restaurants in Metro DC**.

Opportunities and Influencers

The split between opportunities and influencers might seem odd. Why have these two kinds of things in motivation modeling instead of just one? Why have both an influencer—a simple factual statement of something that can hinder or assist our business—and an opportunity—an opinion that that this influencer can be exploited?

Often influencers and opportunities come in pairs (as in Figure 3.7) with a single influencer and a single opportunity related together. But influencers and opportunities are not always joined in pairs. Sometimes a single influencer can help achieve more than one goal, and so it is judged to be more than one opportunity. Consider Figure 3.8. The same influencer, **Innovative Restaurant Shortage in Western Suburbs** is judged to be both an opportunity to open a Portia branch there and an opportunity to attract western suburban residents to Nola, a Portia sister restaurant that is an easy drive from the western suburbs. In fact, there could be a useful debate within Cora Group about how to best exploit the lack of innovative restaurants in the western suburbs. Do we open a new restaurant, promote our existing restaurants, or both?

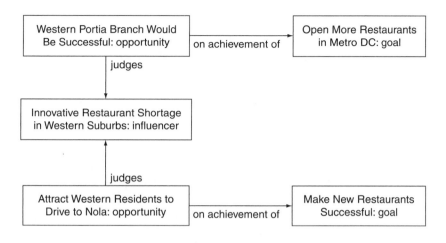

FIGURE 3.8 An influencer and two opportunities

Opportunities and Strategies

An opportunity can affect the application of a strategy as well as directly affect the achievement of a goal. Consider Portia's strategy of offering seasonal menus. In the past, time worked against this seasonal strategy. By the time people had heard of the details of this season's menu, it was too late; a new season and a new menu had arrived. But with the emergence of diner restaurant reviews on the Internet, a potential customer can learn about this season's menu from someone she doesn't know, from someone who took the trouble to review it for her and for everyone else. With the diner restaurant reviews, word spreads more quickly, providing the restaurant an opportunity for making more frequent changes to the menu. Figure 3.9 shows how this new opportunity **affects employment of** the strategy. An opportunity can affect a tactic in a similar way.

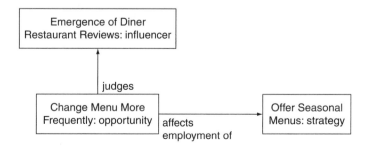

FIGURE 3.9 An opportunity affecting a strategy

THREATS

Not every influencer that affects an organization's goals or strategies can be exploited as an opportunity. For example, consider the trend of customers increasingly eating ethnic food when they dine out. Cora Group recognizes that trend as the influencer **Increasing Public Interest in Ethnic Fare**, shown in Figure 3.10, and judges it to be a *threat* to Nola, that Nola may lose customers to Thai, Peruvian, and other more ethnic restaurants.

A threat is modeled like an opportunity: a threat judges an influencer. A threat is an assessment of how the influencer will affect the business. An organization recognizes the influencer and makes an assessment that the influencer is a threat. Threats are just like opportunities except they're negative instead of positive. Whereas an opportunity can lead to a business advantage, a threat can lead to a disadvantage.

Like an opportunity, a threat can affect a goal. Figure 3.10 shows the threat **Potential to Lose Business to Ethnic Fare** to be a threat to the achievement of the goal **Establish Regular Customers**. Note that the organizations involved are different in this case. Cora Group makes the assessment, recognizing the influencer as a threat to *another organization*—to Nola and its goal of establishing regular customers.

Threats and Opportunities

A single influencer can be judged to be both a threat and an opportunity. Nola recognizes the same influencer of customers eating more ethnic fare but sees

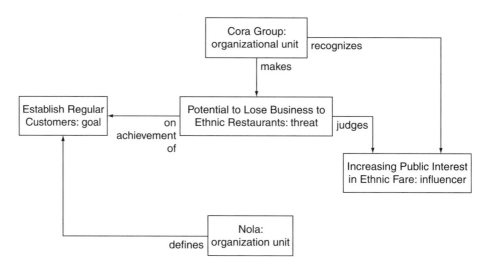

FIGURE 3.10 A threat affecting a goal

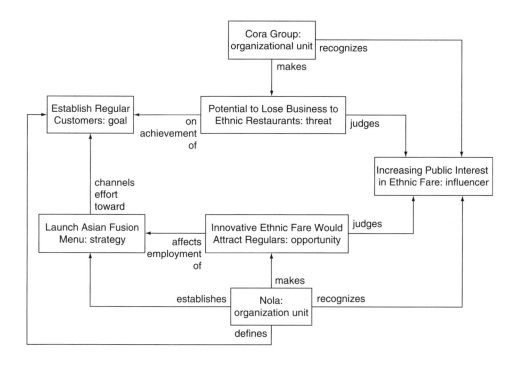

FIGURE 3.11 An influencer judged to be both a threat and an opportunity

the influencer as an opportunity to exploit by offering innovative ethnic food. Figure 3.11 shows the result, with Nola creating a new strategy, **Launch Asian Fusion Menu**, around the opportunity it sees.

An influencer is simply a statement of what is happening, but threats and opportunities are judgments about how an influencer affects the business. In our experience, differences of opinion like that shown in Figure 3.11 are very common. Sometimes the differences are disagreements between different organizations, as in Figure 3.11. In other circumstances, various people within a single organization will have different opinions about how to judge an influencer. Motivational models are very convenient for making these differences of opinions explicit and for (when appropriate) facilitating consensus.

ASSESSMENTS

Threats and opportunities are very similar; they are both *assessments*. An assessment is an evaluation of an influencer's potential effect on a business. If the influencer is both external to the organization—about a competitor, a market trend, or

Table 3.1 The Four Varieties of Assessment		
	Internal	**External**
Positive	Strength	Opportunity
Negative	Weakness	Threat

something else outside the organization itself—and judged to be favorable, it is an opportunity. If the influencer is external to the organization and judged as unfavorable, it is a threat.

Influencers can be internal to an organization, and an internal influencer can have an assessment, also positive or negative. A positive assessment of an internal influencer is a *strength*, and a negative assessment of an internal influencer is a *weakness*. Table 3.1 shows the four varieties of assessments.

You may be familiar with the four varieties of assessment from their acronym: SWOT, for strength, weakness, opportunity, threat. *SWOT analysis* is a popular method of creating business strategy by identifying and analyzing the strengths, weaknesses, opportunities, and threats of a business and using those identified assessments to create a strategy.

Motivation modeling does not prescribe SWOT analysis. Instead, motivation modeling is agnostic to the method by which strategy is formed. Strategies can be created through a formal SWOT analysis process and then modeled. Or, more commonly in our experience, strategies can be formed, refined, and rethought in a series of informal conversations among key leaders over a period of months and years. Or strategies can be created in the modeling process itself, in a series of model-based workshops, as described in Chapters 8 and 9. Modeling can be applied at any step of the way, to make explicit the current discussion and show the current disagreements.

STRENGTHS AND WEAKNESSES

Some influencers are internal to the organization. An internal influencer can be judged as either a strength, if it helps the organization achieve its goals and strategies, or as a weakness, if it inhibits the organization from such achievement.

For example, Adelina is a fairly new restaurant in the Cora Group with a small space—only eight tables. They have exploited the intimate setting of their small space by focusing on romance, by becoming the Cora Group restaurant that couples go to for a romantic evening. By catering to couples focused on romance instead of business dinners or larger parties, Adelina has prospered.

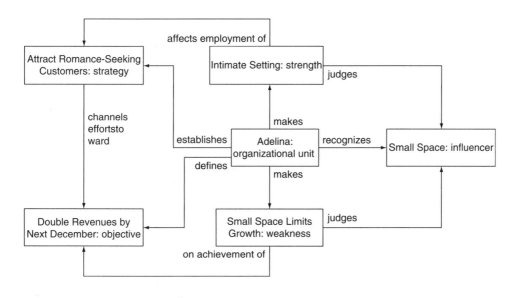

FIGURE 3.12 A strength and a weakness

Figure 3.12 shows a model of this situation. The influencer **Small Space** is a simple statement of the fact that Adelina has only eight tables. (The description attribute of this model element would no doubt include details about the small space, including the dimensions and layout of the dining room and how it is usually configured for eight two-person tables.) The strength **Intimate Setting** represents how Adelina uses the small space to its advantage in setting a romantic mood. This strength affects the employment of Adelina's strategy **Attract Romance-Seeking Customers**.

Unfortunately Adelina's success is also limited by its space; they turn away many people every night because they have only eight tables and they have become very popular. If they had a larger space, they could do more business. But moving is always risky. What if their customers don't move with them or they don't find the new larger space as charming as the existing one?

Figure 3.12 also shows this limitation on their success. The same small space that leads to the strength **Intimate Setting** is also judged to be a weakness, **Small Space Limits Growth**. This weakness affects Adelina's objective, **Double Revenues by Next December**.

In this example there is a single influencer that is judged to be both a strength and a weakness. This is common. Often factors that help our businesses succeed later inhibit further success. Models are useful for spotting these subtle, counterintuitive relationships. They are sometimes hard to notice when talking or thinking about a situation but easy to identify when creating a visual model.

COMPARING ALTERNATIVES

Motivation models are most often used for *strategy capture*. Someone creates the strategy in a process that does not involve modeling. Modelers are called in later to capture that strategy after it is created. The model represents the strategy that is already agreed, and the purpose of the model is to support the communication of the strategy, or its analysis, or one of the other purposes discussed earlier.

But sometimes motivation models are used to help create the strategy. As part of the process of deciding what strategy is best, modelers create models of the alternatives and then analyze them. For example, suppose the management team is trying to decide how to increase Adelina's revenue. Three alternatives are discussed: Adelina could move to a new location, Adelina could cater to business events that rent the whole restaurant for an evening, or Adelina could raise prices, attempting to capture new revenue from the existing business. For the most part, these alternatives are mutually exclusive. If Adelina moved, it would be a risky time to raise prices or to cater to a new audience.

Figure 3.13 shows the first alternative: moving to a new location. The influencer **Restaurant Moves Often Strand Customers** is a reflection of the reality of the restaurant business. Many customers remember a restaurant by its location. Moving the restaurant will lead some customers to show up at the old place and others to forget about the restaurant entirely. Some customers will be lost.

This influencer is *evoked* by the strategy **Move to New Location**. The influencers we have seen so far are all observations about the world—trends, competitors, etc.—or observations about our business. This one is different; it is a *potential* observation, something that is not happening yet but that we expect to happen if we adopt this strategy. It is related to the strategy by the association **evokes**.

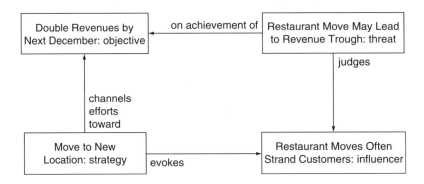

FIGURE 3.13 One alternative strategy

If the restaurant move does strand some customers, Adelina will see a revenue trough—a decline in revenue for some time until existing customers learn about the new location and new customers discover the restaurant. This potential revenue shortfall is modeled by the threat **Restaurant Move May Lead to Revenue Trough**. The threat in turn affects achievement of the objective **Double Revenues by Next December** that is the original motivation for the restaurant move strategy.

Another Strategy

Figure 3.14 shows the second strategy, **Market to Business Events**— marketing to businesses that are interested in reserving the whole restaurant for an evening, to host a business event. These business events often involve much drinking and typically result in more revenue for the restaurants that host them.

But there is a drawback to this second alternative. Some customers who are looking for an evening of romance at Adelina will be disappointed to learn that the whole restaurant is closed that night for a business event and that they must find another venue. This consequence evoked by the strategy is modeled as the influencer **Closing for Events Disappoints Some Customers**, judged by the threat **May Lose Disappointed Regulars to Competitors** that will affect the objective of doubling revenues.

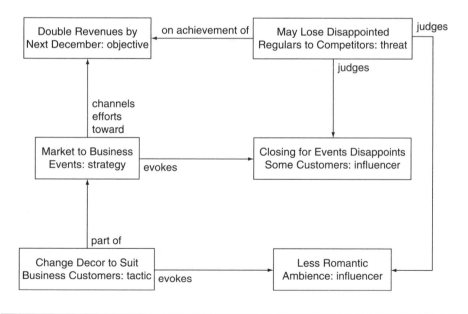

FIGURE 3.14 Another alternative strategy to achieve the same objective

There is another drawback. Adelina's decor reinforces its current strategy of high romance. If Adelina wants to attract a business audience for events, it needs to tone down the romantic decor to something more business-appropriate. The tactic **Change Decor to Suit Business Customers** is part of the new strategy. This tactic evokes its own consequence, the influencer **Less Romantic Ambience**, that also threatens to lose disappointed regulars to more romantically focused alternatives.

A Third Strategy

Figure 3.15 shows the third alternative: raising prices. **Raise Prices** is modeled as a tactic rather than a strategy because it is quick to implement and easy to reverse. The tactic evokes an obvious consequence: that some regular customers will reevaluate their patronage, modeled as the influencer **Price-Sensitive Customers Reevaluate**. (And in the usual manner of luxury goods, the higher prices may even signal increased desirability to some customers.) The influencer is assessed by the threat **Lose Customers to Less-Pricey Competitors**.

But there is also another more serious threat involved in raising prices. If the price rise leads to Adelina earning a reputation of being overpriced (modeled as an influencer), this could lead to customers becoming indignant, also affecting the objective of doubling revenues.

Three Strategies in a Single Diagram

Figures 3.13, 3.14, and 3.15 show three alternative courses of action—two strategies and a tactic—to the objective of doubling revenues. The three courses of action are shown in three separate diagrams. They can also be shown in the same diagram, as shown in Figure 3.16. The three courses of action are alternative approaches to channel effort toward the objective, and the three **channels**

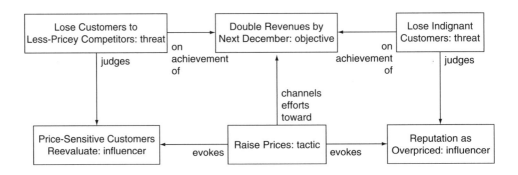

FIGURE 3.15 A third alternative strategy

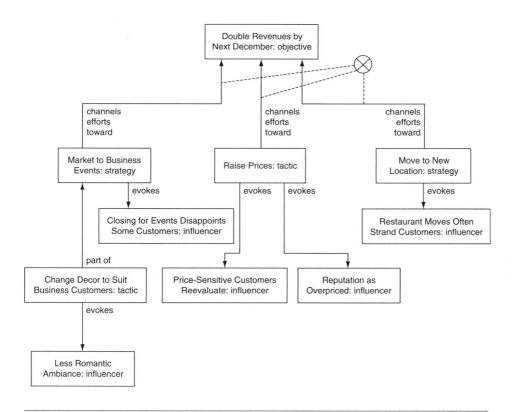

FIGURE 3.16 Three alternative courses of action

efforts toward relationships are labeled with an exclusive-or symbol, to indicate that they are mutually exclusive. If they were not so labeled, someone could interpret the diagram as showing three courses of action that Adelina intends to pursue in tandem.

The influencers that are evoked by the three courses of action are also shown in Figure 3.16. The resulting threats are omitted, so the diagram shown is not overly complicated. (A version of this model with the threats included was shown in Chapter 2 as an example of an overly large and complex model, one at the limit of understandability.)

CAUSAL LOOP DIAGRAMS

Influencers are connected to opportunities and other assessments through the **judges** relationship and the **evokes** relationship, as described earlier in this chapter. Influencers also support another relationship—at least some influencers do.

Some influencers can be connected to other influencers to show cause and effect. These special influencers that can be connected to each other are called *actuators*. An actuator is an influencer that represents a quantity, something that is large or small, growing or declining. Portia's competitor is an influencer for Portia, as it could be a threat (or even an opportunity), but it is not an actuator since it is not a quantity. But the competitor's annual revenue is an actuator; it's a quantity that has an effect on Portia's world. Similarly, the competitor's critic ratings are an actuator, as is their customer reputation.

Note that an actuator may be easy to measure—like annual revenues—or difficult to measure—like critic ratings. How do you average a good rating in a newspaper with a middling rating in Zagat's™? Some actuators, such as customer reputation, are perhaps not even measurable. An influencer can be an actuator without being measurable. An actuator need only be inherently a quantity, even if it can't actually be measured.

A network of actuators connected together is called a *causal loop diagram*. A causal loop diagram shows how potential business actions lead to complex dynamic effects. For example, consider neighborhoods that become restaurant districts, with dozens of restaurants all within a few blocks. How does this happen? Initially, a couple of restaurants are located in the neighborhood. In an effort to be noticed, another new one opens nearby. The neighborhood gets the reputation as a minor restaurant district, and some customers travel to the neighborhood and then walk around to decide where to eat. More restaurants open there, and the reputation of the restaurant district increases.

Figure 3.17 shows a model of this situation. The actuator **Neighborhood Is Known for Restaurants** increases, and that actuator causes increases in the actuator **Restaurant Customers Dine in Neighborhood**. That in turn causes increases in the actuator **Neighborhood Attractiveness to Restaurant Owners**. Greater attractiveness of the neighborhood to restaurant owners

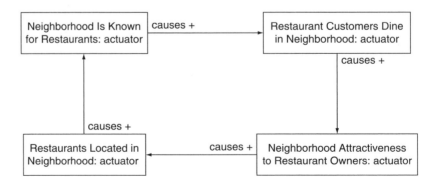

FIGURE 3.17 A causal loop

causes increases in the actuator **Restaurants Locate in Neighborhood**, which in turn causes increases in the original actuator **Neighborhood Is Known for Restaurants**. The neighborhood becomes increasingly concentrated with restaurants.

Connecting Actuators

The relationship that connects the two actuators is **causes+**, meaning that increases in one actuator lead to increases in the other. It also means that decreases in one actuator lead to decreases in the other; the same causal loop can run in reverse. Suppose a local crime wave (not modeled) leads to the neighborhood becoming less popular with customers this year. The neighborhood is now less attractive to restaurant owners and fewer restaurants now locate there; some restaurants will close and others will choose to locate elsewhere. Now the neighborhood is a bit less known for restaurants than it was before, and even fewer customers seek it out. The neighborhood spirals down.

An increase in one actuator can alternatively lead to a decrease in another. For example, if business rents increase in a neighborhood, the neighborhood will become less attractive to restaurant owners. As a result, fewer restaurants will locate there; some existing restaurants will move to other, cheaper locations, and owners considering opening a new restaurant will also choose other locations. The negative causality between rents and attractiveness is identified with a **causes−** relationship, the negative twin of **causes+**.

Figure 3.18 shows a **causes−** relationship between business rents and attractiveness, as part of a causal loop. This causal loop is *balancing*; a rent increase causes a decrease in the neighborhood attractiveness to owners, causing fewer restaurants to locate there and leading to declines in the rent. In a balancing loop,

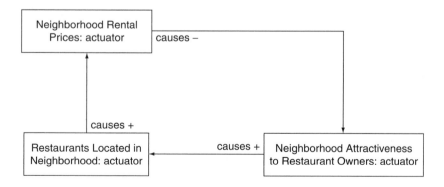

FIGURE 3.18 A balancing causal loop

changes in one direction cause changes in the other direction, tending toward either moderation or (in some cases) cycles. By contrast, Figure 3.17 is a *reinforcing* causal loop diagram: Things get more and more extreme over time.

Delayed Causality

Some causality happens quickly and some happens slowly. Rising rents will cause a neighborhood to become immediately less attractive to restaurant owners, but the number of restaurants there won't decline immediately. Owners are reluctant to decide to relocate their restaurants, and even when they decide to move, executing the move takes months. Restaurants will close due to the high rent or for other reasons, but only over time, and others will fail to open there, but again only over time. There are significant delays in this link of the causal loop.

Causal loop models indicate which causal links happen slowly, with the relationships **causes delayed+** and **causes delayed−**. Figure 3.19 shows the same balancing loop as Figure 3.18 but with the delays annotated. Now **Neighborhood Attractiveness to Restaurant Owners** causes a delayed response to **Restaurants Located in Neighborhood**.

There are four causality relationships. Table 3.2 summarizes them.

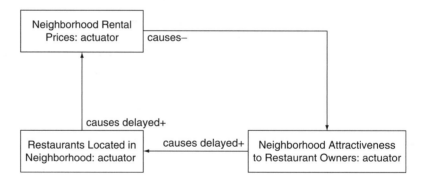

FIGURE 3.19 A causal loop with delays

Table 3.2 The Four Varieties of Actuator Causality		
	Immediate	**Delayed**
Positive	causes+	causes delayed+
Negative	causes−	causes delayed−

Complex Dynamics

The causal loop diagrams so far are fairly simple and easy to understand, and it's easy to predict what will happen. They show simple dynamics. But causal loop diagrams can also exhibit complex dynamics that are hard to predict. Consider what happens if we combine Figures 3.18 and 3.19 into a single model, shown in Figure 3.20.[3]

The neighborhood wants to become more concentrated with restaurants, making it attractive to restaurants owners and leading to additional restaurants. But the neighborhood becomes expensive (at least in terms of business rent), making it less attractive to restaurant owners and leading them to look elsewhere. What will happen?

Note that the **Neighborhood Attractiveness to Restaurant Owners** has two causality links coming in—one for the positive effect of restaurant customers dining there, the other for the negative effect of rental price increases. What does the causality mean when there are multiple incoming relationships? How can we say that an increase in rental prices will lead to a less attractive neighborhood (to the restaurant owner) when that effect may be overwhelmed by the increasing number of restaurant customers choosing to dine there?

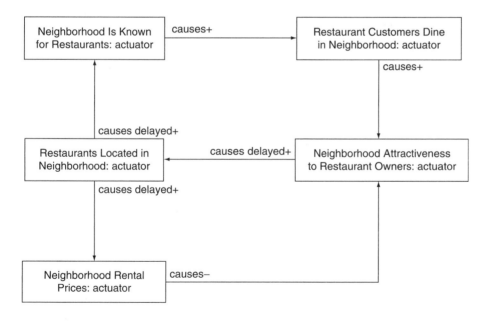

FIGURE 3.20 Combining two loops into a single model

---

[3]Actually, Figure 3.20 can exhibit some different outcomes, depending on how the delays interact.

There is a wrinkle in what the causality links mean. If actuator A is linked via a **causes+** relationship to actuator B, that means that increases in A lead to increases in B *if everything else is equal*, and decreases in A lead to decreases in B *if everything else is equal*. For actuators with multiple incoming causality, everything else is not equal. The combination of the causal links can result in complex dynamics.

There are several different ways the Figure 3.20 dynamics can play out. One possibility is that the neighborhood becomes more popular until the high rents halt the increase in popularity. Another possibility is that the neighborhood becomes more popular for restaurants, leading to some big rent increases, which in turn lead to many established restaurants departing, the neighborhood becoming a much less desired destination, and more restaurants leaving, finally resulting in no restaurants at all. Another possibility is that the rent negative causality is not enough to diminish the enthusiasm for the neighborhood, and it becomes increasingly popular until other dynamics take over (e.g., the restaurant concentration leads disgruntled residents to complain to city authorities about the noise and traffic). And there are other possibilities; many outcomes exist.

Causal Loop Diagrams and Management Discussion

Causal loop diagrams are useful for eliciting discussion among members of a management team. The Portia management team can dig into Figure 3.20 and (perhaps) predict how the neighborhood will evolve over time.

A causal loop diagram can also be simulated to resolve issues about how the dynamics will play out. However, causal loop diagrams are rarely simulated directly. They simply don't have enough information to resolve the uncertainties. Instead, a causal loop model is used as an intermediate step in building a system dynamics model, and the system dynamics model is simulated. Chapter 11 describes system dynamics models and simulation.

THE BMM STANDARD

In 2006, the Object Management Group adopted a standard for business motivation modeling: the Business Motivation Model (BMM). Prior to BMM, there was much variety. In practice, business analysts used many different techniques to model business goals and strategies. There was little agreement among all the variety of techniques, and people had difficulty translating models from one technique to another. Also, some modeling tools supported the modeling of goals and strategies, but different tools supported it in different ways with different kinds of model elements. Again there was little agreement among all the tool variety, and people had difficulty porting models built in one tool to another. The OMG stepped in to fix this problem with the BMM standard.[4]

The motivation models described in this chapter are largely consistent with the BMM. As with all the standards described in this book, we have not endeavored to be complete. There are several corners of the BMM that are not covered in this chapter. For example, the BMM describes a rather elaborate categorization of influencers, including suppliers, infrastructure, implicit corporate values and management prerogatives. (For more details you can read the specification [OMG 2007]. For a standards specification, it is remarkably clear and readable.) Instead of providing complete coverage, we have covered the parts of the BMM standard that are (in our opinion) the most useful for everyday business modeling, endeavoring always to keep the discussion simple and useful.

In addition to goals, strategies, and influencers, the BMM also specifies business policies and business rules as well as the way policies and rules are related to goals and strategies. Rather than describing business rules and business policies in this chapter, we describe them in Chapter 6. Similarly, the BMM specifies the way business processes are related to strategies. We cover that topic in Chapter 5, when we describe business processes.

As we write this book, BMM is a new standard: BMM 1.0 was adopted in 2006. In our view the standard is good but incomplete. One shortcoming of BMM 1.0 is that it does not specify a graphical look for BMM diagrams. The standard says how goals and strategies are related but is silent on how a diagram showing goals and strategies should be drawn. But in our experience, business motivation models are inherently visual. It is not enough to *read* how their goals and strategies relate; people like to *see* how they relate in a diagram.

We created our own graphical look for BMM diagrams and used that look for the diagrams in this chapter. This look is meant only to be a stopgap, an attempt to show diagrams in the absence of a standard. Hopefully a future edition of the book will be able to use the BMM graphical standard when it is developed in a future version of the BMM.

We also took the liberty of changing the cardinality of one of the relationships. In the BMM each assessment judges a single influencer. But we have found that the same assessment is sometimes convenient for more than one influencer—for example, as in Figure 3.14. So we changed the cardinality of **judges,** to allow an assessment to judge more than one influencer.

The BMM was developed to model a single strategy for a business: either today's strategy or a desired strategy described in a business plan. The BMM is silent on alternative strategies, on supporting the sometimes messy process of deciding which influencers are important and which tactics to employ. In our

---

[4]There is a potential confusion between the Business Motivation Model—the standard—and business motivation modeling—the practice of creating models of goals and strategies and the focus of this chapter. To avert this confusion, we use the acronym to refer to the standard and spell out the practice: BMM is the standard used for business motivation modeling.

use of the BMM to model strategy alternatives, we found a need for a couple of extensions. One extension is the relationship **evokes** between a course of action and an influencer. As described earlier in the chapter, a potential course of action **evokes** an influencer when someone believes that the course of action will lead to the influencer. Figures 3.13, 3.14, 3.15, and 3.16 all use this new relationship.

Figure 3.16 shows a second extension for modeling strategy alternatives. As discussed earlier, when several course-of-action alternatives are shown in the same diagram, we use a symbol to show that the relationships are mutually exclusive. This approach to modeling mutually exclusive relationships is adapted from Terry Halpin's work with Object Role Modeling [Halpin 2001].

BMM 1.0 does not support modeling of causality networks among influencers. You simply cannot create a causal loop diagram in BMM. To support causal loops, we added the influencer subclass actuator and the four causality relationships among actuators shown in Table 3.2. Our notation for these causal relationships was adapted from the standard notation for causal loop modeling in system dynamics [Sterman 2000], modified to be more consistent with the form of model elements and relationships in BMM.

Case Study

Unisys Corporation performs IT infrastructure services and IT outsourcing for other companies and for government agencies. Many organizations recognize that their own IT departments do not perform services such as desktop support very well, so they outsource that responsibility to Unisys. When an client employee's desktop computer misbehaves, the employee calls tech support and talks to someone at Unisys.

In 2007, Unisys had a problem. Unisys had many existing clients who were happy and satisfied with Unisys, but the company was having increasing difficulty winning work from new clients. Unisys lacked the numeric evidence from its existing work—the before and after numbers about cost reduction and time savings that would motivate new clients to choose Unisys over another IT services vendor. When writing proposals, Unisys personnel wanted to be able to make claims that client X saved $23 million by hiring Unisys and that client Y cut the time waiting to resolve IT support issues by 38%. Unfortunately, no one at Unisys was collecting the evidence to support those claims.

Unisys assembled an "evidence team" to solve this problem. This team included both sales and marketing professionals who understood the kinds of evidence needed as well as field managers—individuals who work with existing clients every day and understand what is easy to accomplish with clients and what is hard. The team was chartered with determining how the engagement delivery process needed to change to collect the evidence.

The evidence team knew they had to create new business processes and modify existing ones to collect the evidence. But they didn't start by examining processes. Instead they started with a discussion of what they were trying to do, digging deeper into the goals they had been asked to achieve and the alternative strategies they could use to achieve those goals. They started by creating a motivation model.

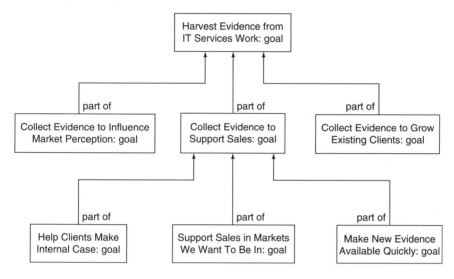

FIGURE 3.21 Goals of the Unisys evidence team

The evidence team modeled the overall challenge as the goal **Harvest Evidence from IT Services Work**, shown at the top of Figure 3.21. The team recognized that there were three distinct purposes for the evidence that they were charged with collecting. First, the evidence was to be used to influence the general market perception of Unisys, to be used in trade publication advertisements and as talking points by the senior management. This was modeled as the goal **Collect Evidence to Influence Market Perception**, a subgoal of **Harvest Evidence from Services Work**. Second, the evidence was to be used to support individual sales. When Unisys writes a proposal for a client, the proposal team should be able to use numeric evidence of past success with other clients in the new proposal. This second purpose was modeled as the goal **Collect Evidence to Support Sales**. Third, the evidence was to be used to grow business at an existing client. For example, if Unisys does desktop support for some business units of a company, numeric evidence of success in those business units would help convince

Continued

Case Study—continued

the client to outsource desktop support of the rest of the business units. The third purpose was modeled as the goal **Collect Evidence to Grow Existing Clients**.

Evidence Collection Subgoals

As they discussed it further, the evidence team uncovered three subgoals of **Collect Evidence to Support Sales**—goals that were important to achieve as part of supporting proposals to new clients. Prospective clients must make the business case inside their own companies; they must persuade various internal client stakeholders of both the wisdom of outsourcing and the merits of outsourcing to Unisys. The evidence team thought it was important to collect the kinds of metrics that would help their clients make those internal cases. This was modeled as the goal **Help Clients Make Internal Case**, a subgoal of **Collect Evidence to Support Sales**.

Unisys has many successful client engagements. There was not time enough to collect detailed evidence from every success. The evidence team knew they must focus. But which client engagements should they focus on? The team decided that they should focus on the markets in which the company wanted to grow and pay less attention to the other markets. This market focus for the evidence was modeled as the goal **Support Sales in Markets We Want To Be In**, another subgoal of **Collect Evidence to Support Sales**.

The kinds of evidence needed to sell new clients changes from year to year. Last year cost saving was important. This year, clients are interested in improving their time to market. Next year, supporting growth will overshadow other concerns. The evidence team realized that new evidence must be available quickly to support new sales needs as they arise. This realization was modeled by the third subgoal of **Collect Evidence to Support Sales**: **Make New Evidence Available Quickly**.

The evidence team turned from discussing goals to discussing how these goals could be achieved. Who should collect the evidence from an engagement? Should it be the existing engagement delivery personnel, already working with the client? Or should it be someone else, perhaps an "evidence squad" whose sole purpose is to dive in, collect evidence from an engagement, and then leave? The evidence team decided it would be easier and simpler for the existing engagement delivery personnel to collect the evidence. This decision was modeled as the strategy **Evidence Collected by Delivery Team**, shown in Figure 3.22.

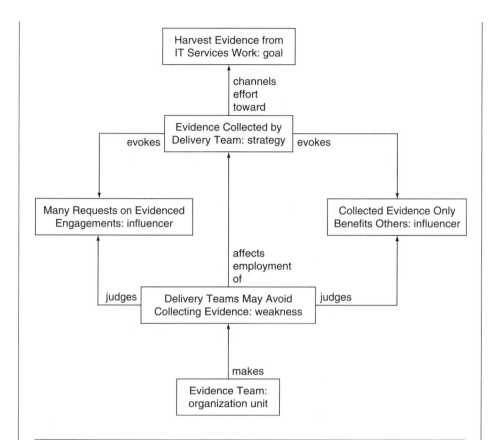

FIGURE 3.22 Using the delivery team to collect evidence

Challenges with Relying on Delivery Personnel

But there are some drawbacks with using the delivery personnel to collect evidence. The field managers described a hidden costs of providing numeric evidence: the engagement team and the client that provides the evidence have to field many subsequent requests by other interested clients—clients who want to verify that the evidence is real and ask questions about how it was achieved. These requests can be a burden on both the Unisys team and the client. This is a significant disincentive to those field managers who collect evidence from their engagements and a reason for them to avoid collecting evidence, everything else being equal. This drawback is modeled as the influencer **Many Requests on Evidenced Engagements** and the weakness

Continued

Case Study—continued

Delivery Teams May Avoid Collecting Evidence, a judgment of the influencer by the evidence team.

The existing delivery incentives also work against the strategy. The delivery personnel are incented to perform well on their engagement: to keep their client happy and satisfied, to deliver the contracted services, and to perform this work within budget and on time. Collecting evidence takes time and effort but does not help the people who are expending this time and effort. All this work is for the benefit of unknown others sometime in the future. In most organizations, such work is usually avoided, short-changed, or performed superficially. This misalignment between who pays for evidence collection and who benefits is modeled as the influencer **Collected Evidence Only Benefits Others**. The weakness **Delivery Teams May Avoid Collecting Evidence** is also a judgment of this influencer.

The evidence team decided they needed to tackle this weakness. They decided on three strategies. First, they tackled the misalignment of incentives by deciding to incorporate evidence collection into performance evaluation. The engagement manager, the leader of the delivery personnel for a client, will be measured on how well he or she collects evidence of success as well as the other measures, such as engagement profitability and client satisfaction. This decision is modeled as the strategy **Incorporate Evidence into Delivery Perf Evaluations**, shown in Figure 3.23 as a sub-strategy of **Evidence Collected by Delivery Team**.

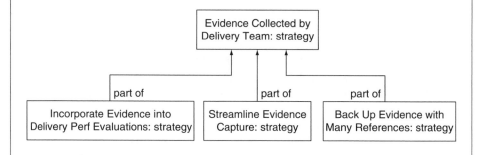

FIGURE 3.23 Evidence strategies

Second, they decided to make evidence collection easy, to reduce the avoidance by lowering its cost. This approach is modeled as the strategy **Streamline Evidence Capture**.

Third, they reasoned that creating a lot of evidence references from existing engagements would spread out the burden of fielding requests.

No one delivery team would have to field too many requests if everyone fielded some. This decision was modeled as the strategy **Back Up Evidence With Many References**.

The Value of the Motivation Model

With their motivation model, the evidence team now had a clear understanding of what they were trying to do and a consensus on how to do it. They proceeded to decide what metrics to collect and how to change the engagement delivery business processes to collect those metrics. This work was also performed via business modeling, using a business process model of the engagement delivery process. But business process models are not the focus of this chapter; instead they are described in Chapter 5. So our description of this case study ends here, with the completed motivation model.

How did the motivation model help the Unisys evidence team? The motivation model helped organize the discussion as it was happening. Meetings of large cross-functional groups often wander. By constructing a motivation model along the way, the team focused their attention on what they were trying to do.

The motivation model served as a record of their discussion later. Too often teams make decisions in workshops and then the members later cannot recall the logic behind the decision. Why did we decide that? What were we thinking? The motivation model is a record of the goals, strategies, and influencers that led to their decisions.

As the evidence team crafted business process activities to collect evidence, they traced these activities back to goals and strategies. For example, early in an engagement, a delivery manager decides whether to try to collect evidence from that engagement. This decision is driven by whether the evidence is likely to help sell other work that Unisys wants to win. So the new activity **Decide Whether to Collect Evidence** is traced back to the goal **Support Sales in Markets We Want To Be In**.

Finally, the motivation model was useful for communicating the evidence collection strategy to others. Many other people would have to understand what the evidence team has done. The many engagement delivery managers across Unisys who will become responsible for collecting evidence metrics need to understand what needs to be done and why. The evidence team used the motivation model to explain these metrics to the engagement delivery managers.

The motivation model built by the evidence team is not concerned with the corporate strategy of Unisys as a whole nor with the strategy of a Unisys business unit. Instead, the motivation model is narrowly focused on the strategy for achieving one goal: collecting evidence from delivery work to support future sales. This is strategy-in-the-small, the strategy for a single

Continued

Case Study—continued

project. While strategy-in-the-large gets much attention, strategy-in-the-small pervades all organizations. Only a few people in any organization perform strategy-in-the-large, but everyone performs strategy-in-the-small.

Motivation models are just as useful for modeling strategy-in-the-small as for modeling strategy-in-the-large. Both involve goals, objectives, influencers, assessments, strategies, and tactics.

A business motivation model describes the broad goals that the business is trying to achieve, specific measurable objectives, and the strategies and tactics by which they are to be achieved. The goals, objectives, strategies, and tactics are affected by influencers—things that are happening in either the world or the business. These influencers are assessed to be strengths, weaknesses, opportunities, or threats to the business. Some of these influencers affect each other in causal loops, the aggregate effect of which impedes or supports the strategy of the business. All these model elements—goals, strategies, influencers, etc.—are related to one another in an interconnected network.

The business motivation model is largely about the "why" of the business. In Chapter 4 we look at the "who"—the organizations that live within a business, how those organizations are related to each other, and how they interact, both with each other and with organizations outside the walls of the business.

Business Organization Models

4

Business organization modeling is the second of the four business modeling disciplines we describe in this book. A business organization model describes how a company is organized—the business units and departments and working groups within it. A business organization model describes the interactions—who interacts with whom to get the work done. A business organization model describes the roles that people play in the company. It also describes the way a company interacts with other organizations outside the company. This chapter explains business organization models.

Now that the decision has been made to acquire Cora Group, it must be integrated into the far larger Mykonos Corporation. Mykonos has acquired many restaurants, but most have been acquired individually. Acquiring an individual restaurant is straightforward. After the acquisition, the general manager of the acquired restaurant reports to the appropriate regional head of restaurants. Purchasing responsibility for bulk food and kitchen equipment is transitioned to Mykonos Purchasing, to take advantage of existing vendor relationships and bulk purchasing agreements. Responsibility for human resources and employee benefits is transitioned to Mykonos HR, always a welcome change for the acquired restaurant.

The acquisition of Cora Group is different. Cora Group is a company of several restaurants, with a small central office that already performs some of the functions to be transitioned to Mykonos Corporate. You expect that both purchasing and human resources could be supplied by Mykonos more cheaply and better than Cora Group performs those functions today. But before you make any changes, you plan to better understand the Cora Group.

You start by exploring the way Cora Group and its individual restaurants are organized. You want to understand who dines at the restaurants and who the competitors are. You need to learn whether Cora Group uses the same vendors as Mykonos so that you can determine whether purchases can simply be consolidated or whether vendor changes will need to be made. By understanding how the individual restaurants function, you can weigh the difficulty of transitioning responsibilities to Mykonos.

To achieve this understanding, you create a business organization model. A business organization model shows the organizations inside a company, how they interact with each other, and how they interact with other companies.

Business organization models include *organizations*—collections of people who work toward a common goal. Some organizations in a business organization model are inside the company.[1] An organization model for Cora Group includes the restaurant Portia as well as the other restaurants that are part of Cora Group Other organizations in a business organization model are outside the company. An organization model for Cora Group includes Sabre Staffing, a company Cora uses to hire waitstaff.

Organization models include *roles*—what people do within an organization. An organization model for Portia includes the role of chef. Each of the people who prepare food at Portia plays the role of chef.

Organization models include *associations*—ways that organizations and roles relate to each other. For example, one type of association in the organizational model of Portia is the reporting relationship between a chef and the Portia general manager.

WHY MODEL BUSINESS ORGANIZATIONS?

To better understand why we want to create business organization models, let's consider the eight purposes of business modeling, first identified in Chapter 1. Of these eight, business organization models can achieve four purposes: communication, training and learning, persuasion and selling, and analysis.

When you return from your exploratory visit to Cora Group and report to Mykonos management, the organization models help you *communicate* what the Cora Group organization does and how it does it. Organization models are also useful to communicate changes. After a corporate reorganization you use an organization model to show the changes in structure and reporting. You also show how interactions have changed between groups within the company and with business partners outside the company.

Companies perform projects. When performing a project, organization models help communicate the project scope. Some of the organizations in an organization model are in scope for the project and some are out of scope. We use organization models to achieve consensus among project stakeholders about what is in and what is out. By including some organizations, some roles, and some

---

[1]Organizational modeling can be performed on government agencies instead of companies, using the same techniques, and to the same ends. Similarly nonprofits, universities, or other sorts of organizations could be the focus of your modeling.

associations in the model and leaving others out, we reach agreement about what to attempt in the project.

Sometimes business organization models are used to *train and learn.* New employees can learn about the other people they must interact with. New employees can learn the roles they must play and their place in the organization.

An organization model can be used to represent a past state of a company, the current state, or a future state. The models of different periods can be compared to each other and *analyzed.* We study a company after a proposed reorganization to understand the impact on the customers. We determine whether the proposed reorganization will simplify the interactions with customers, or make them more complex.

These same organization models are used to *persuade* senior management which alternative reorganization should be performed. Employees can be persuaded of the benefits of a planned reorganization. They can see where they will be located in the new organization, and they can see how their responsibilities and interactions will change. Some responsibilities and interactions will change and some will not.

ORGANIZATIONS

An *organization unit* (or more simply stated, an organization) is a collection of people who work together toward a common goal. An organization has a clear boundary. Some people are part of Portia and others are not. An organization usually has structures within it. Mykonos has Mykonos Purchasing, Mykonos Finance, Mykonos Atlanta—for the restaurants in the Atlanta metropolitan area—and so on. An organization can be part of another organization. For example, before the acquisition, Portia was part of Cora Group.

A corporate holding company provides another good example of organizations that are part of other organizations. Within a holding company, each company has its own management structure, its own performance goals, and its own budgets and resources. But all the companies within the holding company are connected. Their performance flows up to the holding company, and their goals are part of a larger plan.

An organization can be a commercial company, a nonprofit, or a government agency. An organization can be a smaller group of people within a larger organization. An organization can even be temporary. A temporary project team is an organization. The team exists while the project is performed and then disappears after the project is finished.

When we model organizations, we look at the way they are structured, the work they perform, and the way they are associated with other organizations. We do not focus on how they perform their work. How they perform their work is instead modeled as business processes and is described in Chapter 5.

As part of your exploration of Cora Group, you create some organization models. Figure 4.1 shows **Cora Group** and the five restaurants that are part of it:

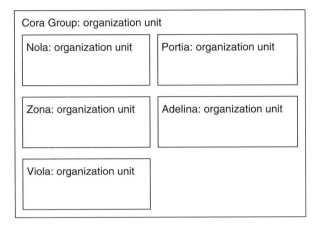

FIGURE 4.1 Business organization model of Cora Group

Nola, **Zona**, **Portia**, **Adelina,** and **Viola**. Cora Group is an organization unit. Each of the five restaurants is also an organization unit. Each restaurant is shown graphically as being enclosed by **Cora Group**. This graphical enclosure means that there is a **part of** association between the two: **Nola** is **part of Cora Group**, as are each of the other four restaurants.

Business organization models are different from organization charts. Compare Figure 4.1 to the organizational chart we first saw in Chapter 2, which is shown again as Figure 4.2. There are two differences. First, the business organization model (in Figure 4.1) shows us the organizations that comprise Cora Group instead of people and their roles. Instead of seeing Dan Hamscher, the general manager of Nola, we see Nola. Second, the organization model shows what organization is part of what other organization rather than the reporting relationships between people. Instead of seeing that Dan Hamscher reports to Sam Coates, we see that that Nola is part of Cora Group.

We use the **part of** association to show the organizations that are part of a larger organization. In Figure 4.1, **Cora Group** is composed of five restaurants, each of which is part of **Cora Group**. Figure 4.1 shows no association between **Adelina** and **Viola** and in fact no associations between any of the restaurants within **Cora Group**.

The size of the rectangle that depicts an organizational unit in an organization model is not significant. In Figure 4.1 **Cora Group** is shown larger than **Nola** not because it is a bigger organization (although it is) but because we want to show **Nola** as enclosed within **Cora Group** to depict the **part of** association between them. The size of the organizational unit in an organization model means nothing.

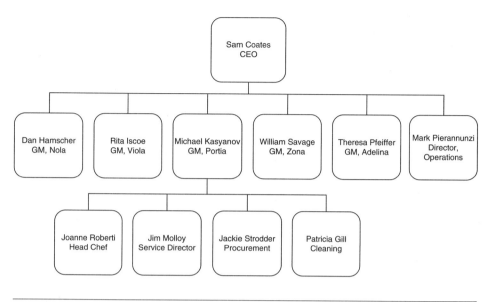

FIGURE 4.2 An organization chart

The location of an organizational unit within an organization model diagram also means nothing. In Figure 4.1, **Nola** is located above **Zona**, but that does not mean that Nola is more important or larger than Zona or anything at all. Location implies meaning in an organization model only when one organization encloses another. All other location matters are purely aesthetics.

Each organization has a name and a description. The description of the organization includes several sentences detailing the purpose of the organization, a bit of its history, and the functions it performs. For example, the description for **Adelina** is:

> *Adelina is the critic's favorite restaurant of the Cora Group. It is located in Washington, DC. Adelina opened in 1997 and specializes in authentic Greek seafood dishes. Adelina has earned a Zagat food rating of 24 and has been ranked as one of* Washingtonian Magazine's *"100 very best restaurants" for eight years in a row.*

Business organization models are inherently hierarchical. An organization is composed of several other organizations, which are in turn composed of other organizations. Figure 4.3 shows **Cora Group** as composed of five restaurants. One of those five—**Portia**—has four more organizations that are part of it: **Diner Services**, **Procurement**, **Cooking Services**, and **Cleaning Services**. Diner Services is responsible for all interactions with the customers of Portia: hosting, reservations, and serving food. Procurement is responsible for all interactions with

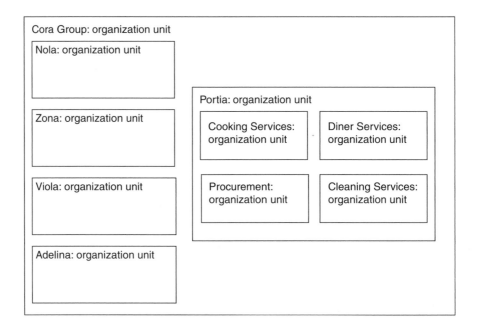

FIGURE 4.3 Organizations and sub organizations

external vendors and suppliers. Cooking Services is responsible for the creation of all meals. Cleaning Services is responsible for cleaning the facilities, including the dining area, bathrooms, and immediate restaurant surroundings.

Of course, there are limits to showing the inherent hierarchy of organizations in a single diagram. Figure 4.3 is a three-level diagram showing **Cooking Services** as a part of **Portia**, and **Portia** as part of **Cora Group**. Three levels is about the limit of a single diagram. If we added a fourth level—**Cora Group** as part of **Mykonos**—the diagram would be harder to understand. **Cooking Services** becomes too small to read. Five levels is even worse.

An alternative to Figure 4.3 is to show the organizations within **Portia** as a separate diagram. Figure 4.4 illustrates this approach. The advantage of a two-level diagram like Figure 4.4 is that it is simpler, and easier to understand.

ROLES

A *role* is the responsibility a person assumes when he or she holds a position in an organization. When a person assumes a role, she is bound by the expected social behavior that accompanies that role. For example, consider the role **Host**.

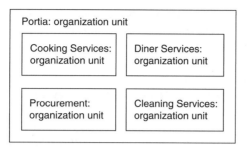

FIGURE 4.4 Organizations within Portia

We expect the host to take reservations, greet diners, and assign the diners to tables. We also expect the host to be pleasant and patient when interacting with the diners, since this role is the initial contact the restaurant makes with diners. The host represents the restaurant to the dining public.

Organizations contain roles. In a business organization model we show the roles contained within an organization using the same enclosing **part of** association that we saw earlier. Just as an organization can be part of another organization, a role can also be part of an organization. Figure 4.5 shows five roles that are part of Portia: **Head Chef**, **Service Director**, **Head of Procurement**, **Director of Cleaning Services,** and **General Manager.**

Note the similarity between Figure 4.5 and Figure 4.4. The **Head Chef** role in Figure 4.5 leads the **Cooking Services** organization in Figure 4.4. Similarly, **Service Director** in Figure 4.5 leads the **Diner Services** organization in Figure 4.4, **Head of Procurement** in Figure 4.5 leads **Procurement** in Figure 4.4, and **Cleaning**

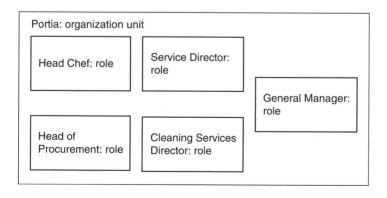

FIGURE 4.5 Roles within an organization

Services Director leads **Cleaning Services**. Figure 4.5 has a fifth role, **General Manager**. In fact the General Manager does not lead one of the organizations within Portia; he leads the whole of Portia.

As with organizations, the placement of roles is not significant when using the enclosing **part of** association. In Figure 4.5, it does not matter whether **Head Chef** is to the left of **Service Director** or to the right of it. Both **Head Chef** and **Service Director** are part of **Portia**.

Figure 4.5 is not so useful because it does not say very much. It only says that Adelina has five roles: **Head Chef**, **Service Director**, and so on. It can be made more useful by adding the reporting relationships that exist between the roles [Harmon 2003], as shown in Figure 4.6. The role **Service Director** reports to the role **General Manager**, as does **Head of Procurement**, **Cleaning Services Director**, and **Head Chef**.

What does it mean for one role to report to another? The supervising role—the role reported to—has some authority over the reporting role—the role that reports. The supervising role can tell the reporting role what to do and when to do it. The reporting role is responsible for informing the supervising role about progress made and issues encountered. The supervising role is ultimately responsible for the actions and work of the reporting role. Everything done on his behalf is his responsibility, even if done poorly by the reporting role.

In depicting reporting relationships, business organization models use the same diagrammatic conventions as do organization charts. The reporting association itself is shown as a line without arrowheads. No arrowheads are needed because the direction of the reporting association is implied by the physical layout. The reporting role is lower in the diagram than the supervising role.

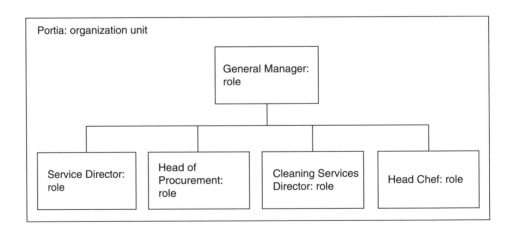

FIGURE 4.6 Organization with roles and reporting

In Figure 4.6, **Service Director** reports to **General Manager** (rather than vice versa) because **Service Director** is closer to the bottom of the diagram and **General Manager** is closer to the top. The line itself is from the top of the reporting role and to the bottom of the supervising role, from the top of **Service Director** to the bottom of **General Manager**.

Reporting only occurs between two roles. A role cannot report to an organization, nor can an organization report to another organization.

Role reporting and organizational composition can be combined. Figure 4.7 shows an example: the reporting structure of a project to deploy a new restaurant reservation system. The project has a project leader and three roles reporting to that leader. All four roles are part of the **Reservation System Project**, and that organization is part of **Mykonos**.

The people who play the roles on this project also play other roles in the organization. For example, the person who plays the **Marketing Support** role—Janice Buckler—has a primary role as **Marketing Manager** reporting to **Marketing Director**. Both **Marketing Manager** and **Marketing Director** are part of **Mykonos Marketing**. (Neither role nor the organization are shown in Figure 4.7.) For her **Marketing Support** role, Janice is responsible for ensuring that the reservation system is implemented in a way that does not hurt the image of the Mykonos restaurants.

Business organization models that only show an organizational chart reporting structure are not very interesting on their own. We can learn a bit about the

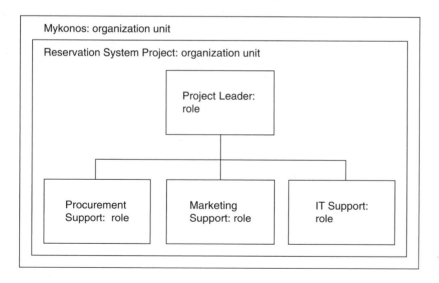

FIGURE 4.7 Project organization model

way the organization is structured and who reports to whom. But we cannot tell who procurement interacts with and which vendors supply the restaurant. We cannot tell who at Portia interacts with the customers. We cannot tell anything about the customers they service, such as whether they are local diners or business travelers. And we cannot tell who Portia's competitors are.

Most organization charts look alike. They have CEOs or presidents at the top; they have departments such as finance and sales and human resources. It is difficult to understand the differences between organizations simply by looking at the reporting relationships.

EXTERNAL ORGANIZATIONS AND EXTERNAL ROLES

The organizations and roles we have investigated so far are inside Mykonos. The organization chart, the organizations within Portia, and Portia's place within Cora Group are all part of the larger Mykonos Corporation. Everything is ultimately part of the same organization.

But of course, Portia interacts with other organizations and roles that are outside Mykonos. Portia serves restaurant customers, acquires supplies from vendors, and competes with other restaurants. Customers, vendors, and competitors are not part of Mykonos. They are external.

A business organization model can show how Portia interacts with external organizations and external roles. External organizations and external roles are shown outside the Portia organization unit. For example, Figure 4.8 shows the role **Customer**. **Customer** is not contained within **Portia**; it is an external role.

In Figure 4.8, **Customer** is shown to the right of **Portia**. In business organization models, the convention is to show customers on the right. But customers of whom, and to the right of what? **Customer** is a customer of **Portia**. **Portia** is the *organization of interest* in Figure 4.8; it is the organization we are focusing on, the reason the model exists. In Figure 4.4, the organization of interest is also **Portia**, but there are no external roles, so the organization of interest encompasses the whole diagram. In Figure 4.8, there is a role, **Customer**, external to the organization of interest.

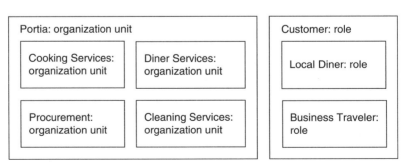

FIGURE 4.8 A business organization model with external roles

The role **Local Diner** in Figure 4.8 is shown as **part of** the role **Customer**. This is a new kind of association. We have seen roles that are part of organizations, and organizations that are part of other organizations, but we have not yet seen roles that are part of roles. When a role is part of another role, the enclosed role—the one inside—plays the part of the enclosing role—the one outside. **Local Diner** plays the part of **Customer** to the organization of interest, **Portia**. **Business Traveler** also plays the part of **Customer**.

Portia interacts with other external roles. Portia has suppliers—companies that provide kitchen equipment and fresh meats and vegetables. Portia has competitors—other restaurants that compete for the same clientele. Some organizations influence Portia; these influencers pass rules or policies that impact the operations of the restaurant. Figure 4.9 shows four roles external to **Portia**: **Supplier**, **Competitor**, **Influencer**, and **Customer.** By convention, the **Supplier** role is shown to the left of the organization of interest, the **Competitor** role is shown below it, and the **Influencer** role is shown above it.

Cortina is a restaurant around the corner from Portia and a clear competitor for Portia's business. In Figure 4.9 the organization **Cortina** is shown as **part of** the role **Competitor.** When an organization is represented as part of a role, it means that the organization plays that role with respect to the organization of interest. The restaurant Cortina plays the role of a competitor to Portia. The organization **Pluperfect** is also part of the **Competitor** role because it is another restaurant competing with Portia.

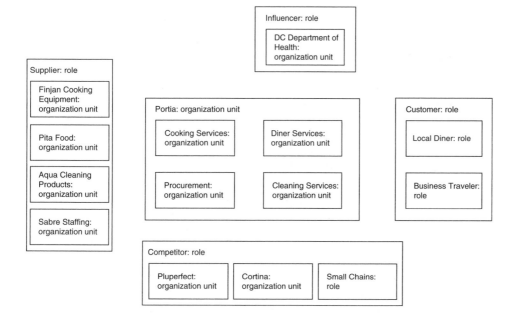

FIGURE 4.9 More external roles

The **Competitor** role has a third model element within it. The role **Small Chains** is part of **Competitor**. **Small Chains** represents mid priced restaurants that do not offer the same atmosphere and dining experience as Portia but compete with it for some customers.

In the **Supplier** role to the left are four organizations that supply products and services to Portia. Finjan Cooking Equipment provides cooking equipment: ovens, steamers, pots and pans, and knives of all varieties. Pita Foods provides food supplies. (Of course, there are many other food vendors not shown in Figure 4.9.) Aqua Cleaning Products provides cleaning services. Sabre Staffing provides waitstaff and other talent for hire.

The **Influencer** role is by convention shown above the organization of interest. Influencers are organizations that affect Portia. In Figure 4.9, DC Department of Health is an influencer; it recently banned smoking in public places, including bars and restaurants. This ban is significant, and Portia personnel must enforce it. The General Manager of Portia is concerned about the effect on diners who like to smoke. Will they go elsewhere, perhaps across the river to other restaurants in Virginia that allow smoking? Should Portia build an outdoor patio for smokers?

The appropriate detail for a business organization model depends on the way the model is to be used. Each situation is different. Sometimes just a **Customer** role is sufficient, without showing specific customer organizations or roles. At other times more detail is needed within **Customer**. For example, in Figure 4.9 we show two customer roles, **Local Diner** and **Business Traveler**. We segment customers into two roles so Mykonos Marketing can explore how competitors interact with different customer segments.

INTERACTIONS

We have seen how an organization can be part of another organization and how the **part of** association works with roles as well: A role can be part of an organization, an organization can be part of a role, and a role can be part of another role. We have also examined the reporting association: how one role can report to another. Now let's look at interactions, a third kind of association between model elements in a business organization model.

An *interaction* shows who works with whom. Two organizations participate in an interaction if they work together, at least sometimes. When two organizations work together, usually something is passed from one organization to the other, some good or service delivered. This *deliverable* can be something final, like a restaurant meal, or it can be some work in progress, like a drink order. It can even be something purely conceptual, like an idea for a new menu item.

Roles can also participate in interactions. A role can interact with another role, and a role can interact with an organization.

Let's consider an example. Figure 4.10 shows a technology user calling a help desk about a problem concerning a software application. The help desk performs

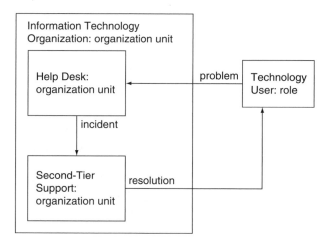

FIGURE 4.10 Three interactions

initial diagnosis on the problem and may refer it as an incident to second-tier sup-port. Second-tier support supplies a resolution back to the user.

There is an interaction between the role **Technology User** and the organiza-tion **Help Desk**. The interaction is shown as a solid line with an arrow. The inter-action is labeled with the deliverable: **problem**. The interaction is directional, from **Technology User** to **Help Desk**. This means that the technology user delivers the **problem** to the help desk, rather than vice versa.

Figure 4.10 shows an interaction between **Help Desk** and **Second-Tier Support**. The help desk organization provides second-tier support with an **incident**, a written description of the problem recorded and tracked. Figure 4.10 shows the resolution of the problem as a third interaction, one between **Second- Tier Support** and **Technology User**. That interaction delivers a **resolution** to the user.

Because **Second-Tier Support** is part of the larger **Information Technol-ogy Organization**, there is an implied interaction between **Information Tech-nology Organization** and **Technology User**. This interaction is not explicitly shown in Figure 4.10 but is implied by the presence of an existing interaction, the one labeled with the **resolution** deliverable. This implied interaction also delivers a resolution. Similarly there is another implied interaction between **Information Technology Organization** and **Technology User** to deliver the original problem.

Note that time is not shown in Figure 4.10. Of course there is a temporal order to the interactions in this example. The technology user shares the problem with the help desk before the help desk escalates it as an incident to second-tier sup-port and before the problem can be resolved. But Figure 4.10 does not show that temporal order. Instead, Figure 4.10 just shows that the technology user works together with the help desk and that as a result, a problem is delivered. From what's shown in Figure 4.10 the problem interaction might happen before, after, or concurrently with the resolution interaction.

The interaction between a role and an organization (or between two organizations or two roles) is labeled with the name of a deliverable, and the direction of the arrow indicates who provides the deliverable and who receives it. But often more than one deliverable is provided, and sometimes deliverables travel in both directions. For example, in the interaction between **Technology User** and **Help Desk** in Figure 4.10, the help desk sometimes provides a resolution for simple problems directly to the user, without involving second-tier support. This second deliverable from **Help Desk** to **Technology User** is not shown in Figure 4.10. It is better to show a single interaction between the two model elements that interact and to label that interaction with the most important deliverable. Between these two model elements, the most important deliverable is the problem that the user provides to the help desk.

Interaction deliverables can take several alternative forms. Information can be a deliverable. For example, Portia provides total sales to Mykonos Finance every day. A request can be a deliverable. For example, when the Portia general manager is preparing schedules for waitstaff, Portia server will request the days she wants to work. A physical good can be a deliverable. For example, the Portia vendor Pita Foods provides fresh basil and lemon grass every day to Portia. And a service can be a deliverable: Aqua Cleaning does a thorough cleaning of Portia every night after closing.

Figure 4.11 shows several interactions. **Local Diner** interacts with **Diner Services** in three distinct interactions. One interaction results in a diner receiving a **reservation**, the second results in **seating**, and the third in a **meal**. The **Business Traveler** role also interacts with **Diner Services** via the same three interactions. Both roles—**Local Diner** and **Business Traveler**—receive a **reservation**, **seating**, and a **meal**.

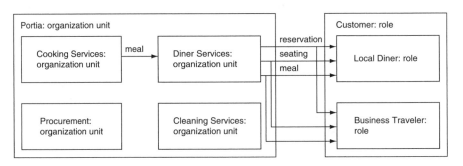

FIGURE 4.11 Interactions between Portia and its customers

Some interactions are between Portia and its customers. Other interactions are internal to Portia, between Portia organizations. In Figure 4.11, **Cooking Services** and **Diner Services** interact. The interaction shows a **meal** as a deliverable from **Cooking Services** to **Diner Services**. The meal is prepared by a **Cooking Services** chef and then served to a diner by a **Diner Services** server.

Figure 4.12 has the same roles and organizations as Figure 4.9 but with interactions between several model elements. Figure 4.12 shows a single scenario: a business traveler enjoying a restaurant meal at Portia. In addition to the interactions we have already seen—those between **Business Traveler** and **Diner Services**—there are some new interactions in Figure 4.12. **Pita Foods** interacts with **Cooking Services**, providing **food** such as olive oil and semolina flour. **Sabre Staffing** provides **waitstaff** to **Diner Services**.

Only the interactions that are part of this business traveller scenario are shown. Although **Cleaning Services** certainly interacts with the cleaning vendor **Aqua Cleaning**, there is no interaction shown in Figure 4.12 because that interaction is not part of the scenario.

Note that there is no interaction between **Business Traveler** and **Pita Foods**. The lack of an interaction association reflects the fact that business travelers simply do not deal directly with this restaurant vendor. In other business organization models customers do interact directly with vendors. For example, when buying

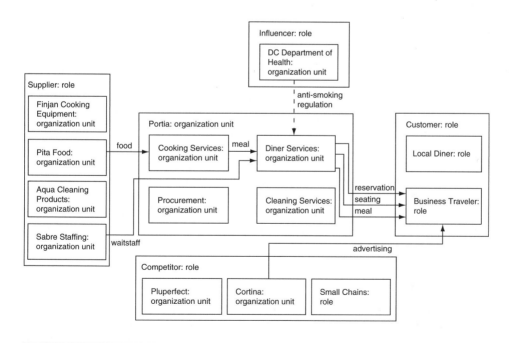

FIGURE 4.12 More interactions

a sweater from a catalog, a customer will receive the sweater from the shipper, a vendor of the catalog retailer.

Business travelers also interact with Cortina, a competitor of Portia. Cortina has placed advertisements in the hotel magazines to attract business diners to its restaurant. That interaction between **Cortina** and **Business Travelers** is shown in Figure 4.12, labeled with the deliverable **advertising**.

Interaction Best Practices

As mentioned earlier, an interaction is labeled with a deliverable, a good or service provided from one interacting organization to the other. The direction of the arrow indicates who provides the deliverable to whom. Usually this direction is clear, as when **Diner Services** provides a meal to **Business Traveler**.

But sometimes it is not so clear which way the arrow should point. Occasionally, both parties in an interaction deliver the same good or service. For example, when the New York Yankees baseball team trades players with the Baltimore Orioles, should the interaction be from the Yankees to the Orioles, or vice versa? For these equal trades of the same kind of thing (e.g., two professional ballplayers), a bidirectional interaction—one with an arrowhead at each end—is appropriate.

Bidirectional interactions are not so common. For the vast majority of commercial transactions, a good is not traded for another good, but sold for money. In this typical situation, the purchased good is shown as an arrow, and the money is not shown at all. Instead it is implied. Money flows upstream, against the direction of the arrows.

When two organizations interact, often a variety of goods and services is provided from one to the other. We have seen business organization models created by novice modelers with six or seven interactions between a single pair of organizations. But too many interactions on a single diagram make it difficult to understand, and obscure the key meaning of who is interacting with whom. Best practice is to limit the deliverable to the single most important one in the interaction.

Some novice modelers mistakenly use interactions to show activities performed by an organization rather than interactions and deliverables. An organization model should show the interaction deliverable **meal**, not the steps of the process to create the meal. Steps such as ordering, serving drinks, serving appetizers, and so on are captured in a business process, as described in Chapter 5.

INFLUENCE

When two organizations work together, we represent that working together with an interaction between them. But an organization can have an influence on another organization, even when they don't work together. This is a different kind of association between the two organizations, not an interaction but an *influence*.

Figure 4.12 includes an example of influence: the dashed line from **DC Department of Health** to **Diner Services**. The organization **DC Department of Health** enforces a ban on smoking, influencing **Diner Services** and indirectly affecting the diner. The health department is not working together with Diner Services. Instead its **antismoking regulation** has influenced the behavior of Diner Services. Because of this influence, Diner Services must now remind people not to smoke and must seat smokers at the bar instead of in the restaurant proper.

One organization can influence another organization, as in Figure 4.12. One role can influence another role. And an organization can influence a role, or vice versa.

Influence is similar to interaction. Both associations are between two organizations (or two roles or one of each). But influence is indirect. The organizations do not work together, as they do if they interact. Instead one indirectly affects the behavior of the other.

WHITE BOXES AND BLACK BOXES

In Figure 4.12, Portia is said to be modeled as a *white box*, revealing details about how it is organized internally. We can see the organizations that are part of Portia, the interactions between those internal organizations, and the interactions between the internal organizations and those outside Portia. Much detail is revealed.

Alternatively, Portia can be modeled as a *black box*, hiding internal details. Figure 4.13 shows a black-box model of Portia. No detail is shown within Portia, no organizations or interactions inside. Interactions and influences are to Portia itself rather than to an organization within. For example, in Figure 4.12 **Pita Foods** interacts with **Cooking Services**, supplying the deliverable **food**. In Figure 4.13, the same interaction is between **Pita Foods** and **Portia** instead of **Pita Foods** and **Cooking Services**.

Black-box models are created when the internal details about an organization are not available. The viewer simply doesn't know how Portia is organized. But more often, black-box models are created when the internal details are not important. Modeling is always a tradeoff between detail and simplicity, and sometimes simple is better. Black-box models are sometimes better than white-box models.

Note that most business organization models have black boxes—organizations that are not detailed. For example, **Pita Foods**, **Cortina**, and **DC Department of Health** are all shown as black boxes in both Figure 4.12 and Figure 4.13. All three organizations have internal detail, but we do not show it. Similarly, in Figure 4.12 there are four organizations within Portia. All four are shown as black boxes.

ASSOCIATIONS

As we have seen, organizations (and roles) can be associated in four different ways: **part of**, **reports to**, **interacts with**, and **influences**. Figure 4.14 shows an example of each of the four associations in the same model. The situation shown in Figure 4.14

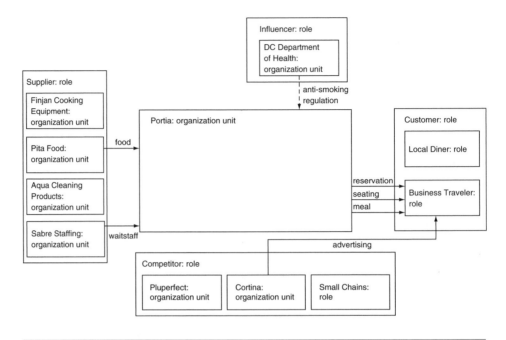

FIGURE 4.13 Black-box organization model

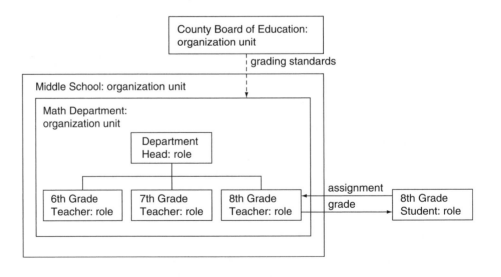

FIGURE 4.14 Four varieties of associations

represents a middle school student interacting with a teacher, turning in assignments and receiving grades.

As you will recall, one organization can be **part of** another, larger organization. The **part of** association is depicted by showing the smaller organization contained within the larger. In Figure 4.14 the organization **Math Department** is **part of** the organization **Middle School**. The roles **Department Head** and the three teacher roles are **part of** the organization **Math Department.** The role **8th Grade Student** is not **part of** the organization **Middle School**, nor is the organization **County Board of Education**.

One role can report to another via the **reports to** association. In Figure 4.14 the role **6th Grade Teacher reports to** the role **Department Head**, as do the other two teachers.

One role can interact with another, and roles can interact with organizations. In Figure 4.14, the **8th Grade Student** interacts with the **8th Grade Teacher**. The deliverable **assignment** is provided from the student to the teacher and the deliverable **grade** is provided from the teacher to the student.

One organization can influence another. Figure 4.14 shows the organization **County Board of Education** influencing the **Math Department**. The Board of Education creates grading standards for all the math teachers, influencing the behavior of the department without interacting with it directly.

CREATING GOOD BUSINESS ORGANIZATION MODELS

Novice modelers often create business organization models that are too big and too complex to understand. Too many model elements—or too many associations between those model elements—renders an organization model useless. When too many associations are shown in one organization model it is difficult to make sense of the whole. To improve readability and simplify the model, it is better to create several separate model diagrams, each with some of the detail but none with all of the detail. Each model can show a single scenario and just the few model elements and associations involved in that scenario. This strategy of *selective revelation*—described further in Chapter 7—is handy for creating models in any of the four business modeling disciplines, but it is particularly useful for business organization models. We often create organization models that reveal only the parts used in a particular scenario and omit the parts that clutter the model and that are irrelevant to that scenario.

Let's consider a Portia example of selective revelation. We create one model that shows the interactions between a customer and Portia. We include **Diner Services**, **Business Traveler**, **Cooking Services**, and the interaction among them. A second model shows the interactions between Portia and the suppliers. A third model shows how the organizations within Portia interact over a longer period of time with other restaurants and with organizations at Mykonos headquarters. Each of these models is understandable on its own. Together they describe how Portia interacts with other organizations.

Creating scenario-based organization models is easy. Each model includes only the organizations and interactions involved in a single scenario. An existing complex model can be changed into several different models, each model showing only the organizations and associations for a single scenario.

Selective revelation is usually performed by scenario for organization models—with different models showing different scenarios—but it can instead be performed by the **part of** hierarchy. We saw this arrangement using **part of** earlier in this chapter. Figure 4.3 showed organizations that are part of Cora Group, including Portia, and Figure 4.4 showed the organizations that are part of Portia. We could have combined Figures 4.3 and 4.4 in a single diagram, but the result would have been too big and would have contained too much information. Selectively revealing organizations is better.

Similarly, selective revelation can be applied to the reporting hierarchy. Rather than showing 30 roles and their reporting relationship on the same diagram, it is better to show the roles in several separate diagrams.

The physical positioning of model elements is also important to make a model readable. If an interaction is shown between two organizations, the interacting organizations should be close to each other so that the interaction is drawn as a short line instead of a long one. Figure 4.15 shows an example of what happens when interacting organizations are far from each other. Figure 4.15 is the same model

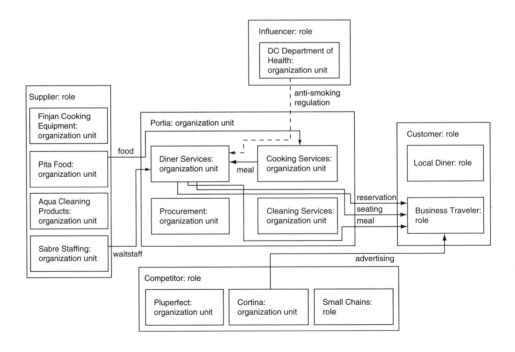

FIGURE 4.15 Interactions at an overly great distance

as Figure 4.12 but with the positions of **Diner Services** and **Cooking Services** swapped. Figure 4.15 has interactions from suppliers to **Cooking Services** and from customers to **Diner Services**. The interactions cross, making it harder to figure out which organizations interact. Figure 4.15 is harder to read than the equivalent Figure 4.12.

Some modeling tools help with readability. Some tools provide different icons to support the visual distinction between organizations and roles. Other tools support the user selection of an organization and the subsequent drill-down to the organizations that are part of the selected organization. Each organization shows only the model elements with which it is associated. Other model elements are revealed on the drill-down, when the sub–organizations are shown.

ORGANIZATIONS AND BUSINESS MOTIVATIONS

In this chapter we explain organization models, showing how organizations can be associated with roles. But we have already seen organizations in Chapter 3 as part of business motivation models. We saw that an organizational unit can define a goal or an objective, can establish a strategy or a tactic, can recognize an influencer, and can make an assessment that an influencer is an opportunity or a threat. The organizations in Chapter 3 that do all this defining, establishing, recognizing, and assessing are the same as the organizations described in this chapter.

Figure 4.16 shows two perspectives on influence, one using a motivation model and the other using an organization model. In a business motivation model, an organization unit can recognize an influencer. As you will recall, an influencer is a

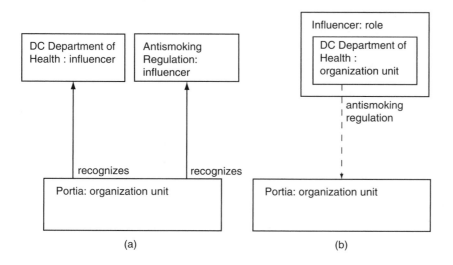

(a)   (b)

FIGURE 4.16 Influence in (a) a motivation model and (b) an organization model

market trend, a law, another organization, or something else that influences the success of the organization. An organization recognizes influencers using the **recognizes** association. In Figure 4.16 (a) the influencer **Antismoking Regulation** is recognized by **Portia** as an influencer. **DC Department of Health** is also recognized as an influencer, as an entity whose actions influence **Portia**.

Figure 4.16 (b) is a business organization model. Instead of showing the *recognition* of **DC Department of Health** as an influencer, Figure 4.16 (b) shows the influence itself. **DC Department of Health** influences **Portia** via the regulation of smoking. The regulation is a deliverable of the influence association, and the influencing organization—**DC Department of Health**—is the source of the influence association.

The traceability between an organization model and a motivation model can be used to better analyze the models. We can compare the goals of a smaller organization with the goals of the larger organization it is part of. Are there missing goals—goals that will not be achieved because no one is addressing them? Are goals in conflict? Similarly, we can compare the strategies of the smaller organization with those of the larger.

STANDARDS

Today no standards exist for organization modeling. Every modeling tool has its own approach to this problem, and every business that performs business modeling does the modeling in its own way. Much variety exists.

The relationship map developed by Rummler and Brache [Rummler and Brache 1995] is perhaps the closest to a standard, albeit a de facto standard with as many variants as practitioners. Rummler and Brache describe a systems view of organizations in which organizations and their components are depicted with rectangles nested within other rectangles. Customers, suppliers, and other external organizations (or roles) are shown by rectangles outside the main organization. Interactions labeled with deliverables connect the organizations (or roles) to show how work gets done, both within and across the organizational boundaries.

Rummler and Brache also introduce the concept of including an organization chart—with reporting associations—within the relationship map view of the organization, much as we have shown earlier in this chapter. Paul Harmon further elaborates on this idea and shows how a chart with the reporting structure of functional units is embedded within the organization model [Harmon 2003].

The organization models presented in this chapter are broadly consistent with the work of Rummler and Brache and with Harmon's extensions. Many commercial modeling tools have also built on the work of these thought leaders, so our presentation is also broadly consistent with commercial modeling tools.

The Object Management Group has started to create a standard for modeling organizations. Currently the OMG organizational modeling work is paused, waiting until more companies (and government agencies) show interest in this standardization. As of early 2008, we believe the OMG is several years away from a standard that will address the modeling of business organization models.

Without standards, modelers will continue to rely on a combination of ad hoc approaches and the proprietary modeling languages built into the modeling tools they use today. Each modeling tool and ad hoc approach is different. Sometimes the differences are obvious. Worse, sometimes the differences are subtle. The model elements and associations that look the same in two tools have subtle differences in meaning. These differences create two problems. Analysts looking at diagrams created in different tools cannot accurately (or easily) interpret and compare the models. And models cannot be exchanged between different tools.

Case Study

A telecommunications services company saw some significant profitability differences between various business units. Some business units were more profitable than others, even for the same services. Why? Were the more profitable business units simply better organized? Should the less profitable business units be reorganized to resemble the more profitable ones? Were either the more profitable or the less profitable business units following industry best practices?

Each business unit had its own sales organizations and its own customer service organization. The North Sales Group and the South Sales Group handled regional sales, one for northern customers and the other for southern customers. The Field Solutions Group handled solutions for new customers and existing customers, and the Equipment Resales Group provided used telecommunications equipment to existing customers. The company also had other corporate departments: Marketing, Finance, Legal, Procurement, and Operations.

To help the company explore organizational alternatives, we created business models. We created business motivation models to capture the goals, problems, and opportunities. We created business process models.

We also created several organization models. We created both an organization model of the existing situation and organization models for each of several alternative scenarios. The model of the existing situation captured the interactions between the current business units and the customers, influencers, and suppliers. The customer interactions included billing and collections, service delivery, inbound sales requests, contract approval, orders, support and maintenance, inquiries, prospecting, and customer qualification. Figure 4.17 shows one of the model diagrams for customer sales inquiries.

The telecommunications services company considered two customer segments: new customers and existing customers. When a new customer made a sales inquiry, they could contact one of three different internal organizations: **Field Solutions**, **North Sales Group**, or **South Sales Group**.

Continued

Case Study—continued

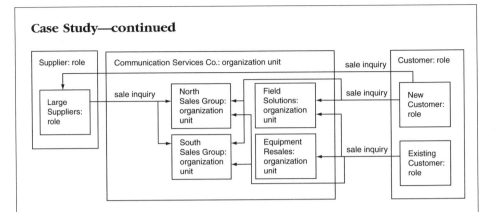

FIGURE 4.17 Customer sales inquiries at a telecommunications services company

Or a new customer could contact a large supplier directly, resulting in an indirect sales inquiry to one of the regional sales groups. Similarly, an existing customer could contact one of four different internal organizations: **Field Solutions**, **Equipment Resales**, **North Sales Group**, or **South Sales Group**. The multiple interaction points made it difficult to understand the customer relationship. Customer information was kept in multiple databases, further impeding a single view of a customer.

Customers who recognized the multiple entry points exploited the duplication by arranging for the organizations to bid against each other. A customer called one team and asked for a bid. With the pricing in hand, they called another, announced the "market price" they had received, and asked the second team to beat it. The internal organizations only later discovered they were being played against each other.

The existing organization was flawed. The company supported its customers poorly and provided that support inefficiently. The organization duplicated capabilities across several organizations, and the duplication was abused by some customers. The organizational structure damaged company performance. But the effect of structure on performance was not apparent from just an organization chart. Only analyzing an organization model revealed the problems.

We helped the company conceive a reorganization. As shown in Figure 4.18, customers are segmented into three groups: top accounts, regional midtier accounts, and other customers. Each customer segment has its own sales organization: **Top Accounts** for the top customers, **Regional Accounts** for the midtier customers, and **Telemarketing** for other customers.

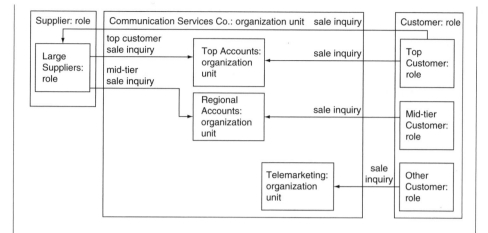

FIGURE 4.18 Redesigned customer sales

The new organization design allowed the company to retain some of the current structure, keeping knowledgeable staff with specific product know-how within their respective business units. The problem of the multiple customer interactions is solved. All customer contacts are now funneled, recorded, and tracked. Customers are not able to maneuver organizations into competing against each other. Overall, customer interactions are streamlined—improving customer satisfaction and increasing efficiency. The new organization allows the company to present a single point of contact, and it promotes cross-selling.

The executive management team used business organization models to understand their current customer interactions and problems. The team evaluated several alternatives and chose one to best fit their company and their goals. The business models allowed the team to see the impact of the organizational changes before reorganizing and possibly discovering that the reorganization did not create the desired results.

A business organization model describes the people who work in and interact with a business. It includes organizations—groups of people with a common purpose. It includes roles—the responsibility people assume in an organization. It shows organizations or roles as part of other organizations or roles. It shows what organizations or roles interact with other organizations or roles. It shows what organizations or roles influence other organizations or roles. And it shows what roles report to other roles.

A business organization model describes both organizations and roles within a business and those outside, including customers, competitors, suppliers, and influencers. Interactions and influences often cross organizational boundaries.

A business organization model is a description of the who *behind a business—the people, their roles, and their organizations. In Chapter 5 we explore the* how—*the business processes that a business uses to get things done.*

Business Process Models

5

Business process modeling is the third of the four business modeling disciplines we describe in this book. A business process model describes tasks and the ordering of these tasks: what work is performed and when it is performed. A business process model also captures who performs the tasks. This chapter explains business process models.

Some businesses run smoothly. Each task is a part of an elegant dance, with employees doing just what they need to do and working together to make a simple and beautiful whole. Other businesses run rough. They get their work done, but every task is a heroic struggle. Chaos reigns. Business processes are the difference between the smooth businesses and the rough ones. The smooth businesses execute good business processes; the rough businesses execute poor ones.

A *business process* is a collection of step-by-step tasks that a business uses when it performs its work. For example, all restaurants pursue the same goals of serving food for hungry customers, but they differ in the details of their business processes. They greet customers differently, they take reservations differently, and they prepare dinners differently.

Now that Cora Group has been successfully integrated into Mykonos, you are charged with growing the revenues of the Cora Group restaurants. You learn that Portia faces a business process problem. Portia's customers are experiencing long delays before they are seated. You are concerned that the delays will result in a poor customer experience and will lead to reduced revenue. You would like to investigate what is happening in this restaurant: Why are customers waiting? Is there an issue with the way Portia takes reservations and assigns tables? Can the problem be solved with a new reservation system? With pagers? With more servers? With more efficient seating arrangements?

You want to understand the business process of Portia customer dining, from the beginning to the end, from the time a dining party arrives until they leave the restaurant. You want to know how customers are greeted, how reservations are handled, how customers are seated, how they are served, and how tables are freed and cleaned so that new customers can be served. You also want to understand who is interacting with the customers along all these steps and how their jobs are performed.

To achieve this understanding, you create a *business process model*. A business process model is a model of a business process—a model of what work is being done and who does it.

WHY MODEL BUSINESS PROCESSES?

Why do we care about modeling business processes? As you will recall from Chapter 1, business models in general are used for eight purposes: communication, training and learning, persuasion and selling, analysis, managing compliance, as requirements for developing software, executing directly as software, and knowledge management and reuse.

All eight purposes apply to business process modeling. Some businesses build business process models as part of their transformation initiatives to capture the way they perform their work today and the way they will perform work in the future. These models are used to *communicate* to the employees what will change and how the change will affect their day-to-day work lives. Sometimes models are used to *train* new employees so that they understand all the tasks they are expected to perform and the order in which they should perform them.

Process models are often *analyzed*. One business process is compared with others to see which process is best. Analysis helps us understand the cost involved with each process, how many people are needed, and where delays occur. Such analysis can also be used to *persuade*. If we think that outsourcing a business function is cheaper than keeping the function in-house, we can show process models with the function in-house and with the function outsourced and demonstrate the difference in cost. Sometimes process models are used to persuade clients or prospective clients—for example, to persuade a client that we understand his business and his challenges.

Process models are useful in *managing compliance* with a new regulation. By modifying an existing process (or by implementing a new process) we ensure that we are complying with a regulation. We can investigate the way we are doing work today and compare it to the work that needs to be accomplished to achieve compliance.

Business process models can provide us with information useful in capturing *software requirements*. By capturing the way users perform the work, we can understand their needs. We can investigate each activity in a process and determine whether the activity is supported by a software application today and whether it should be supported by an application in the future. We can trace the software requirements of the future applications back to the activities they support. (Chapter 12 explores the relationship between business process activities and software requirements.)

Business processes can be *executed as software*. A business process executed as software becomes workflow. A user is presented with user interfaces that walk her through the steps she must perform. To execute a business process as workflow, a specialized tool must be used to convert from the business process to code that can be executed in a business process engine. The tool then ensures that the modeled workflow is realized and followed. Execution of business processes as workflow is explained in Chapter 12.

When an organization practices *knowledge management*, it applies knowledge gleaned in one part of the organization to another part of the organization. Often this knowledge includes how to perform a business process. Business process models capture how work is performed and who performs it. They also show how a person interacts with others—both others within their organization and others external to it.

ACTIVITIES

People in organizations perform work. For instance, help desk employees handle incoming customer calls. An accountant updates a company's balance sheet. A distributor ships an ordered product. And in the Mykonos restaurants, a restaurant host takes reservations and seats parties of diners. Business process modeling is about modeling work that is being performed—modeling what people do, how they do it, and the activities they perform along the way.

What is an activity? An *activity* is a discrete chunk of work, something with a beginning and an end, that is performed one or more times. For example, **Serve Appetizers** is an activity. At every Mykonos restaurant, the activity **Serve Appetizers** is performed many times every evening.

Typically an activity is one step of a larger business process. For example, **Serve Appetizers** is part of the larger business process **Serve Meal**. There are other activities within **Serve Meal**, including **Serve Entrees** and **Serve Desserts**.

Every activity performs work. For example, when a call is made to a help desk, a help desk support person starts by opening a trouble ticket and by asking the caller for his personal information—his name and phone number. **Open Ticket** is one activity in this process, and **Get Caller Info** is another. The incoming call itself is not an activity, since no work is performed. Instead the call is a trigger for the first help desk activity, **Open Ticket**. The ticket itself is also not an activity; it is a record that is created by **Open Ticket**.

Figure 5.1 shows the activity **Welcome Diner**, performed by the restaurant host. Figure 5.1 is atypical; activities rarely appear by themselves. Instead,

```
┌─────────────┐
│  Welcome    │
│  Diner      │
└─────────────┘
```

FIGURE 5.1 An activity

FIGURE 5.2 Three related activities

several activities typically appear together as part of a larger process, as in Figure 5.2. Once the host welcomes the diners, she asks for a name and whether they have a reservation. The host then checks the information against the reservation records to see whether the diners indeed have a reservation.

SEQUENCE FLOWS

A sequence flow is a connection between two activities, showing that one activity is performed before the other. A sequence flow is shown as a solid line with an arrow, from the activity performed first to the activity performed next. In Figure 5.2 there is a sequence flow between the activity **Welcome Diner** and the activity **Get Diner Information**, and another sequence flow between **Get Diner Information** and **Check Reservations**. First the activity **Welcome Diner** is performed. When this activity finishes, the next activity, **Get Diner Information,** begins. After the **Get Diner Information** finishes, the activity **Check Reservations** begins. When this last activity finishes, the process is complete.

This process is used to greet many parties that are arriving at different times. The host might be checking on the reservations of one party before welcoming another party. However, for a particular party, the sequence of activities that are performed is clear and definitive. First the party is welcomed, then the party information is collected, and then reservations are checked.

As you will recall from Chapter 4, a business organization model can include an interaction between two organizations, showing that they work together. An interaction is depicted much like a sequence flow. Both are arrowed lines from one model element to another. But a sequence flow has a very different meaning than an interaction. An interaction is an association between two organizations (or two roles, or an organization and a role). A sequence flow is an association between two activities. An interaction means that the two organizations work together. A sequence flow means only that one activity occurs after the other. An interaction is labeled by the deliverable that one organization delivers to the other. A sequence flow is usually unlabeled and is never labeled with a deliverable.

ACTIVITY ATTRIBUTES

Every activity has *attributes*, which capture details of the work. Activity names are short, typically no longer than four words, and better when they are two or three words. **Check Reservations** is a good name; it is simple and easy to understand. The name of an activity need not convey the details of the way the activity is performed. From "check reservation" we do not know how the reservations are checked, whether there is a reservations system or a big leather-bound book. Rather, the name simply describes the work being performed.

The description of an activity gives more detail about the work, what it means, and how it is performed. For example, a description for **Check Reservations** states:

> *Check the reservation book to see whether the reservation exists. Verify that the party arrived before the reservation time.*

A description typically notes whether a software application is used to perform the activity. If an application is used, the description includes the way the person interacts with the application. For example, if the restaurant has a reservations system instead of a book, the description for **Check Reservations** is instead:

> *Use the reservation system to check whether the reservation exists, searching for the reservation by name or by time. Verify that the party is not late, that they have arrived before the reservation expires.*

Descriptions should have at least a sentence to describe the activity, and two or three sentences are better. Descriptions are an excellent place to capture subject matter expertise.

Activities are temporal. Each activity takes time to complete. Some activities are fast, taking seconds. Other activities are slow, taking months. Often there are delays—delays before the work, delays during the work, and delays because of the work. It is important for subsequent process analysis to capture these times—both the work times and the delay times. If the business process is simulated, the activity times are used by the simulation engine. (Business process simulation is described in Chapter 11.)

Typically an activity is performed by a person, the person who does the work of the activity. This person is called the activity's *resource*. Of course different people perform the same activity at different times. Jessica might greet people today and Austin tomorrow. So the resource of an activity is not a single person but a role. As you recall from Chapter 4, a role is the responsibility a person assumes when he holds a position in an organization. For example, the role **Host** is the resource of the activity **Check Reservations**. When a particular party arrives, their reservations are checked by a single person who plays that role.

People do not work for free. Every resource has a cost, and the cost varies from role to role and from person to person. Details about costs of the resources are useful to understand the end-to-end cost of a process.

Some activities are *manual* work, performed by a resource without any assistance. When a host welcomes an arriving party, she does so without the assistance of any technology. On the other hand, some activities are supported by technology. When a host checks for the party's reservations, she looks up their name in a reservations system. In analyzing a business process model, it is useful to understand what work is performed with the assistance of a system. We can then analyze how new technology could be used and how the activity's resource would interact with that new technology in performing the activity.

Some activities are *solely software*, performed entirely by a software application, with no person involved. For example, Mykonos orders staples for all the restaurants—mineral water, olive oil, and cleaning supplies. These restaurant staples are ordered automatically whenever inventory is low, without anyone involved in the ordering activity. In this solely software activity, the application does not support a (human) resource who is performing the activity. Instead the application is the sole resource performing the activity.

It is occasionally useful to model solely software activities as part of a larger business process, but most activities involve people. Business process modeling is not about modeling software; it is about modeling the work that people do. Solely software activities are uncommon in good business process models.

EVENTS

A business process has a beginning and an end. A process begins with a *start event* and ends with an *end event*. All the activities of the business process— the actual work performed—occur after the start event and before the end event.

When the restaurant host welcomes an arriving party, the welcoming is the first activity. However, to greet the party, something must have happened: the party walked into the restaurant. This arrival is what starts the first activity and is the trigger for everything that happens afterward. That arrival is a start event. A *start event* is something happening that begins a business process. **Diner Arrives** is the start event of the restaurant dining process, as shown in Figure 5.3.

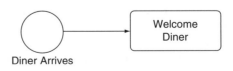

FIGURE 5.3 A start event

FIGURE 5.4 A simple end-to-end process

Note the name of the start event **Diner Arrives** sounds different from the names of the activities, such as **Welcome Diner**. Activity names are typically imperative sentences; they sound like commands. The verb is at the beginning of the name. The name of a start event is typically a declarative sentence, describing something that happens. The verb is at the end.

The *end event* of a process is when the process ends, after the last activity. Sometimes the process has a natural end, and sometimes we end a process because we are not interested in modeling anything beyond. Our modeling scope determines where we end. For example, suppose we care only about how diners are greeted. Then our process is simple, as shown in Figure 5.4. We have a start event to show the diner arriving; we have activities to greet the diner and to check reservations, and we end with **Diner Seated**.

But suppose instead that we intend to capture many more activities and finish only when the party leaves the restaurant. In that situation our restaurant dining process will be much larger than the simple process shown in Figure 5.4.

Most processes have multiple end events. Diners might leave after eating and paying, or they might leave early, disgruntled by long delays in their restaurant experience. They might even leave before they are seated, after waiting too long for a table, or because they are called out to perform emergency surgery. A process can also have multiple start events, showing different ways that work begins.

Some processes have an *intermediate event*, an event that happens after the process starts but before it ends. Many intermediate events model delays. For example, when the first person of a large party arrives at Portia, she waits. Portia's policy is to seat a party only when everyone is present. When the first diner arrives, the host checks the reservations, but she does not seat the diner until the rest of the party arrives. Figure 5.5 shows the process with the intermediate event **Party Arrives** after **Check Reservations**. The diner waits at **Party Arrives**

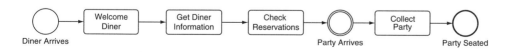

FIGURE 5.5 A process with an intermediate event

Order
Arrives

Midnight
Cleaning

FIGURE 5.6 A message start event and a timer start event

until everyone is present. Once the rest of the party arrives, the host collects the party and they are seated.

Like start events, the name of an intermediate event is also a declarative sentence. For example, the intermediate event in Figure 5.5 is **Party Arrives**, much like the name of the start event, **Diner Arrives**.

Events of all three varieties can have descriptions, just as an activity can have a description. For example, the description of **Party Arrives** explains the Portia policy of making the party wait until everyone has arrived. (Alternatively, the policy might be modeled as a business rule, as described in Chapter 6.)

Events also support other attributes. Start events record detail about when work starts. For example, **Diner Arrives** includes attributes modeling how often dining parties arrive, how many on which night of the week, the sizes of the parties, and so on. These attributes are used for process simulation, as described in Chapter 11. Intermediate events have similar attributes about how long work is delayed.

What triggers a start event? Some start events are triggered by the arrival of a message from elsewhere. For example, a customer order at a catalog retailer begins when an order arrives from a customer. This start event begins with the receipt of a message. A start event with a *message trigger* is depicted graphically as a little envelope within the start event, as shown on the left of Figure 5.6.

Some start events are trigger by a temporal cycle—something that happens every night or every month. For example, the complete cleaning of Portia starts every night at midnight. Temporally started events are said to have a *timer trigger*. A start event with a timer trigger is depicted with a little clock, as shown on the right of Figure 5.6.

An intermediate event can also have a timer trigger if it happens at a particular time, or a message trigger if it sends or receives a message. There are other useful event triggers, including process cancellation, process termination, error condition, and aborted transaction. These event triggers are described later in this chapter.

LANES

A business process model graphically shows who performs which activities. Each role that performs activities in a business process has a *lane*—a horizontal stripe like a lane in a swimming pool. Figure 5.7 shows a process for collecting a

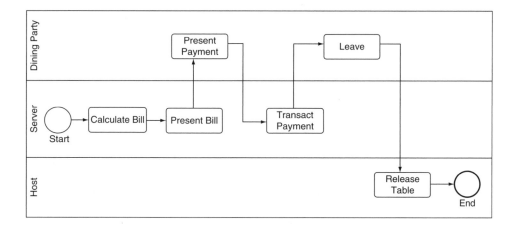

FIGURE 5.7 Lanes in a business process

payment from a departing dining party. Figure 5.7 has three lanes: one for the dining party, one for the server, and one for the host. The dining party performs the activities in the **Dining Party** lane: **Present Payment** and **Leave**. Similarly, the server performs the activities in the **Server** lane, and the host performs the activity in the **Host** lane. Each lane is named by the role or organization who performs the work. This role (or organization) is called the *participant* of the lane.

Some activities have an outgoing sequence flow to another activity in the same lane, when the same person performs the next activity. For example, the activity **Calculate Bill** is followed by **Present Bill**, both performed by the server. Some activities have an outgoing sequence flow to an activity in another lane, when the next step is performed by a different role. For example, after the diner leaves in **Leave**, the host releases the table in **Release Table**.

In Figure 5.7, the participant of the top lane is **Dining Party**, the customer of this process. Figure 5.7 is typical. When a customer is shown, the customer is usually the top lane. The other participants who serve the customer are situated in lanes below. Putting the customer on top is a common convention that makes business process models easier to read.

Not every process model has a customer on top. Sometimes a model is less visually complex if the customer lane is in the middle, neither on top nor on the bottom. And sometimes a process is completely concerned with internal matters and has no participant who can be called a customer. But these exceptions to the customer-on-top convention are not so common. In most models, the customer is on top.

When a process model has more than two lanes, the modeler must decide which lane is placed where. Should the **Server** lane be above the **Dining Party** or below? A good rule of thumb is to place lanes to minimize sequence flow.

When a sequence flow is from an activity in one lane to an activity in another lane, it is better if the two lanes are adjacent so that the sequence flow is short. If the two lanes are distant from each other—e.g., separated by three other lanes—the sequence flow is long. It is harder to read the resulting diagram.

GATEWAYS

Our processes so far follow a single path, one activity at a time, from the start event to the end event. For example, in Figure 5.4 the host finds the reservation, a table is available, and the diner is seated. In reality work is always more complex: conditions arise that cause the sequence flow to diverge, either to one sequence flow or to an alternative. The diners either have a reservation or they do not. Different activities occur depending on whether they have a reservation. Similarly, the diners order appetizers or they do not.

We use a *gateway* to model sequence flow alternatives. A gateway is depicted as a diamond shape. Multiple sequence flows exit a gateway. The actual sequence flow taken in a particular situation depends on the condition modeled by the gateway.

The business process fragment in Figure 5.8 shows what happens after the host checks reservations. There are two alternative outcomes of the reservations check: either the party has reservations or they do not. These two outcomes are shown as two outgoing sequence flow of the gateway **Reservation?** If they have a reservation, the host assigns a table in **Assign Table**. If the party has no reservation, the customers are turned away in **Turn Customers Away**.

Gateways are named. The name of a gateway is a question, with the alternative answers to the question as labels on the outgoing sequence flows. In Figure 5.8,

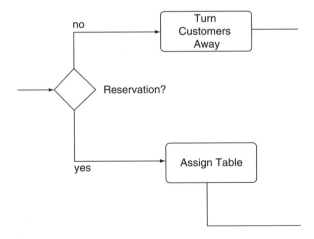

FIGURE 5.8 A gateway

the gateway is **Reservation?** and the two outgoing sequence flows are labeled **no** and **yes**.

Of course, Portia turns customers away only as a last resort. Instead the host checks whether a table is available. If a table is available, the party is seated anyway, as though they had a reservation. The process fragment Figure 5.9 shows this more accurate process, with a second gateway **Seat Now?** showing the result of the table availability.

Figure 5.10 shows more of the same process. If the party has no reservations and no table is available, the host looks for a way to arrange tables. If no such rearrangement exists, the party will wait for a table, perhaps waiting 20 minutes or an hour. Ideally the party simply waits until a table is available, but in practice many parties are impatient and ask periodically about the status of their table. So the process in Figure 5.10 shows the host checking for availability after a wait, only to sometimes ask the party to wait some more. The activities **Check Availability, Check for Rearrangement**, and **Wait for Table** are part of a *sequence flow loop*, a cycle of activities connected by sequence flow.

Some gateways model decisions, where someone decides which sequence flow to take. **Seat Now?** in Figure 5.10 is such a decision. The host decides whether to seat the party now or whether to check for a rearrangement of tables. The decision is not difficult or time-consuming; one can hardly imagine the host laboring over this simple choice on a busy Saturday evening. But it is a decision nonetheless.

As we describe in Chapter 6, gateways that model decisions can be guided by one or more business rules. The decision **Seat Now?** is guided by a business rule that describes what to do when a table is available. Other business rules provide further guidance in other situations—for example, when the party includes regulars, friends of the owner, or celebrities.

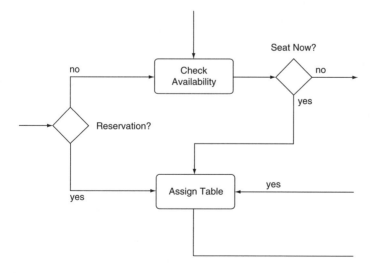

FIGURE 5.9 Two gateways

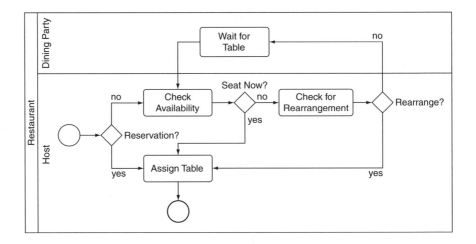

FIGURE 5.10 Seating flow

Parallel Gateways

The gateways in Figures 5.8, 5.9, and 5.10 are *exclusive gateways*. With an exclusive gateway, either one sequence flow is taken or the other is taken. But not every gateway is an exclusive gateway. A *parallel gateway* starts parallel work—two (or more) sequence flows that then progress at the same time, perhaps to be later joined back together by another parallel gateway.

Consider the process shown in Figure 5.11, with detail on the preparation of appetizers, entrees, and desserts. In Figure 5.11, the chef prepares the appetizers and the entrees at the same time. The appetizers can be prepared quickly and are served to the customers when they are ready. The parallel gateway **Split Order** splits the work into two parallel flows, one traveling the upper sequence flow to **Prepare Entrees**, and one traveling the lower sequence flow to **Prepare Appetizers**. After the appetizers and entrees are served, the sequence flows arrive at the other (unnamed) parallel gateway. At this point they are combined back together, and the subsequent activity **Serve Desserts** is performed only once.

Inclusive Gateways

Figure 5.11 assumes that each party orders both appetizers and entrees. But what happens if a dining party orders just entrees, without any appetizers? Figure 5.11 is not a good model of that situation because the parallel gateway mandates the use of both sequence flows. Figure 5.11 says that both entrees and appetizers are prepared.

Instead of using a parallel gateway, this situation can be modeled with an *inclusive gateway*, as shown in Figure 5.12. An inclusive gateway allows either

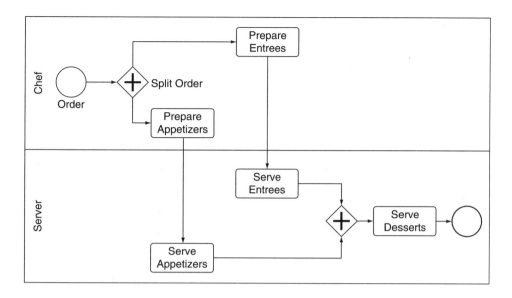

FIGURE 5.11 Using parallel gateways to prepare dinner

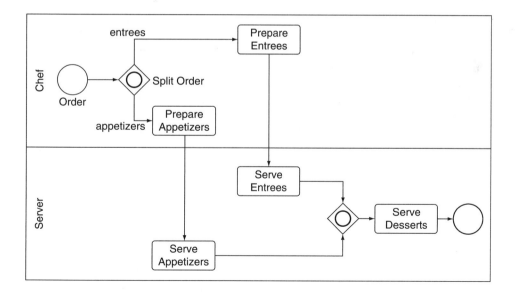

FIGURE 5.12 Using inclusive gateways to prepare dinner

outgoing sequence flow to be taken or both to be taken in parallel. A party can order just appetizers, just entrees, or both appetizers and entrees.

The behavior of the first gateway—**Split Order**—is a bit complex. When a work arrives at **Split Order**, sometimes it needs to travel the upper path, sometimes the lower path, and sometimes work needs to be split so that the two paths can occur in parallel. Chapter 11 describes how to simulate an inclusive gateway, providing percentages (for example) for how often the upper and lower paths are taken.

The behavior of the second inclusive gateway—the unlabeled gateway in Figure 5.12—depends on the behavior of the first, **Split Order**. For a party that orders only appetizers, when the appetizers are served, the second gateway passes the work through to the next activity, **Serve Desserts**, as though the gateway did not exist. Similarly, for a party that orders only entrees, the second gateway passes the work through to **Serve Desserts**. But for a party that orders both appetizers and entrees, the second gateway behaves like the unnamed parallel gateway in Figure 5.11. After the appetizers are served, the outgoing sequence flow waits at the gateway for the entrees to be served. Only when both the appetizers and the entrees have been served will the activity **Serve Desserts** be performed.

DEFAULT SEQUENCE FLOWS AND CONDITIONAL SEQUENCE FLOWS

One of the outgoing sequence flows from a gateway can be marked as a *default*. A default sequence flow is the one taken if there is no reason to take another sequence flow. Consider the process fragment on the left of Figure 5.13, showing what happens after drinks are offered to the diners. Either the diners order wine or they order mixed drinks or they order both. The default—indicated by the slash on the sequence flow—is that they order mixed drinks.

There is an alternative notation to using an inclusive gateway—an alternative way of showing the same process. The process fragment on the right of Figure 5.13 behaves the same as the fragment on the left, despite the different notation. There is no gateway on the right. Instead of a gateway, the sequence flow

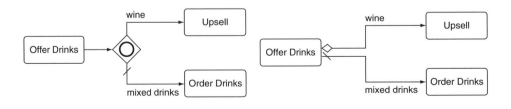

FIGURE 5.13 Identical process with a gateway and without

from **Offer Drinks** to **Upsell** is a *conditional sequence flow*. A conditional sequence flow is a sequence flow that includes a condition, a description of the situation under which it is permissible to take that sequence flow. The conditional sequence flow is depicted with a miniature diamond at its beginning.

SUBPROCESSES

Some activities are atomic; there is no more detail about the activity than its name, its description, and its attributes. Such activities are called *tasks*. The activities we have considered to this point are all tasks.

Often we are interested in understanding an activity in further detail. We want to break it down to a more detailed set of activities. A *subprocess* is an activity that has this extra detail, that can itself be described as a process. Figure 5.14 shows an end-to-end restaurant dining process. The party is greeted, is seated, orders dinner, dines, and pays. Each of the five activities is itself a subprocess, as shown by the + icon at the bottom of each activity.

Figure 5.15 shows one of the subprocesses—**Seat Party**—in detail. Figure 5.15 has the same activities, gateways, and sequence flow as the process fragment in Figure 5.10, but in Figure 5.15 the activities, gateways, and sequence flow are framed as a subprocess. Figure 5.15 has a start event and an end event. The start event in Figure 5.15 is not the start of the whole process. Instead it is only the start of **Seat Party**, the subprocess. Similarly, the end event in Figure 5.15 is only the end event for **Seat Party**.

How do Figures 5.14 and 5.15 work together? Figure 5.14 provides the context and launching points for the subprocesses, including **Seat Party**. After the dining party is greeted, they arrive at the subprocess **Seat Party**. The party then continues to the beginning of the **Seat Party** subprocess, the start event in Figure 5.15. The party moves within the subprocess, though the activities and gateways, until a table is assigned. When the party reaches the end event in Figure 5.15, the party returns to Figure 5.14, continuing to the next activity, **Take Order**.

Figure 5.15 shows the subprocess detail within one of the activities in Figure 5.14. When one diagram shows the subprocess of an activity from another diagram, the two diagrams are often referred to as the *lower-level process* and

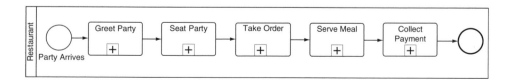

FIGURE 5.14 Five subprocesses

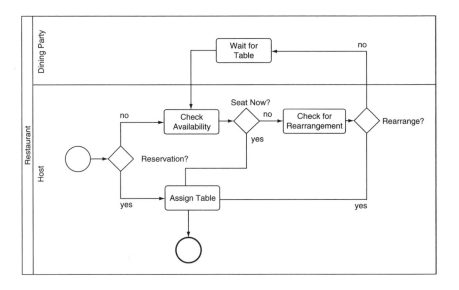

FIGURE 5.15 The subprocess within **Seat Party**

the *upper-level process*. The lower-level process—Figure 5.15—shows the detail of one of the activities in the upper-level process—Figure 5.14.

Figure 5.15 is an *independent subprocess*. The lower process is shown as a separate free-standing diagram. Some subprocesses are *embedded* instead of independent. The lower process details of the subprocess are shown in the context of the upper process, on the same diagram. Figure 5.16 shows **Greet Party** as an embedded subprocess. The **Greet Party** activity is large and contains three activities, joined by sequence flow. In many business process modeling tools, the embedded subprocess can be expanded by pressing the + icon. For example, in Figure 5.16, the user could press the + icon on **Seat Party**, causing the **Seat Party** activity to be expanded into an embedded subprocess, akin to **Greet Party**. The detail can subsequently be compressed back into the activity by pressing the − icon.

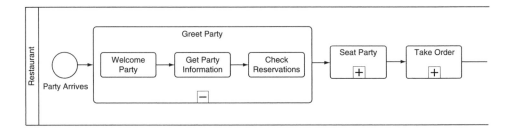

FIGURE 5.16 An embedded subprocess

The drawback of embedded processes is spacing: The diagram must be drawn with sufficient space to allow for the expansion of the subprocess. If **Seat Party** in Figure 5.14 were embedded, the whole process would have to be redrawn to provide space for **Seat Party** to be expanded within the lane. Embedded processes are impractical for modeling anything more complex than a few activities. It is also difficult to model an embedded subprocess within another embedded subprocess. In practice, most subprocesses are independent.

Figure 5.17 shows **Collect Payment**, another subprocess of Figure 5.14, originally shown as Figure 5.7. Unlike Figure 5.15, Figure 5.17 has no start event and no end event. A subprocess without a start event begins at an activity that has no incoming sequence flow. In Figure 5.17, there is one such activity, **Calculate Bill**, so the subprocess starts there. A subprocess without an end event finishes with activities that have no outgoing sequence flow. In Figure 5.17, **Release Table** is the sole activity without outgoing sequence flow. Omitting the start event and end event removes visual clutter while the process flow remains clear and understandable. Figure 5.18 shows the same **Collect Payment** subprocess with a start event and an end event. Figures 5.17 and 5.18 are equivalent; they behave the same.

In more complex subprocesses it is common to have two or more activities where the process ends. It is also possible to have two or more activities where the process starts. In such cases it is helpful to show all the start events and end events. Otherwise someone examining the process needs to locate all the activities that do not have an incoming flow and understand that they all start concurrently, and locate all the activities that do not have outgoing flows and understand that they are all possible end points.

Subprocesses provide several benefits. Subprocesses hide detail so that models can be divided up into chunks that are easier to manage and understand. A model with too many elements in a single diagram is difficult to understand.

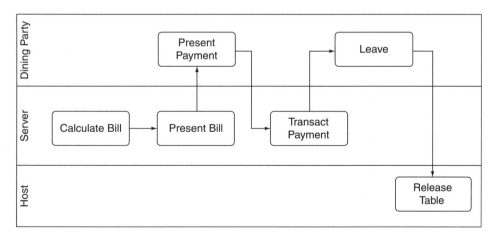

FIGURE 5.17 A subprocess without a start event or an end event

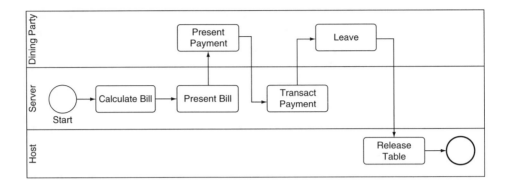

FIGURE 5.18 The same subprocess with a start event and an end event

Subprocesses are useful for modeling common process fragments that are used in several different locations. Rather than create the same process fragments several times, the same lower-level subprocess can be part of several different upper processes. Subprocesses reduce the modeling work that must be performed.

Subprocesses are also easier to maintain. If we add new activities, e.g., to implement a restaurant paging system (as described later in this chapter), we can add the activities within the **Seat Party** subprocess without affecting the rest of the overall restaurant process.

COMPENSATION AND OTHER CONDITIONS

A dining party might leave rather than wait for a table. Actually, a party could leave at any time—just after they arrive or when they learn of a wait, while waiting or after they see a menu. They might leave during the meal because their child is misbehaving or because someone in the party becomes sick.

There are many potential departures. It is possible to model all these potential departures with gateways. One could introduce a gateway after every activity, asking whether the dining party leaves now. The process model would then be full of gateways, all to model the situation of a dining party leaving early. Obviously, such a model is awkward.

Instead of using dozens of gateways, we model the potential for departure at any time with a single *exception flow*. An exception flow is a sequence flow triggered by an exception—an intermediate event that occurs sometime during the course of a subprocess. Figure 5.19 shows an exception flow. Attached to the boundary of the **Seat Party** activity is an intermediate event with a zig-zag icon. The intermediate event can occur at any time during the **Seat Party** activity. **Seat Party** has a subprocess shown in Figure 5.15, so the intermediate event can occur during any of the activities in the subprocess. The single intermediate event in Figure 5.19 eliminates the need to add several gateways to Figure 5.15.

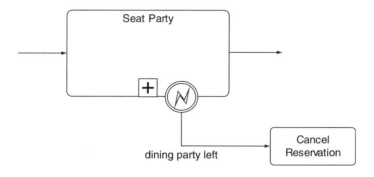

FIGURE 5.19 An exception and an exception flow

If the exception occurs in Figure 5.19 and the dining party leaves, their reservation needs to be cancelled. This cancellation is indicated by the activity **Cancel Reservation**, downstream of the intermediate event.

Business Transactions

Sometimes a business process includes a *business transaction*. A business transaction is a collection of activities that must either complete successfully or must be rolled back in their entirety, as though none of the activities had never been performed [Fowler 2003]. A business transaction can take hours, days, or even weeks to complete. Business transactions are common in business.

Let's consider an example. Some of the Mykonos restaurants have special event rooms that can be rented in their entirety for an evening. The reservations for these special event rooms are not performed using the usual dining reservations process at the individual restaurants. Instead Mykonos provides a centralized service for reserving special event rooms, so if a customer wants to reserve such a room in one restaurant and that room is already booked that evening, the centralized service can suggest reserving a special event room in another Mykonos restaurant across town.

Figure 5.20 shows the process for reserving a special event room. The normal process is quite simple. Mykonos takes a reservation for a room in the activity **Take Special Event Room Reservation**. Some customers want entertainment—a comic or musicians—for their event. Rather than allow customers to book their own entertainers, Mykonos prefers to handle those reservations as well, to ensure that only appropriate entertainment is performed at their restaurants. So the next step of the process is optionally booking entertainment in the activity **Reserve Entertainment**. Finally the customer is charged, two weeks before the event.

But the customer can change his mind before he is charged. If he cancels, Mykonos must cancel the reservation at the individual restaurant and cancel the

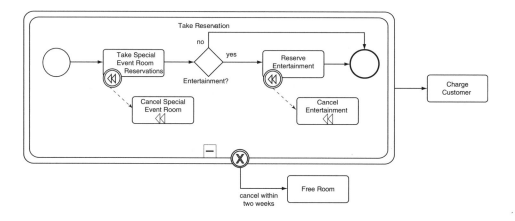

FIGURE 5.20 A transaction, a cancellation and some compensation

reservation for the entertainment. Figure 5.20 shows how this cancellation is modeled. **Take Special Event Room Reservation** and **Reserve Entertainment** are contained within the embedded subprocess **Take Reservation**. The subprocess is a transaction, as shown by the activity's double hull. The intermediate event with the cancel trigger—the outlined X—indicates that the transaction can be cancelled.

If **Take Reservation** is cancelled after the **Take Special Event Room Reservation** has occurred, the room will need to be cancelled. This cancellation happens in the activity **Cancel Special Event Room**. This activity is called a *compensation activity*, meaning that it compensates for activities that have already occurred, bringing the transaction back to the situation before anything happened. **Cancel Special Event Room** compensates for the activity **Take Special Event Room Reservation**. That compensation association between the two activities is depicted with a compensation trigger, the rewind marker on the boundary of **Take Special Event Room Reservation**. The corresponding compensation activity **Cancel Special Event Room** is also marked with a rewind marker. The two activities are connected with a dashed line, depicting the compensation association between them. Similarly, **Cancel Entertainment** compensates for the activity **Reserve Entertainment** if the customer cancels his reservation and entertainment has been reserved.

Only transactions can be cancelled; the cancel trigger is only allowed within a transaction activity. The intermediate event in Figure 5.19 is not a cancel trigger but is instead an exception trigger. So when a dining party leaves, no compensation activities will be performed.

The example shown in Figure 5.20 is rather simplistic—good for illustrating transactions and compensation but more simple than real-world situations.[1]

---

[1]Readers with a software engineering background will notice the difference between the business transaction in Figure 5.20 and database transactions. Database transactions are similar to business transactions but at a vastly different timescale—in milliseconds instead of days and weeks.

POOLS

Sometimes activities in a process must interact with another process. Supplies must be ordered via a separate procurement process. Taxes must be prepared and filed with national and local governments, each of which has its own processes for finding mistakes and violations. Leases are renewed for restaurants, involving negotiations with the real estate owners over price and terms.

We model multiple processes and the interactions between those processes using *pools*. A pool is a horizontal container for other process elements: activities, events, and gateways. A pool is a bit like a lane—as you recall, also a horizontal container for process elements—except that a pool can contain lanes, and usually does.

Consider an example in which a Mykonos procurement specialist orders kitchen equipment (e.g., a stove) from a distributor, shown in Figure 5.21. The process begins when the procurement specialist places an order for the equipment. The distributor's sales department receives the request and verifies with the warehouse that the item is in the inventory. Sales then calculates the price and creates an invoice that is sent to the restaurant. The procurement specialist receives the invoice and issues a deposit payment for the equipment. Once Sales receives the deposit, it approves the order and instructs the warehouse to ship the equipment. The process ends when the restaurant receives the equipment.

Like many of the restaurant example models in this book, the process shown in Figure 5.21 is simple. It is meant to illustrate, not to be complete. We did not

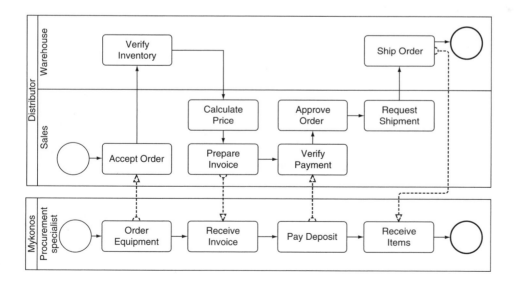

FIGURE 5.21 A process with two pools

include what happens if the warehouse is out of stock or if partial payment is received. Similarly, when the equipment is received it is inspected and if inspection reveals something wrong, it is returned. This process Mykonos employs is more complicated than the model shown in Figure 5.21.

Figure 5.21 has two pools: a pool at the top and a pool at the bottom. The pool at the top shows the distributor's process. That pool has two lanes: one for the warehouse and one for sales. The pool at the bottom shows Mykonos's activities and has a single lane for the procurement specialist.

You might be wondering why pools are necessary. Why not model the process of Figure 5.21 with three lanes and no pools, as shown in Figure 5.22? What's the difference between the two models? The difference between Figure 5.21 and Figure 5.22 is profound. The process shown in Figure 5.22 is managed as a single process. Some organization—perhaps Mykonos—has the responsibility for the whole end-to-end process. If something goes wrong, the responsible organization (i.e., Mykonos) is charged with fixing the problem. So, if sales cannot calculate a price for some reason and the order sits at the **Calculate Price** activity, Mykonos has the authority to solve the problem, perhaps to help them calculate the price and then to move the order along to the next activity.

But in fact Mykonos does not have that authority over the activities in the sales lane. The sales participant is an employee of the distributor, a different company, over which Mykonos has no control. And the distributor has no authority over the activities in the procurement specialist swimlane. Figure 5.22 is a poor model of the equipment procurement process because it implies that some organization has authority over the whole end-to-end process. That single organization does

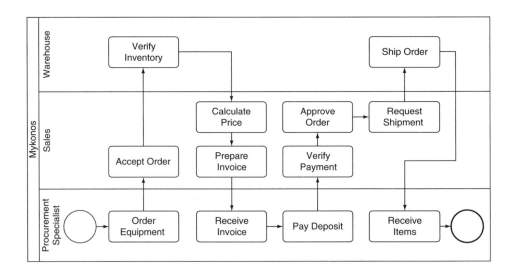

FIGURE 5.22 Three lanes instead of two pools

not exist. Figure 5.21 is a much better model. Mykonos has responsibility for the activities the bottom pool, and the distributor has responsibility for the activities in pool at the top. No single organization manages procurement as a single process. Instead it is managed by two different organizations, as two processes that interact.

The interaction between the pools occurs in *message flows*, shown as the dashed lines in Figure 5.21. For example, there is a message flow between the activities **Order Equipment** and **Accept Order**. A message flow is different from a sequence flow. A message flow is used to connect activities (or events) that are in different pools, modeling a flow of messages between the two activities. For example, as part of the **Order Equipment** activity, the procurement specialist sends a fax to the distributor. That fax is read and interpreted in **Accept Order**. The sending of the fax is a message and is modeled with a message flow. Message flows also model other means of messaging, in addition to faxes: emails, Web service invocations, telephone calls, even in-person visits. All are messages; all are modeled with message flows.

Message flows are only used between pools. Two activities in the same pool are never connected by a message flow, because both activities have access to the same information. All activities in the same pool are assumed to have access to whatever information they need, through IT systems, paper, or verbal communication. Similarly, sequence flows are never used to connect activities in different pools. As you recall, a sequence flow between one activity and another means that the second activity happens after the first is completed. A single organization manages that process, even when the two activities are in separate lanes. In Figure 5.21, **Verify Inventory** and **Calculate Price** are connected by a sequence flow, so **Calculate Price** happens after **Verify Inventory** is complete. The distributor organization ensures that **Calculate Price** takes place at the right time. But as we have discussed, there is no single organization with authority across pools. Sequence flows are inappropriate between pools because there is no one to ensure that the sequencing occurs.

In Figure 5.21 both pools are shown as *white boxes*. A white-box pool is one in which all the activities are modeled. In Figure 5.21 we can see all the activities in the distributor pool and all the activities in the Mykonos pool. Everything is visible.

White-box modeling is often impractical. Often you do not know how your business partners do what they do. You know only how your own process interacts with their process. And it is often not so important to understand the internal details of your business partners' processes. For these situations, *black-box* modeling is more appropriate. In a black-box business process model, the internal details of the external organizations are not shown. Figure 5.23 shows the same process as Figure 5.21 but with the distributor pool as a black box.

Figure 5.23 has the same messages as Figure 5.21, connecting to the same activities in the Mykonos pool but connecting to the distributor pool, not to activities but to the pool as a whole. For example, in Figure 5.21 there is a message flow from **Order Equipment** to **Accept Order**. The same message flow is shown in Figure 5.23, but the message flow is from **Order Equipment** to the black-box

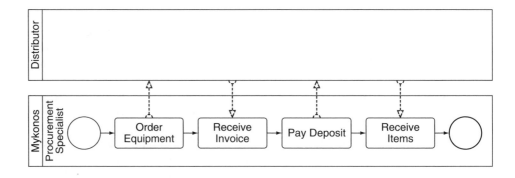

FIGURE 5.23 A black-box pool

distributor pool. In Figure 5.23 we can see exactly how Mykonos is interacting with the distributor, but we cannot see inside the distributor's process.

How do you decide whether a business process should be modeled using multiple pools interacting with message flows or as a single pool using sequence flow? The key question to answer is: Who manages the process? If the whole process is managed by a single organization, a single pool is appropriate. If multiple organizations manage their own processes that then interact, multiple pools are important.

As we write this chapter, there is some difference of opinion in the business modeling community about when pools are appropriate. Some modelers think participants who are part of different organizations must always be in different pools. So these modelers consider the process shown in Figure 5.15 to be invalid, since the dining party is certainly not part of the restaurant organization. These modelers would draw Figure 5.15 in two pools, with a message flow between **Wait For Table** and **Check Availability** modeling the verbal communication that occurs when an impatient dining party asks whether a table is ready now.

We think this approach is overly restrictive, and leads to overlay complex models. We believe it is appropriate to include an external participant within a pool as long as a single organization is managing the whole process. In Figure 5.15, **Dining Party** is included in the **Restaurant** pool because the restaurant is managing the whole process. As always, you are free to use either approach, as long as you are consistent.

AS-IS AND TO-BE PROCESSES

A model of today's business is often called an *as-is model*, to contrast with a model of a desired future situation, a *to-be model*. The terms "as-is" and "to-be" work for all business modeling disciplines. One can have an as-is process model and a to-be process model, showing activities, gateways, and sequence flow for today and for the planned future. Similarly, one can have an as-is organization model and a to-be organization model, showing today and tomorrow for the organization. One can even have as-is and to-be motivation models if the strategy is to be changed.

It is common to have a single as-is process model and several different to-be processes models. Several alternatives are evaluated to decide which is the best business processes for the future. Depending on the evaluation goals, we could decide on a to-be process that takes the least amount of time to complete the work. Alternatively, we might decide on the to-be process that best improves customer quality.

It is also possible—albeit less common—to have several as-is processes. For example, Mykonos restaurants perform customer reservations differently. Some restaurants call the customer on the day of the reservation to confirm and some do not. Some restaurants only take reservations two weeks in advance, some limit reservations to one month forward, and Portia will take a reservations one year in advance. When Mykonos implements a reservation application across all its restaurants, they will standardize on a single reservation process, modeling all these alternative as-is processes to understand what is involved in the standardization.

Let's look at an example of an as-is process. Figure 5.24 shows a single as-is process: the subprocess for seating customers. The as-is process is purely manual; No technology supports the host in her job of seating the customer. A dining party waits until a table is available, and they either check periodically with the host or just wait until the host informs them that a table is available.

Studying the as-is process provides an understanding of how work is performed today as well as some insight into problems. For example, when a table is not available, the dining party waits in the **Wait for Table** activity. For some customers, this is an anxious wait because they are unsure whether they have been forgotten.

At some family-oriented Mykonos restaurants, pagers are provided to waiting diners. Pagers make the waiting less anxious for some diners, because they do not have to periodically ask the host if they have been forgotten. Diners have a feeling of assurance that they are queued in a system, and they can relax and enjoy waiting for their pager to buzz.

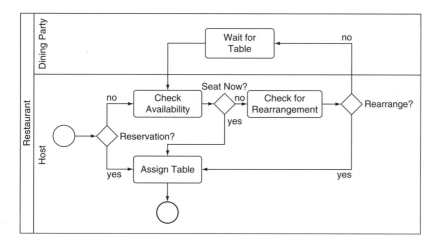

FIGURE 5.24 Seating subprocess

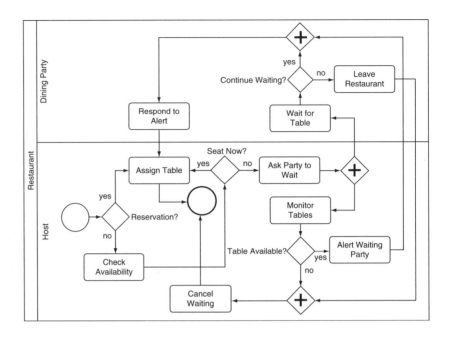

FIGURE 5.25 The to-be process with a pager

Figure 5.25 shows a revised **Seat Party** subprocess, incorporating activities that use a paging system. Figure 5.25 is a to-be process, one potential future. When a dining party is asked to wait in **Ask Party to Wait**, they are given a pager. At any point the party might choose to leave. If they leave they return the pager. If they stay, when the pager notifies them that a table is available, they return the pager, the host assigns the table and the diners are seated.

By comparing the to-be process of Figure 5.25 with the as-is process of Figure 5.24, we can see which activities are performed differently and which new activities are needed.

BUSINESS MOTIVATIONS AND PROCESSES

In Chapter 3 we described goals, courses of action, strategies, and other elements of business motivation models. As you will recall, a goal is something an organization is trying to achieve, a course of action is something an organization does to achieve a desired result, and a strategy is a broad, lasting course of action. Figure 5.26 shows the restaurant **Portia**, an organization unit; the goal **Improve Customer Experience** that Portia defines; and the strategy **Use Pagers** that Portia establishes to channel efforts toward the goal.

Organizations are responsible for business processes. An organization is responsible for a business process if the organization is charged with the successful completion of the process and with fixing any issues that arise along the way. In Figure 5.26, **Portia** is responsible for the process **Seat Party with Pagers**, the business process detailed in Figure 5.25.

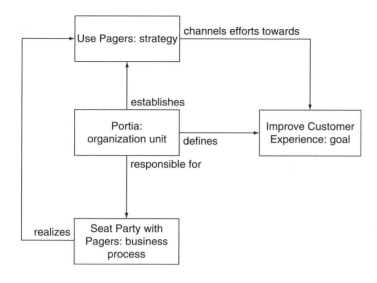

FIGURE 5.26 Business motivation and business processes

Business processes *realize*[2] courses of action. Realizing a course of action means that the business process implements the course of action—that the activities, gateways, and sequence flow in the business process achieve the course of action. Figure 5.26 shows that the **Seat Party with Pagers** business process **realizes** the strategy **Use Pagers**.

An individual activity can also realize a course of action. Figure 5.27 shows the individual activities within the **Seat Party with Pagers** business process that realize the strategy **Use Pagers**. Although the process as a whole realizes the strategy, only some of the activities within the process realize it.

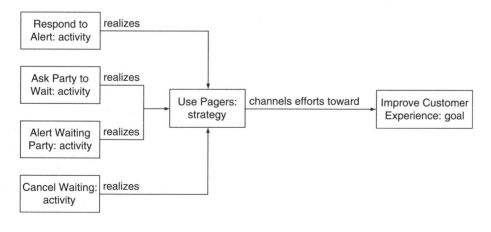

FIGURE 5.27 Business motivation and activities

[2]As you will recall from Chapter 3, BMM is the OMG standard for business motivation models. The **realizes** association between a business process and a course of action is introduced in BMM.

BUSINESS PROCESSES, ORGANIZATIONS, AND INTERACTIONS

In Chapter 4 we described organizations, roles, and other elements of business organization models. As you will recall, an organization is a collection of people who work together toward a common goal. A role is the responsibility a person assumes when he holds a position in an organization. Business process models also show organizations and roles. Each lane in a business process model is labeled with the participant who performs the activity. The participant is either an organization or a role. Similarly, each pool is labeled with the participant who manages that process. That participant is also either an organization or a role.

Figure 5.28 shows the relationship between a business organization model and a business process model. At the bottom of Figure 5.28 is the business process model of the Mykonos procurement of kitchen equipment, originally shown as Figure 5.21. At the top of Figure 5.28 is a business organization model that describes the relationship between Mykonos and the distributor, the same distributor role shown in the process model at the bottom. Between the top and bottom are arrows showing which model element at the top is the same as which label at the bottom.

The organization Mykonos is shown at the top of Figure 5.28. The **Operations** organization unit is within **Mykonos** because it is part of the larger restaurant company. Within **Operations** are three organizations: **Human Resources, Finance**, and **Procurement**. The **Procurement Specialist** role is part of the **Procurement** organization. There is an arrow from the **Procurement Specialist** role at the top of Figure 5.28 to the lane label of the lower pool at the bottom. The **Procurement Specialist** role is the participant of that lane; all the activities in that lane are performed by someone who takes that role. There is also an arrow from **Mykonos** to the pool label of the same lower pool. Mykonos is responsible for the process of the lower pool.

Figure 5.28 also shows the **Distributor** role. **Distributor** has two organizations within: **Sales** and **Warehouse**. Both of those organizations are participants of lanes in the upper pool, as shown by the arrows. The distributor is responsible for the upper pool process as a whole.

Not every organization or role in a business organization model corresponds to a participant in a business process model. Instead only the relevant organizations and the relevant roles are participants. For example, **Human Resources** is an organization within Mykonos but not a participant of any lane or pool in the equipment procurement process, since no one from Human Resources does any of the work in this process.

There are two interactions in the business organization model of Figure 5.28. One interaction is **order**, between **Procurement Specialist** and the **Sales** organization. The other interaction is **kitchen equipment** delivered by the **Warehouse** organization to the **Procurement Specialist**. As described in Chapter 4, the direction of an interaction is from the organization (or role) delivering the value to the organization (or role) receiving the value.

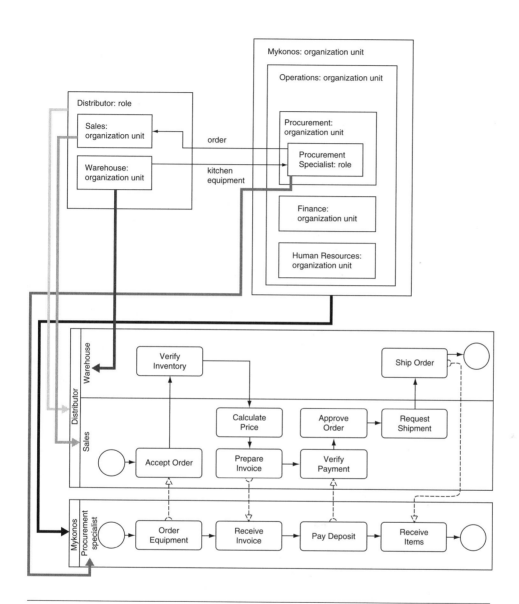

FIGURE 5.28 Business organizations and business processes

An interaction between two organizations in a business organization model can correspond to a business process in a business process model, with the business process detailing the way the two organizations actually work together. The business process at the bottom of Figure 5.28 details the **order** interaction between the distributor's sales organization and Mykonos's procurement specialist, showing all the activities that result in the order being placed. The same process also details the **kitchen equipment** interaction between **Warehouse** and **Procurement Specialist**.

THE BPMN STANDARD

The Business Process Model Notation—commonly known by its acronym, BPMN—was originally published in 2004 by the organization Business Process Management Initiative. BPMN is a graphical modeling notation for business processes that is independent of a specific implementation environment. BPMN was officially adopted as an OMG specification in 2006, and updated in 2008 [OMG 2008b].

BPMN is a good standard with modeling constructs for all the common business process modeling needs and for many less common needs as well. BPMN is a successful standard, becoming widely adopted in the business process modeling community. The business process models in this chapter, and through this book, are shown in BPMN. As with other business modeling standards, we make no attempt at completeness in our description. We use only some of the elements of BPMN—the elements we find most useful in our everyday business process modeling.

Prior to the emergence of BPMN, modeling practitioners created business process models using a great variety of notations. There are several other standards and many nonstandard proprietary methods for the visualization of business processes. In our experience, each of these standards and proprietary methods has shortcomings that limit its usefulness and in practice have limited its use.

IDEF was one of the standard notations used for modeling business processes. IDEF was developed by the US Department of Defense (DoD) in the 1980s, primarily for the modeling of information and software but also widely applied to business processes. IDEF includes 15 modeling methods—IDEF0 through IDEF14—to support a variety of purposes. IDEF0 and IDEF3 have been used for business process modeling.

IDEF0 shows business process activities but does not show their sequence or timing. In practice, many readers of IDEF0 models found them difficult to understand because it was not apparent what activities occurred when. IDEF3 was later developed to show sequence flow among activities. Today IDEF is still used by DoD and its contractor community but is not popular in other organizations. Businesspeople find IDEF difficult to understand.

UML is another standard notation that has been used for modeling business processes. As described in Chapter 1, UML is a software modeling language. One of the diagrams of UML—activity diagrams—has been used for modeling business processes [Eriksson 2000]. UML activity diagrams are functionally similar to BPMN diagrams, and can be used to model business processes. But UML looks quite different from BPMN. BPMN was designed to be understood by businesspeople—people without training in software development. By contrast, UML users are technical people: software developers, software architects, and system architects. UML diagrams look technical, and in practice they are much harder for businesspeople to understand than BPMN diagrams. Furthermore, BPMN has a richer set of model constructs for business process modeling—constructs including pools, compensation, and timer start events.

BPMN is designed for business modelers and provides those modelers with a rich but simple notation to create business process models. As of this writing the tool support for BPMN is still evolving. Though many tools claim to implement BPMN, some have implemented only portions of the standard—the portions that are most similar to the proprietary modeling techniques they already support. Business process models cannot yet exchange models; a model created in one tool cannot yet be read into another tool. At the time of this writing, the BPMN standard is being refined within the OMG. We expect future versions of BPMN will provide guidance for tool interoperability, as well as provide additional modeling features.

As more tools support BPMN and provide for conversions between their own formats and BPMN, we expect BPMN to be an excellent choice for avoiding dependence on a single vendor's proprietary modeling method or tool. And today BPMN already provides a rich set of modeling constructs, providing all the constructs available in proprietary tools and several that are unique, including business transactions and compensation. We find no reason to use any other business process modeling notation.

OMG has also adopted a second standard for business process modeling: Business Process Definition Metamodel (BPDM), adopted in 2007. BPDM is not an alternative to BPMN. Instead it complements BPMN. Whereas BPMN specifies the notation, the visual look of a business process model, BPDM supports the representation of process models independently of any notation. BPDM provides a serialization capability for BPMN, so a model can be saved to a file in a standard way. BPDM also deals with the synchronization and execution order of a business process and describes the way participating organizations in a process define their agreements and interactions so that they can collaborate.

BPMN and BPDM address different audiences. Though BPMN addresses business modelers, BPDM addresses tool vendors that need to support import and export capability of the models in their tools.

Because they are complementary standards, OMG plans to merge BPMN and BPDM into a single standard, with the merging planned for BPMN version 2. Today, even when a tool supports portability to another tool, the model elements can be moved, but their visual layout is lost. A modeler must recreate the model diagram, repositioning each model element. Version 2 of the combined standard will include support for diagram layout interchange so that model layout is also preserved.

Case Study

The United States shares a 2,000-mile border with Mexico. That 2,000 miles is the most frequently crossed international border in the world, with 250 million legal crossings every year. In addition to the many legal crossings, there are also some illegal ones. Every year an unknown number of people—perhaps as many as a million, perhaps more—cross the border from south to north, from Mexico to the US. Most of the people crossing are economic migrants, attempting to create better lives for themselves by working in the United States. Some of the people are smugglers, carrying illegal drugs and other contraband. And among the large numbers of economic migrants and smugglers, it is believed that terrorists, planning to inflict religiously-inspired violence on Americans, might also try to cross the southwest border.

US Customs and Border Protection (CBP) is responsible for preventing illegal border crossings. At the time of this writing, CBP has only partial success in catching people who cross the border illegally. Historically, most people who attempted to cross ultimately succeeded (even if it took several attempts). In 2006, CBP sought technology solutions for improving their performance, for catching significantly more illegal crossers, enough to deter crossers from attempting to cross. They were looking for a private sector partner to create something—a wall, a fence, electronics, or something else—that would help them spot and apprehend all the illegal border crossers.

CBP created a competition among prospective private sector partners to determine who could propose the best solution to their challenges. Five companies responded. Four recommended mixes of sophisticated technologies, including watching the border with blimps or unmanned aerial vehicles. Our approach was different. Instead of merely providing a technology-centered approach, we also focused on the business processes. We learned as much as we also could about the everyday life of border patrol agents, the law enforcement officers who patrol the border. Our approach involved five steps:

1. Understand the government agencies involved, how each works, and how each interacts with other agencies.
2. Capture as-is business process models, to understand how work is being done today and the challenges with the existing process.
3. Create alternative to-be business process models, to investigate how work will be performed after the deployment of various solutions.
4. Simulate the alternative to-be process models, to understand which are most effective.
5. Map the proposed technology solutions to the to-be business processes, to understand how the technologies will be used.

The business processes we modeled encompass the entire cycle of handling illegal border crossers—everything from the detection of an illegal crosser to that person's ultimate removal from the United States. The entire cycle includes detection, identification and classification, response, apprehension, detention, and removal. Detection is the initial spotting of a group of illegal crossers. A group might be detected by sight, or technology such as radar and cameras can be used. Once a group is detected, the illegal crossers are identified and classified. Are the crossers a family with children carrying luggage, economic migrants who are likely nonviolent? Or are they four fast-moving individuals carrying suspicious backpacks, smugglers who are likely to be dangerous? Response involves dispatching the appropriate number of border patrol agents and dispatching them to the right location. Apprehension involves arresting the border crossers and transporting them to a border patrol station. After they arrive at the station, the border crossers are fingerprinted to identify whether anyone is wanted for another criminal activity. The border crossers are interviewed to determine who is a Mexican citizen and who is a citizen of another country. Mexican citizens are returned to Mexico in a bus, but anyone from another country cannot be returned to Mexico. They are instead deported to their country using a far longer process, based on international laws and agreements.

CBP was interested in solutions for detection, identification and classification, and response. But we went much further in our investigation, looking at the downstream processes of apprehension, detention, and removal. These downstream processes were important for providing us with a complete understanding of the situation and the challenges facing CBP.

We worked with border patrol subject matter experts—retired border patrol agents who provided us with detail about the activities they performed and the challenges of their day-to-day work. Working with subject matter experts provided insight into how they performed their work. For example, we learned that each geographical location along the border is different, with different terrain, different weather, and different socioeconomic situations. One technology solution cannot fit all the locations.

We explored the suitability of new technology with the subject matter experts, looking at ways different technology solutions would affect the agents' work. Would a particular new technology help or hurt them? Agents already carry a good deal of equipment: radio, multiple cellphones, flashlights, and weapons. Adding more equipment weighs them down. It is better to replace equipment, to make the whole load easier to carry. Also, most illegal crossing happens at night, under the cover of darkness. If an agent uses an electronic device with a lighted screen, the device will illuminate the face of the agent, exposing his location to all the illegal border crossers, and making it easier for

Continued

Case Study—continued

them to avoid him. The lighted screen would even make him an easy target for those border crossers who are violent.

Figure 5.29 focuses on the transportation activities, showing the embedded subprocess **Transport Crossers**. Transportation historically has been performed by border patrol agents but does not require their specialized tracking and apprehension skills. For a small group of illegal crossers, the agent drives the group to the border station. But if the group is too large to fit in his truck, he must wait with the apprehended border crossers for another agent to bring a van or a bus. While the agent is waiting and while he is driving, he cannot intercept any more border crossers.

We explored several alternatives to the current process. The best alternative was a combination of technology improvements, resourcing improvements, and process improvements. One improvement was a set of technologies to keep the agents in the field in constant communication with the stations. Other improvements included the ability to track positions of agents, track incidents they are handling, and track assets such as transport vehicles. This allows the dispatcher to determine the best and most efficient pick-up point, minimizing the wait and transportation time.

Resource combinations were also explored. What is the best number of vehicles to handle the expected number of crossers and minimize the overall wait times? Who should drive the vehicles so that the agents can spend their time catching illegal crossers?

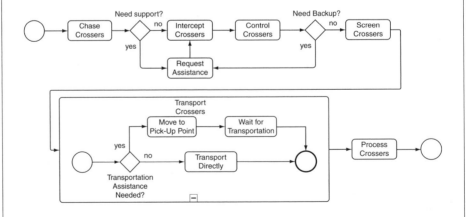

FIGURE 5.29 Transport Crossers subprocess

We used business process simulations to analyze the process, resulting in proposal recommendations. These recommendations involved the outsourcing of transportation, the number of buses, and technologies to better support the agent.

In September 2006 CBP awarded the contract to our team. Our proposal was recognized as having the best approach. In particular we were recognized for our deep understanding of CBP's business and needs.

Business process models are useful for understanding how activities are accomplished today but also for creating good approaches for how they should be accomplished in the future. They are useful for conveying and communicating an approach and for showcasing an understanding of the issues and solutions.

A business process model describes the work that is being performed, the order in which work is performed, and who performs the work. A business process model includes a rich set of modeling elements—activities, gateways, events, and flows— that describe the complexity of a process.

A business process model is about how work is accomplished. In Chapter 6, we examine the rules that govern a business process—the business guidelines that restrict what should be done when performing the business process.

CHAPTER

Business Rule Models

6

Business rules are the fourth and last business modeling discipline described in this book. Business rules shape the behavior of a business and guide the behavior of the business's employees. Business rules explain what is allowed and what is not allowed. A business rule model also explains the consequences of violation: what happens when a rule is violated. This chapter describes business rule models.

Sometimes customers at a Mykonos restaurant leave before they finish their dinner. Perhaps there is an emergency at home, and they must leave to tend to the emergency. Or someone in the party became ill while they're at the restaurant. Or they were disgruntled, unhappy with the wait for their dinner, and leave before their dinner arrives.

There are many legitimate reasons for a restaurant party to leave early. There is also one illegitimate reason: Like all restaurants, Mykonos occasionally suffers from dine-and-dash, a form of theft where a restaurant party leaves early without paying, effectively stealing the restaurant meal.

What should a Mykonos server do if one of her parties leaves early? Should the party have to pay for their dinner? What if the service truly was bad or if the waits truly were long? And how should Mykonos separate customers who legitimately must leave early from those who would dine-and-dash?

There are additional issues around customer payment. Maybe the customers are surprised by the size of their bill, and question one or more of the charges. The server needs to resolve the situation, and if she cannot, the manager will attempt to do so.

And sometimes, a customer is willing but unable to pay. None of his credit cards have enough credit. Or he's left his wallet behind at home. What happens now?

Mykonos Dining Corporation provides instructions to their restaurant employees about what to do in these situations. These instructions are called *business rules*. The business rules guide the servers and managers when confronting payment situations. By providing business rules, Mykonos can take advantage of the shared experience of many people, to provide best-practice solutions to all employees.

Mykonos also provides business rules for other circumstances—circumstances that do not involve payments. There are business rules to protect the health of the Mykonos restaurant customers and to ensure that the local health codes are satisfied. There are business rules around safety, to ensure that no employees are hurt, especially since the restaurant business involves both fire and knives. There are business rules around staffing and scheduling employees, to promote both fairness and efficiency and to reduce employee dissatisfaction. There are business rules about seating customers at tables and managing customers that are waiting to be seated. And even though menu design for a restaurant is largely left to the discretion of the restaurant head chef, there are some business rules about menu design—for example, to ensure that vegetarian customers always have at least two entrees from which to choose.

BUSINESS RULES SHAPE BEHAVIOR

What is a business rule? A business rule is "a directive intended to influence or guide business behavior" [Ross 2003]. As a directive, a business rule can be an order—"This must be done"—or a suggestion—"This should be considered"— or something between an order and a suggestion. The purpose of a business rule is to shape behavior: Do this and don't do that. And the guidance is business guidance: For Mykonos there are business rules about payments and cleanliness and appropriate attire for customers but not about who an employee dates or what a customer does after he leaves the restaurant. Employee dating and customer behavior after they leave the premises are outside the scope of the restaurant business.

Consider a Mykonos business rule about payments:

> ***Charging for Orders****:* It is obligatory that a party is charged for a menu item if the party orders the menu item and the menu item is served to the party.

Charging for Orders is a business rule. It is a *directive:* it says what must be done. If Joe orders a glass of pinot noir and the glass is served to him, his party must be charged for it. If the wine is served and Joe starts drinking it but leaves before he finishes, his party must still be charged. If the wine is served but the party later leaves because they are dissatisfied with the service, the wine must still be charged. The **Charging for Orders** business rule applies to all these situations.

But some situations are not covered by **Charging for Orders**. What if Joe orders a glass of pinot noir, but Joe and the rest of his party leave before the wine is served? **Charging for Orders** is silent on that situation; presumably other business rules apply. Similarly, if a glass of pinot noir is served to Joe's party but neither Joe nor anyone else ordered it, **Charging for Orders** does not say whether it must be charged.

Business rules travel in groups. It is rare for a single business rule to exist by itself, without 5 or 20 others that apply to related situations. There are many other Mykonos business rules about payments. For example:

> *Splitting Bills:* It is permitted that a server may split a bill only if the party agrees to bill splitting and the bill is split equally.

The **Splitting Bills** business rule provides guidance about bill splitting—the conditions under which it is permissible for customers to split a bill. There are two conditions that must be true if a bill is to be split. If the party does not agree to split the bill, the bill may not be split. And the bill may not be split if it is to be split 60-40 or anything other than equally.

Splitting Bills seems quite understandable, but only because we are relying on our existing knowledge about servers, parties, and restaurant bills—knowledge that we all have gained from eating in restaurants. Someone who has never eaten in a restaurant might wonder what these words really mean. If a person eats by himself, is that a party? What about 11 people who eat at two separate tables because there is no room to seat them all together? What is a bill, really? A complete business rule model that includes **Splitting Bills** needs to define some nouns: server, party, and bill. **Charging for Orders** also uses two nouns that need definitions: party and item. Is a glass of pinot noir an item? Is a cigar? A shoe?

There are some other mysteries about **Charging for Orders** and **Splitting Bills**—mysteries at least to our fictional person who has never enjoyed a restaurant meal. What does it mean for a party to incur a bill? Can a server incur a bill? Can a bill incur another bill? What does bill splitting mean? What does it mean for a bill to be split equally? A complete business rule model needs to define verbs like *incur* and concepts like *equal splitting*. Later in this chapter, we show how all these terms are defined as part of a business rule model.

Why No Diagrams?

You might have noticed that the business rules **Charging for Orders** and **Splitting Bills** are shown here as sentences in English, not as diagrams. The business motivation models in Chapter 3 were diagrams, as were the business organization models in Chapter 4 and the business process models in Chapter 5. Why are business rules textual when the models in the other three disciplines are graphical?

In fact, a business motivation model can be described in text instead of in a diagram. Consider the simple motivation model shown in Figure 6.1 (and

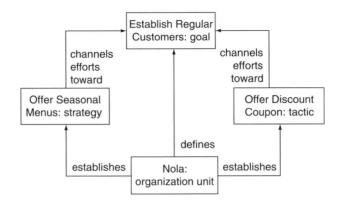

FIGURE 6.1 A simple motivation model

originally presented as Figure 3.5). Figure 6.1 can be expressed textually instead of visually:

> *The organization unit **Nola** defines the goal **Establish Regular Customers**. **Nola** establishes a strategy **Offer Seasonal Menu** that channels efforts toward **Establish Regular Customers**. **Nola** also establishes a tactic **Offer Discount Coupon** that channels efforts toward **Establish Regular Customers**.*

The text is equivalent to the diagram; from either you could create the other. In reviewing a business motivation model with a subject matter expert, it is often convenient to show him the diagram and walk him through it by saying the equivalent text so that he understands each element in the diagram. Diagrams are (usually) easier and faster for people to understand, so business motivation models are usually expressed graphically.

Business organizational models can also be expressed textually, in much the same way. So can business process models. Every model in this book can be expressed in English[1] instead of in lines and boxes and other graphical elements. As with business motivation models, the usual practice is to express organization and process models graphically; as you've seen the resultant diagrams are easier and faster to understand than the equivalent words.

Business rules are different. Some experts have proposed graphical languages for business rules (e.g., Terry Halpin's work [Halpin 2001]), but most people find the

---

[1]Of course, when we say English, we really mean any natural language: Japanese, Portuguese, Hindi, or any other of the world's 7,000 written tongues.

words easier to understand than the diagrams. In our experience, a business professional will more quickly understand a well-written business rule than she will understand a business process of equivalent complexity. Why? The reason is not clear. Perhaps our brains are just wired to comprehend rules. Perhaps in our ancestral past there were advantages to quickly learning tribal rules articulated by a tribal elder, and advantages to quickly recognizing when a rule was violated. Presumably the East African savannah offered no such advantages to the quick learning of business processes.

Even though business rules are in practice written as sentences instead of diagrams, they are still business models. Not all models are visual. With business rules, the model is expressed in the logic of the text rather than in a diagram.

A business rule is a model because it fits the definition we introduced in Chapter 1: it is a simple representation of a complex reality. For example, the **Splitting Bills** rule we examined earlier is simple guidance that applies to thousands of different restaurant situations, many of which are complex.

But there are some diagrams in this chapter. Although the business rules we examine are all shown as text, we do show diagrams of how those rules relate to other model elements, just as we showed diagrams in Chapter 5 of how activities relate to goals and to objectives. We also include some simple diagrams that show how rules are constructed, that show the components of a rule and the ordering of those components. And we include *fact type diagrams*. As we explain later in the chapter, fact types are verbs used in rules and the nouns those verbs tie together. Fact types lend themselves to diagrams. So although there are no diagrams of business rules themselves, this chapter has many diagrams for other purposes.

WHY BUSINESS RULES?

Why model business rules? As you recall, there are eight purposes for business modeling in general. Of these eight, business rules can achieve six: communication, training and learning, managing compliance, software requirements, direct execution, and knowledge management. But one of these six is by far the most common. Today, when a business rule model is created, it is usually for the purpose of specifying *requirements* for application software. Business rules are not a traditional means for specifying software requirements, but they complement the traditional techniques by capturing something that those techniques do not. Business rules capture constraints on behavior. They capture what is allowed and (more important) what is not allowed.

Of course, writing software from requirements is always slow, since it involves people understanding requirements and using those requirements to write and test code. A faster approach for implementing business rules in software is emerging: business rules can be *directly executed*. Instead of a person reading the business rule and translating the rule to code, a software application reads the rule and directly applies the rule when appropriate. New rules can be added and existing rules changed, and these changes are effected immediately.

At least that's the promise of direct execution. Today, direct execution is rare, since the technology is not widely understood. But in the future we expect direct execution to be widespread.

Business rules are used for *communication*—to communicate guidance to company employees. Business managers and proprietors guide employees about what to do and what not to do. Managers and proprietors have been crafting policies and other guidance for hundreds of years; one can imagine Benjamin Franklin writing lists of dos and don'ts for the employees of his printing businesses in the 18th century. But this managerial guidance has—until recently—been informal. There is little similarity from one company to another in the format and wording of their policies and guidance.

We are seeing some change here. Informal approaches to employee guidance famously suffer from misinterpretation. Joe and Jerry can interpret the same policy in different ways. Business rules offer precision, providing a way to guide employee behavior that avoids misinterpretations. So some companies are investigating the use of business rules for employee guidance.

Similarly, when a new recruit starts with a company, she must learn all the rules and policies of her new employer. She must learn all about "how we do things here." A business rule model is a good way to capture those rules and policies so they can be easily understood. Business rules are useful for *training and learning*.

Regulatory *compliance* is more important now than it has ever been. New laws and regulations require changes to company behavior. These company behavior changes usually then require changes in the behavior of individual employees. When a new law takes effect, there are actions that employees are no longer allowed to perform. This translation from a legal change to an employee behavior change is the path by which compliance is implemented.

Business rule models support compliance implementation, and support it easily and gracefully. When new regulation occurs, the regulation is analyzed for its impact on the business rules. Then new rules and changed rules are published so that employees are aware, and change their behavior. Sometimes applications must also change to support new regulatory requirements. If the applications are tied to business rules through a manual requirements process, the new rules and changed rules identify the components of the application that must change. Alternatively, if the applications directly implement the business rules, the new rules and changed rules are directly executed and the change occurs.

Business rules support *knowledge management*. Business rules are a good form for capturing much of the tacit knowledge that organizations want to preserve.

RULES

Let's consider some simple rules about customer payments, to better understand how business rules work and the forms they can take.

> ***Greenbacks Only:*** It is obligatory that each cash payment employ US currency.

Like all business rules, **Greenbacks Only** shapes behavior. It says what should occur. The Mykonos restaurants accept payments in cash, but only greenbacks can be used. No euros or yen are accepted.

> ***No Checks:*** It is prohibited that a payment employ a personal check.

No Checks says what should not occur. Mykonos restaurants do not accept any personal checks for payments.

> ***VISA Only:*** It is permitted that a payment employ a credit card only if the credit card is backed by VISA™.

VISA Only says what is allowed and the conditions under which it is allowed.

These three business rules illustrate three forms. The guidance captured by a business rule says what should be—*it is obligatory that;* what should not be—*it is prohibited that;* or what is allowable and the conditions under which it is allowed—*it is permitted that . . . only if.*

These three business rules sound absolute. No exceptions will be brooked and any server who accepts payments in euros will be fired on the spot. But in truth **Greenbacks Only** says absolutely nothing about whether it is strictly enforced with severe penalties or whether it is merely a recommendation, to be followed at the server's discretion. The same rule is written the same way in either case. Similarly, **No Checks** might be as strict as it sounds, or it might be merely a recommendation for individual behavior, or it could be somewhere in between.

Later in the chapter we describe *level of enforcement*, the degree to which a rule is actually enforced by an organization. But for now, just note that the level of enforcement is separate from the rule itself; that a rule is written in the same absolute way whether it is to be strictly enforced or merely a guideline.

Just as a business rule does not say to what degree it is to be enforced, it also doesn't say who does the enforcement. **Greenbacks Only** is silent about who tells the customer that only US cash can be used. Maybe it is enforced by the server, maybe by the restaurant manager. The rule can also be used by the restaurant host—for example, if a prospective customer calls and asks whether euros are accepted. In a similar way, **VISA Only** is silent about who enforces the guidance that only VISA cards are accepted.

Some rules are automatable. They can be enforced by an application or perhaps by several applications. For example, in addition to being enforced by a server or a manager, **VISA Only** could be enforced by the payments application. When an American Express™ card is swiped, the application rejects the attempt, perhaps showing a dialog box that displays the rule "It is permitted that a payment employ a credit card only if the credit card is backed by VISA." The rule is the same, regardless of whether it is enforced by people or machines.

Business rules change. For example, Mykonos restaurants might start accepting MasterCard™ and American Express. If they do, **VISA Only** must be changed to reflect the new cards accepted.

> ***Credit Cards Accepted:*** It is permitted that a payment employ a credit card only if the credit card is backed by VISA or the credit card is backed by MasterCard or the credit card is backed by American Express.

Business rules change more often than other business models. In an organization as large as Mykonos, every week will see at least one rule changed or added. Sometimes things will change even more quickly. Discover™ cards will become accepted on Monday, a new safety policy to prevent customer falls will start on Tuesday, a new rule around scheduling servers will be implemented on Wednesday. This is a much faster pace of change than that of business processes, business organizations, or business motivations. Business organizations and business motivations typically change far more slowly, with a few changes each year instead of a few changes each week.

BUSINESS RULE FORMS

Some of the business rule examples in this chapter have started with the phrase "It is obligatory that" and then continued with a statement of what is obligatory. These business rules use the same "It is obligatory that" *form*. There are six business rule forms, one of which uses the phrase "It is obligatory that." We will describe each of the six, giving examples of business rules for each.

Obligation Statements

Many business rules oblige people (or software applications) to ensure that something is true. These truth-ensuring rules are *obligation statements*. An obligation statement begins with the phrase "It is obligatory that" and then continues with what is demanded.

Earlier we considered **Greenbacks Only**, a simple obligation statement.

> ***Greenbacks Only:*** It is obligatory that each cash payment employ US currency.

As an obligation statement, **Greenbacks Only** implicitly acknowledges the possibility that a customer might attempt to use another currency. For example, a customer might think he could pay his bill with euros. A server might accept the euros, either as a mistake or in ignorance or as a knowing violation of the rule. All this is possible, and in practice might happen. But as a company, Mykonos

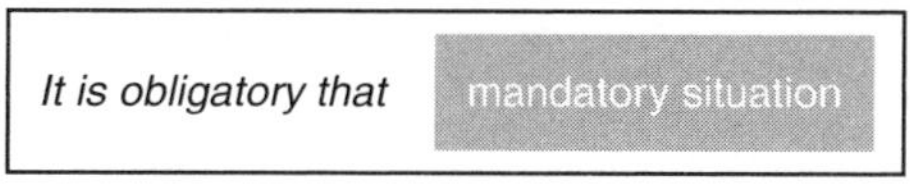

It is obligatory that	mandatory situation

FIGURE 6.2 The structure of a simple obligation statement

mandates that it must not happen. **Greenbacks Only** says that each Mykonos employee has an obligation as part of his or her job to accept only US dollars for cash payments. Further, each Mykonos employee has an obligation to inform customers of this restriction if there are questions or confusion.

Figure 6.2 shows the structure of a simple obligation statement such as **Greenbacks Only**. The expression that follows "It is obligatory that" is called the *mandatory situation*. In **Greenbacks Only**, the mandatory situation is "each cash payment employ US currency." That mandatory situation itself may be either true or false. The mandatory situation is true if a cash payment in a Mykonos restaurant in fact employs US currency, and it is false if a cash payment in a Mykonos restaurant employs euros or yen or sterling. **Greenbacks Only** says nothing about whether the mandatory situation is true or false. Instead, **Greenbacks Only** states that the Mykonos employees have an obligation to make the mandatory situation an actuality.

Greenbacks Only is a simple obligation statement. Let's consider a more complex variant of **Greenbacks Only**.

> *Greenbacks Only B:* It is obligatory that each cash payment employ US currency if the payment amount of the cash payment is at least 20 dollars.

Greenbacks Only B insists on US currency for larger amounts but says nothing about what should happen for payments of less than $20. Either other rules apply for those smaller payments or a server is free to accept other currencies.

Like **Greenbacks Only**, **Greenbacks Only B** implicitly acknowledges the possibility of customers paying with more than $20 in non-US currency as well as the possibility of servers accepting such currency. But **Greenbacks Only B** indicates that such behavior must not happen.

Figure 6.3 shows the structure of **Greenbacks Only B**. Figure 6.3 includes an optional *condition* as well as the mandatory situation. The condition is the scope of when the mandatory situation actually applies—when it is mandatory.

It is obligatory that	mandatory situation	if	condition

FIGURE 6.3 The structure of an obligation statement

For example, in **Greenbacks Only B**, the condition is "the payment amount of the cash payment is at least 20 dollars." If the condition is true—if the cash payment is at least 20 dollars—then the mandatory situation applies. For those payments the employees of Mykonos have the responsibility of ensuring that US currency is used. If the condition is false—if the cash payment is less than 20 dollars, nothing is mandated. The Mykonos employees are not obligated to do anything, at least nothing to satisfy this rule. The "if" in **Greenbacks Only B** effectively reduces the concern to just those payments where the condition is true—just those payments that are $20 or larger.

Greenbacks Only B is not a good business rule because there are situations in which it is not clear whether the rule applies. Suppose a customer pays €15 for a couple of drinks at the bar. Is this payment more than $20? How is a server to know, unless she carries the daily currency conversion rates with her? **Greenbacks Only C** is a better rule with the same intent.

> *Greenbacks Only C:* It is obligatory that each cash payment employ US currency if the cash payment is applied to a bill and the amount of the bill is at least 20 dollars.

Now a server need only know the amount of the bill to determine whether euros are allowable. Of course, if the payment is accepted, someone will have to make a calculation of whether €15 is a sufficient payment and what the change should be. Other rules apply.

Greenbacks Only B and **Greenbacks Only C** have the same mandatory situation: "each cash payment employ US currency." But the conditions of the two rules are different. The condition of **Greenbacks Only C** is "the cash payment is applied to a bill and the amount of the bill is at least 20 dollars." Where the condition is true, the employees of Mykonos have the responsibility of ensuring the mandatory situation—of ensuring that cash payments employ US currency. No obligation results where the condition is false. For example, if the account of a bill is less than $20, it does not matter whether US currency is used. Similarly, a cash payment that is applied to something else (other than the bill) can also be done in a non-US currency. A customer might pay greenbacks for his bill, but leave a tip in Mexican pesos, knowing that the server is leaving the next day for a vacation on the Mayan peninsula. Such an action does not violate the rule because the action falls outside the scope of the condition. The rule is only violated when a cash payment is in non-US currency, it is applied to a bill, and the bill is large enough, at least $20.

Obligation statements are the most common of the business rules. When do you use an obligation statement? An obligation statement is used when you want the business—the employees and perhaps the software applications—to ensure that something is true. You first determine the expression that must be kept true, make it the mandatory situation, and (if necessary) create a condition that captures the scope of when the mandatory situation applies.

Prohibitive Statements

Some business rules are meant to prevent. These preventative business rules are called *prohibitive statements*. We have seen several prohibitive statements in this chapter (e.g., **No Checks** a few pages back). Let's look at a prohibitive statement that is a variant of our obligation statement **Greenbacks Only**.

> *No Loonies:* It is prohibited that a cash payment employ Canadian currency.

Instead of insisting that cash payments employ US currency, **No Loonies** insists that such payments do not employ Canadian currency. (Perhaps this rule is for a Mykonos restaurant in Buffalo, New York, in which customers often try to pay their bills in Canadian dollars instead of greenbacks.)

As with its obligation statement counterparts, **No Loonies** does not claim that there are no cash payments that use Canadian currency. Rather **No Loonies** states that Canadian currency *should* not be allowed for payments. Employees have a duty to reject cash payments in Canadian currency. Software applications such as payment applications should reject such payments as well.

The structure of **No Loonies** is shown in Figure 6.4.

A prohibitive statement starts with the phrase "It is prohibited that." After that phrase is the *banned situation*, an expression of what must be false. The banned situation of **No Loonies** is that "a cash payment employ Canadian currency." A prohibitive statement says that employees (and perhaps software applications) have a responsibility to prevent the banned situation. Employees can prevent the banned situation of **No Loonies** by rejecting cash payments in Canadian dollars and by advising customers that Canadian dollars are not accepted.

As with obligation statements, prohibitive statements can be more complex than **No Loonies**. Many prohibitive statements make the prohibition conditional on some other expression. Consider **No Loonies B**.

> *No Loonies B:* It is prohibited that a cash payment employ Canadian currency if the cash payment is applied to a bill and the amount of the bill is at least 20 US dollars.

No Loonies B prohibits the use of Canadian currency for larger bills—those of more than 20 dollars. The structure of **No Loonies B** is shown in Figure 6.5. It includes a condition in addition to the banned situation. The condition is a scope of the ban, a description of when the ban must apply and when it need not.

FIGURE 6.4 The structure of a simple prohibitive statement

It is prohibited that | banned situation | if | condition

FIGURE 6.5 The structure of a prohibitive statement

The condition of **No Loonies B** is "the cash payment is applied to a bill and the amount of the bill is at least 20 dollars." When the condition is true, the banned situation must be prevented. Employees and applications have a duty to examine the payment of bills of more than $20 to ensure that Canadian dollars are not used for those payments.

When do you write your intended business rule as a prohibitive statement? You use a prohibitive statement when you want the business—the employees and perhaps the applications—to prevent something. You write the banned situation—an expression that describes what must be prevented. If necessary, you write the condition—an expression of the scope of the ban.

Restricted Permissive Statements

Another business rule form is the *restricted permissive statement*. A restricted permissive statement specifically allows something but restricts the condition under which it is allowed. Let's look at an example, a variant of the same cash payment rule.

> ***Euros Allowed:*** It is permitted that a cash payment employ European Union currency only if the cash payment is applied to a bill and the amount of the bill is at most 100 U.S. dollars.

Two Mykonos restaurants are located close to embassies of EU countries. Many of the customers of those restaurants are foreign service officers and other members of the foreign embassy community. For the convenience of those customers, the two Mykonos restaurants accept euros. **Euros Allowed** says that euros can be used for bills that are $100 or less but that larger bills cannot employ euros. **Euros Allowed** is violated when a customer attempts to use euros to pay for a large bill, one of more than $100.

The structure of a restricted permissive statement is shown in Figure 6.6. The restricted permissive statement includes a *permitted situation*. The

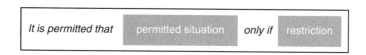

It is permitted that | permitted situation | only if | restriction

---

FIGURE 6.6 The structure of a restricted permissive statement

permitted situation describes what is allowed. In **Euros Allowed**, the permitted situation is "a cash payment employ European Union currency." Mykonos allows the cash payment to employ EU currency. The restricted permissive statement also includes a *restriction.* The restriction describes the scope of the permission—what must be true for the permission to occur. The permitted situation is only allowed to be true if the restriction is also true. In **Euros Allowed**, the restriction is "the cash payment is applied to a bill and the amount of the bill is at most 100 dollars." Mykonos allows a cash payment to employ euros only under the restriction that the cash payment is applied to a bill of $100 or less.

The condition in an obligation statement is optional. You can create an obligation statement that has no condition, and it is still a valid business rule. The condition in a prohibitive statement is also optional. But the restriction in a restricted permissive statement is required. Without a restriction, the restricted permission statement does not actually shape any behavior. Consider our example without a restriction: "It is permitted that a payment employ European Union currency"— euros are OK. But if the rule does not exist, then EU currency is OK anyway. Without a restriction, the rule does nothing.

What violates a restricted permissive statement? A violation occurs when the permitted situation is true even though the restriction is false. The other combinations do not matter. If the restriction is true, it doesn't matter whether the permitted situation is true or false; no violation occurs. For example, if the amount of the bill is $57, the restriction is true, and it doesn't matter (to this rule) whether European currency is used or not. **Euros Allowed** is not violated. And if the permitted situation is false, no violation occurs. If a cash payment does not use euros, it does not matter whether the bill is for $57 or $570. **Euros Allowed** remains not violated.

When do you write your business rule as a restricted permissive statement? You use a restricted permissive statement when you want the business to permit something only under certain conditions. You write the permitted situation first. Then you write the restriction—what must be true for the situation to be allowed.

Necessity Statements

We have considered three forms of business rules: obligation statements, prohibitive statements, and restricted permissive statements. These forms have different semantics, but they are similar in one respect. They all describe what should be. An obligation statement describes what a business should try to ensure. A prohibitive statement describes what a business should try to prevent. And a restrictive permissive statement describes what a business should allow under certain conditions.

But some business rules are not concerned with what should be. Instead they describe what is. Consider the business rule **Single Payment Network**.

> *Single Payment Network:* It is necessary that a credit card is backed by exactly one payment network.

VISA is a payment network, as is MasterCard and American Express. Being backed by a single payment network is fundamental to the meaning of a credit card. That is exactly what a credit card does; it provides access to a payment network. Each card is back by exactly one payment network. Capital One may issue both VISA cards and MasterCards, but a single card is either one or the other. A VISA card provides no access to the MasterCard network, or vice versa: a MasterCard cannot access the VISA network.

Single Payment Network does not state what Mykonos employees or customers should do. Instead it states something that is always true; it states a general truth rather than a responsibility. No actions of a Mykonos employee or customer will violate **Single Payment Network**. In fact, only a major industry change—e.g., an inter-access agreement between payment networks—will affect **Single Payment Network**, and that major industry change will not violate the rule so much as render it entirely invalid.

Single Payment Network is a *necessity statement*. Each necessity statement is a statement of something that remains true. Some necessity statements express truths about the world, like **Single Payment Network**. Others express truths not about the world but about the way the organization defines the world. **Large Party** is an example of this latter situation.

> *Large Party:* It is necessary that a party is large if the size of the party is at least 8.

A party of 8 or 9 people is considered by Mykonos restaurants to be large. A party of 6 or 7 is not considered to be large, at least not by **Large Party**. (Another rule may of course apply.) This division between 7 and 8 is how Mykonos chooses to structure its work. Other restaurants will divide party size differently, and some will not even have the concept of a large party.

The structure of a necessity statement is shown in Figure 6.7. A necessity statement starts with the phrase "It is necessary that." A necessity statement includes an *assured situation*, the description of what is necessarily true. The assured situation of **Large Party** is "party is large" and the assured situation of **Single Payment Network** is "credit card is backed by exactly one payment

FIGURE 6.7 The structure of a necessity statement

network." The necessity statement also includes the word "if" and a *condition*. The condition of **Large Party** is "the size of the party is at least 8." As with obligation statements, the "if" and the condition are optional. For example, **Single Payment Network** has no condition.

A necessity statement is structurally a bit like an obligation statement. Both are about something positive. Just as an obligation statement states something that must be, a necessity statement states something that is always true. But the two forms of business rules are quite different in intent. An obligation statement expresses something that the organization mandates. A necessity statement is simply a statement of what is always true, either in the world or in the way the organization structures its knowledge about the world.

Necessity statements express *structural business rules*. Structural business rules are statements about what is. They cannot be violated and need not be enforced. Structural business rules are fundamentally different from *operative business rules,* those rules that state what should be. Obligation statements, prohibitive statements, and restricted permissive statements are all operative business rules. Operative business rules can be violated and must be enforced.

When do you write your business rule as a necessity statement? You use a necessity statement when some situation is always true by definition. You write the true-by-definition situation as the assured situation. If a condition applies, you add it.

Impossibility Statements

Necessity statements are not the only structural business rules. *Impossibility statements* are also structural business rules. Instead of stating what is always true, an impossibility statement states what is always false. For example, **Single Payment Network B** is an impossibility statement.

> **Single Payment Network B:** It is impossible that a credit card is backed by two payment networks.

A single credit card cannot be backed by two different payment networks. For example, the same credit card cannot be both a VISA and a Discover.

The structure of **Single Payment Network B** is shown in Figure 6.8. The impossibility business rule starts with "It is impossible that" and then continues with the *incorrect situation*, the situation that is always false. For **Single**

FIGURE 6.8 The structure of a simple impossibility statement

FIGURE 6.9 The structure of a more complex impossibility statement

Payment Network B, the incorrect situation is "a credit card is backed by two payment network."

More complex impossibility business rules are also possible. Consider **Vegetarian Menu Items**.

> ***Vegetarian Menu Items****:* It is impossible that a vegetarian menu item includes an ingredient if the ingredient is meat or the ingredient is fish.

Vegetarian Menu Items is true by definition. A vegetarian menu item contains no ingredient that is meat or fish.

The structure of **Vegetarian Menu Items** is shown in Figure 6.9. In addition to the *incorrect situation,* Figure 6.9 includes a *condition,* the scope of the impossibility. If the ingredient is meat or fish, then it is impossible that that the menu item is vegetarian. But if the ingredient is neither meat nor fish, the rule does not apply.

You might have noticed the parallel between impossibility statements and prohibitive statements. Both say what cannot be. But impossibility statements are structural, explaining what cannot be by definition. Prohibitive statements are operative, explaining what should not be by policy.

When do you write your business rule as an impossibility statement? You use an impossibility statement when some situation is always false by definition. You write the false-by-definition situation as the incorrect situation. If a condition applies, you add it.

Restricted Possibility Statements

The last of the business rule forms is the *restricted possibility statement.* A restricted possibility statement is also a structural statement, describing something that is true by definition. Instead of describing what is always true (like a necessity statement) or what is always false (an impossibility statement), a restricted possibility statement describes what can be true only under certain conditions.

Let's look at an example. **Vegetarian Menu Items** described earlier is an impossibility statement about vegetarian menu items. The same rule can instead be expressed as a restricted possibility statement, as **Vegetarian Menu Items B**.

> ***Vegetarian Menu Items B****:* It is possible that a vegetarian menu item includes an ingredient only if the ingredient is not meat and the ingredient is not fish.

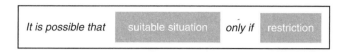

FIGURE 6.10 The structure of a restricted possibility statement

If an ingredient is neither a meat nor fish, it can be included in a vegetarian menu item. But if the ingredient is meat (or if it is fish), it cannot be included.

The structure of **Vegetarian Menu Items B** is shown in Figure 6.10. A restricted possibility statement starts with "It is possible that." Next is a *suitable situation*, the situation that might be true. The suitable situation of **Vegetarian Menu Items B** is "a vegetarian menu item includes an ingredient." After the suitable situation is "only if," then the restriction that needs to be true for the suitable situation to be possible. In **Vegetarian Menu Items B** the restriction is "the ingredient is not meat and the ingredient is not fish."

Restricted possibility statements are structurally similar to restricted permissive statements. Just as a restricted permissive statement describes a situation that is permitted, a restricted possibility statement describes a situation that is possible. Just as a restricted permissive statement has a restriction—a condition that must be true for the situation to be permitted—a restricted possibility statement has a restriction that must be true for the situation to be possible. The difference between the two is that a restricted permissive statement is an operative business rule, expressing what is permitted and the condition that needs to be true for it to be permitted. By contrast, a restricted possibility statement is a structural business rule. It expresses what is possible and the condition that needs to be true for it to be possible.

When do you write your business rule as a restricted possibility statement? You use a restricted possibility statement when a situation is allowed by definition but only under a restriction.

Business Rule Statements Summary

The six business rule forms are shown in Table 6.1. Note the parallel between the obligation statement and the necessity statement, between the prohibitive statement and the impossibility statement, and between the restricted permissive statement and the restricted possibility statement.

When you are writing a business rule, how do you decide which form to use? First you decide whether the rule you are writing describes a situation that must always be or whether it describes a situation that should be. In the former case, it is a structural rule; in the latter case, it is an operative rule. Then you decide which of the forms provides the simplest expression of the rule. Often the same rule can be expressed in multiple forms, but one form leads to a simpler expression. When writing business rules, simpler is better.

Table 6.1 The Six Business Rule Forms

Operative Rule Form	Operative Rule Example	Structural Rule Form	Structural Rule Example
Obligation statement	*It is obligatory that each cash payment employ US currency if the cash payment is applied to a bill and the amount of the bill is at least 20 dollars.*	Necessity statement	*It is necessary that a party is large if the size of the party is at least 8.*
Prohibitive statement	*It is prohibited that a cash payment employ Canadian currency if the cash payment is applied to a bill and the amount of the bill is at least 20 dollars.*	Impossibility statement	*It is impossible that a vegetarian menu item includes an ingredient if the ingredient is meat or the ingredient is fish.*
Restricted permissive statement	*It is permitted that a cash payment employ European Union currency only if the cash payment is applied to a bill and the amount of the bill is at most 100 dollars.*	Restricted possibility statement	*It possible that a vegetarian menu item includes an ingredient only if the ingredient is not meat and the ingredient is not fish.*

NOUN CONCEPTS

A business rule is expressed as an English sentence, but it is more formally stated than most sentences you encounter in everyday life. We have already examined one way business rules are more formally stated—the six business rule forms. Another way that business rules are more formally stated is how nouns are treated in a business rule. Just like any sentence in English, business rules contain nouns: words or word phrases that describe persons, places, things, animals, or abstract ideas. In business rules, the meaning of a noun is called a *noun concept*. There are many noun concepts at Mykonos. Just in our discussion in this chapter we have used more than 10: menu item, appetizer, ingredient, customer, order, bill, credit card, payment, personal check, cash payment, payment network. And there are hundreds of other noun concepts used in other rules at Mykonos restaurants and at Mykonos headquarters—noun concepts about ingredient freshness and spoilage, about unhappy customers, about waits and pagers.

Noun concepts are defined in a business rule model. Some noun concepts are defined with a definition from a dictionary, either a specialized technical dictionary for a technical term or an everyday dictionary for a common term. For example, the noun concept **payment** is defined as follows:

> *payment*
> *Definition: an amount paid*
> — **American Heritage Dictionary of the English Language, Fourth Edition**

There are dictionary definitions for many of the other Mykonos noun concepts. But some terms are not defined in any dictionary. Consider **cash payment**. This is a useful term, an important building block for Mykonos business rules like "A cash payment must employ US currency" and in fact for business rules at any retail establishment that accepts cash. But **cash payment** is a bit too specialized for any everyday dictionary. Instead, we define it ourselves, using the definitions for **payment** and for **cash**.

> *cash payment*
> *Definition: **payment** that employs **cash***

This definition means that **cash payment** is a specialization of **payment** and that any payment that employs cash is a cash payment. This definition is built on the noun concepts **payment** and **cash**. The latter is defined with a dictionary definition, as **payment** is.

> *cash*
> *Definition: money in the form of bills or coins; currency*
> — **American Heritage Dictionary of the English Language, Fourth Edition**

Similarly, **gratuity**—used in the rules about allowable gratuities—is also defined with a dictionary definition.

> *gratuity*
> *Definition: a gift of money, over and above payment due for a service, as to a waiter or a bellhop; tip*
> — **Random House Unabridged Dictionary**

Every noun concept used in a rule must be defined. There are two ways of defining a noun concept. Either you can use a dictionary or you can create your own definition, using other noun concepts you have already defined. Of course each of those previously defined noun concepts was itself defined, either via a dictionary or with other noun concepts. So ultimately everything depends on dictionary definitions.

Noun Concepts and Structural Rules

A noun concept can be detailed with a structural rule. As you will recall, a structural rule is a business rule that cannot be violated. It expresses a truth about the world or about the way the organization structures its knowledge about the world. It is true by definition.

Consider what happens when a party of 10 chooses to sit at two tables so they do not have to wait for one of the big tables to be available. When they sit at their tables, they become a separated party. The structural rule **Parties 1** is true by definition. A separated party must be seated at two or more tables. Otherwise it is not a separated party.

Parties 1: It is necessary that a separated party is seated at two or more tables.

A structural rule is inherently definitional instead of prescriptive. Instead of expressing the behavior that Mykonos wants, it serves to detail a noun concept and the way the noun concept relates to other noun concepts.

FACT TYPES

Another way that business rules are more formally stated than most English sentences is their use of *fact types*. A fact type characterizes the way noun concepts may be related. For an example, consider again the prohibition on personal checks in **No Checks**.

No Checks: It is prohibited that a payment employ a personal check.

Implicit behind the rule is the idea that a personal check is the kind of thing that is conceivable to employ as a payment. Somewhere in the world there are restaurants that accept personal checks as payments—just not the Mykonos restaurants. By contrast consider the following statement that is not a rule at all:

Nonrule 2: It is prohibited that a payment employ autumn leaves.

Mykonos does not need to state **Nonrule 2** because no fact type relates payments and autumn leaves. There is no restaurant in the world that accepts autumn leaves as a payment for burgers and fries. Autumn leaves are not a kind of thing that is possible to employ as a payment for a restaurant meal.

Behind **No Checks** is the *fact-type diagram* shown in Figure 6.11. A fact type diagram is a summary of what is expressible in rules. The sole fact type in Figure 6.11 can be read as **payment employs personal check**—that in principle a payment can employ a personal check.

Figure 6.11 is not a diagram of **No Checks** or in fact a diagram of any specific rule. Instead Figure 6.11 is a diagram of a single fact type that rules can build on. Figure 6.11 says that any rule that includes the noun concept **payment** and the noun concept **personal check** can relate those two noun concepts via the verb *employs*.

FIGURE 6.11 The single fact type on which **No Checks** is built

Table 6.2 Other Potential Rules That Use the Same Fact Type

Potential Rule	Interpretation
It is obligatory that a payment employ a personal check.	For that odd restaurant that requires all payments be made in personal checks.
It is permitted that a payment employ a personal check only if the personal check is drawn on a local back.	A personal check is acceptable if another condition holds: the check is local.
It is obligatory that a customer be photographed if the customer makes a payment and the payment employs a personal check.	For the careful restaurant that wants to collect forensic evidence from customers who might bounce checks.

In addition to **No Checks**, the fact type of Figure 6.11 supports a huge variety of other potential rules. Some of these other potential rules are shown in Table 6.2.

Note that the fact type diagram of Figure 6.11 complements the business rule form diagrams shown in Figures 6.2 through 6.10. Each of the business rule form diagrams shows the structure of one of the business rule forms. For example, Figure 6.3 shows the structure of an obligation statement—that an obligation statement begins with the phrase "It is obligatory that," continues with a mandatory situation, then includes the word "if" and finishes with a condition. Figure 6.11 shows a fact type that can be used in the mandatory situation or in the condition, or in both.

Multiple Fact Types

A business rule can be built on more than one fact type. Actually, a rule like **No Checks** that is built on only a single fact type is an exception. Most business rules are built on multiple fact types. Consider **VISA Only**, the rule that restricts credit card acceptance to those that are backed by the VISA payment network.

> *VISA Only:* It is permitted that a payment employ a credit card only if the credit card is backed by VISA.

VISA Only is built on two fact types: **payment employs credit card** and **credit card is backed by payment network**. Figure 6.12 shows the two fact types and the way they relate to each other. The noun concept **payment** is related to the noun concept **credit card** via the fact type **payment employs credit card**.

FIGURE 6.12 The two fact types on which **VISA Only** is built

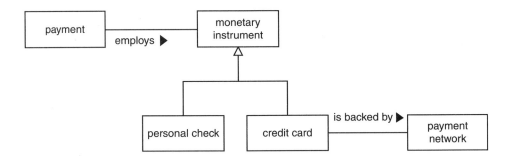

FIGURE 6.13 Fact types for both **No Checks** and **VISA Only**

The noun concept **credit card** is also related to the noun concept **payment network** via the fact type **credit card is backed by payment network**.

There is some overlap between Figures 6.11 and 6.12. Both include **payment**; both include **employs**, and both use it in the same way. Figures 6.11 and 6.12 can be combined into a single diagram shown in Figure 6.13. Figure 6.13 shows the fact types that both **No Checks** and **VISA Only** build on.

Figure 6.13 shows **personal check** as a *specialization* of **monetary instrument**. The specialization association is expressed in the diagram by the arrow with the hollow arrowhead, and it is expressed in English as *"personal check" is a category of "monetary instrument."* The specialization means that a personal check is one kind of monetary instrument. Any associations that apply to monetary instruments also apply to personal checks. So we have a general fact type *payment employs monetary instrument*, and because of the specialization, we know that rules can be written about a payment using (or not using) personal checks. In the same way, **credit card** is a specialization of **monetary instrument**, and rules can be written about payments using credit cards.

Note that the association **is backed by** is between **payment network** and **credit card**. The **employs** association is at the more general level between **payment** and **monetary instrument**, applicable to all monetary instruments, but **is backed by** only applies to credit cards, not to other monetary instruments. With the fact types of Figure 6.13, we can write a rule about credit cards being backed by VISA, but we cannot write a rule about personal checks being backed by VISA.

Fact Type Consistency

Figure 6.13 combines Figures 6.11 and 6.12 into a single diagram. This combination is important. The rules that guide an organization should use a single coherent set of fact types. Consider what would happen if they did not—if each rule used whatever fact types made sense for that single rule, without reference to the fact types used by other rules. Instead of the previous payment rules, Mykonos might end up with these payment rules:

No Checks B: It is prohibited that a payment use a personal check.

Visa Only B: It is permitted that payment utilize a credit card only if the credit card is backed by VISA.

Greenbacks Only: It is obligatory that a cash payment employ US currency.

No Checks B is more or less the same as **No Checks** except that the underlying fact type is **payment uses personal check** instead of **payment employs personal check.** Similarly, **Visa Only B** is more or less the same as **VISA Only** except for the use of **utilize** instead of **employ**. In practice a server could figure out when an event violated one of these rules.

But what if Mykonos now wants to proscribe the use of multiple monetary instruments for small debts? Suppose Mykonos wants to prohibit the use of both credit cards and cash, unless the amount is large enough to warrant the trouble. A new **One Monetary Instrument** could be written to ban that activity.

One Monetary Instrument: It is prohibited that a payment employ more than one monetary instrument if the amount of the payment is less than $50.

But does **One Monetary Instrument** really do what we want? If a customer is both utilizing a credit card (per **Visa Only B**) and using a personal check (per **No Ohecks B**), is she really *employing* more than one monetary instrument? We are leaving much to the interpretation of individuals, and their interpretations will vary. It is better to have all rules build off a single coherent set of fact types.

Fact types that are more or less the same—but not quite identical—introduce problems into the business rules that build on them. These problems are a manifestation of a more general truth about business rules. Every business rule must conform to two different standards: It must be understandable to a business professional who reads it, and it must be written precisely, with each noun concept and each fact type defined consistently with the other business rules that use the same noun concepts and fact types. Only a business rule that is both understandable and precisely defined is useful for shaping behavior.

Properties

Consider the fact types that **One Monetary Instrument** builds on. We have already seen **payment employs monetary instrument** in other rules. But the other fact type is new: **payment has payment amount**. A payment has a payment amount, some quantity of money, perhaps more than $50, perhaps less.

The fact type **payment has payment amount** is treated a bit differently from other fact types we have seen. **Payment amount** is a *property* of a payment. A property means that one noun concept is dependent on the existence of the other. Without a payment, there is no payment amount. There is no such dependency between payment and monetary instrument. The VISA card in your wallet exists on its own,

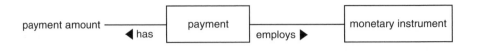

FIGURE 6.14 Fact types for **One Monetary Instrument**

whether or not you use it today to make a payment. But if you don't make a payment today, there is no payment amount. The existence of a payment amount is entirely dependent on the existence of a payment.

Figure 6.14 shows the fact types that **One Monetary Instrument** builds on. Note that the fact type **payment has payment amount** looks different from the fact type **payment employs monetary instrument**. The property **payment amount** is drawn without a rectangle surrounding it. It is drawn that way because it is a property—a property of **payment**. The association between **payment** and **payment amount** is labeled with "has," and the fact type **payment has payment amount** also uses the word "has." "Has" indicates that payment amount is a property of payment. "Has" is reserved just for properties. No nonproperty fact types use "has."

RULE VIOLATIONS

Earlier in this chapter we mentioned rule violation several times, relying on your intuition of what violation means. But now we need to be more precise. A business rule is said to be *violated* when an event or state of affairs occurs that should not, according to the rule. For example, when a customer pays a bill with Japanese yen instead of US dollars, the rule **Greenbacks Only** is violated. The server advises the customer that cash payments must be in US currency.

The customer might then attempt to pay for the bill with his JCB™ card—a credit card used widely in Japan and accepted by many US merchants but not by Mykonos restaurants. Thinking the card is a VISA, the server attempts to process the payment. Then the payments application notes another rule violation—a violation of the rule **VISA Only**. The application rejects the JCB card. Now the server takes the card back to the hapless customer and explains the second rule. One violation was spotted by a person, the other by an application. Either people or software can notice business rule violations.

Every operative business rule can be violated, at least in principle. Since the purpose of an operative rule is to describe what should be, a rule violation occurs whenever what should be does not actually happen—when people do not live up to the standards of the rule. For example, consider again the operative rule **No Checks**.

No Checks: It is prohibited that a payment employ a personal check.

Whenever a payment employs a personal check, **No Checks** is violated.

Only operative business rules can be violated. Structural rules cannot. Structural rules are true by definition, so a violation of a structural rule is impossible. To see why, consider again the structural rule **Vegetarian Menu Items B**.

Vegetarian Menu Items B: It is possible that a vegetarian menu item includes an ingredient only if the ingredient is not meat and the ingredient is not fish.

Suppose a vegetarian menu item included a meat ingredient. That seems like it might be a violation of **Vegetarian Menu Items B**, but it is not. If a menu item includes a meat ingredient, the menu item is not vegetarian at all, by definition. There is no violation because there is no vegetarian menu item.

Directly Enforceable

It must be possible for someone to decide whether a rule is being violated. If Joe knows a business rule and sees Emily do something, it should be possible for Joe to decide whether Emily's action violates the rule or not. If a proposed rule does not admit this kind of decision, it is not a rule at all.

Let's look at an example. At any Mykonos restaurant a customer can choose to give a tip to his server—a tip of any size. If the service if good, he might give 20 percent of the bill or even more. If the service is bad, he might give 5 percent or even nothing at all. It is all his choice. Unfortunately, in a large party, the server often gets stiffed; the customers collectively pay a small tip, much less than 10 percent. So, like many other restaurants, Mykonos specifies a minimum tip if the party is large. **Nonrule 1** is an attempt to regulate that behavior through a business rule, but it does not succeed because **Nonrule 1** is not a well-formed rule.

Nonrule 1: It is obligatory that the gratuity is at least 15% if the gratuity is applied to a bill and the bill is incurred by a party and the party is large.

The problem with **Nonrule 1** is that it is not always possible to know whether the rule is being violated. Certainly a party of 24 is large, so if that party gives an 11 percent tip, **Nonrule 1** is violated. And certainly a party of two is not large, so even if they give nothing, **Nonrule 1** is not violated. But what if a party of six gives a 9 percent tip? Is a party of six large? What about a party of eight? A party of seven?

Nonrule 1 is said to be not *directly enforceable*. A rule is directly enforceable if someone who knows the rule and sees some behavior can decide whether the rule is violated. **Nonrule 1** needs to be replaced by the directly enforceable rule **Large Party Gratuity**.

Large Party Gratuity: It is obligatory that the gratuity is at least 15% if the gratuity is applied to a bill and the bill is incurred by a party and the size of the party is greater than 7 people.

(Alternatively, the noun concept **large party** could be defined as a party whose size is greater than seven.)

Large Party Gratuity is directly enforceable. If Joe knows **Large Party Gratuity** and sees a party of six people apply a tip of 11 percent, he can determine that **Large Party Gratuity** is not violated. The party might be stingy, but they are not violating this rule.

Multiple Violations

Most operative rules can be violated in more than one way. Consider the following rule about menus, meant to ensure that vegetarians always have at least two choices on every menu at a Mykonos restaurant.

> *2 Vegetarian Entrees*: It is obligatory that each menu include at least two vegetarian entrees.

Obviously, **2 Vegetarian Entrees** is violated when Angela Glaser—the head chef at Zona—creates a new menu with only a single vegetarian entree. But there is a second, not so obvious situation when **2 Vegetarian Entrees** is violated. Suppose a menu has two vegetarian entrees: linguini puttanesca and grilled eggplant with goat cheese. Now Angela decides to add anchovies to enhance the linguini puttanesca. This addition may well improve the taste of the dish, but it also makes the entree no longer vegetarian. Her change to the entree violates the **2 Vegetarian Entrees** rule.

A business rule shapes behavior when it is violated. Someone enforces the rule by noting the violation and explaining the rule to the violator. Or if the rule is enforced by an application, the application notes the violation and presents a dialog box to the violator. But a business rule also shapes behavior before it is violated, by the mere potential for violation. When our anchovy-happy Angela talks about her plan to a colleague, the colleague reminds Angela of **2 Vegetarian Entrees**. Or Angela remembers the rule on her own and adds another vegetarian dish to the menu when she improves the linguini with anchovies. In either situation, the mere potential for violation triggers the business rule.

A single change can violate more than one rule. Consider the rule **Visible Allergens**, meant to protect people who have food allergies.

> *Visible Allergens:* It is obligatory that the description of a menu item includes an ingredient if the ingredient is a common allergen.

Fish is a common allergen, one of the eight recognized by the US Food and Drug Administration. If Angela adds anchovies to the puttanesca sauce and does not change the menu, she is not only making things more difficult for vegetarians, she is also endangering anyone allergic to fish. Her one seemingly innocent change violates two business rules: **2 Vegetarian Entrees** and **Visible Allergens**.

A violation of a business rule should be recognized as soon as possible. It does little good to recognize the violation of **Visible Allergens** after someone has an allergic reaction to a menu item that is inadequately described on the menu. It is better for the server to recognize the violation before the allergic customer orders the linguini. It is even better to recognize the violation before the menus are printed. And it is still better yet to recognize it when the change is being first contemplated, while the violation is still only a potential. With business rule violations, early recognition is better.

ENFORCEMENT

A rule does not specify what happens when it is violated. **2 Vegetarian Entrees** is written solely about the behavior that is to be shaped by the rule. It is not written as **Nonrule 3**, with an explanation of the process by which it can be waived.

> *Nonrule 3:* It is obligatory that each menu include at least two vegetarian entrees, unless an exception is authorized in advance by Mykonos Headquarters.

Instead of **Nonrule 3**, there is an *enforcement level* applied to **2 Vegetarian Entrees**. The enforcement level indicates whether a rule is strictly enforced, whether it is merely guidance for the interpretation of people on the ground, or whether it is somewhere between. **2 Vegetarian Entrees** is in fact somewhere between strict enforcement and guidance. **2 Vegetarian Entrees** has an enforcement level of **pre-authorized**, meaning that the rule is enforced but exceptions can be authorized in advance.

> *2 Vegetarian Entrees:* It is obligatory that each menu include at least two vegetarian entrees.

> *Enforcement level:* pre-authorized

Why separate the enforcement level from the statement of the rule itself? In practice, the enforcement level of a rule will change more often than the rule itself. Mykonos might decide initially to enforce **2 Vegetarian Entrees** strictly by setting the enforcement level to **strict**. After some experience is accumulated, the enforcement level is downgraded to **pre-authorized**.

Separating the rule from the enforcement level also supports different enforcement levels for different parts of the organization. There are more vegetarians in California than Texas, so Mykonos may decide to set enforcement to **strict** for the California restaurants and to merely **override** for the Mykonos restaurants in Texas. The rule is the same for all Mykonos restaurants, but the enforcement level is localized.

Every rule has a level of enforcement, one of the five valid enforcement levels shown in Table 6.3.

Table 6.3 Valid Rule Enforcement Levels

Enforcement Level	Meaning
Strict	The rule is strictly enforced. Anyone who violates the rule will be penalized.
Pre-authorized	An exception is allowed to the rule if the exception is authorized before the rule is violated.
Post-justified	An exception is allowed to the rule if the exception is approved after the violation. If the rule is violated and an exception is not later approved, the violator may be penalized.
Override	The rule may be violated as long as the violator provides an explanation.
Guideline	The rule is a suggestion but not enforced.

The **pre-authorized** and **post-justified** enforcement levels require the existence of an authorizing organization—an organization that has the authority to grant exceptions to a rule. The **strict** enforcement level may also require an organization, one to administer the penalties. These are two ways that a business rule model and an organization model need to work together. Later in this chapter we will look at both these relationships between business rules and organizations as well as other relationships.

BUSINESS POLICIES

Earlier in the chapter, we examined **2 Vegetarian Entrees**, the business rule mandating vegetarian entrees on menus.

> *2 Vegetarian Entrees:* It is obligatory that each menu include at least two vegetarian entrees.

Why does **2 Vegetarian Entrees** exist? Why is it important to include two vegetarian entrees on menus at Mykonos restaurants? The reason is a *business policy*. Mykonos has a business policy of making their restaurant menus vegetarian-friendly. They want to ensure that vegetarians feel welcome at Mykonos restaurants and that there are multiple options for them.

> *Vegetarian-Friendly Menus.* All menus must be friendly to vegetarians.

Vegetarian-Friendly Menus is a business policy. Like a business rule, a business policy shapes behavior. But a business policy is less precise than a business rule and more subject to interpretation. **2 Vegetarian Entrees** is a precise statement of what is allowed and what is not allowed. **Vegetarian-Friendly Menus** is more vague. It leaves open to interpretation whether a particular menu is friendly to vegetarians.

Earlier in the chapter we described how all operative business rules must be directly enforceable—that if someone knows the rule and sees a situation, she is able to tell whether the situation violates the rule. **2 Vegetarian Entrees** is directly enforceable, but **Vegetarian-Friendly Menus** is not. If you know the rule and see a menu, how can you tell whether the menu violates the rule? In general, business policies are not directly enforceable.

A business policy can be the reason that a business rule exists. For example, the business policy **Vegetarian-Friendly Menu** is the reason that the business rule **2 Vegetarian Entrees** exists. **2 Vegetarian Entrees** is an implementation of the business policy, a translation from the vague intention of the business policy into the precise, directly enforceable language of an operative rule. Figure 6.15 shows the business policy, the business rule, and the **derived from** association between them. The **derived from** association means that **2 Vegetarian Entrees** is an implementation of **Vegetarian-Friendly Menus**.

More than one business rule can be derived from a single business policy. Consider the rules **4 Vegetarian Appetizers** and **Visible Meat And Fish**. The first is much like **2 Vegetarian Entrees**, except for appetizers instead of main courses. It ensures that there are at least four vegetarian options among the appetizers on any Mykonos menu. **Visible Meat and Fish** ensures that it is obvious from the description of a menu item whether it is vegetarian or not. Both serve to make Mykonos menus friendly to vegetarians.

> *4 Vegetarian Appetizers:* It is obligatory that each menu include at least four vegetarian appetizers.
> *Visible Meat and Fish:* It is obligatory that the description of a menu item include an ingredient if the ingredient is a meat or the ingredient is a fish.

Figure 6.16 shows the relationship of the three business rules and the business policy. All three rules are derived from **Vegetarian-Friendly Menus**.

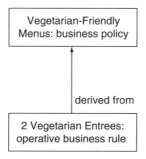

FIGURE 6.15 A business policy and a business rule

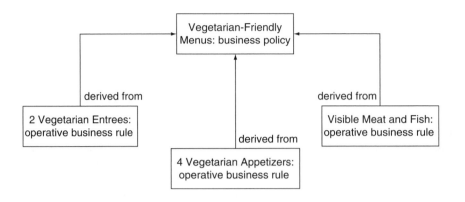

FIGURE 6.16 A business policy and three business rules

Composing Business Policies

A business policy can be part of another business policy. Consider the business policy **Dietary Restriction Menus**.

> *Dietary Restriction Menus:* All menus should cater to people with common dietary restrictions.

The business policy **Vegetarian-Friendly Menus** is a part of this larger policy of catering to people with common dietary restrictions. Figure 6.17 shows this **part of** relationship between **Vegetarian-Friendly Menus** and **Dietary Restriction Menus**. Also shown are two other business policies: **Allergy-Sensitive Menus** and **Menus Friendly to Lactose Intolerant**. Some people have food allergies and some people cannot digest milk or dairy products. Mykonos strives to make menus friendly to both these groups, in addition to vegetarians.

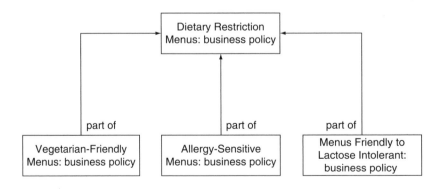

FIGURE 6.17 Composing business policies

Mykonos has business rules that implement **Allergy-Sensitive Menus** and other business rules that implement **Menus Friendly to Lactose Intolerant**. Of course, there are many other dietary restrictions. Some people avoid beef for religious reasons; others avoid pork or shellfish. Some people shun all red meat; others avoid anything cooked in alcohol. Each of these dietary restrictions could have its own Mykonos policies and its own business rules to implement. The general policy **Dietary Restriction Menus** results in many business rules to guide the creation of menus.

Directives

Both business policies and business rules are *directives*. A directive is an element of guidance under the control of the business. Consider again the business rule **4 Vegetarian Appetizers**. It is an element of guidance intended to shape the behavior of the Mykonos chefs (and others) designing menus. And it is under the control of the business. Mykonos has developed the business rule on its own, for its own reasons. Similarly, the business policy **Vegetarian-Friendly Menus** is a directive. It is an element of guidance intended not to shape the behavior of those creating menus but to be implemented in business rules that shape their behavior. And like **4 Vegetarian Appetizers** it is under the control of Mykonos. No outside organization is commanding Mykonos to offer vegetarian-friendly menus; instead Mykonos personnel have decided on their own to offer them.

BUSINESS MOTIVATION, POLICIES, AND RULES

As you recall, in Chapter 3 we examined courses of action—ways that an organization achieves its goals and objectives. Courses of action come in two varieties: strategies—larger and more difficult to change—and tactics—smaller and easier to change.

Business rules *govern* courses of actions. Consider the Mykonos strategy **Create Innovative Menus**. Mykonos management wants all Mykonos restaurants to create innovative menus. (Presumably this strategy channels efforts toward Mykonos goals, such as **Expand Menu Variety**.) But **Create Innovative Menus** is governed by the **2 Vegetarian Entrees** rule. Mykonos wants innovative menus at its restaurants, but innovative menus that include at least two vegetarian entrees. Similarly, **Create Innovative Menus** is also governed by the business rule **Visible Meat and Fish**. Figure 6.18 shows the **governs** association between **Create Innovative Menus** and the two business rules.

What does it mean for a business rule to govern a strategy? The business rule shapes the way the strategy can be applied. The rule constrains the strategy; Mykonos intends to create innovative menus but will not do so in ways that result in menus with fewer than two vegetarian entrees.

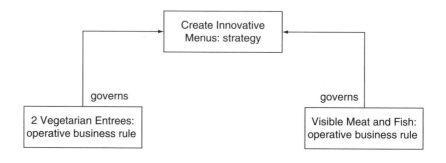

FIGURE 6.18 Business rules govern strategies

Business policies also govern courses of action. As you will recall, the business policy **Dietary Restriction Menus** requires that menus at Mykonos restaurants cater to people with common dietary restrictions. Figure 6.19 shows that business policy governing the strategy **Create Innovative Menus**. In practice this means that innovation in menus is constrained by many different business rules—all the business rules that are derived from **Dietary Restriction Menus**. The rules shown in Figure 6.18 are derived from this business policy, so Figure 6.19 is a simpler way of showing the associations of Figure 6.18. All directives—business policies and business rules—can govern courses of action, but it is often simpler to focus on the business policies.

Directives and Desired Results

In Chapter 3, we also introduced desired results—the goals that an organization seeks to achieve and the objectives that quantify those goals. Sometimes a directive supports the achievement of a goal. The most common situation of this kind of support is a structural rule defining a noun concept that is used in an objective. An objective is too vague to measure if the noun concepts it uses are not precisely defined. Structural rules can help define those noun concepts.

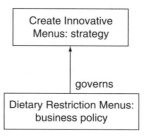

FIGURE 6.19 Business policies govern strategies

Let's consider an example. The restaurant Nola has an objective **4 Positive Reviews**, garnering four positive reviews in major periodicals in 2009. But what is a major periodical? Certainly *The Washington Post* is a major periodical. Is the much smaller weekly *Washington City Paper* a major periodical? And what exactly is a positive review? This objective needs support from some structural rules.

> ***Major Periodical:*** It is necessary that a periodical is major if the periodical has a circulation and the circulation is at least 50,000.

> ***Positive Starred Review:*** It is impossible that a review is positive if the review uses a five-star scale and the review has fewer than three stars.

Major Periodical supports the achievement of the objective **4 Positive Reviews** by providing some precision about determining whether a periodical is major. **Positive Starred Review** also supports the achievement of **4 Positive Reviews**—at least for reviews that are based on a star metric. Other metrics are supported by other structural rules. Figure 6.20 shows the associations between the objective and the two rules.

Directives and Assessments

Also introduced in Chapter 3 were assessments: the strengths, weaknesses, opportunities, and threats faced by an organization. An assessment will often motivate the establishment of a directive. An organization recognizes a threat, and to counter that threat it creates a new business policy. For example, in Chapter 3, Cora Group recognized the threat **Increasing Public Interest in Ethnic Fare**. This was a threat to the Cora restaurants; as the interest in ethnic food increases, Cora Group restaurants could lose customers to competitors that feature Thai food, Ethiopian food, Bolivian food, and so on.

Since then Cora Group has been acquired by Mykonos, and Mykonos creates a new business policy, **Ethnic Menu Items**, to counter this threat. The new policy requires that menus feature some menu items inspired by ethnic cuisines.

> ***Ethnic Menu Items:*** Menus must feature ethnic-inspired menu items.

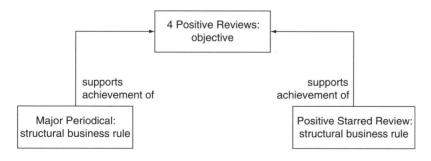

FIGURE 6.20 Directives support achievement of desired results

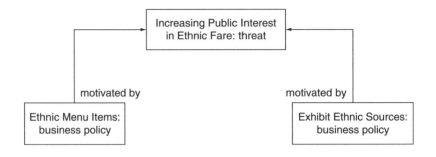

FIGURE 6.21 Business policies motivated by a threat

Ethnic Menu Items is a reasonable policy, but it is not precise enough to be a business rule. From the policy it is not clear what it means for a menu item to be ethnic-inspired or how many menu items on a menu must be so inspired. **Ethnic Menu Items** is the basis for several business rules that define and implement this policy.

Figure 6.21 shows the **motivated by** association between the business policy **Ethnic Menu Items** and the threat **Increasing Public Interest in Ethnic Fare**. The **motivated by** association means that the directive is established because of the assessment—the assessment motivates the directive.

Figure 6.21 shows a second business policy motivated by **Increasing Public Interest in Ethnic Fare**. Mykonos leadership considers the ethnic fare threat to be as much image as reality. They say "all food is ethnic food", certainly a bit of an exaggeration but no doubt one with some underlying truth. So they establish a second policy, one of illustrating the existing ethnic background of menu items in Mykonos menus. This business policy is **Exhibit Ethnic Sources**.

For example, Nola's menu already includes orecchiette chicken mole, a dish with roots in both the Apulia region of southern Italy and the Oaxaca region of Mexico. With an explanation of the ethnic connections of the dish on the Nola menu, customers who are attracted to ethnic fare will be attracted to Nola.

Directives can also be motivated by assessments that are not threats: by strategies, strengths, or weaknesses or even by other assessments that do not fit the SWOT framework. (If you recall from Chapter 3, SWOT analysis is a method of creating business strategy by identifying and analyzing the strengths, weaknesses, opportunities, and threats of a business.) For example, many executive chefs who lead Mykonos restaurants have local name recognition, at least among those who know food. This name recognition is clearly a Mykonos strength. Mykonos can build on that strength with another business policy about menu design, a policy that the menu of a Mykonos restaurant should include the name of the executive chef of the restaurant. Figure 6.22 shows the trace association between the business policy **Feature Chef Name in Menu** and the strength **Well-Known Chefs**.

FIGURE 6.22 Business policy motivated by a strength

Tactics and Business Rules

Earlier in this chapter we explained that every operative business rule has an enforcement level. Some rules have an enforcement level of **strict**; those rules are strictly enforced. Other rules have enforcements levels of **override** or **guideline** or one of the other choices for an enforcement level.

The decision to apply a specific enforcement level to a rule is itself a tactic. For example, Mykonos might decide that the business rule **2 Vegetarian Entrees** is to be only a guideline, with chefs of the individual restaurants free to violate the rule without penalty. Figure 6.23 shows the association between the business rules and the tactic that specifies the enforcement level. The tactic **Vegetarian Enforcement as Guidelines** determines the enforcement level of the business rule **2 Vegetarian Entrees** using the association **affects enforcement level of**.

Figure 6.23 shows a second business rule, **4 Vegetarian Appetizers**. The enforcement level of **4 Vegetarian Appetizers** is also set to **guideline**. In fact, the same tactic sets that enforcement level as well, also using an **affects enforcement level of** association.

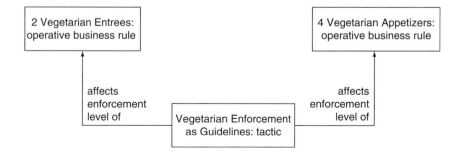

FIGURE 6.23 Tactic sets enforcement level of business rules

BUSINESS ORGANIZATIONS AND BUSINESS RULES

In Chapters 3 and 4, we examined how an organization establishes a strategy and how an organization defines a goal to be achieved. An organization can establish a tactic, determining a smaller and more changeable course of action to achieve some desired result. Every strategy and every tactic is achieved by some organization; someone has set this strategy in place.

Organizations also establish directives. For example, the business policy **Vegetarian-Friendly Menus** is established by the organization **Mykonos**, as shown in Figure 6.24. Mykonos also establishes a business rule derived from that business policy, **4 Vegetarian Appetizers**.

The other business rule in Figure 6.24—**Visible Meat and Fish**—is derived from the same business policy, but it is not established by Mykonos. Instead it is established by Nola, one of the Mykonos restaurants. Rita Iscoe, the general manager of Nola, is concerned that her vegetarian customers will not be aware which menu items are vegetarian and which are not, so she creates an additional business rule in her restaurant to assist them.

The multi-organization situation shown in Figure 6.24 is typical. Business policies and business rules are established by a mix of organizations from different parts of the enterprise. A server at Nola has to pay attention to business rules established by Nola, business policies from Mykonos Finance, business rules from the Cora Group, and so on.

The **establishes** association between an organization unit and a directive is the same association as the **establishes** between an organization unit and either a strategy or tactic. Just as Mykonos can establish the business rule **4 Vegetarian Appetizers**, Mykonos can also establish the strategy **Create Innovative Menus**. The **establishes** association is from an organization unit to a *means*. Strategies and

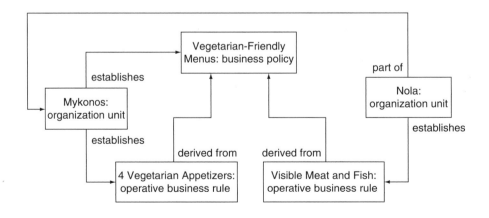

FIGURE 6.24 Organization units establishing directives

tactics are means. So are directives. Strategies, tactics, business policies, and business rules are all means, all ways that an organization tries to achieve its goals and objectives.

BUSINESS PROCESSES, BUSINESS POLICIES, AND BUSINESS RULES

In Chapter 5, we examined business processes. As you will recall, a business process is a collection of step-by-step activities that a business uses to perform its work. Business policies govern business processes. They guide how the work is done, and they constrain how it is done. This relationship between a business policy and a business process is through the **governs** association.

Let's consider **Seat Party** again, a process we first examined in Chapter 5. **Seat Party** is the business process by which customers arriving at a Mykonos restaurant are seated. **Seat Party** is governed by the business policy **Customer-Friendly Seating**, as shown in Figure 6.25.

> *Customer-Friendly Seating:* Customers must be seated promptly, in a fair manner.

Also shown in Figure 6.25 are two business rules about customer seating, **Reservation Seating** and **Regulars Seating**. Both these rules guide the **Seat Party** process.

> *Reservation Seating:* It is obligatory that a party is seated if the party has a reservation and the reservation is ripe and a table is available and the table is an appropriate size for the party.

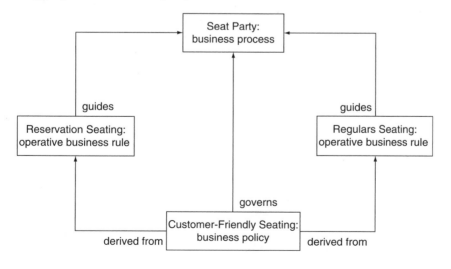

FIGURE 6.25 Business rules guide a business process

Regulars Seating: It is obligatory that a party is seated if the party includes a regular and a table is available and the table is an appropriate size for the party.

Reservation Seating says that a party must be seated if they have a ripe reservation—one for the current time—and an appropriate table is available. **Regulars Seating** says that a party must be seated if someone in the party is a restaurant regular and an appropriate table is available. Of course, all the noun concepts and fact types used by these rules must be defined. There are also structural rules defining when a reservation is ripe, when someone is a regular at a Mykonos restaurant, and whether a table is an appropriate size for a party. These definitions and structural rules are omitted here for the sake of brevity.

As customers arrive they must be seated promptly and in a fair manner—a matter of some judgment on the part of the host. But in particular, a party with reservations must be seated if an appropriate table is available, as must a party with a regular customer.

Business Rules and Gateways

Figure 6.25 shows how the whole of a business process is governed by a business policy and how it is guided by business rules. Those relationships are useful, but even more useful are the relationships between directives and the individual model elements that are part of a larger business process. Gateways in particular are often governed by business rules.

Figure 6.26 shows the internals of the **Seat Party** business process, as originally presented in Chapter 5. At the gateway **Reservation?** the host determines whether a party has a reservation (and whether the reservation is ripe). At **Seat Now?** the host determines whether an appropriate size table is available. These two gateways

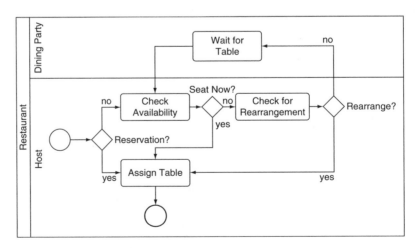

FIGURE 6.26 The **Seat Party** business process

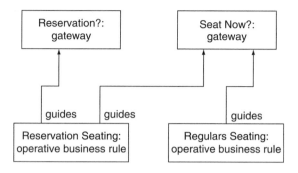

FIGURE 6.27 Business rules guide gateways

are guided by the business rules, as shown in Figure 6.27. **Regulars Seating** guides **Seat Now?**, and **Reservation Seating** guides both **Seat Now?** and **Reservation?**

Note that the gateways are depicted as diamonds in the business process model of Figure 6.26, and as rectangles in Figure 6.27. Figure 6.27 is another trace diagram, like the many we have seen in this book. It shows how individual model elements associate with one another, and it uses the visual conventions of those diagrams. In these trace diagrams, all model elements are shown as rectangles, with both the name of the model element and the kind of model element it is.

The existence of business rules can simplify the business process. The **Seat Party** process can be modeled with a single gateway instead of three, as shown in Figure 6.28. The gateway **Seat Party?** determines whether the party is immediately assigned a table, whether tables are rearranged to provide an appropriate table for the party, or whether the party must wait. That decision is guided by business rules, by the rules **Reservation Seating** and **Regulars Seating** as shown in Figure 6.29. (Other rules also guide the seating of a party—for example, rules about the circumstances in which tables should be rearranged.)

Business Rules and Activities

Business rules can guide activities as well as gateways.[2] An activity is guided by a business rule when the business rule helps the person performing the activity do his or her work. For example, let's consider again the business rule **Large Party Gratuity**, about mandatory tips for large parties.

> ***Large Party Gratuity:*** It is obligatory that the gratuity is at least 15% if the gratuity is applied to a bill and the bill is incurred by a party and the size of the party is greater than 7.

---

[2]As you will recall from Chapter 5, a conditional sequence flow is an alternative visual presentation of an inclusive gateway. Business rules can guide a conditional sequence flow, in the same way as they guide the equivalent gateway.

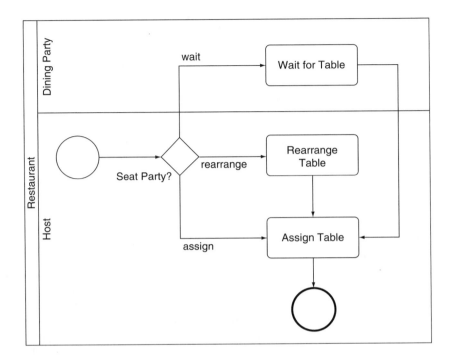

FIGURE 6.28 Business rules simplify **Seat Party**

When the server performs the activity **Produce Bill**, she uses this business rule. If the party has more than seven people, she includes a line item on the bill for the mandatory gratuity. Of course, she might be using a software application to produce the final bill—an application that automatically includes the mandatory gratuity. In that situation, the application must be aware of the **Large Party Gratuity** business rule.

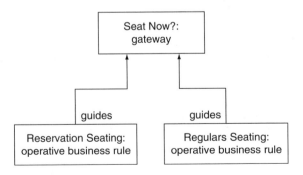

FIGURE 6.29 Business rules guide a gateway

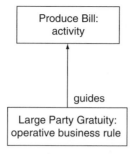

FIGURE 6.30 A business rule guides an activity

Figure 6.30 shows the relationship between the **Large Party Gratuity** business rule and the **Produce Bill** activity. The rule guides the activity.

THE SBVR STANDARD

SBVR is a standard for formally describing business rules. SBVR stands for *semantics of business vocabulary and business rules*. (Somehow the second *B* is not part of the acronym.) SBVR includes both means for defining vocabulary—noun concepts and fact types—and means for defining business rules that use that vocabulary. SBVR is another OMG standard, adopted by the Object Management Group in 2008 [OMG 2008].

SBVR is a large specification. It supports multiple natural language expression of the same rule, e.g., the same rule expressed in English, Korean, and Portuguese. It includes elementary concepts useful for expressing rules, concepts such as sets and integers. It precisely defines the meaning of rules, with ties to mathematics that are beyond this scope of this book. And it explains how to transform business rules and vocabulary expressed in SBVR into other standards.

The content of this chapter is consistent with SBVR. You should be able to use the vocabulary and rules in this chapter with any SBVR-compliant tools. But our ambitions in this chapter are more modest than the ambitions of SBVR. We have only used some of SBVR, concentrating on the elements and structures that are most useful for everyday business modeling. Much of SBVR is more advanced and so is not described in this book.

Prior to the development of SBVR, there was no standard for business rules recognized by any standards organization. But there was a de facto standard style of writing business rules—RuleSpeak—developed over 10 years by Ron Ross and his colleagues at Business Rules Solutions [Ross 2005]. RuleSpeak is perhaps the most widely practiced style for business rules, understood by many business rules practitioners and compatible with several business rules tools. RuleSpeak is also consistent with SBVR, which is no surprise since Ron Ross was a significant contributor to the SBVR standards effort.

SBVR is a standard for describing business rules, but it does not describe the way rules relate to strategies, goals, organization units, and other model elements. Those relationships are specified in BMM, the OMG standard for business motivation models. As you will recall, BMM is the standard behind the model elements in Chapter 3.

The adoption of an OMG standard for business rules changes things. Software applications that use business rules will be able to exchange those rules with other applications. It's the usual standards story: standards allow different applications to work together. But the adoption of SBVR is also a milestone. Business rules have come of age. They always deserved to be a first-class member of the business modeling toolkit, along with business processes, business motivations, and organizations. With SBVR, they are now recognized as such.

THE BUSINESS VALUE OF BUSINESS RULES REDUX

Why business rules? Why are they worth the trouble? Early in this chapter, we looked at the business value of business rules. We showed how business rules are used as software requirements, how they can be directly executed, and how they are used for communications, training and learning, and managing compliance. But now that we have examined business rules in some detail, we can say more.

Capturing business rules simplifies business process models. When the rules around decisions are modeling separately, outside the business process, the business process becomes simpler. We saw an example of this in Figures 6.26 and 6.28, where we modeled the decision rules for when to seat parties and when they should wait, removing that logic from the business process. The resulting business process was simpler, and hence more valuable.

Business rule models provide greater agility. Today many organizations want the ability to change faster when they need to, to quickly react to changes in the business environment: market opportunities and threats, or new laws and regulations. With a business rule model, many of the desired changes are implemented as new business rules. Other desired changes are implemented as changes to existing business rules. Business rule models separate the part of the business that naturally changes the quickest—the rules—from everything else that changes slower.

Business rules are also useful in the modernization of legacy applications. Most organizations have legacy software: applications written 10, 25, or even 40 years ago. These legacy applications cannot be retired; they perform important business functions. But they were created using technologies that are now either obsolete or are simply too expensive to maintain. There is a great interest in modernizing these applications.

Legacy modernization is risky. When a new application is written to replace the old, it's easy to overlook important business logic encapsulated in the legacy code. The new application is missing the hard-won knowledge that the old one accumulated over its lifetime. The result is a brand-new application that is worse than the legacy application because it is missing business rules. Many legacy modernization efforts fail for just this reason.

Business rules mitigate this risk. The legacy modernizer examines the legacy code—typically with tools for just this purpose. He mines the code for the business rules encapsulated within it. Then he models those business rules. Either the business rules become requirements for the new application, or they are executed directly.

Business rules are useful and valuable, but not widely practiced today. We expect this to change. We expect business rules to go mainstream. In the future, every company and every government agency will model its business rules.

Business rules guide behavior. Operative business rules guide behavior by stating what is obligatory, what is prohibited, or what is permitted only under certain conditions. Structural business rules guide behavior by defining what is necessary, what is impossible, or what is possible only under certain conditions. Operative business rules can be violated. Violations are prevented through enforcement.

Business rules are precise—precise enough to be directly enforceable. If someone knows a rule and sees relevant behavior, that individual can determine whether the behavior violates the rule. Business policies are the less precise and more abstract cousins of business rules. Business rules are often derived from business policies.

Business rules are richly connected to other business model elements. Business rules govern strategies. Business rules support the achievement of goals. Business rules are established by organizations. And most important, business rules guide business processes and the gateways and activities within those processes.

Business rules are the last of the four business modeling disciplines. In Chapters 7–9, we explain how to create a business model. There are some techniques to creating a good business model—techniques that are common to all four disciplines. Chapter 7 describes the techniques for creating a good model.

Creating a Good Model

7

There is no simple formula for creating a good business model. In fact there are lots of ways to fail—many different methods of creating a bad model. These bad modeling methods cross all four model disciplines. For example, one can build an overly complex motivation model, an overly complex organizational model, an overly complex process model, or an overly complex rules model. Similarly, model elements can be given bad names in any of the four model disciplines. Creating a good model involves avoiding all the paths of failure. This chapter explains the different paths of failures and some techniques for avoiding those paths.

Business modeling can deliver significant value. As we described in Chapter 1, there are eight different kinds of purposes that a business model can achieve. Often a business model will accomplish several of these purposes at the same time.

But in some organizations, business modeling has a bad reputation. "We tried that ten years ago," the old timers say. "There was a team of business modelers on the fifth floor. Lots of models were built, but nothing useful happened." The old timers described how the models became increasingly elaborate and complex until no one could understand them. "Finally, we axed the group."

So why is there a discrepancy between the promise of business modeling and the actual experience of business modeling? What gave business modeling its bad reputation in some organizations?

Leo Tolstoy begins his epic novel *Anna Karenina* with the sentence, "All happy families are alike; every unhappy family is unhappy in its own way." By this he means that to achieve happiness a family must avoid a host of dangers: alcohol abuse, infidelity, overspending, depression, and so on. An unhappy family of drunks is different from an unhappy family of spendthrifts. But the happy families have avoided all the dangers and for that reason are somewhat alike.

Business modeling is like the situation Tolstoy describes. There are many dangers to business modeling. Each danger can contribute to a bad reputation for business modeling. These dangers include model value destruction, scope failures, straight-through modeling, creeping complexity, ugly models, and incompetent modelers. Only by avoiding all these dangers can business modeling succeed.

Fortunately it is possible to avoid all these dangers. With some careful attention and governance, you can build a good model rather than a bad one.

MODEL VALUE DESTRUCTION

Not every model should be built. Sometimes the costs of creating and using a model are greater than the benefits that are gained from its use. In finance the term *value destruction* is used for situations in which a company takes an action that has a smaller economic benefit than the cost of the action. For example, a company that continues to sell a money-losing product line is said to be destroying value. Some models destroy value in exactly that way and should not be built at all. *Model value destruction* is one reason for the bad reputation of business modeling.

Creating a model always takes time: time interacting with the subject matter experts, time spent constructing the model with modeling tools, time spent making the model simpler and more understandable, time spent finding and fixing problems with the model, and time spent verifying a model with subject matter experts. Further time is spent using the model: time spent analyzing the model for business implications, time spent explaining the model to others, time spent maintaining the model when things change, and so on.

The act of modeling sometimes adds value on its own, when the modeling leads to greater understanding of a business situation. More often, the mere act of modeling adds no value. The value of modeling comes from the benefits that the model delivers, one or more of the eight purposes described in Chapter 1: communication, training, persuasion, analysis, compliance checking, requirements for software development, direct execution, or knowledge management and reuse. And some models do not deliver enough of these benefits to make up for the time and effort of creating the model.

The decision about whether to create a model is ultimately an economic decision: Do the anticipated benefits outweigh the anticipated costs? Are we going to deliver more value using this model than we will spend creating it?

Model Value Analysis

For small models, ones that can be built in an hour or four, we typically make a quick informal analysis. Do we expect to realize enough benefits to offset the time and trouble of creating the model? If it looks like it will add value, we build the model. In any case, the risks are low. At worst we have wasted half a day.

For larger models, we create a more formal analysis. We employ a simple technique to decide whether the model is worth building: We create a *model value analysis* before modeling. A model value analysis is just a summary of the expected costs and the expected benefits, and a comparison of the two. A model value analysis is typically created as a spreadsheet. One sheet of the spreadsheet estimates the costs of creating the model, another estimates the expected benefits, and a summary sheet compares the two.

Consider an example. Like all companies, Mykonos has to pay invoices. The payment process involves receiving invoices from bakeries, restaurant supply companies, and vineyards; checking the invoices; resolving issues with them; paying them; and managing the funds to cover the payments. Mykonos provides this process as a shared service to all the individual restaurants. Portia and Adelina and all the other restaurants that are part of Mykonos Corporation do not have to pay invoices on their own. Instead the payments work is done by a team of seven Mykonos personnel in the Chicago headquarters, and the individual restaurants interact with this headquarters team to answer questions and resolve issues.

Bill Mayo, Mykonos's controller, manages the accounts payable team. Bill is considering creating a business process model of the payments process. One reason for modeling the process is that the accounts payable team suffers from personnel turnover: Bill loses three or four people every year to transfers or departures. This turnover means significant training for the new people, and Bill believes that a process model will make the training easier and faster.

Bill also thinks a payments process model will make it easier to explain the process to the individual restaurants. They are often confused about their role in the process, and time is spent explaining the process to them. Finally, Bill thinks that a process model will reduce the time spent auditing the process every year.

Figure 7.1 shows Bill's estimates of the benefits of having a business process model of the payments process. The benefits are expressed in hours that Bill or his team will save every year in each of the eight different categories of business modeling benefit. Bill thinks he will save 80 hours a year in training with the model and another 80 hours each year in communicating with the restaurants. He thinks he will save a couple of days each year—16 hours—working with the auditors.

Many of these categories show nothing—no benefit. For example, Bill does not intend to analyze the model to make improvements to the process, so the analysis row shows nothing. Similarly, Bill does not intend to use the model as the basis for software requirements, so there is nothing in that row of the benefits table.

Figure 7.1 also shows estimates of the costs of building, using, and maintaining the business process model. These costs include both the time spent by a modeler and the time spent by people who know the accounts payable process, the subject matter experts who need to work with the modeler to build an accurate model. Building the model is a one-time expense, whereas maintaining the model is something that must be done every year, as the process changes. Socializing the model is both an expense while the model is built and an ongoing expense to explain it to new people.

Benefits	Hours saved	
	one time	each year
Communication		80
Training		80
Persuasion		
Analysis		
Compliance checking		16
As software requirements		
Direct execution		
KM and reuse		
Total benefits	**0**	**176**

Costs	Hours spent	
	one time	each year
Constructing the model	80	
Socializing the model	40	20
Maintenance		40
Total costs	**120**	**60**

FIGURE 7.1 A model value analysis

The model value analysis shows a total one-time cost of 120 hours and an ongoing annual cost of 60 hours each year. The benefits to Bill and his team are 176 hours per year. The model will almost pay for itself in the first year and will deliver 116 hours of net benefits each year thereafter.

Building a model of the payments process seems to be a good investment on the whole, but it is something of a close call. Often business models deliver significant net value within six or nine months, but this model is not expected to deliver net value until the second year. The benefits are rather modest for this model since the scale of the modeled enterprise is so small: only seven people.

The benefits that Bill expects from the model are all cost savings—hours that he and his team can avoid spending if they have a good model of the payments process. Cost savings are one example of the benefits that can be achieved by a model, but there are many others. In a different situation, a model can lead to additional revenue by persuading a customer to make a purchase. A model can lead to a business process change that results in higher customer satisfaction. A model can lead to better business controls that reduce risk.

Making a Decision Based on Model Value Analysis

Once Bill examines the model value analysis, he must decide what to do. If Bill is cautious, he may decide to forgo modeling his process, since the benefits are small. Or Bill could refine the rather coarse detail of the model value analysis, perhaps translating the hours into dollars. If the analysis was expressed in dollars, Bill could better compare dollars to dollars instead of hours to hours, since hours represent the time of different people who have different salaries. Or the model value analysis could prompt Bill to look for additional benefits—for additional ways to leverage the model, such as implementing a business process management system solution to connect his team with the individual restaurants. (Chapter 12 describes BPMS solutions.) And of course if Mykonos continues to acquire restaurants, the benefits of the model could increase substantially: Bill's payment team will grow and more time will be saved with a business process model.

Note that a model value analysis does not make a decision for Bill. Rather it informs his decision, providing additional information that helps him better understand the costs and benefits of creating a model. A model value analysis frames the decision of whether to build a model in the terms of a business decision, in costs and benefits, in hours or dollars.

The payments process value analysis shows no (estimated) value for reuse. This is typical. Most business models cannot be used beyond their original scope and purpose. When reuse is possible, it is usually hard to anticipate.

A model value analysis is a useful tool for deciding whether to create a business model. A model value analysis can also help guide the development of a model. A model should be built in ways that help achieve the estimated benefits. For example, the Mykonos payments model will be used for communication, training, and (to some extent) compliance checking.

The simple model value analysis in Figure 7.1 took Bill perhaps an hour to construct and use. That small investment is appropriate for the scale of the decision to be made, since Bill is deciding to invest about 120 hours. Suppose you are considering creating a bigger model—for example, a business process model of all the accounting and finance processes at Mykonos, not just the payments process. In considering a larger model, more time should be spent on the model value analysis. A good rule of thumb is 1 percent: spend 1 percent of the total anticipated modeling time on the model value analysis, to decide whether the other 99 percent makes economic sense.

SCOPE FAILURES

Some people find modeling to be very consuming, almost addictive. Modelers grow to like the models they build, and spend more and more time tinkering with them, refining them, making them more accurate and of higher fidelity. Clients of a modeling effort also like the models that are built for them, encouraging further refinement. More and more time is spent modeling. This is another path to model value destruction: spending too much time building and refining a model, more time than the value that can be delivered from the model you are building.

You cannot model everything, and you should not try. To avert model value destruction, you must manage the scope of the models you build. Managing the scope of a model means managing the *breadth* of the model—what the model includes and what the model does not include. Managing the scope also means managing the *depth* of the model: for the elements that are included, how detailed should the model be?

For example, suppose you are creating an organization model of the Mykonos Corporation and you want to manage the scope of the model. You decide to model only the internal functions of Mykonos, such as accounting and procurement, not the hundreds of individual restaurants that are managed individually. That is your model breadth: internal functions are in, individual restaurants are out. You also decide to only model organizations down to a certain size—five full-time people, ignoring smaller organizations and functions. That is your model depth: everything down to those that have five full-time people or the equivalent.

Figure 7.2 shows a *scope table* for the modeling Mykonos's organization. The scope table shows what is in and what is out for the breadth: you intend to model only internal functions, not individual restaurants or organizations outside Mykonos. The scope table also shows what is in and what is out for the depth: You intend to model only organizations of at least five full-time equivalents (FTEs).

Model scope is not something you decide once, when planning the model, and then blindly execute. Instead scope is something that you reexamine periodically. Does the scope still make sense? Did we overlook some line items in the breadth, items that are neither in-scope nor out-of-scope? Do some aspects that were once out of scope need to be moved in?

For example, once you have built part of the Mykonos organizational model, you might decide to augment it with the interactions between the organizations. But which interactions are important enough to warrant modeling? You decide to include only those interactions that occur monthly or more often and that involve at least 10 hours of work monthly, either directly or indirectly. You refine your scope table.

How do you decide what should be in scope? The scope should be driven by the reasons you are building the model. If you are building your model to better communicate to the individual restaurants how the Mykonos shared services work, then that purpose of communicating with the restaurants should determine what is in and what is out. The restaurants need to see the shared functions they will be using and how a typical restaurant within Mykonos Corp. will interact with those shared services. The individual restaurants will be out of scope—the model does not need to differentiate between Adelina and Zona—but a

	In	Out
Breadth	▶ internal functions	▶ individual restaurants ▶ orgs outside Mykonos
Depth	▶ 5 FTEs or bigger	▶ less than 5 FTEs

FIGURE 7.2 A scope table

	In	**Out**
Breadth	▶ internal functions that are shared services ▶ a generic individual restaurant ▶ interactions between the individual restaurant and the shared services	▶ individual restaurants ▶ internal functional that are not shared services ▶ orgs outside Mykonos
Depth	▶ 5 FTEs or bigger ▶ interactions monthly or more frequent ▶ interactions of at least 10 hours of work per month	▶ less than 5 FTEs ▶ less frequent interactions ▶ smaller interactions

FIGURE 7.3 A further refined scope table

typical restaurant should be in scope so that there can be interactions between it and accounting, between it and procurement, and between it and the rest of the shared services. Figure 7.3 shows a refined scope table, reflecting the purpose of the model. The increasing complexity from Figure 7.2 to Figure 7.3 is very typical: as the model is built and new issues are examined, the once simple scope table itself becomes increasingly complex.

Managing scope requires both business judgment and some ruthlessness. Everyone—modelers, clients, and subject matter experts—will want to expand your model. Each person will want to include new items in the breadth, and more detail in the depth, to include the model elements that are important to them and to make the model a closer fit to the world they see. You must be firm in rejecting these well-meaning desires, increasing the scope of the model only when it makes business sense, not when someone wants it. Models are by their nature never correct. Your job when managing scope is to make models useful on a budget of limited time and effort.

STRAIGHT-THROUGH MODELING

Some models are small, requiring an hour or four to build. A modeler works with a single subject matter expert for an hour and creates a small model. Or perhaps a modeler works with a team in a half-day facilitated session (as described in Chapters 8 and 9) and creates a model. These one-session models can be created with a simple straight-through process, shown in Figure 7.4. First decide the purpose of the model. Then determine the scope. Then create the model elements and associations. Finally, check the model, make corrections, and clean the model up. After a few hours, your model is done.

Some models are larger, requiring 50 hours or even 500 hours to create. Many novices attempt to use the same straight-through process of Figure 7.4 for creating larger models. They spend 10 hours determining the purpose of the model,

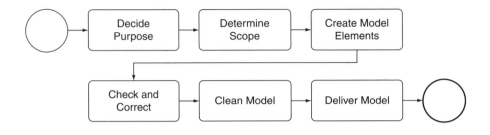

FIGURE 7.4 A straight-through process for creating a small model

8 hours on its scope, 22 hours creating elements and associations, and then another 10 hours checking, making corrections, and cleaning.

But the straight-through process in Figure 7.4 does not scale. Novices discover that they learn more about the real purpose later, as they are creating model elements, and they need to change their initial understanding. They discover that they learn more about the appropriate scope later, as they are checking and correcting their model. For a 500-hour model, the purpose, scope, and model value analysis must be reexamined again and again as more is learned about what the model needs to accomplish and how it needs to work. In the same vein, when the novices wait to check a large model until they are done modeling, they discover more problems than they can hope to fix. For building a larger model, an iterative process is needed.

Iterative Modeling

Figure 7.5 shows an iterative process for creating a business model.[1] The iterative process performs all the activities of the straight-through process (Figure 7.4) many times, once each iteration. Each iteration is a small amount of work, perhaps 8–40 hours in total across all the activities.

Each iteration should leave the model in a deliverable state. The gateway **Model Complete?** asks whether the model is complete enough against your planned scope and purpose. Most of the time it will not be complete and you will cycle back for more. But even if it is not complete, it should be ready to deliver at the point of the gateway. Why be ready for delivery at the end of each iteration? In essence the process of modeling means delivery all the time. You will need to show the model to others: to subject matter experts, to stakeholders, to other modelers. They do not want to see a model that is in a state of disrepair. They want to see a model that is finished, albeit incomplete. So at the end of every iterative, you should leave the model in a presentable state.

---

[1]Readers with a background in software development may recognize this need for iterative development [Larman 2004] [Cockburn 2001]. Business modeling has some of the same drivers as software development and the same risks of straight-through processes.

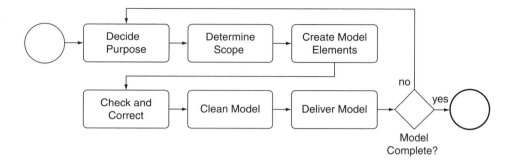

FIGURE 7.5 An iterative process for creating a larger model

There is another reason for leaving the model deliverable at the end of each iteration: situations change. The modeler might be pulled off the model for a while, onto a more pressing need. The model itself might no longer be important, or the work could be postponed to a later date. If the model is deliverable at the end of each iteration, it can be delivered at the end of any iteration.

At the end of every iteration, your model should deliver some value. Consider Bill's model of the payments process, described earlier. After two iterations, he has a model that shows how an invoice is checked and paid, as long as there are no problems or issues. The model does not deliver all the value estimated in his model value analysis from Figure 7.1. The model is not useful for communicating with the restaurants since most of their issues are with the exceptions and problems. And the model does nothing for the auditors, who are mostly concerned with how problems are handled. But the model, even in its incomplete state, would help him train new payments employees. It delivers value—not all the value he anticipates from the final model, but some of the value.

MODEL COMPLEXITY

Business models must be kept simple so that they can be easily understood by others. A simple model is easier to understand than a complex one, easier to communicate to others, and easier to maintain. Because it is easier on all dimensions, a simple model is much more valuable than a complex model. Simple is better—often much better.

Creating simple models takes skill. Novice modelers create overly complex, incomprehensible models because the world they are modeling is always complex. There is a fundamental tension between the natural complexity of the world and the need for model simplicity. Without the skills to craft simplicity, novices resort to modeling everything and creating complexity.

In addition to skills, keeping models simple requires effort. It is much easier to build a complex model than to build a simple one. This is a bit like Cicero's "I didn't have time to write you a short letter, so I wrote a long one."

But how do you create simple business models? There are three simplifying techniques:

1. Model element omission
2. Selective revelation
3. Hierarchy and decomposition

Model Element Omission

A model with fewer model elements is naturally simpler, and so one way to build a simple model is just to omit unnecessary model elements. Leave them out. Focus on the seven or nine most important elements and ignore everything else. Then once you have created the best simple model you can, ask whether the fidelity is high enough for the task at hand. Often it is; often, less is indeed more.

Consider the motivation model shown in Figure 7.6. The restaurant Adelina has six influencers, including its small space (limiting its success, as described in Chapter 3), its neighborhood becoming more important as a restaurant destination, and the concern in recent national media coverage about bacteria spread in restaurants. These six influencers are not the only things that influence Adelina's goals and strategies. There are many other influencers that could have been modeled. We could have easily created a model with 20 influencers, but these six are the most important ones. The other, less important ones are omitted because they can be ignored. Figure 7.6 is a better model than the 20-influencer version.

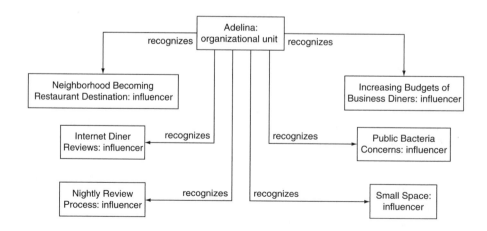

FIGURE 7.6 Six influencers

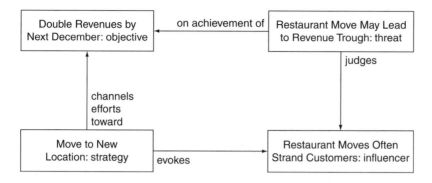

FIGURE 7.7 One alternative strategy

Selective Revelation

Omitting model elements is usually not enough by itself. Even after omitting the less important model elements, you might need to keep many model elements, more than can be easily understood in a single diagram. *Selective revelation* is one approach to the problem. The model might be large, but the model is shown in several diagrams, each one of which is simple enough to understand on its own. The model is selectively revealed, one diagram at a time.

Consider Figures 7.7 and 7.8, both first shown in Chapter 3. They show two alternative strategies for Adelina: a move to another location and an expansion

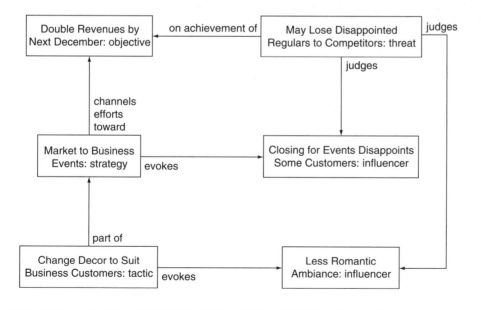

FIGURE 7.8 A second alternative strategy

to a different customer base. Each strategy has its own consequences. If Adelina moves (Figure 7.7), some existing customers might be stranded. If Adelina expands its customer base (Figure 7.8), it will need to change its décor and close for business events, both risking the loss of disappointed existing customers. These two diagrams are from the same model and could be combined into a single diagram, but the result would be too big and complex, and might lead to misinterpretation. It is better to show the two alternatives in separate diagrams, selectively revealing the model elements.

Note that Figure 7.7 and 7.8 share a model element. Both diagrams include the objective **Double Revenues by Next December**. That model element sharing diagrams is typical of good selective revelation because it lets the reader of the models understand how the different diagrams relate to each other.

With selective revelation, the model can be big and complex with hundreds or even thousands of model elements as long as each diagram from the model is simple, with no more than 9 or 10 elements. You need multiple diagrams to show the whole model, but each one is comprehensible on its own. By understanding each diagram in the model, a reader can understand the whole model.

Selective revelation can be done well or it can be done poorly. Figure 7.9 shows another approach to the same Adelina strategy alternatives. Instead of showing each alternative in a separate diagram, Figure 7.9 has the two alternatives together, along with the two threats that may result. The influencers and tactics that connect each strategy to its threat are not shown, to keep the diagram simpler. But Figure 7.9 is hard to understand because it is not clear which strategy leads to which threat, or why. Does moving to a new location lead to the threat **May Lose Disappointed Regulars to Competitors**? Figure 7.9 does not say. It is an example of selective revelation performed poorly.

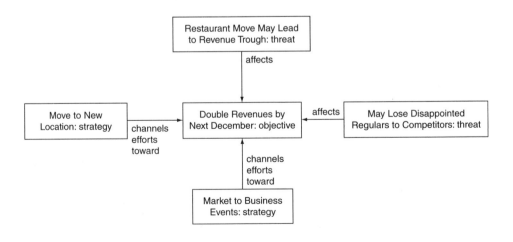

FIGURE 7.9 Selective revelation performed poorly

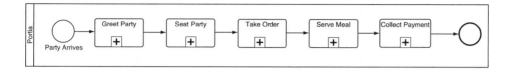

FIGURE 7.10 The upper level of the restaurant dining process

What is the real difference between Figure 7.8 and Figure 7.9, between selective revelation done well and done poorly? Both Figure 7.8 and 7.9 are subsets of the same underlying Adelina strategy model. But Figure 7.8 supports a clear and compelling narrative. Using Figure 7.8 you could tell a story about Adelina pursing a strategy of supporting business events. By contrast, there is no good story in Figure 7.9. It shows the two strategies, but because it does not link the strategies to the threats, the story is not clear, not complete, and not compelling. Good model diagrams tell a story. Figure 7.9 does not.

Model Hierarchy and Decomposition

A third approach to the complexity-comprehension tension is to use hierarchy. Some model elements are aggregated together into a composite model element. The details are underneath.

Consider the business process shown in Figure 7.10, the process for customer dining at Portia that we first explored in Chapter 5. A restaurant party arrives, is greeted, seated, orders, dines, and then settles his bill. All five activities are subprocesses, with more detail not shown in Figure 7.10. Figure 7.11 shows

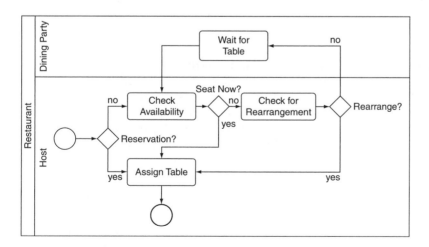

FIGURE 7.11 Inside one subprocess of the customer dining process

the expansion of the subprocess **Seat Party**. The other four subprocesses from Figure 7.11 are not shown, but they are similarly complex. Figure 7.10 could have included all the detail of all five subprocesses, but it would be horribly complex, with too many model elements to be easily understood. Instead that detail is pushed down into a hierarchy, and Figure 7.10 is quite simple.

Note that the lower-level business process in Figure 7.11 has two lanes, whereas the upper-level process has only a single lane for the restaurant as a whole. The subprocess is not just a decomposition of the activity **Seat Party** but also a selective revelation of the organizations that perform the activities.

When you explain a hierarchical model to someone else, you must explain more of the model mechanics. You must explain that the activity **Seat Party** has more detail and that the detail is in another diagram, and that everything shown in Figure 7.11 is inside the single **Seat Party** activity in Figure 7.10. Despite your best explanation, some businesspeople will have trouble understanding hierarchically organized models. Our experience is that model decomposition is fundamentally more difficult for businesspeople to understand than the other two simplifying techniques. Be patient and be willing to explain every time you talk about your model.

Refactoring Your Model

As you build a model, it gets more complex. New model elements are added; new associations are made between existing elements. Unless you maintain the simplicity along the way, your model will naturally become too complex. Furthermore, you might become responsible for someone else's model, a model that is already too complex.

Making a model simpler and easier to understand without changing the meaning of the model is called *model refactoring*.[2] Refactoring involves applying one or more of the simplification techniques described earlier: omitting model elements, using selective revelation, or creating model hierarchy. Often a single refactoring will include several applications of the techniques: e.g., omitting three model elements, creating two new hierarchies, and transforming one diagram into three via selective revelation. Refactoring a model leaves its semantics unchanged; it merely makes the model easier to understand.

For example, consider Viola, one of the restaurants that was originally part of Cora Group. Viola was started two years ago, but it has struggled to find a large enough clientele and has not yet reached financial breakeven. Some in the Cora Group attribute Viola's difficulties to the unusual focus of its cuisine: food of the Visegrád region of Eastern Europe. Others blame the high rent Viola pays

---

[2]Some readers with a background in software development might be familiar with *software refactoring*—changing the design of working software [Fowler 1999]. The concept of model refactoring was originally borrowed from software, and the intent and practice are similar, even if the techniques of changing a business model are quite different from the techniques of changing software.

and think the restaurant could have been a financial success in another part of town with cheaper rent.

The general manager of Viola convenes a strategy session to discuss Viola's situation, to consider the issues and strategic alternatives and decide what Viola should do. The result is the model shown in Figure 7.12. There are three alternative strategies to reach the restaurant's goals: **Grow Via Word of Mouth, Grow Via Restaurant Reviews**, and **Close and Reopen with New Name and Menu**.

But Figure 7.12 is a complex jumble. There are too many model elements to understand what is modeled. There is little logic in the arrangement of model elements—in what element is placed where. It is hard to understand what is missing: Are there missing influencers or perhaps missing connections between the assessments and the strategies It is difficult to tell.

Figure 7.12 should be refactored. One approach is to refactor into three diagrams using selective revelation, one for each of the three strategies. Figure 7.13 shows one of the resulting diagrams, with the strategy **Grow Via Word of Mouth** and the model elements that are related to it.

The nine elements in Figure 7.13 tell an interesting story. Viola has a small customer base, but those customers return often to dine there. Typically, intensely

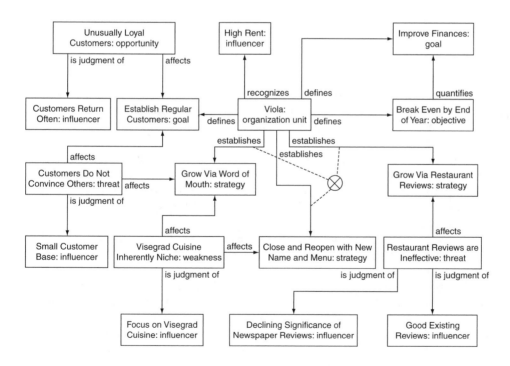

FIGURE 7.12 An overly complex motivation model

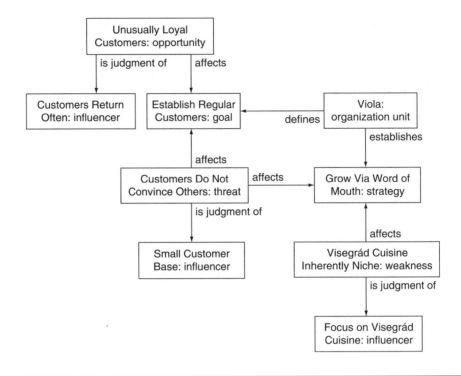

FIGURE 7.13 A single strategy

loyal customers of a restaurant tell the people they know, and the loyalty translates into many new customers via word of mouth. But that is not happening at
Viola. Somehow their existing customers are failing to convince others to try
the restaurant.

The workshop participants explored the theory that Viola's cuisine was preventing good word of mouth. Visegrád food—the food of Poland, Hungary, Slova-
kia, and the Czech Republic—is inherently a niche market. Few people know
Visegrád food or want to try it. This unusualness of the food limits the effectiveness of word of mouth.

All the model elements in Figure 7.13 are present in Figure 7.12. Figure 7.13 is
a pure selective revelation refactoring. But Figure 7.13 tells a clear story that is
buried within all the detail of Figure 7.12.

The other two strategies within Figure 7.12 deserve their own diagrams as
well. There is some overlap among the three diagrams; some model elements
are appropriately in more than one diagram. The weakness **Visegrád Cuisine
Inherently Niche** plays a role in both Figure 7.13 and in the diagram showing
the strategy **Close and Reopen with New Name and Menu**. The organization
Viola itself is in all three diagrams.

There also needs to be a diagram that shows the goals, objectives, and all three strategies together, without any of the influencers or assessments. The influencer **High Rent** can be omitted altogether since it seems to have no impact on any of the strategy alternatives.

We refactored Figure 7.12 by employing selective revelation, creating a new diagram for each of three strategies. But selective revelation by strategy is only one of many different ways that an overly complex model diagram can be refactored. Each overly complex model is different and deserves its own creative approach to make it simple.

Novices often try to build a model first, let it become complex, and then refactor at the end to make it simple. This approach can work for small models, but it does not work for larger ones. The model gets too complex to easily make changes. Even the people who built it become confused. And if the model happens to be delivered early—for example, if the modeling effort is cut short because the modelers are called away on another activity—the model will be too complex for anyone else to understand. A better practice is to periodically refactor along the way, to spend an hour simplifying every day or two. Refactoring wants to be an iterative activity, folded into the rest of the iterative construction of a model.

It is tempting to combine refactoring with other changes. For example, you might want to refactor a business process model as you add some activities. But it is better to separate refactoring from changes in the meaning of the model, to first refactor and then change the semantics later, after the refactoring is done. The refactoring itself should leave the meaning of the model unchanged and just make it simpler to understand. Refactoring without introducing an unintended change is difficult enough. If you are not careful with your refactoring, you might inadvertently change the logic of a business process or disconnect a goal from a strategy. It is better to focus on refactoring by itself, without the added challenge of intentionally making semantic changes at the same time.

BAD NAMES

Most model elements are named. An activity in a business process might have a name like **Inspect Produce.** An objective in a business motivation model might be named **Double Revenues by December.** A business rule might be named **Employee Theft Notification.**

Model elements can be named poorly and often are. Consider the following names we have seen in models:

- **CAC.** This is an organizational unit in a business interaction model. Six months later, will anyone remember what the acronym stands for?

- **Inquire MPI and Initiate 'Register Once', Local Eligibility Verified, and if eligible, Initiate Patient ICN creation**. This is a single activity in a business process, albeit one that sounds like a whole process itself.

- **Receive/Send New/Updated Enrollment/Registration data from system**. This is another business process activity, something about updating a system. Rather than using the slash character as an all-purpose conjunction, the modeler needs to pick some appropriate words for the name.

Good names are important. Models are used for communication with other people, and model elements with bad names make that communication unnecessarily difficult. People refer to model elements by name, and a bad name makes it tough to refer to the element you mean.

What are the characteristics of a good name for a model element? A good name is short: two, three, or four words are best. Longer names make it harder to understand the meaning of the model element and harder to refer to the model element when you're talking with other people. If you are tempted to write a long model element name to explain details, you should instead describe those details in the model element description.

The name should describe the intent of a model element, not the implementation. The implementation might change over time, even as the intent stays the same. "Validate Customer" is better than "Run search for customer name in CRM system." You may later validate the customer using another system.

Slashes, punctuation, and acronyms should be avoided in a name. Slashes and punctuation just make model element names awkward. An acronym is acceptable if it is already universally understood among the readers of the model. But if it is not universally understood—and many acronyms are not—some readers must decode the acronym every time they see it. Decoding slows down their comprehension of the model.

Overloaded words should be avoided. For example, "Process Exceptions" is a bad name for a business process activity because the word "process" already has too many meanings.

Capitalization should be handled consistently across your model. We prefer model elements with initial capitals, e.g., "Validate Customer," but other standards are also common. Inconsistent letter casing is confusing; readers of the model will wonder whether you mean something different by your inadvertent differences in capitalization.

Model element names should generally be unique—different from the name of any other model elements. If there are different model elements with the same name, confusion can result when someone refers to a model element. But uniqueness of model element naming can be difficult, particularly for larger models. If you have a model of 1,000 model elements, it can be tough to enforce uniqueness: You might not be aware that there is already a "Validate Customer" activity somewhere else. (Some modeling tools support the enforcement of name uniqueness by identifying when a name is not unique.) Furthermore, in a large model, you might be able to create unique names only by resorting to numeric suffixes, e.g., "Validate Customer 23." So we regard model name uniqueness as good but not absolutely required.

The characteristics of a good name of a model element also apply to names of lanes and pools in business process models. A short name is better than a long name. A name with no acronyms is better than one with acronyms. A unique name is better than a duplicated one. And so on. Since a lane is named by the organization that performs the work and the organization may be a model element in an organization model, the guidelines for naming are the same. Similarly, a pool is named by the organization that is responsible for the pool's process, and that organization may be a model element in an organization model. The naming guidelines apply.

WEAK DESCRIPTIONS

A model element can have a description, a paragraph or two that explains the details of the model element. For example, earlier in this chapter we introduced the challenges faced by the restaurant Viola and its failure to grow despite winning a loyal clientele. One of the model elements in the motivation model is the influencer **Declining Significance of Newspaper Reviews.** Someone reading the model might wonder about this influencer. Is Viola not getting the restaurant reviews it once did? Are newspapers reviewing more restaurants and so watering down the effect of each review? The description explains:

> *Traditionally, newspaper reviews were significant for restaurants. A good review could triple a restaurant's business overnight and leave it popular for as long as two years after the review was published. But over the last few years, newspaper reviews have gradually lost much of their former influence. Customers are less likely to read local newspapers at all and much less likely to read the reviews of restaurants. Now customers typically find good restaurants via the Internet reviews of other customers, by local dining blogs, or by professional review books like Zagat or Michelin™ guides.*

This description explains what the influencer means and the richer context behind it. The description includes the most important things a model reader needs to know about the model element.

In practice, many modelers write weak descriptions—a sentence fragment that explains a bit more than the name of the model element but not much more. But descriptions are important because they are read on several different occasions. Model element descriptions are read when a modeler is exploring a model she created some weeks earlier, trying to recall what the different model elements mean and how they are related. Descriptions are read when a modeler is modifying a model created by someone else. She tries to understand what the previous modeler has done and how the model works. Model element descriptions are read by subject matter experts, who check a model to determine whether it matches their understanding of the situation. Descriptions are read by other non-modelers who are learning the content that the model represents. These people are learning a new business process or learning the new policies.

To serve these different purposes, every named model element should have a written description. The description of a model element should be a paragraph or two that is easy to read and easy to understand by someone who is not a modeler. Any model element should be a good starting point for a model; someone should be able to start his tour of a model by examining any model element, reading its description, and working out across its associations to other model elements.

A model element description should be about the model element, not how the model element is associated with other elements. For example, suppose you are describing a business process activity, **Take Dinner Order,** an activity that follows the activity **Serve Drinks.** The description of **Take Dinner Order** should describe how the server takes the order, how long it takes, and some of the common scenarios that happen. The description should not describe how **Take Dinner Order** follows **Serve Drinks** since that following is represented by the sequence flow between the two activities. A modeler should be able to change the process by rearranging the sequence flow—e.g., by having the server take the dinner order first, before serving drinks—without changing the descriptions of individual activities. The model element description describes the model element itself, not how it is used in the model.

Model elements have associations between them, such as a sequence flow between two activities in a process model or a **quantifies** association between a goal and an objective that provides more detail about the goal. The associations between model elements can also be described. The same guidelines that apply to a model element description also apply to the description of an association between model elements: The description should be understandable, well written, and long enough to explain the association.

UGLY MODELS

In Chapter 2, we explained why model aesthetics matter—that attractive models are more readily accepted by people than ugly models. As humans, our neural wiring causes us to have emotional responses to the models we see, independently of cognitive questions such as whether the model is accurate or whether it is relevant for our problem.

There are no scientific studies to back up our claim that attractive models are more effective. To our knowledge, no one has looked carefully at this question. Our claim is based on personal experience and some speculation. But the experience is powerful. In one situation, subject matter experts rejected a particularly ugly model as inaccurate. The model was given a "makeover": Model elements were rearranged, and fonts and font sizes were changed. All substantive matters stayed the same. After the makeover, the same subject matter experts who rejected the ugly model accepted as plausible the new one. The subject matter experts moved beyond their initial repulsion and started to look carefully at the actual semantics of the model, objecting to individual model elements or individual associations between model elements, rather than rejecting the model as a whole.

Improving Model Aesthetics

What actions can you take to make a model attractive? You can:

1. Change the size of model elements. For example, a business process model looks better when all the activities are the same size.

2. Rearrange model elements. A model looks better when related model elements are close to each other, making the associations or flows between them short and straight.

3. Draw the associations without kinks or crossing lines. For example, an interaction model with simple straight lines that do not cross looks better than one with intersecting interactions.

4. Draw sequence flows in business process models from left to right. By convention, activities in business process models are generally arranged such that earlier activities are to the left of later activities.[3] Most sequence flows start on the left and finish pointing to the right, showing time flowing from left to right.

5. Align and distribute model elements. For example, a motivation model that has a goal and three subgoals underneath looks better when the subgoals are vertically aligned and evenly distributed.

6. Change the font size. A model looks better when it has uniform font size that is large enough to read.

7. Arrange the names of model elements. The names of the model elements are displayed as text on the diagram. Text looks better when it does not overlap with model elements, associations, or other text.

8. Use a complementary color palette. Color is often used in a motivation model, with goals, strategies, influencers, and assessments distinguished

---

[3]This left-to-right convention is common in cultures that read left to right. Other cultures may have different conventions.

by different colors. Colored models look better when the colors complement each other rather than clash.

These actions are intended as guidance rather than rules. Sometimes it is better to
have subgoals that do not align. Sometimes fonts of different size are useful. You
must use your judgment to improve the look of your model.

Iterative Aesthetics

Some modeling novices accept the importance of model aesthetics but approach it
by performing a one-time model makeover at the end of modeling. They build an
ugly model, work with subject matter experts through many work sessions without
considering the model aesthetics, and then clean up the model as a last step before
they deliver it. If they follow an iterative approach at all, the iterations are performed without any aesthetic improvements to the model, as shown in Figure 7.14.

The novices reason that they are saving time—that it will be faster to work on the
aesthetics once at the end rather than continually messing with fonts and colors and
other aesthetic matters through the whole model development process. But like
many novice modeling approaches, cleaning a model at the end does not work. It
is a false economy; it wastes time rather than saving it. The ugly model is used along
the way. It must be explained and justified to the subject matter experts as it is built.
Much more time is spent on these explanations and justifications than would be
spent if the model looked better. Even with the explanations, the subject matter
experts might not accept the ugly model. Model aesthetics matter not just to the
end users of the model after it is delivered but also when you work with the subject
matter experts in the process of constructing the model.

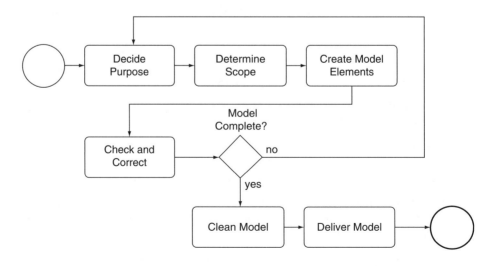

FIGURE 7.14 Improving model aesthetics at the end

A better approach is to improve and maintain the aesthetics of the model on every iteration, to make your model look good every time you deliver it. Of course, if you are in the midst of building a model on the fly with a subject matter expert in a live modeling workshop (as described in Chapters 8 and 9), you will not spend time improving the aesthetics during the workshop. But after the workshop, before you deliver the results, you should clean it up.

You should not only model iteratively, you should iteratively maintain and improve the look of your model. Figure 7.5 shows that process, with the activity **Clean Model** performed repeatedly, once every iteration. Yes, sometimes that aesthetic improvement work will be wasted. Sometimes you will carefully arrange and align model elements only to delete them in your next meeting with a subject matter expert. But usually the time spent improving the look of the model will be a good investment in improving its understandability and acceptance.

Improving the look of a model is a kind of refactoring—an aesthetic refactoring instead of a semantic refactoring. Just as semantic refactoring should be done iteratively to keep the model well organized and understandable, aesthetic refactoring should be done iteratively to keep the model attractive.

FAILURES OF QUALITY

Model quality is important. A high-quality model is a reasonably accurate representation of the understanding of your subject matter experts. An as-is model needs to match their understanding of today's situation, and a to-be model should match how they think the future should be designed.

A model also needs to be *accepted* by subject matter experts. They need to put their stamp of approval on the model, to signal to others that they believe it to match their understanding. If the subject matter experts do not accept a model, even a high-quality model, others will not take it seriously. It will fail to persuade, its analysis results will be dismissed, and people will create obstacles to its deployment.

Model Verification

Model verification is a technique for achieving both model quality and model acceptance. When you verify a model, you ask the subject matter expert about the model, whether it is consistent with her understanding. You ask her about every model element and about every relationship between model elements, diagram by diagram. When she questions a model element or a relationship, you either explain it and try to convince her, or you change it until she is satisfied.

Depending on the corporate culture, it can be useful to formalize the subject matter expert's acceptance with a signoff. For example, the simple statement

This model reflects my understanding of the situation.

can be placed on each model diagram, with a line for her signature underneath.

Of course, there is no legal significance to signing a model (at least in most circumstances). But the mere presence of a signature by a recognized expert will lead to acceptance of the model by others. And by asking her to sign, you focus her attention on the model and how important it is that the model reflects her understanding.

Readers with a background in software development might see model verification as similar to user acceptance testing of a new software application. In fact, both model verification and user acceptance testing seek confirmation by a subject matter expert. Of course, the two processes aim at the acceptance of different things. User acceptance testing is about the acceptance of a software application, whereas model verification is about the acceptance of a business model. But there is also a deeper and more fundamental difference between the two processes. Subject matter experts are first-class members of the team that creates a business model. A modeler and a subject matter expert work together to create a model. They are partners in the creation. The model verification is only a confirmation at the end, a last chance for the subject matter expert (SME) to change his mind about some details.

User acceptance testing is different. The SME does not create the software; he is not a first-class member of the team. Rather he is asked after the software has been created to verify that it does the right thing.[4] The subject matter expert accepts the work of the team rather than being part of the team himself.

Model verification is more complex when multiple SMEs are used to create a model. Sometimes SMEs disagree, and you need to facilitate consensus among them. The workshop techniques described in Chapters 8 and 9 are useful for creating that agreement. Sometimes there is no overlap among the fields of expertise, and you can organize the model so that each diagram reflects only a single SME's view.

While you are verifying your model, you might want to solicit comments and advice from other modelers. Your modeling colleagues are (likely) not subject matter experts in the domain you are modeling, and they cannot help you make the model a better reflection of the SME's understanding. But other modelers often have suggestions for improving a model in other ways: designs to better organize the model elements, ideas for what is missing or what can be omitted, and thoughts for better presentation of the model elements you have. Model improvement fits naturally with the process of model verification.

---

[4]In some agile software development processes, the SME is a first-class member of the software development team [Beck 1999]. But most software is created with more traditional processes, with a SME in a supporting role.

Model verification is a laborious process. It takes time to work with each SME, to check that each model element reflects her understanding, and to make the model changes needed. But the time is usually well spent, and the results of model verification are valuable. The results are a higher-quality model, one that is officially approved by your SMEs and accepted by the rest of your stakeholders.

Model Validation

Model verification is improving the quality of a model by working with SMEs to check every model element in a model. *Model validation* also aims at improving the quality of a model but does so through simulation or analysis instead of static model checking. The idea is that a model is simulated and the resulting simulation statistics are used to find problems with the model. The problems are fixed, and the model is simulated again.

For example, suppose you simulate your business process model of diners eating at Portia and discover an ever-increasing line of people waiting for tables. The longer you simulate, the longer the line. Ultimately in your simulation, people wait several days for a table. Clearly this is not occurring in the real world; no one camps out in front of Portia, waiting for days. You need to change the model to remove the ever-increasing line. Chapter 11 describes the details of how to use simulation to validate a model.

Not every model discipline supports simulation; we are aware of no modeling tool that simulates business rules, and it is not even clear in principle how business rules could be simulated. But every model can be analyzed, and analysis results can also be used to validate a model. For example, suppose you have a business motivation model and a business rule model, with each individual rule traced to the goals it achieves and traced to the strategies that it is based on. Are there business rules that are not traced to any goals or strategies? What are these disconnected rules trying to achieve? Are they really needed? Do they indicate missing strategies or missing goals? Many of the model analysis techniques described in Chapter 10 can be used for validating a model.

Verification, Validation, and Model Fidelity

All models are wrong, as we discussed in Chapter 2. A model can be of high fidelity or of low fidelity, but it is never of perfect fidelity. No model ever reflects all the complexity of the business situation being modeled.

The intended fidelity of your model provides a natural limit to verification. When verifying a model, your SME needs to understand and accept the fidelity you intend and not try to make the model more accurate than that intent. Her approval that the model is an accurate reflection of her understanding is always within the limits of fidelity. Managing the level of fidelity of the model is part of your responsibility, not hers. You might need to adopt the modeling stance (as described in Chapter 8) and remind her that managing the level of fidelity is part of your expertise.

There are also fidelity limits to validation. When you simulate a business process model, the simulation will produce very detailed results. You need to determine how close is close enough, when to regard the differences between the simulation and the world as significant, and when to regard them as within the limits of your intended fidelity.

Consider again the line for tables at Portia. Suppose you refine the model and it no longer simulates an ever-increasing wait. Instead the line for tables rises and falls over the course of a Friday evening, sometimes reaching seven or eight parties. Your SME objects, saying that there are never more than five parties waiting for a table, even on a busy Friday night; that people go elsewhere rather than wait. Should you change the model? It depends on your intended level of fidelity. If you want a model that reflects the actual activity counts to within 2, you should tune this model, figuring out why there are sometimes too many people waiting. Perhaps you need logic about when potential customers give up and eat elsewhere.

Verification, Validation, and Iteration

Verification and validation are better when performed iteratively. Verification and validation can be done just once, after a model is completed, but if you wait until the end you might discover big problems in your model. It is better to perform verification and validation periodically through the construction of a model, so that you can discover the problems and correct them before they are big.

Your first verification should be as soon as it is possible, as soon as you have enough of the model built that it will stand on its own and make sense to a subject matter expert. Similarly, you should validate a business process model as soon as you can simulate part of it, and you should validate other models as soon as you can create useful analysis. As a rule of thumb, you should never go more than two days without verification and never more than a week without validation.

Of course, the best approach depends on the size of the model you are building. If you build a small model in a few days, you might need only a single round of verification and validation at the end. If you build an even smaller model in a few hours, you might be able to skip verification and validation altogether.

Some models are maintained for months or years and are changed from time to time as the world they model changes. When you make changes to maintain a model, you will need to periodically reverify and revalidate.

TEAM CHALLENGES

A small model can be created by one modeler, a single person working with SMEs. A larger model can only be built by a team of modelers. Once a model is big enough, it is too large for a single person to create in the time required. But modeling teams have their own challenges and their own failures. The team must be organized to work on different sections of the model. When different modelers work on different sections of a model, they can end up creating inconsistencies, making one section of the model look different than another section, and function differently as well.

Model Design

A team of modelers cannot all work on the same section of a model at once. The model must be divided up in some way, to let multiple people work on different parts. The *design* of a model describes the way the model is organized into those parts that can be developed independently. For example, a natural design for a business process model is to divide it into separate end-to-end processes. Suppose there are four end-to-end processes. Then a team of four can divide the work by process, with each modeler working on one of the four processes. Another natural design for a business process model is to divide a single large end-to-end process into sections, with an upstream activity that is performed first, a midstream activity that is performed second, and a downstream activity that is performed last. Then a team of three can divide up the work by sequence, with one modeler working the upstream, one the middle stream, and one the downstream.

To divide the work effectively, the modelers must first agree on the model design, and then the modelers can work more or less independently. But there are risks with any up-front design. Often a better design—the "right design"—becomes apparent only after some work has been done. The team learns by building the model, and one thing that is learned is the best design.

The emergence of a better design introduces a hard decision: Do you change the design and reorganize the team, or do you stick with the original inferior design so each member of the team can continue working on his or her part of the model, as originally architected? There are costs with either approach, but usually the better approach is to embrace the change and refactor the model, rather than patching the legacy design.

Modeling Conventions

Different parts of the same model should look the same. They should look like they are parts of the same model rather than parts of different models. For example, color is often used as a visual indicator of model element type. If strategies are blue in one part of a model and green in another part of the same model, people will be confused. They will wonder if the green strategies mean something different than the blue ones. Strategies should be either blue everywhere or green everywhere.

One way to achieve consistency in the look of a model is for the modeling team to agree on conventions before the model is built. The team might agree that goals are red, strategies are dark blue, tactics are sky blue, and so on. Then everyone on the team needs to adhere to the conventions.

What aspects of a model should the conventions address? In our experience, the following are important:

- Model element naming (i.e., maximum length, form of name, capitalization, etc.)
- Model element color
- Model element size
- Model element shape (for situations in which shape could vary)
- Maximum number of model elements on a diagram
- Font sizes
- Association shape (e.g., rectilinear, rounded corners, etc.)
- Model element arrangement and spacing

As with an up-front model design, often the conventions agreed to up-front prove to be insufficient. Often the team learns about what the conventions really need to be as they create the model. In our experience, it is not uncommon for a team to change model conventions and spend an hour or an afternoon modifying the model to make it compliant with the new conventions.

INCOMPETENT MODELERS

Not everyone who tries to create a business model can create a good one. Over the years we have worked with many bad modelers—individuals who had other skills and strengths but created truly awful business models.

What does it take to become a good modeler? All good modelers we know share three key characteristics:

- An interest in business problems
- Logical or mathematical rigor
- Good communication skills

Our experience is that all three qualities are necessary. Someone who has an interest in business problems and good communication skills, but is not mathematical will not become a good modeler.

Business modeling requires immersing oneself in business problems. You do not need an MBA to become a good modeler, but you do need to be intensely interested in everyday business problems, the problems of supply chains and merger integration and policies with unintended consequences. Someone who finds *The Wall Street Journal* to be dull reading is not a good candidate for becoming a business modeler.

Business modeling requires some logical or mathematical rigor. There is no higher mathematics in business modeling—no calculus or topology is required, at least not with the four modeling disciplines described in this book. But business modeling is fundamentally about creating abstractions of the messy world of business. Creating abstractions requires logical or mathematical rigor. Some people are simply not good at this activity.

Business modeling requires good communications skills. Building a model involves talking with subject matter experts, asking questions and listening carefully to their answers. Building a model involves reading background documents. Facilitating a model-based workshop requires on-the-fly facilitation skills, as described in Chapters 8 and 9. And most important, building a model involves creating a visual artifact—a model—that will communicate to others on its own, without explanation. Modeling is a communication-intensive activity, using both verbal and spatial communication. Some people simply do not have the communication skills needed to create good models.

These three characteristics—business interest, mathematical rigor, and good communication—are all necessary for a person to become a business modeler. But these qualities are not sufficient. Business modeling requires knowledge of the business modeling disciplines. Someone who has all three characteristics but does not understand business processes will not be a good business modeler, not until she has studied more, using resources such as Chapter 5 of this book.

Business modeling also requires practice and experience. Someone with all three characteristics and knowledge of the four disciplines is a good candidate for becoming a business modeler, but she will only become a good business modeler once she has two years or five years of experience actually building business models. Like practicing law or developing software or cooking gourmet meals, experience is critical to developing business models.

In our experience, fewer than 25 percent of the people who want to create business models have the three necessary characteristics. Of those people who have the three characteristics, most know only one or two of the business modeling disciplines, and some know none at all. And of the people who have the characteristics and know the disciplines, most are beginning modelers, eager but with little experience. A good business modeler is hard to find.

It is a good time to become a good business modeler, to learn the disciplines and grow your skills. There are far more opportunities for business modeling today than people qualified to create the models.

Creating a good model is a matter of employing several techniques to avoid the dangers. Before you create a model, a model value analysis will help you avoid destroying economic value with your model. Managing the scope will help you avoid modeling too widely or too deeply. An iterative process will help you adjust your purpose and scope as you learn more. Model element omission, selective revelation, decomposition, and refactoring will help you create a simple model. Good names and descriptions will make your models easier to understand. Some attention to size, arrangement, fonts, and colors will make your models presentable. Verification and validation will improve the quality of the models and improve their organizational acceptance. Managing the model design and modeling conventions will help a modeling team work together effectively. And good hiring, screening, training, and mentoring will improve the quality of modelers, ultimately improving the quality of the models they build.

In practice, one of the best ways to create a good model is to host a model-based workshop. Chapters 8 and 9 describe model-based workshops.

Model-Based Workshops

8

Models are often built interactively in facilitated modeling workshops, with subject matter experts talking about the business and a modeler changing the models on the fly. Workshops are group activities. Several subject matter experts—each with different knowledge and understanding—collectively build a model. Together they reach a common understanding.

We describe model-based workshops in two chapters. In this chapter we detail what a model-based workshop is, and in Chapter 9 we explain how to run one effectively.

In Chapters 4 and 5 we explored how the restaurant Portia is organized, who performs business processes at the restaurant, and what those business processes are. We examined organization models and business process models to understand why customers are experiencing delays before they are seated. But in practice how are these models created? What approach is used to create them?

One approach is to create models from documents that already exist. You start by studying the written policies of the restaurant and the training material for new hires. You then create the models in isolation. All the work can be done without leaving your office.

Creating models in isolation is a poor modeling approach. The existing written materials are always incomplete. Usually they are wrong as well—out-of-date and at odds with actual practice. And in interpreting the written materials, you will make mistakes as you try to understand material created by others—material they understand better than you do. Later we discuss when it is appropriate to create models in isolation, but in general this isolated approach is a poor way to create business models.

Another approach is to create the models in one-on-one sessions with subject matter experts. You meet with the restaurant host and understand how she handles reservations and how she assigns a table to a party of diners. You separately meet with a server and understand how she takes an order, serves the meals, and processes a payment. You meet with the manager to get her view on these processes. You then combine what you have learned into a single model.

213

When you model one on one, you are not completely isolated from the subject matter experts (SMEs), but you are working in *lane isolation*. You attempt to understand what each person does in his own business process lane, in isolation from everyone else. You then integrate the model fragments into a single model. After that, you verify the model with each SME, either individually or together as a group.

The one-on-one method presents three challenges. First, it takes time because you need to repeatedly rework the model. You rework the model after each meeting with a SME. You rework the model after you integrate it, because each SME has comments on the new sections of the model she has not seen before. She might have never considered how her activities fit with the activities of others.

Second, in a one-on-one meeting it is difficult to listen to what the SME is saying, to create a model, and to write notes all at the same time. To do all that, you need assistance.

Third, SMEs often disagree. When you work one on one, any disagreements will require you to engage in shuttle diplomacy, working back and forth between the disagreeing subject matter experts to resolve the differences. Disagreements are easier to resolve when the disagreeing SMEs are in the same room at the same time.

A better approach to business modeling is to perform the modeling in a workshop. You collect several SMEs in a room at the same time for a modeling session. You work together to create a model. In a workshop, you can create models in less time, reach consensus quicker, and see how everyone's work fits together.

In a workshop, you cannot do everything yourself. It is difficult in a one-on-one modeling session to listen, model, and take notes all at the same time, but it is completely impossible when you work with multiple subject matter experts. You will need help. A workshop always involves multiple people playing different roles, in addition to the SMEs.

Workshops also introduce a new challenge: group dynamics. Getting people to agree—people with different agendas and personalities—is hard. It can also be hard to convince a subject matter expert (e.g., a server at Portia) to speak freely in front of her supervisor. Without good management, a workshop is chaotic, accomplishing nothing except the generation of ill-will. Workshops require order. They require someone to manage them. They require facilitation.

FACILITATED WORKSHOPS

Over the last 30 years, some practical techniques have been developed to organize productive meetings. A meeting using these techniques is called a *facilitated workshop*. The model-based workshops we describe in this chapter are a special kind of facilitated workshop, one in which business models are created and used.

A facilitated workshop is an organized meeting run by a facilitator. A facilitated workshop will last at least a few hours and could span days. Each of the attendees in a facilitated workshop is an active participant. The participants interact with each other and with the facilitator.

The facilitator manages the workshop and leads the participants. The facilitator is responsible for being objective and impartial. He intervenes when he thinks the workshop is going off-track—for example, when he thinks that a participant is dominating the discussion. But he does not express his own opinions on the topic of the workshop. The facilitator leads the participants in exercises and activities to achieve the workshop objectives. Being an effective workshop facilitator is difficult; it requires training and practice.

The facilitator also has the daunting task of maintaining the social order. Sometimes conflicts arise between workshop participants. The facilitator intervenes, defusing the conflict and depersonalizing the disagreement. The facilitator leads the participants toward consensus.

A good facilitated workshop has a clear agenda and a timetable. No one likes wasting time, and no one likes to participate in a workshop that is unproductive. To be effective, a facilitated workshop must be time-bound and must achieve a particular goal. The facilitator must manage the time carefully, orchestrating the work sessions within the workshop so that the results are valuable and are produced in the time planned.

Facilitated workshops use visual tools. During a workshop, participants observe information created on a white board and recorded on flip-charts. Projectors are used to display slides, demos, and other documents. Visual tools make a workshop more interesting and keep the participants engaged. They also allow participants to track what they have accomplished and where they are headed.

Facilitated workshops use special techniques to build consensus and special techniques to actively involve everyone. A workshop with one active participant and many silent participants is worse than a one-on-one meeting. Like a one-on-one meeting, it reflects the views of a single person, but it is worse because it wastes everyone else's time. No true consensus is reached. The facilitator must ensure that everyone is involved and that all opinions are heard. At times, the facilitator will silence one participant while urging another to provide her opinion. Sometimes the facilitator will circle the room, asking for each person's opinion in turn. Sometimes the facilitator will use a voting technique to ensure that every opinion is counted.

A facilitated workshop has a clear desired outcome. The facilitator manages the meeting to achieve a goal or to answer a question, typically a goal posed or a question asked by the sponsor of the workshop. The facilitator does not drive towards a predetermined result. Rather, the facilitator helps the group arrive at an answer to the question or a solution to the goal that reflects their judgment and expertise.

Much has been written about workshop facilitation and the techniques used. In this chapter our focus is solely on model-based workshops—on using the techniques of facilitated workshops to create, correct, validate, and improve business models. To learn more about workshop facilitation in general, we recommend reading some of the many books on the topic [Schwartz 1994, Conklin 2006].

MODEL-BASED WORKSHOPS

A *model-based workshop* is a facilitated workshop that results in the creation of a business model. The workshop has a business goal—for example, deciding how to comply with a new government regulation—and business models are created to support the decision making about how to achieve the goal.

A small team runs a model-based workshop. The team includes a *facilitator* who facilitates the workshop, asking questions, managing time, and drawing out participation from everyone. The team includes a *modeler* who creates models and captures model-relevant detail. The team includes a *scribe* who takes notes while the facilitator and modeler are busy performing their tasks. The team may also include an independent subject matter expert, someone who has particular domain knowledge useful for communicating with the workshop participants. (Chapter 9 includes more detail about the roles required to run a successful model-based workshop.)

Suppose you are to facilitate a model-based workshop at Mykonos. The workshop is intended to capture organization models and business processes on the way work is performed at the Portia restaurant. Your stakeholder, the CFO of Mykonos, wants to understand how the long delays that diners are experiencing can be removed, and by removing delays how revenue can grow. In particular he wants the participants to consider whether restaurant pagers will help shrink the delays.

You have reserved a room that has a white board, a projector, and screen. The tables and chairs are arranged in the shape of a U, to create a casual and interactive atmosphere. You greet the participants as they arrive.

A few days earlier, you had sent email to the participants, reminding them of the workshop and its purpose. The participants understand that the workshop is about analyzing how work is performed at the restaurant so that delays can be reduced. They know that pagers for waiting diners are to be evaluated. You expect that this is the extent of their knowledge when they arrive at the workshop. And you expect them to know little about business modeling.

You start the workshop by reviewing the agenda. You explain the purpose of the workshop, who asked for it, and why everyone is here. You explain that the group will first capture the as-is state of interactions and processes at the restaurant and try to understand where delays occur. You mention that in the afternoon the group will explore how pagers could improve the process—how they could make the process easier not just for the customers but for the employees as well. Some in the group laugh in nervous acknowledgment; dealing with angry customers is unpleasant. The explanation also eases their fears. No one is going to be fired and no one is in trouble. Everyone understands that the delays are not their fault and that a solution is likely to improve their working conditions.

Introductions are made around the room. Some people they already know as colleagues; others they are meeting for the first time. You introduce the modeler and the scribe and explain their roles and yours.

You begin the workshop with a short presentation that describes both what a model is and the purpose of the models that will be created today. The participants become excited. They want to share what they do and the problems they are facing. You show some examples of models—similar to the ones that will be created. You also describe the model elements you will use.

To you this might seem straightforward; you have facilitated many similar sessions. But to the participants this is new. They know little about modeling and have never been part of a model-based workshop. They are uncertain. You convey that they need to trust you; models are useful and things will become clearer as the workshop progresses.

You then start the first modeling work session, one to create an organization model. You ask the participants to describe where they fit within the organization, who the different groups are, and with whom each group interacts. As they answer, you draw what they are saying on the board and ask them to validate the correctness of what you are capturing.

While you are facilitating, the modeler is creating the model on a laptop. The scribe is taking notes and occasionally asking for clarification. You are facilitating a model-based workshop.

WORKSHOP USES

Model-based workshops help realize the business value of modeling. They can be used to deliver and address seven of the eight purposes of modeling we described in Chapter 1. The workshop you are facilitating is a workshop for *analyzing* a problem and evaluating possible solutions.

A model-based workshop can be used to present models already created. In this case the models are used for *communication*. The already created models are presented to subject matter experts for validation or to a decision maker to provide supporting material in their decision-making process.

A model-based workshop can be used for *training and learning*. For example, employees can be trained on a new business process by working through the process in a model-based workshop. Or a workshop could be used to ensure *compliance* of policies and guidelines.

Workshops are also used for *persuasion and selling*. In fact, you worked with a pager vendor to design this workshop. For you the workshop is about analyzing the problems, but for them it is about selling pager systems.

If the workshop does result in acquisition of a pager system, the system must be integrated with other IT at Mykonos. The models created in the workshop can be used to understand how employees perform their work and how they will use these systems. The usage scenarios can be used as *requirements* for the system development.

A workshop can capture intellectual property for use elsewhere at Mykonos: *knowledge management* and *reuse*. For example, you might run a model-based workshop with your most skilled servers about how to upsell wine. If you capture information on the way the best servers do this, you can train new servers to use the same methods. Knowledge management is particularly important for companies facing the "big crew change," when many older employees are about to retire. The models created in the workshop ensure that legacy knowledge is not lost forever.

Model-based workshops support seven of the standard eight purposes of modeling. But model-based workshops also provide other benefits. A model-based workshop is a facilitated workshop, and all well-run facilitated workshops promote *collaboration*. Employees from different groups—from different restaurants and corporate headquarters—work together in the workshop. They exchange ideas and create models. They learn from each other.

Workshops help participants reach *consensus* in a collaborative environment. Everyone has a say; the facilitator manages the session and ideas are captured. A model is refined until all agree the model represents their collective understanding.

As the SMEs create the models in the workshop, they develop a sense of *ownership* of the models. They try to improve the models on their own, finding problems and raising issues. Later they explain the models to others. Models created outside a model-based workshop often lack this kind of ownership. The SMEs feel that the model is someone else's understanding, not theirs. The models are critiqued, and the consequences of the models are ignored.

Workshops create a *common vocabulary*. Staff at the newly acquired restaurants use different terms than staff at the existing Mykonos restaurants. The restaurant staff use different terms than the headquarters employees. For example, at one restaurant the person greeting diners is called a "host," but at another she is called a "receptionist." At one restaurant there are "servers," at another "waiters." At the workshop the participants create a common language that all understand and agree on. When models are created, the participants agree on the name of each model element.

Workshops help participants *understand the impact of a change*. By evaluating and comparing the as-is and the to-be, the participants can understand how their work will change. They understand the way their organization looks after the change. For example, the Cora Group staff understand how they interact with Mykonos corporate accounting now that they have been acquired.

Workshops are used to *validate assumptions.* Your stakeholder might have a strategy he would like to test. For example, he could assume that outsourcing information technology to a third-party vendor will save money. Or he could assume that the business process Portia uses for scheduling waitstaff is more efficient than the process used at other restaurants. In a model-based workshop, an assumption can be tested with various SMEs, resulting in either validation or disproof. It is common for a stakeholder to enter a workshop with one assumption and in the process of the workshop discover that their assumption was wrong. For example, your stakeholder might learn that Portia's waitstaff scheduling business process is unpopular with the waitstaff because it does not reflect when they want to work. As practiced, the business process includes much later schedule rearrangement. A simple simulation reveals how much time and effort are actually spent correcting schedules, and the true costs of the process are revealed. Simulations can inform decisions, often producing results that might at first seem counterintuitive. Chapter 11 explains simulations in more detail.

A workshop can be used to *understand the scope* of a problem and *build a business case.* You can use a model-based workshop to evaluate several alternate projects. During the workshop, you evaluate motivations, capture goals, and map goals to the alternative projects. You compare the schedule and cost of each project. You can even perform ranking exercises to help the participants determine which alternative is best.

THE TIMING OF MODEL-BASED WORKSHOPS

A project can be understood to have two natural phases. A project starts with a *conception phase* and is implemented during a *realization phase*. In conception, the project is evaluated and planned. In realization, the project is started, performed, and concluded. Of course, real projects implement a bit at the beginning, as the project is conceived, and plan (or replan) a bit later, as the project is realized. Projects are often messy, not conforming to the neat separation between conception and realization.

A model-based workshop can support either conception or realization. A model-based workshop can be performed during conception, to evaluate an opportunity. The purpose of the workshop is to understand the opportunity—the requirements for the project and the way to best address those requirements. If the project itself involves business modeling, a model-based workshop can produce a model value analysis (as described in Chapter 7) to determine whether a modeling effort should proceed.

Sometimes a vendor or outside consultant proposes to perform the project for a client. When there is such as vendor/client relationship, the vendor often performs a model-based workshop during project conception, either for free or for a nominal charge. To the client, the workshop helps evaluate the proposed project. To the vendor, the workshop helps sell the project; the workshop is part of the sales effort. In these situations, care must be taken to ensure that the workshop honors the client's goals. If the workshop is not performed in an objective and high-integrity manner, the client might not realize value from the workshop.

Sometimes a vendor performs a model-based sales workshop internally, evaluating a sales opportunity. The modeling in this kind of workshop helps understand what a prospective client might need or what an anticipated request for proposal (RFP) might include. It helps the proposal team understand the client, the client issues, and what the proposed solution needs to address. (See Chapter 5 for a related case study.)

Model-based workshops can also help a vendor write an effective proposal. Models can be created to trace and map the proposed solution to the client requirements and business processes to demonstrate how the technologies and solution will be used. Diagrams from these models can be used in the proposal itself; they help convey the solution in a way that client personnel can understand.

Model-based workshops are also useful during project realization. If the project itself involves business modeling, workshops can be used to create and validate those models. But model-based workshops can be useful even for projects that are not attempting to deliver any business models. For example, consider a project to develop a new IT system. While collecting requirements for the new system, it is important to understand the business process activities that each software requirement supports. In this way proposed requirements that do not match the business process can be avoided. A model-based workshop can be used to perform this mapping from proposed requirements to business process activities.

Some people believe that model-based workshops increase project costs. This is the view of inexperienced project managers who do not understand the value of modeling or who do not understand the effectiveness of model-based workshops to create business value. In our experience model-based workshops save time and reduce risk by creating consensus around important business challenges, by providing an avenue for raising issues, and by allowing participants to work together to resolve the issues.

MODEL-BASED WORKSHOPS FOR VARIOUS BUSINESS PURPOSES

Every project has a business purpose. Some projects have purposes involving strategy—for example, creating a strategy for a business unit. Other projects have purposes involving execution—for example, deciding whether to outsource a function. Still other projects have purposes involving information technology implementation.

During a single project, multiple model-based workshops can serve different business purposes. One workshop can clarify business goals, another can evaluate alternative strategies, and a third workshop can align technology requirements with business needs.

Model-based workshops are useful in a wide range of different business purposes. In this section we explore some of the modeling workshops that we have delivered and how to create a model-based workshop that is appropriate for the purpose. This list is not exhaustive. There are other business purposes we have not described. But we have found these purposes to be the most common.

Strategy Workshop

Organizations are driven by goals, and by strategies to achieve those goals. Some organizations pick a strategy and execute it for long periods of time. Other organizations change direction every few years and some change more frequently, hopping from one strategy to another in an attempt to discover the right one.

A workshop for picking a strategy focuses on the influencers on the organization, and the goals and strategies that best address those influencers. As you recall in Chapter 3 we explored a business motivation model for doubling revenue in a restaurant. There were three alternative strategies: move to new larger location, raise prices, and market to business events. A model-based workshop was used to surface and evaluate those three strategies. First, the alternatives were modeled: What are the competitors doing? What are the problems and goals we are addressing with each alternative? What does the organization look like now, and how might it change after the new strategy is deployed? What are the steps we must take—the roadmap—to deploy the strategy?

Next, a facilitator used a scoring technique to allow workshop participants to rate the strategies. In this situation, people rated on a numeric scale from 1 to 5. The alternatives were rated on several categories: risk, time to execute, difficulty, and perceived benefit.

Finally, the strategies were ranked. The restaurant management team decided that marketing to business events was the best strategy to doubling revenue. Moving to a new location had the biggest revenue upside, but it was judged to be risky and difficult to execute.

Technology Alignment Workshop

All companies need to ensure their technology initiatives meet business needs. In an alignment workshop, participants explore their business goals and strategies and the planned technology initiatives and look at which initiatives achieve which goals and strategies.

Small organizations typically have one technology initiative, or at most a few. Large organizations have many operating concurrently. A huge organization like Citibank or the US Department of Defense will have hundreds of initiatives. But no organization—even the US Department of Defense—has enough money and time to do everything. Picking the right initiatives is important. What are the right initiatives? The right initiatives are the ones that best serve the business goals and strategies.

In an alignment workshop, the participants explore their business motivations, their problems and goals. Then they explore the technology initiatives that are underway and those that are planned. For each initiative, they consider what goals and strategies the initiative addresses.

Often the initiatives are rated and ranked. The initiatives are rated for the coverage of goals and strategies, for risk, for cost, for duration, and for difficulty. Then they are ranked, from the most important and valuable initiative to the least important and least valuable.

An alignment workshop exposes mismatches between the goals and problems of the organization and its technology projects. Participants will discover some projects they are already executing that do not address any goals or solve any problems. They also discover goals and problems they need to address for which they have no project planned.

Sometimes a technology initiative is discovered to have an unfortunate scope. For example, consider an initiative that is intended to meet a short-term goal, but that is scoped to finish after the goal is no longer relevant. This initiative is not useful as it is scoped; it needs to be either rescoped or cancelled.

Solution Rollout Workshop

Sometimes the business challenge is to roll out a solution across a large organization. This challenge is addressed by the solution rollout workshop.

Consider the restaurant pager system we explored in Chapter 5. As we discovered, the to-be business process with the pager system looks quite different from the as-is business process. We need to communicate the new business process to the general managers of the individual restaurants so that they can train the staff.

We also create business interaction and organizational models to show how the pager system will be supported. The general manager needs to know who to contact when the pager system malfunctions. The corporate IT department needs to know how to support the pagers and what processes to use to provide that support. Corporate IT also needs to understand when to interact with the pager vendor and how that interaction works.

The developers or integrators of the solution benefit from the models created in the workshop. By studying the models, they can understand how employees will perform their work and how they will use the system. The usage scenarios become requirements for the system development and deployment.

Mykonos Finance is interested in understanding the impact on the organization. How will the product be supported? Who maintains and operates it? What impact does it have on resources and staffing?

An associated work breakdown structure details the set of activities that must be performed to perform the rollout. Together with business rules, the organization can ensure that budget plans are created for accounting and that legal documents, licenses, and contracts are established by the legal and procurement departments. A smooth rollout depends on many departments within an organization and on a well-orchestrated set of activities.

Outsourcing Workshop

Most organizations outsource some of their work. Some organizations outsource software development; some outsource help desk and customer support; some outsource human resources, accounting, or legal work. Some outsource all these functions and business processes, and other functions as well.

Making good business decisions about outsourcing is often difficult. Will the new outsourcer deliver the same quality? What should be outsourced and what should be kept in-house? How will the rest of the organization adjust to the outsourced processes? Complicating the business decisions are the human resource issues. Will today's people be reassigned or laid off? How will the outsourcing change the power dynamics in the organization?

To make good outsourcing decisions, you must understand the organizational goals, and how those goals are being accomplished. Like other model-based workshops, an outsourcing workshop involves creating a business motivation model, looking at the problems, goals, strategies, and influencers.

Outsourcing always has a knowledge effect. When functionality is outsourced, the knowledge about how to perform that function is outsourced as well. For example, many organizations outsource the information technology help desk; when an employee has forgotten his laptop password and calls the help desk, someone in the outsourcing company will reset the password. The knowledge and expertise of how to handle IT help desk calls has passed from the organization to the outsourcer. If the organization later wants to insource the IT help desk function, it will be difficult because they no longer have the knowledge in-house.

For the IT help desk function, that knowledge transfer is rarely significant. Most organizations want good help desk support, but few regard the help desk as a core component of their business. They don't care if they lose the knowledge of how to provide good help desk service as long as they can get that service from someone. But every organization has some functions and some processes whose knowledge is too important to lose. Motivation models play an important role in an outsourcing workshop. When you explore what knowledge is deemed important, you can capture that learning as a goal in a motivation model.

Outsourcing usually changes business processes. The outsourcer performs the IT help desk differently, with different escalation processes and different reporting processes. In an outsourcing workshop you can examine the effect of the process change, looking at what employees need to do, who they will work with from the outsourcer, and how their work must adjust.

The business process changes are affected by the geography of the outsourcing relationship. Sometimes the outsourcer's employees work side by side with their clients. Sometimes the outsourcer's employees work across town or across the country. Sometimes the outsourcer's employees are on the other side of the world. The business processes are different in each of these cases. In the outsourcing workshop, you investigate who does the work and where it is done as part of business process modeling.

System Transition Workshop

Most organizations have a mix of information technology—some new systems and some old systems. Old systems sometimes need to be replaced, either because they are no longer supported by vendors or because they have become too expensive to support—or simply because new alternatives offer important new functionality.

Transitioning from an old system to a new one involves technical challenges, of course, but it also presents issues of acceptance. Sometimes the transition is welcomed by employees: a system is so old that its use slows employees in their work. Sometimes the transition is not welcomed: employees are accustomed to the old system and they resist the change.

System transition always impacts the business. Employees must be trained to use the new system. Business processes are often affected. Sometimes there is an extended transition period when both the new and old systems are run concurrently and employees must use both until it is clear the new system works properly and ties to the older system can be severed.

A system transition workshop allows the participants to explore and understand the impact of the transition. As-is and to-be business process models are created to understand the business process changes. As-is and to-be business rule models are sometimes created to help the organization understand how the new system implements policies and other guidance.

Often organizational models are developed to explore which parts of the organization will be impacted by the new system. These organization models can also include IT organizations to investigate who will manage the new system and who will support it.

Regulatory Workshop

Every organization is affected by governmental laws and regulations. For example, many cities ban smoking in restaurants and bars. Some government regulations affect government agencies themselves. For example, the US Federal Information Security Management Act requires that US Federal agencies manage information securely and certify and accredit information security. And every publicly traded company in the United States is required by the Sarbanes-Oxley Act to have effective internal controls.

Internal organizational policies can be like a law or regulation. When the CEO decides that every improvement project must be justified with a cost-benefit analysis, to the rest of the organization his decision feels like a new law passed by Congress.

A regulatory workshop is a model-based workshop for understanding the consequences of a new regulation or a new policy. A new regulation (or a new policy) will have many consequences. It will affect business processes. It might affect organization and interactions. It will usually affect systems. And of course it affects business rules: The new regulation must be operationalized into the 10 or 100 business rules that implement the new regulation. Other existing business rules must be changed as a result of the new regulation.

In a regulatory workshop, participants begin with understanding the new regulation: What does it mean? They create organization models to understand how the regulation changes existing interactions. They create business process models to understand the business process impact. They might perform simulation to understand the cost and time implications of the new regulation. Finally, they operationalize the new regulations in business rules.

Reorganization Workshop

Businesses often reorganize. Some companies reorganize every six months. Others reorganize less often, but they implement far-reaching changes when they do. Some reorganizations work well and some do not. A bad reorganization slows a company down and makes it less effective.

A reorganization workshop is used to design a reorganization. The participants in the workshop might be starting fresh, considering what new organization would better suit the needs of the business. Or the new organization might have already been announced and the participants need to determine how to make it work.

The focus of the reorganization workshop is to understand the business interactions—which organizations interact with which. Organization models are used. The as-is interactions are compared to one or more to-be models. Participants explore the alternatives and try to understand which is best.

Once the interactions are understood, the participants create process models to examine how work will change. Often the focus of the business process models is the people: who now performs what work?

A business process model can also suggest ways to reorganize. Let's consider a Mykonos example. At Mykonos the IT organization includes a help desk, application support, and field services. The help desk team takes IT support calls from the restaurants. Application support solves problems with the applications, servers, and databases. Field service personnel are dispatched to the restaurants to physically fix problems and to perform maintenance. The help desk has three people, application support has ten, and field services two.

When we look at the Mykonos IT processes, we discover something interesting. We find that most of the people handle security issues most of the time. Sixty percent of the total labor hours are consumed by security: dealing with viruses, spam email, botnet infections, installing security patches on existing software, and other security-related activities. These security tasks consume all three organizations.

This interesting finding suggests a reorganization. Rather than distributing responsibility for security across the three existing IT organizations, a new centralized security organization is created, with the responsibility of all IT security. This central security organization leads to somewhat better efficiency and much better visibility into IT security.

Merger Integration Workshop

When two companies merge, they combine their businesses to create a single larger business. When one company acquires another, the acquiring company folds the business of the acquired into its own, absorbing the employees, products, customers, and other assets. Mergers and acquisitions are legally different activities, but they have similar business processes. For either a merger or an acquisition, the laborious task is not deciding to combine but performing the *merger integration*—integrating the operations after the decision to merge is made.

According to several studies, large mergers usually fail: they fail to achieve the economic goals that motivated the merger [DePamphilis 2003]. The merged companies would have both been better staying separate. When a merger or an acquisition fails, the failure is almost always because merger integration was performed poorly.

Merger integration is difficult. The merging companies have different business processes, different policies and rules, different goals and objectives, and of course, they are organized differently. There are often other challenges to overcome: differences in geography, regional or national differences, and different corporate cultures. The merging companies will inevitably use different information technology. To merge effectively, all these differences must be addressed and reconciled.

A merger integration workshop is a model-based workshop that plans merger integration. Typically, a merger integration workshop is held just after the merger (or acquisition) has been announced. The workshop includes participants from both entities to be merged. They work together to design their new company.

The participants examine business processes. Often they decide to adopt all the business processes of one company, but sometimes they adopt some processes from one and some from the other. For example, one company might have a strong recruiting process and the other a superior new product development process. The new combined company will then have both better recruiting and better product development.

The business process decisions have systems implications. The strong recruiting process from the first entity is supported by their recruiting application and so that application is retained in the combined company. The weaker recruiting process of the second entity is supported by a different recruiting application, and that application can be discontinued. But there are inevitably complications. The data from the discontinued recruiting application must be migrated to the retained application. The recruiting application is part of a larger HR package—other components of which are being kept. The recruiting application is also integrated with other applications that are being retained.

Merger integration is simpler when a large company acquires a small one. The business processes and systems of the large company are retained and the small acquired company discontinues its processes and systems and adapts to being part of the acquirer. But even this simpler situation deserves examination. Some of the processes and systems of the small might be better—more agile processes and systems with better architectures that are a better baseline for the future.

In a merger integration workshop the participants create two as-is models and one to-be models. The as-is models represent how the two entities operate today. As-is organization, business process models, and business rule models are created. Multiple to-be models can be created to examine alternatives for the merger. But typically the merger integration must happen quickly. There is no time for alternatives, and the workshop participants create a single to-be model of their vision of the combined entity.

Often merger integration workshops are contentious. The best design for the combined company will differ from the career interests of the some of workshop participants. Conflicts will occur, sometimes even battles as employees fight for their positions. In Chapter 9, we describe some techniques for facilitating contentious model-based workshops.

Business Continuity Workshop

The terrorist attacks of 9/11 exposed which Wall Street banks had good plans for business continuity and which did not. Both the threat of further attacks and the threat of unrelated events—e.g., a pandemic or a hurricane—are leading not just Wall Street banks but many organizations of all sizes to consider how they can function in a crisis or disaster.

Business continuity involves having redundant infrastructure and data backup. It also involves having the processes and extra staff to perform the work when some people are ill or otherwise unavailable. In some situations, remote operations are sufficient. For other situations, work cannot be performed remotely because of security restrictions or other constraints.

The purpose of a business continuity workshop is to create a business continuity plan the business can follow if disaster strikes. Most plans include advanced preparation, some investments the business needs to make before any disaster strikes. The plan is communicated to stakeholders, so it can be widely understood and the mitigating investments can be made.

The participants in a business continuity workshop explore the business implications of a disaster. They try to understand the impact of various disaster scenarios. What if we lose power for several days? What if 60 percent of our employees are either sick or caring for sick loved ones? What if our suppliers are unable to make deliveries? The participants might also explore the IT implications of various scenarios. Can database server support be performed in one instead of two shifts? Can five instead of 12 people accomplish that work? Can three?

The participants typically create motivation models to debate and explore the real goals of continuity. For example, must critical business operations be recovered within 24 hours after a disaster, or is 72 hours good enough? Different continuity goals suggest different strategies.

Workshop participants create organization models to explore which organizations are involved in recovering from a disaster and how those organizations interact with each other. Interactions with customers are also considered, as are those with suppliers, government personnel, and other outside parties. Sometimes business process models are examined to see how the as-is processes are affected by a disaster. Processes can be simulated to see where bottlenecks will emerge under different scenarios.

Performance Improvement Workshop

Most organizations try to improve their own performance. They try to deliver goods or services faster. They try to reduce their own costs. They try to improve their quality or customer satisfaction. They try to reduce the capital tied up in their operations.

A performance improvement workshop is a workshop focused on improving organizational performance. The participants start by creating a motivation model of the objectives for the workshop—e.g., that this workshop is focused on improving customer satisfaction in the order-to-cash process and not focused on other processes or other measures. Constraints are also considered, for example that proposed improvements in customer satisfaction cannot raise the cost of the order-to-cash process.

In a performance improvement workshop, participants construct many to-be models. The participants compare these alternative to-bes with each other and compare them to the as-is model of the existing situation. The participants explore what would happen if they did the same work the same way but were organized differently. They explore what would happen if they changed the business process. They explore what would happen if they incorporated new methods or new technologies to obviate manual work that is done today.

Sometimes these explorations lead far from the as-is situation. For example, consider an IT support organization that is performing a lot of work responding to help desk calls. The workshop participants want to reduce the cost of this technical support and examine outsourcing the work to an offshore business unit, considering how much costs would be saved. They look at handling some of the easier problem with lower-cost (and less skilled) people. They also examine the possibility of reducing the number of tech support calls by eliminating the root causes for the calls, solving the problems before the problems ever occur.

In some performance improvement workshops, the participants identify bottlenecks to remove. For example, in a sales process an engineer is needed to design a solution as part of a proposal. If the right engineer is not available, fewer proposals can be generated, fewer sales will be made, and less revenue can be realized. While investigating the sales process, the workshop participants discover that the engineers also format the proposals, work that can be performed by staff without the key engineering skills. By reallocating work, more sales can be made.

Pursuit Workshop

When a small business makes a small purchase (e.g., a $100 desk), they purchase it off-the-shelf at a retailer. The entire transaction takes a few minutes. But when a large company makes a large purchase (e.g., a $40 million capital markets trade settlement system), a much longer and more careful acquisition process is involved. The large company talks to several prospective vendors. Each competing vendor tries to understand the purchase—what is needed and what is valued by the company. Often the large company creates a *request for proposal* (an RFP), a document describing what they would like to acquire, asking for proposals to be submitted by the vendors. Each competing vendor submits a proposal, including a description of its solution, what it will achieve for the large company, why it is the best choice, and how much it will cost. Sometimes the competing vendors perform *orals*, in-person presentations and demonstrations. The large company then chooses which proposal to accept and enters into negotiations with the winning bidder. For a prospective vendor, this is a *large pursuit*—a multimonth process to try to win a big deal.

Model-based pursuit workshops are useful for vendors engaged in these large pursuits. A pursuit workshop can increase the likelihood of success—the likelihood that a winning bid will be created. It can also reduce the risk of the *winner's curse*, the risk that a winning bid will be created that subsequently loses money for the vendor, or cannot be performed as described. The pursuit team chasing a large acquisition will use several sales strategy workshops to shape their pursuit and improve their odds.

The participants in a pursuit workshop create motivation models to explore the goals and objectives of the customer, the purchasing company. Why are they purchasing? What change in their business are they trying to accomplish? What are the constraints they must live within? The pursuit team likely has an imperfect understanding of these motivational issues—unless they are already deeply involved with the customer performing other business. But in any case the participants create a model from what they do understand.

Once the motivation model is understood, the pursuit team uses the motivation model to design a winning bid. Large companies (and government organizations) typically select a winning bid based on a combination of four factors:

1. Price
2. Technical quality of the solution
3. Business impact of the solution
4. Perceptions and prejudices of the individuals involved in the purchase decision

The motivation model guides each factor.

The motivation model guides the pricing. Pricing a large proposal is largely a matter of deciding what solution components to include and what to exclude. For example, does the customer value 24×7 support, or would they prefer a cheaper proposal that includes support only 10 hours each day and only Monday through Friday? Only by understanding the customer's motivation can good decisions be made.

The motivation model guides the technical solution. When technical alternatives are considered, the one that best addresses the motivation is selected.

The customer is purchasing to accomplish some business performance benefits: perhaps lowered cost, perhaps reduced risk, perhaps improved customer satisfaction. Once these benefits are captured in the business motivation model, exploring the business impact is a bit like the performance improvement workshop described earlier in this chapter. The workshop participants explore alternative business process models, alternative business rule models, or alternative business strategies to see which accomplish those benefits. The resulting models are used in the proposal to illustrate the business benefits of the solution. Simulations can be run to show how the reduced cost or improved customer satisfaction is achieved. These simulations are particularly effective in demonstrations.

Sometimes a customer is interested in how well each vendor understands the business of the customer. Does this vendor really understand our world enough to perform well if we select them? Including business process models and business organization models in a proposal can address these concerns, proving deep understanding.

Finally, big purchases are always human decisions. Some people at the purchasing organization work together to write an RFP, listen to the oral presentations, and select a winner. Each of these people brings his own career goals, prejudices, and preferences to this decision. The pursuit team explores these human dynamics at the pursuit workshop. Who are the critical decision makers? Who is involved in shaping the proposal, and what are the critical concepts and ideas they care about that the proposal should address? What is each decision maker trying to achieve? These human dynamics are captured in organization models.

WORKSHOP BENEFITS IN SUMMARY

Earlier in this chapter we listed and described the various benefits of model-based workshops: analysis of a problem, communication, training and learning, and so on. Some of these benefits are realized at every model-based workshop. For example, every workshop promotes collaboration. Every workshop serves to create a common vocabulary among the workshop participants. Some benefits are realized only at some workshops and not at others. For example, not every workshop builds a business case. Merger integration workshops do not create business cases. Instead the business case for the merger has already been made, and the task is figuring out how best to implement.

Figures 8.1 and 8.2 summarize the business purposes to which a model-based workshop can be applied: strategy, technology alignment, solution rollout, and so on. For each business purpose, Figures 8.1 and 8.2 list the benefits that apply. A full circle indicates that the benefit is often realized for workshops designed for that purpose. A half circle indicates that the benefit is sometimes realized in that type of workshop. A hollow circle indicates that the benefit is rarely realized.

Figure 8.3 shows which models are created in which workshops. In some workshops you will create models from all four disciplines: business motivation models, business organization models, business process models, and business rule models. But more typically in a workshop you will create models in one or two of the modeling disciplines. A full circle in Figure 8.3 indicates that the

	Analysis	Communication	Training and Learning	Ensuring Compliance	Persuasion and Selling	Eliciting System Requirements	Knowledge Management
Strategy workshop	●	◐	○	◐	◐	○	◐
Tech alignment workshop	●	○	○	●	◐	○	○
Solution rollout workshop	●	●	◐	◐	◐	◐	○
Outsourcing workshop	●	●	◐	○	◐	◐	●
System transition workshop	●	●	◐	○	○	◐	●
Regulatory workshop	●	◐	◐	●	○	○	○
Reorganization workshop	●	●	◐	◐	◐	○	◐
Merger integration workshop	●	●	●	●	○	●	◐
Business continuity workshop	●	●	●	○	◐	●	○
Performance improvement workshop	●	●	○	◐	◐	●	◐
Pursuit workshop	●	◐	○	◐	●	◐	◐

FIGURE 8.1 Workshops and purposes

	Promote Collaboration	Promote Consensus	Promote Model Ownership	Create Common Vocabulary	Understand Impacts of Change	Validate Assumptions	Build Business Case
Strategy workshop	●	●	●	●	●	●	●
Tech alignment workshop	●	●	●	●	●	●	●
Solution rollout workshop	●	●	●	●	●	○	○
Outsourcing workshop	●	●	●	●	●	●	●
System transition workshop	●	●	●	●	●	●	◐
Regulatory workshop	●	●	●	●	●	◐	○
Reorganization workshop	●	●	●	●	●	●	●
Merger integration workshop	●	●	●	●	●	◐	○
Business continuity workshop	●	●	●	●	●	●	◐
Performance improvement workshop	●	●	●	●	●	●	●
Pursuit workshop	●	●	●	●	●	●	●

FIGURE 8.2 Workshops and benefits

model is usually created, typically because it is critical for the success of that kind of workshop. A half circle indicates that the model is sometimes created, and a hollow circle that the model is rarely created.

Figures 8.1, 8.2, and 8.3 are based on our experience. They are meant as heuristic advice, not as rigid rules. As you acquire your own experience with model-

	Business Motivation	Business Organization	Business Process	Business Rules
Strategy workshop	●	◐	◐	◐
Tech alignment workshop	●	◐	◐	○
Solution rollout workshop	◐	●	●	○
Outsourcing workshop	●	●	◐	○
System transition workshop	○	●	●	●
Regulatory workshop	◐	●	●	●
Reorganization workshop	●	●	◐	○
Merger integration workshop	●	●	◐	●
Business continuity workshop	●	◐	●	●
Performance improvement workshop	◐	●	●	●
Pursuit workshop	●	●	●	○

FIGURE 8.3 Workshops and models

based workshops, you will tackle new problems, and to solve those problems you will apply different models to these workshops purposes. You might even create entirely new workshop purposes. You will want to refine this advice with the heuristics from your own experience.

WORKSHOP FOCUS AND DELIVERABLES

Workshops must be focused. A model-based workshop needs to target a particular business problem and focus on understanding that problem and solving it. A workshop without a clear focus is confusing to the participants. When a participant is not clear why she is performing the workshop activities, her attention wanders. The resulting models are not useful.

Some workshops are internally focused: focused on issues within your own organization. For example, you might be asked to facilitate a model-based workshop to improve a business process. Your stakeholders want to evaluate a particular process change. What are the impacts of the change?

Some workshops are externally focused: focused on issues at another organization, your client, or your business partner. You can run a workshop at your client's organization to help them solve a problem. Or you can run a workshop to show how your company's product can help your client.

Every model-based workshop must produce value. Discussions by themselves are generally not valuable; the discussions are soon forgotten. Instead, a workshop must create a product, a deliverable from the workshop that can be used by others. Some workshops create more than one deliverable.

Not surprisingly, one common deliverable of a model-based workshop is a model. Workshops can produce business motivation models capturing goals, problems, and strategies. They can produce organization models. They can produce business process models, as-is and to-be. They can produce business rule models, capturing policies and guidelines. Sometimes a workshop produces models from several disciplines.

After the models are built, someone creates a *workshop report*, another deliverable from the model-based workshop. The workshop report is a presentation that distills and summarizes the models for others: for senior management and other stakeholders. In addition to explaining the models, the workshop report also summarizes the model analysis, what the models mean, and what has been learned. Who creates the workshop report? Usually the facilitator does the work after the workshop is over. He sends the result to the workshop participants for their comments and suggestions. Sometimes the participants create the workshop report together as the last activity in the workshop itself.

The workshop report generally includes the business context of the workshop. It describes how the model-based workshop fits into the larger overall project. It describes the accomplishments of the workshop. The workshop report can include a business case for further workshops.

Sometimes simulation results or simulations themselves are deliverables of a model-based workshop. Simulation results are powerful in conveying information about the cost effectiveness or efficiency of different alternatives. Delivering a simulation itself—via a playable user interface—is also powerful. The stakeholders can run what-if scenarios on their own and evaluate the various scenarios from their own perspectives. Chapter 11 describes simulations.

Model-based workshops can produce other deliverables. A workshop that involves business process change may also examine the system impacts of the proposed process change. The resulting system impact assessment is a deliverable that analyzes the systems and other IT technology that are impacted by the proposed process changes. A system impact assessment is not a business model, but it is a natural outcome of some business model-based workshops.

A model-based workshop can also produce project planning deliverables: a high-level roadmap, a prioritization of what should be done next, a detailed project schedule, or a work breakdown structure. The high-level roadmap is a collection of activities, grouping activities by project phase. It shows what activities need to be done and the order in which those activities need to be performed. The detailed project plan describes the proposed project activities, resources, and schedule in greater detail.

When a model-based workshop delivers more than one model, the models can be traced together. For example, a strategy workshop may deliver both a to-be motivation model and a to-be business process model, showing the process that is designed to achieve the strategy. Some of the activities in the process model are intended to achieve particular objectives in the motivation model. Each of those activities is traced to the objectives it is intended to achieve.

THE VALUE OF MODELING IN FACILITATED WORKSHOPS

Why are model-based workshops better than more traditional facilitated workshops? In other words, what business value does a business model provide in a facilitated workshop?

Models are useful in workshops because they provide a mechanism for the participants to capture their thoughts in a visual way. It is much easier to view the constructed model on a white board or projected from a laptop than to write it down as notes for review later.

Modeling in a workshop helps the participants reach consensus. Instead of each participant keeping his or her own version of the notes, each individual's ideas become additions to a single model created collaboratively. The model can be changed during the workshop as participants have new insights and new realizations.

Modeling during workshops allows the workshop participants to explore cause and effect before they actually do anything. The participants explore different policies, different organizational structures, and different business processes and explore the consequences of each. It is cheaper and safer to explore these in a model-based workshop (perhaps with subsequent analysis and simulations) than to actually implement the new policy or change the organization and see what happens. Models are cheaper and safer than reality.

By creating models during a workshop, the participants are creating intellectual property. Often the business models remain useful over time. Others—people not in the original workshop—can later refer to the business process models to understand the way a process is intended to work. A business motivation model can be used to later create a business plan or a business case.

WHEN ARE MODELS CREATED?

When should business models be created? Should they be created during a workshop itself? There are advantages to creating them during a model-based workshop. The workshop participants feel that they are part of the creation. They perceive that they are adding value. They take ownership of the models, feeling that the models represent their beliefs and ideas.

But creating models during a workshop involves some scope uncertainty. The facilitator might not know what modeling is required until the workshop is underway. Is procurement a single process or three? The workshop can run out of time, and additional workshops might need to be scheduled with the participants. Scheduling time with participants is always difficult. Typically, busy participants do not welcome additional workshops that take them out of their day-to-day jobs and beyond their original commitment to the workshop stakeholders.

Another approach is to create some models before the workshop starts. Creating models in advance mitigates the scope uncertainty. With models in hand, it is clear that procurement is a single process, and the size and the shape of the process are clear as well. Models created in advance can make a workshop faster and more productive. The models are modified by the participants rather than created in their entirety, an easier and faster job. Modeling in advance also eases the facilitator's job as the created models become a natural starting point: is this gateway accurate? Do you perform this activity next? Finally models created in advance make the facilitator look good. They demonstrate her knowledge of the business situation.

Creating models in advance does have a drawback. The participants feel less ownership of the models. Rather than creating the model, the participants modify something that was created by someone else. Instead of collaborating and feeling creative, the participants are commenting and critiquing. The workshop has a negative tone, like a complaint session.

Often a combination is best. You build models before the workshop and then you start the workshop fresh, without those models. The facilitator uses the knowledge of the already created models to drive the workshop. If participants become stuck, the facilitator can ask, "What if we added this activity here?" or "What about this business unit? Are there interactions with them?" Using this before-and-during method, the facilitator is ready when he starts the workshop. He understands the scope of the models that need to be created, but he is not asking the participants to comment on the models that already exist. The facilitator guides the participants to create models that they own.

Modeling is iterative in nature. Often one workshop is not sufficient to create the necessary models. Depending on the size and complexity of the models, a series of workshops might be necessary.

Between one model-based workshop and the next, you refine and improve the models. Typically, models created during a workshop are overly complex and need to be simplified and refactored. Typically, they are also ugly and need aesthetic improvements. Sometimes there are other problems: model element naming or scope issues. After a single eight-hour workshop, you might spend 20 hours improving the resulting models. (Chapter 7 explains techniques for creating a good model.)

After models are refined and improved, you must present them to the participants. They need to see the changes you made to their models—the models they created at the workshop and that they feel they own. If you present them, usually participants accept the changes, seeing those changes as improvements that retain the knowledge and spirit of their original work. Of course, your refinements could have introduced errors, and when you present the newly refined models, they can spot the errors.

Case Study

Healthcare is financed differently in the United States than in other parts of the world. Most people in the United States subscribe to health insurance from a private company, a health insurer. Some of these health insurers cover subscribers across the whole United States, in all 50 states. Other health insurers have more limited geographical coverage, offering health insurance to people who reside in some localities but not to those who reside elsewhere.

A client of ours is a healthcare company offering health insurance coverage to employees of companies across the country. Our client does not run its own business processes to receive health claims or to issue payments. Nor does it own the necessary information technology to support those claims or payment. Instead, our client contracts with another company to perform these services. This *services company* receives health claims and issues payments to members—patients—and to healthcare providers— physicians, hospitals, labs, and pharmacies—on behalf of our client.

As with any partnering relationship, our client wanted to ensure that if the services company became unable to provide services for any reason, our client could switch to a *backup entity* for claim processing and payment services. The backup entity was to be another services company, selected ahead of time, ready and willing to provide those services on short notice. To mitigate the risk of over-dependence on the services company, our client was willing to pay a suitable backup entity, just for the ability to be ready to take over if needed. Our client prepared an RFP for those backup services.

But a potential transition from the services company to a backup entity would not be easy. The healthcare insurance company's program was performed by the services company staff and run on the services company computers—computers that also support other healthcare customers. If a transition were to occur, how could our client's members be separated from other members? Could patient privacy be maintained if operations were to transition to the backup entity?

We worked with our client to explore the issues surrounding this potential transition (or *portability*) and to reach consensus among the stakeholders on a portability approach. We conducted 18 workshops to explore the issues and reach consensus and to help our client prepare the RFP for the backup entity.

We conducted business continuity workshops with key stakeholders and department heads, including both business subject matter experts and information technology subject matter experts. The focus of the workshops was to ensure that both the goals and timing of the transition were clearly understood and that the participants agreed on those goals and timing. The workshops also looked at the ways a transition would impact IT. The results of the workshops were captured as a business motivation model, with goals, problems, and strategies.

The modeling team facilitated a second series of workshops to understand how our client interacts with the services company today in providing health coverage for its members. They created an organization model with interactions between the two organizations. The purpose of this model was understanding what service a backup entity would need to provide if the transition were to occur. The model also examined the dependencies of our client on the services company. Each of the dependencies would have to be untied if a transition happened.

Business process models were created as well—not of every process performed on behalf of members but of a few critical processes. These business

Continued

Case Study—continued

process models showed who in our client and who in the services company performed what activities. In the event of a transition, the services company activities would need to be performed by someone from the backup entity instead.

The workshops provided several benefits for our client. First, some previously unrecognized dependencies on the services company were identified at the workshops. Each dependency needed to be addressed in the go-forward plans, and each had an impact on the RFP for a backup entity. Second, over 50 gaps were identified. These gaps were problems that had to be solved before a transition could occur. Most of these gaps were technical problems. For example, one gap involved IT backups and patient privacy. Every IT organization periodically creates backup tapes to make it easier to recover from a variety of IT problems. The services company tapes included patient data from our client's members as well as patient data from other services company customers. During a transition the tapes would need to be shared with the backup entity, but since the tapes contained patient data from other customers, the privacy of patients would be violated if the services company shared the tapes. To prepare for portability, the tape copy process had to be changed.

Third, the workshops supported better mutual understanding between senior management and operations. The cross-functional team was able to better understand the goals and objectives and the impact of those goals and objectives on the transition plan. For example, operations originally assumed that any transition would span 90 days. However, during the early strategy workshops, a senior manager explained that only the contract transition could span 90 days. The business processes for processing claims and issuing payments must be transitioned within 72 hours so that there are no significant interruptions to the patients and their healthcare providers. Obviously, a 72-hour transition is more difficult than a 90-day transition: it requires different processes and a different approach.

The workshops produced additional value beyond the identification of dependencies and technical gaps, or the promotion of mutual understanding of the business motivations. The workshops identified several transition processes that needed to be created—one-time processes to perform a rapid transition from the services company to a backup entity. The models produced in the workshop documented the way our client did its work. When a transition to a backup entity occurs (if it occurs), the models will be used for training that backup entity.

The workshops also looked at the technical infrastructure: the software and hardware that supports the transitioned business processes. Each application in the technical infrastructure was traced to the gaps and to the business process activities. The tracelinks help answer impact questions. If a gap is not addressed, what issues arise? If claims are transitioned first before other processes, what hardware and what applications are affected? Which organizations use that process? Which organizations use those systems? Exploring these impact questions is important to creating good plans.

Our client saw benefit in model-based workshops and benefit in the rigor that the workshops provided. The workshops helped the management team shape their approach. The workshops helped achieve consensus. The modeling allowed the company personnel to understand and articulate the scope of the RFP and required transition. Finally, the model-based workshop allowed the company to create a timely RFP.

A model-based workshop is a facilitated workshop performed for the purpose of creating business models. Model-based workshops can be performed during the conception of a project—to scope its effort—and during the execution. Model-based workshops have proven useful for many different business purposes, including developing strategy, aligning technology to business needs, rolling out solutions, implementing outsourcing, transitioning to a new software application, ensuring compliance with regulations, reorganizing, merging, planning for business continuity, improving performance, and pursuing new business.

Chapter 9 explains how model-based workshops are run. We describe phases of a workshop and types of participants as well as how to create an effective workshop and avoid some common pitfalls.

Running a Workshop

Model-based workshops can be effective if run properly. But they can fail to produce results if challenging personalities prevail. A good model-based workshop requires planning, including work before the workshop starts. A good model-based workshop involves multiple people filling different roles in the workshop itself. And the workshop facilitator must be ready with countermeasures when difficult situations arise, to ensure that the modeling effort is a success and the sponsor gains the expected results. This chapter explains how to run an effective model-based workshop.

In Chapter 8 we described workshops and explored the role of a model-based workshop. In this chapter we focus on how to run a model-based workshop: how to prepare, what to do during the workshop, and what to do afterwards.

A MODEL-BASED WORKSHOP EXAMPLE

As you recall from Chapter 8, the Mykonos CFO—Dan Massa—is concerned about the delays experienced by diners at Portia. Dan would like to explore using a restaurant paging system to both reduce those delays and improve the diner experience. In the past when Dan has proposed pagers to his colleagues on the Mykonos management team, they dismissed the idea as inconsistent with the high-end image of their restaurants. But recently they have become more receptive as they begin to notice the use of pagers at fancier restaurants—restaurants they consider their competition.

So Dan has tasked two employees in his organization with analyzing the costs of rolling out pagers at Portia. Their analysis is based on the costs incurred at Elma, another Mykonos restaurant that has already implemented pagers. Elma has a different clientele than Portia; Elma is popular with families, whereas Portia is a more typical Mykonos restaurant with a clientele of adults looking for high-end food.

You are not sure a pager system will fix Portia's problems or fit with its operations. You realize that the question is larger than technology or its cost. Mykonos management needs to understand how pagers will fit the Portia business processes and whether they are consistent with Mykonos strategies and goals. You would like to run a model-based workshop to further explore these issues and ultimately to build the business case for pagers if they look promising.

Now you need approval and buy-in for the workshop itself from your intended sponsors, the Mykonos management team. You must convince them to support the modeling effort. You pitch a model-based workshop using a short presentation detailing the reasons that the workshop will be useful. You cover what a model-based workshop will accomplish, who will be involved, and how long it will take. In the presentation you include a model value analysis (as described in Chapter 7) detailing the costs and benefits of creating business models for analyzing these questions.

You also prepare a scope chart, more for your own benefit in managing the workshop than for your sponsors. The scope chart captures the breadth and depth of modeling that will be covered in the workshops. Figure 9.1 shows the scope chart you create.

The modeling effort will focus on the two restaurants: Elma—already with pagers—and Portia. It will focus on the diner experience—the business process where diners experience delays.

After you receive the sponsor backing, you produce a detailed workshop plan. Mykonos management would like to know some details about the model-based workshops. How many are needed? How long will they take? How much will they cost? Will employees be disrupted? How many employees will be involved?

You call people you know at Portia so that you can understand how many people work there and how many business processes they support. With this knowledge you plan a sequence of three workshops. First you will hold

	In	**Out**
Breadth	▶ Elma and Portia ▶ diner business process ▶ as-is and to-be ▶ goals and strategy	▶ other restaurants ▶ Mykonos operations ▶ interactions between restaurants and Mykonos corporate
Depth	▶ diner experience from arrival to departure ▶ lunches and dinners ▶ every day of the week	▶ special events ▶ large parties ▶ holidays

FIGURE 9.1 Scope chart for a pager model-based workshop

a half-day workshop with Dan Massa and the finance organization so that you can understand their goals, approaches, and drivers. The second workshop is with Elma employees, to capture the business processes and organization of a restaurant that uses pagers. You estimate that second workshop will take a whole day. The third workshop is with employees of Portia, and it will take two whole days. Day 1 is to be spent on capturing as-is models, including the strategy and motivations of the restaurants, their organization, and their business processes. On day 2 you will evaluate the to-be models and compare the as-is and the to-be.

In your calls you identify who is to be present at each workshop and you check availability. You also have a timing dependency: the Elma workshop must occur before the Portia workshop. You schedule the workshops and create a detailed project plan.

Once your plan is approved, you execute it. You prepare for the workshop, collecting material. Finance provides you with their cost analysis of the pager systems. You call the restaurants and discover how they are organized, learn about their mission and goals, and collect their training booklets. You also get the pager system manuals from the vendor.

You work with a modeler to prepare preliminary organizational, process, and business motivation models based on your interpretation of the material you collected. You plan to use the models during the workshop if needed to help guide the discussion. You also schedule a scribe to support you during the workshops.

You talk to the general managers of Elma and Portia, explaining your plans and asking for their support. They commit to identify the subject matter experts you need. Together you work out a schedule for the workshops.

Once all your pre-work is completed, you finalize preparation for the workshops. You confirm that everyone can still attend the workshops and that an appropriately equipped conference room has been reserved. You need a white board, a projector and sufficient space for eight people.

You conduct all three workshops. You facilitate all three, with the modeler and scribe supporting you. You run the workshop according to the steps presented in Chapter 8: you make introductions, review the agenda, introduce the modeling concepts the model disciplines, and the model elements. Then you model.

After each workshop you meet with your scribe and modeler. You combine your notes, perform model cleanup and modify the models based on the notes. After the third workshop you meet again to consolidate everything you learned.

When you create the business process models during the workshops you ask how long each activity takes, who performs it, and you identify the delays—all the detail important for a business process simulation. The modeler creates a simulation to explore efficiency, resource utilization, and cost. The simulation allows you to evaluate whether the pagers reduce the delays that diners experience. (See more on simulations in Chapter 11.)

After each of the three workshops, you conduct a verification session, a two-hour meeting to verify the model. During the workshops the participants saw the models as they were created. The models were messy: sequence flows were crossed and it was not easy to see everything on a single page. Now the models have been cleaned up and are simple and attractive. Model elements are neatly placed. Each model element is described using the notes taken during the workshop. As you verify, you move through the model, clicking on elements, showing the participants what the description says and making changes in real time. You also present the simulation results. Some results are surprising and cause the participants to rethink the activity times and delays they originally provided.

The model verification sessions are shorter than the workshops. The participants are already familiar with the model they helped create. The purpose of the verification is to show them the final model and to ensure that your team did not misinterpret something or introduce errors. It also gives the participants a chance to review what they previously said and change anything that they feel does not represent their intentions.

One of the three model verification sessions is conducted remotely, using the Web conferencing application WebEx™. All the original model-based workshops were in person; workshops are more effective when conducted that way. But Elma is located in Charlotte, NC. To save on travel costs, the follow-on model verification with Elma is performed remotely, since you have already met the participants and they are familiar with the models and techniques.

The three model-based workshops are straightforward and do not require iteration. In Chapter 7 we discussed the need to create large models in iterations. If the Elma models had been more complex, multiple workshops would have been needed to complete the models. Or if some of the Portia participants had not been available for one workshop, multiple workshops would have been needed to include everyone.

Once the workshops are complete and the models verified, you conduct your final analysis and simulations. According to the models, the pagers reduce the delays by 18 percent, a significant improvement. There is also a small but real increase in efficiency as servers and waitstaff are asked less about when a table will be available. The reservations and seating processes are changed, but other business processes are unaffected. And you conclude that pagers will be accepted by the Portia clientele, with no impact to Portia's strategy, and without hurting Portia's business.

You produce a final presentation for your sponsors. In the presentation you reiterate the purpose of the workshops. You cover each workshop and who attended. You include some model diagrams to show what was created. And you share the analysis and simulation results. As a result of your work, your sponsors decides to implement pagers, first at Portia and then across other Mykonos restaurants.

PROCESS DETAILS OF MODEL-BASED WORKSHOPS

There is more to a model-based workshop than merely conducting the workshop itself. There is both preparation before the workshop and analysis and other activities after. Furthermore, a workshop rarely stands alone. As with the Portia pager experience, there are usually multiple workshops, and some smaller verification sessions. Figure 9.2 shows the process details of model-based workshop

First you pitch the idea. You will have to convince someone—a sponsor—that the workshop is worth the effort, that it will bring him value and that it should be funded and supported.

The second activity is **Scope and Plan**. You determine what will be covered in the workshop and what will not. You secure the people you need and schedule the workshop. You create a project plan: when meetings will occur and when results will be delivered from each.

During **Workshop Preparation**—the third activity—you collect existing materials: training manuals, org charts, old strategies. You use these materials to gain a better understanding of the organization, how it runs today, and the history of how it arrived at its current state. You plan the specifics of the way you will run the workshop. And you also prepare preliminary models.

The next three activities are iterative, performed once for each workshop you conduct. In the Portia pager example, there were three iterations—one for the workshop with the finance organization, once for the Elma workshop, and once for the longer Portia workshop. Within each iteration, you conduct a workshop, you combine models across workshops, and you verify the models with the workshop participants.

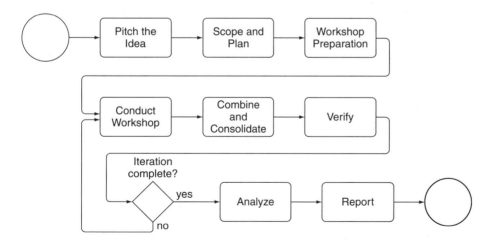

FIGURE 9.2 Process details of a model-based workshop

Then you analyze the models. You might simulate them and investigate the simulated results (as described in Chapter 11), or you could use a variety of static analysis methods (as described in Chapter 10). Sometimes you do both.

When the models and analysis are complete you prepare your final report, the last step in the process. You summarize and present the results back to the sponsor and his team.

ROLES IN A MODEL-BASED WORKSHOP

The facilitator works all activities of the model-based workshop process, from pitching the idea at the beginning to analyzing and reporting at the end. Other people support him in this end-to-end process. For example, the modeler creates models during workshop preparation and in the workshops and analyzes those models afterward. The scribe takes extensive notes. But most people involved in a model-based workshop only work the single task **Conduct workshop.** They do not help plan the workshop. They do not participate in the analysis and reporting afterward. Most people are only involved in the workshop as participants, to add their expertise and judgment to help create a better model. Most people in a model-based workshop are *participating subject matter experts*.

Participating Subject Matter Expert

A participating subject matter expert (SME) knows the area being modeled. He might know the details of the business process because he has personally worked it. Or he might know details of the business rules because he wrote some of them and enforces many of the others. A participating SME is at the workshop because his knowledge is being modeled; in a sense the facilitator and modeler and other people at the workshop are helping him create a model of what he knows.

During the workshop, the participating subject matter expert talks. He explains how he performs the business process. He explains the conditions under which a particular business rule applies. He explains the content of the work he knows. The other roles in a model-based workshop all serve to manage, organize, and model what the participating SME says: the scribe takes notes on what he says, the modeler creates models of what he says, the facilitator probes with questions or redirects to a related topic. None of these roles would be useful without the participating SME; everything revolves around him.

Every model-based workshop has at least one participating subject matter expert, and typically more than one is involved. Usually there are three to seven, each with an intimate knowledge of a different aspect of the problem. Of course, some models reflect a greater breadth of expertise; more than seven SMEs are needed. But a workshop with more than seven participating SMEs becomes hard to manage. It is better to organize multiple workshops when more than seven participating subject matter experts are needed.

The participating SMEs are the final arbiters of the content of the model. But most SMEs are not modelers, and they are not good judges of how best to model their own knowledge. There is a separation of responsibilities in a model-based workshop: the participating SMEs are ultimately responsible for the content of the model, but the facilitator and modeler are responsible for creating a good model from that content.

A participating SME needs no special training or preparation. He shows up with his knowledge of the domain and a willingness to work with the rest of the workshop participants to turn his knowledge into a model.

Contributing Subject Matter Expert

Some workshops involve another kind of SME: a *contributing subject matter expert*. The contributing SME might not know the company-specific details of the business process being modeled—she is often an outside consultant—but she knows how other companies perform that process. She might not know the business rules at this restaurant, but she knows the business rules of other restaurants.

The contributing SME brings general domain knowledge to the workshop. She understands what other companies are doing; she knows the market trends; she has the outside perspective.

Not every workshop needs a contributing SME. Sometimes the scribe can perform that role because of his deep external expertise. Sometimes no external perspective is needed. There is rarely more than a single contributing SME involved. A single outside voice suffices.

Though the participating SMEs are involved only during the workshop itself, the contributing SME helps the facilitator prepare before the workshop and helps with analysis and reporting afterward. Her perspective is useful for evaluating and understanding what the participating SMEs said.

Facilitator

In Chapter 8 we described workshop facilitation. But what does a facilitator actually do during a workshop? The facilitator stands in front, calling on participating SMEs, moving from topic to topic and from model to model. The facilitator nurtures honest discussion, and identifies and depersonalizes disagreements. The facilitator seeks consensus, and employs many techniques to achieve that consensus.

The facilitator manages conflict. Some workshops are contentious. Sometimes participants argue. Sometimes participants have different political goals and use the workshop to push their own agendas. Without facilitation, conflict can prevent a workshop from achieving its goals.

But when managed, workshop conflict can be productive. As Ronald Hiefetz notes, "conflict [within an organization] is the primary engine of creativity and innovation" [Avery 2001]. The workshop can provide a safe setting where differences of opinion can be discussed and argued. The facilitator must keep the workshop safe for conflict, defusing and depersonalizing. At times, the facilitator must have a strong personality and governs the workshop strictly, yet have a gentle demeanor and be able to get his point across. He disassociates himself from any conflict without taking sides. The facilitator sometimes asks someone to stop talking; sometimes he tries to resolve conflict directly. In difficult situations, participants in conflict can be separated into smaller concurrent sessions or into follow-on workshops held separately.

The facilitator manages time, both keeping the workshop on schedule and managing the scope against the time. This is a fundamental responsibility that is always required. Workshops always threaten to take too much time. Sometimes participants wander off topic. Sometimes participants want to dive deeper into one model, deeper than the scope of the workshop requires. The facilitator must take action, reminding the participants of the scope they all agreed to.

The facilitator manages breaks. Modeling is a thought-intensive activity that tires the participants. Breaks are important to allow everyone to stay alert. But the workshop must restart promptly after each break. All the participants are busy with their day jobs. Without careful time management of the breaks, they are likely to take too long.

Sometimes a model is not completed within the planned time. That can be OK. It is better to move on to the next model, finish it on time, and get more models completed. This situation is similar to getting stuck on one problem when taking an exam. Staying with one model and taking up a lot of extra time might allow you to complete that model but at the price of not getting to the others you could have completed. You might complete one model instead of completing half a model and five others. The facilitator makes these tradeoff judgments, deciding when it is better to move to the next model and when completion is better.

The facilitator manages voting. Often the state of the participants needs to be sampled. Does everyone agree that the process is correct as it is displayed? What are the right priorities for goals and problems? What is the best order for proposed initiatives to address the needs of the organization? The facilitator needs to use voting techniques to ensure that voices are heard. In an open, uncontentious workshop, a vote can be as simple as a show of hands or going around the room asking for each participant's opinion. In a more politically charged workshop, some attendees are reluctant to express an opinion that differs from that of their management. Then a secret vote might be required. And though voting techniques are useful to sample the opinion of a group, the facilitator needs to be savvy about the relative importance of the people voting. Not every vote in a workshop is equal. For example, a sponsor's vote is usually more important than the vote of someone else.

Facilitating a model-based workshop requires skills, both skills in general workshop facilitation and skills in business modeling. Of course, workshop facilitation skills are important: the facilitator must be accomplished at managing groups, managing conversations, navigating politics, and steering through difficult social situations. But model-based workshops require more. A facilitator must understand how to create and analyze business models. The facilitator of a model-based workshop must be able to listen and model at the same time.

One way for the facilitator to acquire the needed skills is to use shadowing techniques, an apprenticeship of sorts. When *shadowing*, the facilitator attends a model-based workshop facilitated by an experienced model-based workshop facilitator. The shadow facilitator observes and learns. The shadow facilitator then facilitates part of a session at the next workshop, and takes on increasing responsibility at each subsequent one.

It is also useful for the facilitator to know something about the industry of the client, the topic of the workshop, or both. He need not be an expert, but if he knows the basics he can avoid asking questions about industry terminology or topic fundamentals.

Modeler

The modeler in the workshop is responsible for creating models. There are three alternative methods of creating those models during a workshop: *note modeling*, *private modeling*, and *live modeling*. The modeler can take notes during the workshop and create the models afterward, employing note modeling. Or the modeler can use private modeling, creating models during the workshop but not showing those models to anyone during the workshop. Or the modeler can employ live modeling, creating the models during the workshop and projecting them onto a screen for everyone to see as they are created. With live modeling, the model takes shape and changes right before the participants' eyes.

Live modeling is by far the best approach. When the facilitator talks about a model element, the modeler points to it with her mouse and everyone can see what is talked about. When a participant describes a new objective—one that hasn't been discussed before—the modeler can create it, name it, type in a few words of description, and associate it with the existing goals. The participants get the sense of creating the model with their discussion. When a participant sees something he doesn't agree with, he speaks up and explains. The modeler corrects the model right then, and the participant can see it fixed as he talks. In our experience, live modeling produces both better models and more deeply invested participants.

Live modeling is the best approach, but it requires skills that most modelers do not have. The modeler must listen to the workshop discussion and model at the same time. She must model quickly—as the conversation turns from point to point, the modeler must keep up. Sometimes she must ask for clarifications, asking questions about naming, timing, delays, or business rules. The modeler needs to know when to ask those questions and when not to interrupt a participant discussion. She must be respectful of the participants and aware of the dynamics in the room.

To employ live modeling, the modeler must know the modeling tool intimately. It looks bad if the modeler is struggling with the tool: credibility is lost. The modeler must be proficient, using the modeling tool as if she has done it all her life. Furthermore, the modeler must be able to explain the models she is creating, answering any questions regarding the model and techniques.

Live modeling also requires a reliable modeling tool. We have encountered tools that crash periodically during a live modeling session. When working privately with a tool, crashes are merely annoying. But during a live-modeling session, they destroy credibility, particularly if time is then lost trying to diagnose the problem.

Often a modeler will use one of the other techniques—note modeling or private modeling—instead of live modeling, because she does not have the skills. She knows how to model, but she is not proficient enough to show everyone the models as she creates them.

Scribe

The scribe takes notes during the model-based workshop, capturing everything that is said. The scribe captures discussions, agreements, timing, organizational details, interactions, issues, and even details about how individual people act during the workshop. It is impossible for the facilitator or the modeler to take good notes; they are busy doing other things during the workshop. So the scribe must take all the notes for all three.

The scribe is at the workshop just to take notes. The scribe must not be selective; he must take voluminous notes about everything since it is often not clear during a workshop what is more important and what is less so. Sometimes the notes are referenced days, weeks, or months later. Unless the notes are detailed, no one will remember what happened at the workshop or why something was modeled the way it was.

The scribe does not need to know how to model, but it is helpful if the scribe is familiar with the model disciplines and the modeling techniques. It is also helpful if the scribe has some familiarity with either the organization or the business problem. It makes the whole modeling team seem more organized and knowledgeable. When the scribe contributes to the discussion—even a little—the contribution avoids questions about the scribe's value.

Sponsor

The sponsor sponsors the workshop. He uses his executive authority to secure the commitments needed to run the workshop. If there are costs involved—for example, if the facilitator and modeler are outside consultants—the sponsor covers the cost. Even if there is no direct cost, there is an opportunity cost of the workshop because the time of every participant is valuable. The sponsor secures their time and their commitments.

Typically, the workshop is motivated by a sponsor's specific need or desired outcome. The sponsor wants a problem resolved, a question answered, or an assumption validated. His desired outcome sets the overall goal for the workshop.

Before the workshop, the facilitator and modeler meet with the sponsor, to get his commitment for the workshop. The sponsor must ensure the right participants are identified, and that they actually attend.

The sponsor also sets the overall tone for the workshop. Typically the sponsor makes the opening remarks, explains the expected outcome, and introduces the modeling team. The sponsor also emphasizes the importance of the effort and his expectation that the participants cooperate, speak freely, and enjoy the experience.

CHALLENGING PERSONALITIES IN A MODEL-BASED WORKSHOP

Most of the people in the workshop have the same role: they are participating SMEs. But in practice the participating SMEs behave differently. Each participant has his own personality. The personalities play off one another in a workshop, making each workshop unique.

The mix of attendees at a workshop sometimes presents challenges. Some people are disruptive; others hijack a workshop to fit their personal causes. Others are quiet and do not participate. If the workshop is disrupted or if the participation is uneven, you will not get consensus and you will not be able to create the models you need. Your workshop will fail.

As the facilitator, the workshop success rests with you. You must identify the various personalities and handle them. To help you envision the personalities you will encounter, we have described a few of the common ones, giving each an animal name based (loosely) on an animal that exhibits similar behavior.

The Mouse

The mouse is quiet. She is a participant, but she does not actually participate much in the workshop. Her lack of participation can be due to a variety of causes. The mouse might be shy and reluctant to talk in a group setting. Or perhaps she feels intimidated by more powerful or more aggressive participants. The mouse is unsure of herself. She has little confidence in her opinions and is afraid of ridicule. So she is quiet rather than risking participation.

To involve the mouse, you must take action. As the facilitator, you must ask her for her opinion. You can use facilitation techniques that require everyone to voice their thoughts—for example, by circling around the room person by person and asking each person in turn for his or her view.

Even when she participates, the mouse might not voice her true thoughts. For example, when you work with the group to model a business strategy, the mouse will agree with everyone else about what the business should do rather than take a stand. To reduce this effect, you can use anonymous voting techniques to ensure that her true voice is heard.

The Bulldog

The bulldog is aggressive. You will recognize the bulldog because he will challenge you and challenge other participants from the beginning of the workshop. Often he will start by questioning the usefulness of the workshop itself because—for some reason unknown to you—he does not want to be there.

The bulldog does not want to be there for one of several possible reasons. Maybe the bulldog wants to be in control. He did not organize the workshop, and he cannot control it. Maybe the bulldog does not like listening to other people's opinions. Maybe the bulldog does not like consensus. He perceives meetings in general—and workshops in particular—to be a waste of time. Maybe the bulldog is unfamiliar with modeling and feels threatened.

The bulldog will disrupt. He will challenge you, asking questions such as "Why are we here?" He will make comments like "This is not useful." or "I think this is a waste of time."

You have to manage the bulldog quickly. You can attempt to ask him to wait and see the value, or say "Let's stick with this for now and you will soon see the results" or even "We can discuss this offline, but for now let's focus on this organizational model."

Sometimes you will need to take action. Sometimes the bulldog must simply be removed from the workshop so that progress can be made with the other participants. You can approach the sponsor (at a break) and ask that the bulldog be removed. If the bulldog is critical to the model you are building, you will need to schedule a separate one-on-one meeting with him. (And bulldogs are much easier to manage one on one.)

For bulldogs, it helps to be prepared. Your sponsor might be able to identify the potential bulldogs, so that you avoid surprises. Prior to the workshop, you can strategize with your sponsor about who to watch for bulldog behavior and how to handle such behavior should it arise.

The Prairie Dog

The prairie dog is nervous and afraid. He has seen business process reengineering efforts that result in workforce reduction. He worries about his job and suspects that he has been invited to the workshop because his job is in jeopardy. The prairie dog is careful about what he says. He is more concerned with protecting his position and with how his statements will be interpreted than with the business problem that motivated the workshop.

Sometimes his concerns are warranted. Sometimes model-based workshops do result in workforce reductions or in other changes that the prairie dog would not welcome. The modern workplace is an uncertain environment. And if a model-based workshop did not have the potential to transform the business, would it really be worth your time and trouble?

But some model-based workshops are not aimed at workforce reductions or at any change that should threaten the prairie dog. If your workshop does not threaten any positions, you should explain that. You can address the prairie dog concerns when you introduce the workshop. When you explain the purpose of the workshop, you will alleviate the prairie dog concerns.

What do you do if your workshop is in fact aimed at efficiency or at reducing headcount? What do you do if the concerns of the prairie dog are valid? There are several approaches. You can introduce the workshop by describing its purpose as *improving* efficiency and understanding what problems the individuals and team are facing. By solving problems and reducing bottlenecks you will help the prairie dog perform his job better. He could then contribute his issues and knowledge and be engaged, understanding you are there to help.

But sometimes it is better to be brutally honest. If the ultimate purpose of the workshop is improving efficiency so that headcount can be reduced, it is better to present that purpose at the beginning. Courage can be contagious, even for prairie dogs.

As the facilitator, you need to be attuned to the audience and the way they will perceive the workshop. Making the participants feel at ease regardless of the workshop purpose is critical to the success of the modeling effort. In some cases being up-front about the real reason for the workshop might be the best approach. You will have to gauge each situation and discuss the right approach with your sponsor because he knows the participants and can predict their reactions.

The Pig

The pig is self-centered. The sponsor has a purpose for the workshop, but the pig is at the workshop for a completely different purpose. The pig wants to control the workshop and use it to push his own agenda. The pig is not open-minded. Most participants contribute their own opinions and then listen to others. But the pig wants only to talk and not to listen to anyone else.

As the facilitator, you must convey how the workshop incorporates everyone's voice. You must pay attention to the pig since he often has good ideas, perspectives, or knowledge. You need to direct the pig and do so constructively. Listen and make sure he is heard, but cut him off and give others an opportunity to be heard as well.

Voting techniques help manage the pig. The voting—whether anonymous or not—shows how the group thinks and exposes the pig for what he is. It lets everyone see that the pig holds a minority view.

The Cat

The cat is independent and has a short attention span. Though attending your workshop, he is really running his own. While you are working with the rest of the participating subject matter experts to capture business rules, he is talking with another participant about the previous model, the rumored corporate reorganization, or what a mutual friend did the week before.

The cat does not mean to disrupt, but his side talk interferes with the workshop progress. He often needs to be brought back to the content of the workshop. You need to catch him wandering off and then politely ask him to end the side conversation, and focus on the model you are creating.

The Crab

The crab always disagrees. Crabs move sideways and backward, but they will not help move your workshop forward. The crab is a contrarian: the topic is not critical; the issue at hand is not important; the model does not matter. The crab will always find something he dislikes or disagrees with.

Unlike the pig or bulldog, the crab is not pushing a personal agenda. His crabbiness is matter of personality rather than political interest. Often a crab is just unhappy—with his job, with how his day is going, with one of the team members, or with you and the workshop. He finds many opportunities to disagree.

A crab often adds value by pointing out the problems and shortcomings with a model or with a proposed solution to a business problem. If managed properly his crabbiness can be useful, but if he is too vocal he can disrupt the workshop. He can also dampen the enthusiasm of other participants, casting a negative shadow on the workshop.

How should a crab be managed? As the facilitator, you can recognize his negative contributions and turn to others for positive solutions to the problems he raises. For example, when he points out a problem with a proposed business process redesign, you can ask other participants how the problem could be addressed. Sometimes a crab cannot be managed in this way, and you simply need to remove him from the workshop.

The Otter

The otter is social and playful. He does not prepare for workshops, he does not bother understanding the purpose of the workshop, and he does not follow the modeling. The otter does what is comfortable for him: he socializes.

A workshop is always a social event. There is always some small talk, some wordplay, and some gossip exchanged at every workshop. For more than a few participants, workshops are fun precisely because they are social; some participants delight in another opportunity to work with their colleagues.

But the otter takes this normal workshop socializing too far. The otter is all play and no work. In the middle of focused discussion about a model, he starts an unrelated conversation. During a debate about the appropriate tactics for achieving a strategy, he segues into a joke. The otter's playful acts do not advance the goals of the workshop.

Table 9.1 Summary of Challenging Personalities

	Behavior	How to Manage
Mouse	Quiet and tentative	Ask for opinion, actively include
Bulldog	Aggressive and challenging	Rebuff, maybe remove
Prairie Dog	Nervous and afraid	Explain workshop purpose and results
Pig	Controls for his benefit	Acknowledge, cut off, and direct
Cat	Independent and wandering	Cut off and refocus
Crab	Disagrees and criticizes	Recognize and involve, maybe remove
Otter	Playful and not serious	Remind purpose

As the facilitator, you must ask the otter to be quiet. You must remind him about the purpose of the workshop. The otter does not have an agenda and is not aggressive; once asked he will stop playing and participate.

The Whole Workshop Menagerie

You can prepare to manage the challenging personalities in a workshop by understanding the range of personalities you can encounter. Table 9.1 lists all the personalities we have described and how to handle each.

You can plan to manage challenging personalities, but planning does not help much. Each workshop has a different collection of participants and a different combination of personalities. Each workshop has different dynamics; you must manage each differently.

Other aspects of the workshop do benefit from planning. There are other actions you can take to run a smooth and productive workshop.

CREATING A PRODUCTIVE WORKSHOP

A model-based workshop consumes time. All the workshop participants spend time at the workshop itself: 4 hours or 8 hours or however long the workshop takes. And as we showed in Figure 9.2, there is further time spent before and after the workshop by the facilitator and the modeler: time scoping and planning, time preparing, time cleaning up and analyzing the models, time creating the report.

A model-based workshop usually incurs expenses as well. Minor expenses include the meals and snacks that are generally provided during a workshop, and the provisioning of a suitable meeting room for the workshop. Larger expenses include travel costs if some of the participants live in other locations. If the facilitator, modeler, or other model-based workshop participants are employed by another company, their consulting time is an expense as well.

Because a model-based workshop consumes time and money, it must produce significant business value—more value than the time and money it consumes. When you facilitate a model-based workshop, the business value you must create is a high hurdle; it drives much of your activity before and after the workshop. There are many things you can do before, during, and after a model-based workshop to make it productive and create the significant business value you need.

As the facilitator, you need to ensure everyone—every workshop participant—has a common understanding of the purpose and expected outcomes of the model-based workshop. Although time-consuming, it is often valuable to call participants individually prior to the workshop. On each of those calls you explain the purpose and expected outcomes of the workshop and why the person you are calling is important to the workshop success. We have found that this individual-by-individual explanation and appeal leads to fewer no-shows and more participation. Then when the workshop is held you start the session by reminding everyone of the purpose and expected outcomes.

It is important to understand the organizational environment you are entering. If you are not already deeply knowledgeable about the organization, you should meet with the sponsor of the model-based workshop and ask him questions about the participants and the organization. Who are the challenging personalities? What are the politics that different participants might push? Are there any topics that should be avoided? Are there sensitive issues—e.g., regarding outsourcing or workforce reduction—that will make the atmosphere more difficult?

As the facilitator, you are responsible for keeping the workshop interesting to the participants. Some workshops are inherently interesting to the participants. When there is uncertainty about the organization's strategy—and interest among the participants about getting the strategy right—a strategy workshop will be inherently interesting. Workshops that employ live modeling are always interesting for participants, no matter what the topic of the workshop. Participants are fascinated watching their words shape a model projected for all to see.

But what do you do if your workshop is not inherently interesting and if your modeler is not skilled enough to employ live modeling? You must employ techniques to keep their interest. You can use a white board and sticky notes to mock up a model, to draw out the new business process. Mocking up a model visually with sticky notes is not as interesting for the participants as live modeling, but it is far better than just listening to each other talk.

Typically one workshop is not enough. As we showed in Figure 9.2, a series of model-based workshops is generally necessary to produce the business models. And the workshops themselves can be part of a larger effort—part of a project or a sales pursuit. But each workshop in the series must in itself produce business value for the participants. If a workshop does not produce value, you will lose commitment for and participation in subsequent workshops. Your sponsor might even lose confidence in your approach and cancel the remaining workshops. So, at the end of a workshop, the models produced should be valuable in their own right.

How can you ensure that the models produced in a single workshop are valuable? Each workshop must have a clear goal. Each workshop must focus on a manageable chunk of the business problem. If the workshop is three days long, you can probably create a motivation model and create some as-is and to-be processes. If the workshop is only three hours long, your goals will be more modest, perhaps only part of the motivation model or a single organization model. But you must organize the workshops so that the models you create are valuable.

Create a clear workshop agenda and an appropriate allotment of time. Do not try to do too much during the workshop. Doing too much tires all the workshop attendees, and reduces the quality of what is produced. At the beginning of each session within a model-based workshop, clarify how long the session will last and what modeling will be performed. For example, you might allot two hours for a business organization model and three hours for each of two business processes. Even if you have not completed the model in the scheduled time, you will get a chance to return to it. As we explained in Chapter 7, modeling is iterative. You will refine the model later.

Take whatever time is offered. You might know that a thorny business motivation model will take six hours, yet your participants will only give you two, either because of scheduling conflicts or due to reluctance to involve themselves in an effort they expect to be waste of time. Don't postpone the workshop until you can get all six hours; you might never get them. Instead, accept the two hours and make them productive and valuable. Once the participants see the value, they will find the remaining four hours in their schedules. They might even find the time that day to stay beyond the two hours scheduled. In our experience, once participants are engaged and they see value, they want to complete the models. Their schedules suddenly clear.

Explain the model elements and the meaning of each. Some of the participants in your workshop will not have seen (for example) a business process model before. Others will have worked with business process models, but models defined in a looser manner, without the precision around activities, sequence flows, message flows, and gateways. If your participants do not understand what they are seeing, they will lose interest and they will not be able to contribute to constructing the models. Explain the basics at the beginning of the workshop or before a new modeling discipline is used. Show a simple example and highlight each of the modeling elements and its purpose.

Take breaks. Modeling is a rigorous mental exercise and can be tiring. Schedule regular breaks between large chunks of modeling. You can also use breaks when you sense that the team is bored or drifting or that conflicts are forming. Allow tempers to cool before you restart.

Manage the breaks with care. If you schedule a 15-minute break, some participants will take 20 or even 30 minutes, catching up on phone calls and email. This *break creep* is natural and understandable: the participants are all busy professionals with many pressures and demands. But break creep reduces the modeling you achieve. And if the whole team is not present you will not be able to reach true consensus on any contentious issues.

Gathering participants after a break is difficult and frustrating, particularly when some are on their phones. Fortunately you have a powerful tool to eliminate break creep: embarrassment. When you take a break, announce the time everyone is expected to return and the embarrassing penalty for anyone who is late. We find that requiring a latecomer to dance in front of the workshop to a classic 1970s funk track is an effective penalty. Then when the break is almost done, you can play the classic song. The music alerts everyone that the break is finishing and reminds them of the embarrassing penalty for being late. Almost everyone wants to avoid dancing in front of their colleagues.

Your preparation before the workshop makes the workshop itself more productive. If the purpose of the workshop is to create a business motivation model, you can collect materials on the business problems and other influencers facing the organization. You can also talk with participating subject matter experts before the workshop to learn more about how they see the influencers. Then, during the workshop, if the conversation stalls, you can inquire about an influencer you learned from your research or from your conversations.

Make sure the participants you need will actually attend the workshop. Often a participating subject matter expert will become too busy and designate someone else to attend "on his behalf." But does the designee actually have the expertise? If not, he will not be able to help create the model. Nothing is as frustrating as asking questions of a purported SME and eliciting the responses "I am not sure" or "I need to ask Joe."

Listen carefully when the SME talks. Novice modelers and facilitators usually miss some of what the SME says. By hearing only parts, they fail to create a good model and then fail to gain the model buy-in from the SME. The SME treats the model as something odd the modeler created rather than something she cocreated with the modeler.

Plan to spend significant time modeling between workshops. We have found that after a two-hour workshop, you must perform one to three hours of modeling before you are ready for the next workshop. Similarly, after an eight-hour workshop, you should plan to perform four to 12 hours of modeling before the next. Alternating in-session time and out-session time is important, to capture everything the subject matter experts said, to refactor the model so it is simple and clean, and to prepare questions and points of departure for your next session.

How many workshops are enough? How many workshops should you plan to complete a model? The answer depends (of course) on what you are modeling and on how large and complex the model will be. But our experience is that one workshop is rarely enough. You will need at least two so the SMEs can see what has been built. Usually three or more workshops are needed.

WORKSHOP ANTIPATTERNS

In the model-based workshops we have conducted, we have seen several recurring problems. We call these problems workshop *antipatterns*. (Some readers with a background in software project management will recognize the origin of this term [Brown 1998].) Each antipattern is a common way for model-based workshops to fail.

Some of these antipatterns can be managed when they happen—during the workshop itself. But others cannot; you must avoid them in your preparation before the workshop or suffer through them when they occur.

Missing Participants Antipattern

You arrive at the workshop location. As the participants assemble you notice that the IT director is missing. Your heart sinks. Without him, the workshop is going to be a waste of time. Only he understands the mission of the IT organization. Only he knows the history of why the IT organization is organized the way it is. You call his cell phone but reach his voicemail. It doesn't look like he is going to be at the workshop.

Your workshop fails before it starts. You already know you will not achieve the workshop goals. As the workshop progresses, the rest of the participants see the failure and start to consider it a waste of time. One leaves at a break and never returns. Some of the others begin to question the usefulness of the workshop.

For a workshop to be productive, all the required participants must show. If the workshop is missing participants, the models will be skewed, lacking the detail that the missing expertise would have provided. You will need to meet afterward with the missing participants to fill in that detail and then verify the resulting model changes with the original group. It is more productive to have all the right people in the room at the same time.

The missing participant might be a bulldog—someone who just does not want to participate. But typically this antipattern arises because of the culture of the organization. You can discover a lot about the organization in planning meetings before the workshop. Are they taking the workshop seriously? Are they enthusiastic about the workshop? Was the scheduling of the planning meeting difficult? Were there no-shows at the planning meeting itself?

As a facilitator, you can mitigate this risk in a couple of ways. You can call each participant the day before the workshop and confirm his or her attendance. You can locate the workshop in a conference room near the work areas of the key participants, so you can walk them to the workshop if necessary.

Missing Equipment Antipattern

You arrive at the workshop early so that you can set up your computer, load your presentations, run the modeling tool, and arrange the room. But when you arrive, you realize that the room is missing equipment. It has neither a laptop projector nor a white board. You begin to panic. How can you do live modeling if you cannot display the models on a screen? How can you create business process models if you do not have a white board? With some difficulty you find another room two floors up with a white board and a projector. Everyone moves. But you have failed the first impression. As a facilitator you need to demonstrate your management skills and introduce your model-based workshop on a positive note. Now the participants think you are incompetent.

Model-based workshops don't require a lot of equipment or supplies. You need only a room with sufficient space and adequate ventilation, a laptop, a projector and a blank wall on which to project, a white board and markers, and perhaps sticky notes for voting. But without the equipment, your workshop is difficult. Participants need to see the models to understand and relate to them. If all you can do is discuss the models abstractly, they will not understand and you will not be able to create good models. The workshop will be confusing.

To avoid this antipattern, find out about the room you will be using. If possible, visit the room before the workshop to see what equipment is available. You don't need much, but make sure you have it all. Another approach to avoiding this antipattern is to bring everything yourself. Create a *workshop toolkit*: laptop, projector and spare bulb, sticky notes, markers, and clear cling sheets that turn any wall into a white board. A digital camera is also useful, to photograph white board model diagrams. A prepared facilitator impresses participants.

Multitasking Antipattern

You are in the middle of running a workshop, describing the elements of a process model in preparation for creating one. Then you notice one participant is not listening. Joe—the information technology director—is typing into his laptop, probably checking email but maybe even playing solitaire. Someone else is distracted. Nancy from Procurement is checking her PDA. Is she looking at her schedule? Texting with a colleague? What is that music? Someone's cell phone is ringing, playing the opening riffs of "Sweet Home, Alabama" as he walks to the hallway to take the call. And he does not even wait until he is out of the room to start talking!

Many business professionals are proud of their "multitasking" skills—of their alleged abilities to do two things at once. Computers multitask well, but for people, multitasking is largely a myth. Doing anything of business value requires focused attention. Or as the Roman philosopher Publius Syrus said, "To do two things at once is to do neither" [Bartlett 1904]. In our experience, people who think they multitask are in fact poor performers.

In particular, to create a valuable workshop, you need the focused attention of all workshop participants. But how can you get this attention in our modern world, with cell phones, PDAs, and laptops? You must be firm. Establish some simple rules at the beginning of the workshop: no cell phones, no laptops, no PDAs, no email. When participants forget these rules during the workshop, reinforce them.

A milder approach is to have the participants discuss and agree on the rules collectively. The participants might decide to ban laptops and turn cellphones silent, but answer emergency calls from Dan related to the quarterly financial close (for example). The advantage of letting the participants decide is that they will police each other, freeing you from cell phone enforcement duty.

Either approach will work, but you must do something. If you do nothing, your workshop will suffer the slow death of 40 phone calls.

Weak Sponsor Antipattern

At the beginning of your workshop, the sponsor stands up and speaks. But instead of explaining the purpose and importance of the workshop and instead of encouraging the participants, he says little. He just introduces you and sits back down. Within an hour, three participants have left. And another participant is showing signs of the bulldog.

A weak sponsor leads to a weak workshop. If the participants do not see enthusiasm from the sponsor, they decide it is not important. They decide to get it done and move on. They see the modeling effort as yet another pointless exercise producing a report that no one will read.

Beyond expressing enthusiasm, a sponsor needs to perform several activities before the workshop. A weak sponsor will fail to act. He will not talk to the participants, explaining to each why her participation is important. He will not send the required emails. He will not ask participants to schedule their time. When you ask him about the hidden agendas and difficult personalities, he will not know.

To avoid this antipattern, you must coach your sponsor. You must tell him what he needs to say. You must ask him to schedule the necessary meetings and check that he does. You can even draft the emails he should send and ask him to send them. It is much easier for some sponsors to revise your email than to compose their own.

Biased Facilitator Antipattern

You are facilitating a strategy workshop for the Mykonos management team. As you create the business motivation models, Harry, the Mykonos Chief Technology Officer, proposes a new strategy for improving customer satisfaction. He proposes to build a portal, a Website where restaurant general managers can share experiences about successful customer-related techniques. But you have seen this before at many different companies, and you know what will happen. The portal will be built, and no one will contribute. The restaurant general managers are busy running their restaurants. Without a strong reason to contribute, they won't. And without contributed material, no one will look there for new techniques. They will talk to other GMs they know, read the trade literature, or even search the Web before they will try the portal again. The portal will die from a lack of interest.

As you look around the room, you wonder if anyone else is aware of this phenomenon. Are you the only person who has seen portals die? You would like to provide some guidance, but is that outside the boundaries of your role as a facilitator? You are torn.

The facilitator is supposed to facilitate, not participate. To retain the trust of the participants, the facilitator needs to stay neutral and even-handed, focused on the processes of facilitation and modeling rather than the content of the workshop. But this is difficult. As the facilitator, you might be from the same company as the participants. You could have an interest in the outcome. Or you could just be knowledgeable about some workshop topics.

Facilitators often become engrossed in the content of the workshop and try to contribute. But when you participate, you are not facilitating. You are not managing the discussion or the time. You are creating content. Worse, the participants will see your actions as corrupt, an abuse of your position. And they will start to suspect everything you do, not just your newly expressed opinions about the content, but even the standard facilitation techniques of asking others for their opinions, calling for votes on open questions, and moving the discussion to a new topic. You will lose their trust.

Like any kind of corruption, this antipattern is completely avoidable if you exercise self-control. Stay in your facilitator role. If you need to influence the discussion, do so discretely through a contributing subject matter expert or a sympathetic participant. If you need to participate, find another facilitator to take your place for that workshop and become either a participant or a contributing subject matter expert yourself.

Rejected Model Antipattern

When you work with SMEs, one of your goals is that they invest in the model you are building together. At first they will think of the model as your model, not theirs. Not feeling comfortable with the modeling tool, the model elements or modeling in general, they will claim the model does not represent their thinking. This can be confusing. You captured what they said, and you showed them the resulting model. Why don't they feel ownership?

At first it is natural for a SME to think of the model as your model, but after two or three workshops, you want her to own the model, to feel like she created it as much as you did, to have her think of it as *her* model. When she feels that she owns the model, verification becomes easier. She will examine the model, find mistakes, and bring them to your attention rather than waiting for you to ask her about the accuracy of each model element.

Even better, when the SME owns a model, she will introduce it to others. The model gains credibility because it is a product of an insider—someone who is recognized inside the company as an expert has loaned the model some of her own credibility.

How do you achieve that kind of SME ownership? Often it happens naturally with time. With each workshop the SME becomes more invested. But you can also increase the likelihood of SME investment by employing *model echoing*, by listening carefully to what she says and attempting to put everything she says into the model. When the SME says something you echo it in the model, perhaps with a new model element, perhaps with a new association between existing model elements, perhaps with a changed description on an existing element. With model echoing, the work session becomes a conversation between the SME talking with words and you answering with model elements.

Model echoing has a much bigger impact when you are live modeling. When the SME sees her words today change the model tomorrow, at the next work session, she might make the connection and feel some investment in the model. But when the SME can see her words taking shape in the model immediately after she says them, there is an opportunity for a much bigger investment. Model echoing via live modeling can have a powerful emotional effect.

Of course, not everything the SME says really deserves to be in the model. SMEs wander out of scope, talking about topics that are not the focus on the model. And SMEs mix the important and the trivial. How do you practice model echoing yet keep a model in scope and on target?

A good approach is to model what the SME says as she says it and then prune the model later. You can prune the model in-session with her, explaining that this element is really not so important and that element is really out of scope. Or you can prune the model later out of session and then explain what you have done at the beginning of the next workshop. Using either pruning method you will attain the benefits of echo modeling and still keep the model in scope.

Participants Modeling Antipattern

You are live modeling an existing procurement business process with a team of participating SMEs and things go awry. You are working with the participants to name an activity, and Nancy insists that the name should be **Review Restaurant Supplies with Each of the General Managers.** You think this name is far too long but you say nothing. Then Beth wants you to include a "box" for the inventory system that is used in the supply review. You explain that in a business process model an application is shown in a swimlane, not as an activity. But Beth says, "I just want a box on that picture to show the RESTINV system. Can't your tool make a box?" So your modeler adds an activity and names it RESTINV, even though the RESTINV is not actually an activity. Then Roger objects to the parallel gateway that joins three sequence flows together. He doesn't understand it, and he asks your modeler to just remove it. You know you are creating a bad model, but you are not sure what to do. Isn't the client always right?

Sometimes participating SMEs want to create and change the models themselves, either using the modeling tools directly or instructing you on what model elements should be created and where they should be placed. This is an encouraging development, since it only happens when the SMEs become deeply invested in the models. They will only want to create a model when they care about it.

However this development is also dangerous. SMEs do not know how to create coherent, simple, and accurate models, and the vast majority of them are not interested in investing the time and trouble to learn. Without training and experience, they think of the model elements as boxes and lines rather than activities and sequence flow, or goals and associations, or whatever the model elements are in the discipline you are using. To paraphrase humorist P. J. O'Rourke, turning over modeling decisions to a subject matter expert is like giving whiskey and car keys to teenage boys.

You must be firm. A good approach is to adopt the *modeling stance* with subject experts. "Ms. SME, you are an expert in the supply chain process of your business, and I trust your judgments on all supply chain matters. I am an expert in modeling, and I ask you to trust my judgments in how to translate your supply chain expertise into an effective model." The modeling stance establishes business modeling as something that has its own expertise and frames the problem of modeling as requiring both their subject matter expertise and yours, both subject matter expertise in a specialized company matter (e.g., their supply chain business process) and subject matter expertise in business modeling. By adopting the modeling stance, you remind them of your deep respect for their expertise but reserve the modeling decisions for yourself.

Case Study

In the United States, each of the 50 states enforces its own labor laws. Each state regulates the way a business located in that state can employ people, and each regulates the wages, salaries, and benefits that a business must provide to its employees. The states enforce safety laws to prevent employees from being hurt. The states enforce laws to prevent employees from being exploited by their employers. And of course sometimes things do not work out as planned. Businesses sometimes shut down or reduce their workforces and employees find themselves looking for new work. The states provide unemployment benefits to those who lose their jobs. To fund these benefits, the states tax employers against the risk of their employees becoming unemployed.

In New York State, these responsibilities are shouldered by the New York Department of Labor. In addition to its regulatory work, NYDOL offers unemployment insurance and other unemployment benefits. Managing unemployment benefits is complex, partly because such benefits must meet the requirements of the US Federal government. The management of unemployment benefits involves registering employers and employees, verifying that employees are eligible for unemployment benefits, processing claims and payment, and handling appeals if benefits are denied.

A few years ago, NYDOL realized that it needed to overhaul its existing computer systems and business processes to meet the evolving needs of New York businesses and the employees of those businesses. NYDOL's older systems could not be easily changed, and this lack of system agility affected the department's ability to perform its mission [Welborn 2006].

A modeling team was enlisted to perform business process reengineering and support the new system implementation. The processes they examined included collecting unemployment taxes, granting unemployment benefits, and the related hearing and appeals process. The modeling team created as-is models and to-be models of those processes. They performed organizational analysis on the to-be future state to develop plans for resources change management. They defined business performance metrics for monitoring the future state. They analyzed the to-be models to determine requirements for the new system implementation.

But the NYDOL subject matter experts rejected the models. They were not familiar with the details of the models and did not feel ownership. They did not understand the modeling approach or the modeling tool.

The models were also inconsistent. Models for different processes were detailed to different extents. Some models were less detailed, some more. It was difficult for the SMEs to understand the models and interpret them consistently.

We were asked to improve the models to make them acceptable to NYDOL. After meeting with the SMEs it became apparent that the models were created in lane isolation—different SMEs had worked on small sections of the models but had not seen the whole. We used a three-step approach to improve the models.

First, we cleaned up the as-is models, refactored them, made them consistent, and improved their visual appeal. We applied the best practices

Continued

Case Study—continued

described in Chapter 7. Common naming conventions, style, and diagram size were used to make the models easy to understand. Simple graphical treatments were applied to make the models attractive.

Second, we held workshops with the SMEs at an offsite location so that there would be no distractions, no phone calls, and no emails. The workshops were held on alternating days, allowing model cleanup on the days between the workshops.

Initially the workshops showed both the original (rejected) models and the improved models (cleaned up, refactored, and made consistent). We wanted to show the SMEs that nothing was lost between the original and improved models. Though the improved models looked different, they still contained all the content of the original models. The NYDOL SMEs accepted the improved models.

Subsequent workshops focused on the to-be processes. We facilitated the SMEs in creating to-be process models, using live modeling to create the models with them. After an opening plenary session, the SMEs were divided among the business processes each understood, and model-based workshops for these business processes were conducted in parallel. A couple of joint workshops were held to handle connection points between two business processes.

Third, some employees of NYDOL elected to learn the modeling tool and become business modelers. We held training sessions, teaching both the tool and more general business modeling principles. By the final workshop some NYDOL employees were able to model themselves and to perform their own modeling modifications and cleanup.

After six weeks of working with NYDOL, we transitioned the models to them. They took complete ownership and maintained the models with their own modelers.

Running a model-based workshop involves several steps—from pitching the value of a workshop to conducting the workshop, analyzing the results, and presenting a report to the sponsor.

A facilitator leads a model-based workshop. She is supported by a team that includes a modeler, a scribe, a contributing subject matter expert, and several participating SMEs. Some participating SMEs have challenging personalities and require careful management to achieve good results from the workshop. There are also common antipatterns that must be avoided or managed.

This chapter and the two previous describe how to create good business models. The next three chapters explain how to use those business models to create business value, starting with Chapter 10, which explains how to analyze a business model.

Business Model Analysis

Much can be learned about a business by analyzing its business models. There are several different techniques for business model analysis—techniques appropriate for different business situations. This chapter explains how to analyze a business model.

The Mykonos attorneys are worried. Last month a prestigious Los Angeles restaurant was sued by a customer who claimed he became sick after eating undercooked beef. The restaurant settled the suit for $3.4 million, despite some doubt whether the customer became sick because of their food or even whether the customer was sick at all. Mykonos was not involved in this lawsuit, but the Mykonos attorneys are worried nonetheless. If restaurant disease lawsuits become popular, Mykonos would seem to be an attractive target: a large cash-rich company with many restaurants cooking a great variety of food that might sound strange to jurors who are only familiar with the more mainstream fare served at Chili's™ and Applebee's™.

The Mykonos attorneys want to reduce the risk of being sued. Mykonos food is already safe; all the restaurants comply with all the local health regulations. But the attorneys want to reduce the legal risk, so they create a small task force to change policies and business processes, a disease lawsuit task force.

Fortunately for the task force, the Mykonos business processes and business rules are already modeled, as these business models—created originally for other purposes—are useful for determining what to do about the risk of lawsuits. The task force examines the business processes, looking for ways to reduce legal risk. They consider the menu creation process and introduce a new activity into the process to review new menu items for legal risk. They examine the new server hiring process and decide to add some new training for servers, so the servers can explain food preparation to customers. And because Mykonos acquires so many existing restaurants, they change the process by which restaurants are acquired, to make sure that they are not acquiring future lawsuits.

The disease lawsuit task force analyzes the existing business models to determine how they can reduce the risk of lawsuits. Their effort is an example of *business model analysis,* mentioned in Chapter 1 as one of the eight ways that a business model can create value. Business model analysis is the work of analyzing existing business models to learn more about the business. Business model analysis is about reaping value from models, using the models to discover new insights. The disease lawsuit task force uses the business process models to discover new insights into how to reduce liability risk—how to make some minor changes to the processes to have a big impact on the risk of a lawsuit.

In Chapter 7 we described several ways to improve a business model to make a model simpler and easier to understand. We analyzed business models in that chapter, but it was analysis with a different, inward focus. In Chapter 7 we were concerned with deciding whether to create a model, and we used model value analysis to make that decision. We were also concerned with improving a model once it is created. All this analysis is about improving the modeling, analyzing a model for the benefit of the model. By contrast, our focus in this chapter is outward. The business model analysis described in this chapter is analysis with the purpose of improving the business being modeled, or at least the purpose of better understanding that business.

ANALYSIS TECHNIQUES

There are several different analysis techniques, several different ways to wring insight from an existing business model. Each analysis technique has its own methods. Each technique is used for a different business purpose. In this chapter we explain four techniques, as shown in Table 10.1. *Improvement analysis* is using a model to find ways to improve the business. *Transformation analysis* is using an as-is and a to-be model to understand how a business must be transformed from the as-is to the to-be. *Impact analysis* is using a

Table 10.1 Model Analysis Techniques

Analysis Technique	Business Purpose	When Applicable
Improvement analysis	Improve the business	Always, because businesses can always be improved
Transformation analysis	Support a proposed transformation to make it easier and more likely to succeed	When there is an existing plan to transform the business
Impact analysis	Discover the consequences of a proposed change	Before a proposed change is made to the business
Acquisition analysis	Determine whether to acquire another business	When a merger or acquisition is considered

model to understand the impacts of a proposed change to the business. *Acquisition analysis* is using a model to determine whether to acquire another business.

Business change is the common thread among the four model analysis techniques. All four techniques are about business change in some way. Improvement analysis is finding useful changes to make to the business. Transformation analysis is about supporting a big change to the business—a sweeping transformation. Impact analysis is about discovering the consequences of a proposed business change. Finally, acquisition analysis is determining whether and how to undertake the dramatic change of merging with another business. Model analysis is always about business change.

Simulation could be considered a model analysis technique. Simulation is certainly a method of extracting insight from an existing model. So Table 10.1 could have included a row for simulation analysis, and we could have described simulation in this chapter on model analysis. But we did not, for two reasons. Business simulation is complex enough—and different enough from the other analyses—to warrant its own chapter, Chapter 11, the longest chapter in our book. And unlike the other model analysis techniques in Table 10.1, simulation is used for a wide range of business purposes. In fact, simulation can be used for each of the four model analysis techniques. Simulation can be used to discover ways to improve a business, to support a transformation, to understand an impact, or to analyze an acquisition. Simulation is one way to realize the model analysis techniques.

Table 10.1 is not intended to be exhaustive. There are other model analysis techniques not listed in Table 10.1 and not described in this chapter. In fact, model analysis is a creative process. When you analyze a model, sometimes none of the existing techniques fit your needs, and you must create a new technique. There is much room for innovation in analyzing business models.

IMPROVEMENT ANALYSIS

Every business can be improved. No business is perfect; there are always opportunities to make business processes faster, to improve the accuracy of decisions, or to change the organization structure in ways that improve customer satisfaction. Even when a business is well designed for a particular environment, it never stays that way. The business environment continually changes. A business that fit the environment yesterday will fail to fit today. Business improvement is a never-ending task.

A business model can be analyzed for improvement opportunities—opportunities to improve the business that is modeled. The analysis of a business model to discover improvement opportunities is called *improvement analysis* (naturally). The goal of improvement analysis is to find ways to improve the business, to use the model to better the business. Improvement analysis is not about improving the model. Improvement analysis is different from the techniques explained in Chapter 7 for making more accurate and more useful models, although sometimes opportunities for improving models are found along the way, as a side effect of performing improvement analysis.

Let's consider an example. Each Mykonos restaurant is responsible for acquiring its own cooking equipment—the ranges and ovens and broilers that it uses to prepare food. Sometimes equipment is replaced, and sometimes new equipment is purchased to augment the existing equipment. A purchasing process is followed to procure the new equipment, a process shown in Figure 10.1. The process starts when a restaurant general manager recognizes that a purchase is required. The general manger decides what to buy and prepares an equipment request. A procurement specialist from Mykonos headquarters analyzes the request and decides whether the equipment is needed. If it is in fact needed, he researches whether an alternative purchase might make more sense, whether an alternative might be cheaper or better. He forwards his recommendations to the purchasing manager, who makes the final determination of whether new

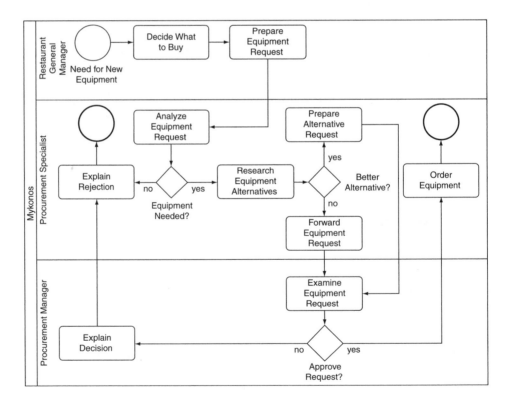

FIGURE 10.1 The equipment procurement business process

equipment is needed. If the purchasing manager approves the purchase, the procurement specialist orders the equipment. The general manager learns about the order after it is placed or after it is rejected.

Mykonos is interested in changing the procurement process. It takes too long and costs too much. There are too many handoffs, too many times that the process is handed off from one person to another. The successful acquisition of new equipment requires four separate handoffs: a handoff from the restaurant general manager to the procurement specialist to analyze the request, a handoff from the procurement specialist to the procurement manager to approve the request, a handoff back from the procurement manager to the procurement specialist to actually order the equipment, and finally a handoff back to the restaurant general manager—or at least a conversation with him to notify him that the order was placed. In one process path, four handoffs are required just to reject the request.

Can some of the handoffs be eliminated? Why are all the activities in Figure 10.1 performed? Are they all truly necessary? These questions can be answered by analyzing the motivation behind each activity. Figure 10.2 relates activities in Figure 10.1 to elements in the Mykonos business motivation model.

In Figure 10.1 the restaurant general manager decides what new equipment to buy in the activity **Decide What to Buy**. This activity realizes the Mykonos strategy of creating kitchens that are customized to the needs of the individual restaurants. Each Mykonos restaurant is different, with a different menu. So each Mykonos restaurants has a unique kitchen, one individually customized for the needs of that restaurant, reflected in the strategy **Individually Customized Kitchens**. The activity **Decide What to Buy** realizes that strategy. The same strategy is also realized by the activity **Prepare Equipment Request** and much later in the process when the equipment is actually ordered from the vendor in the activity **Order Equipment**.

Mykonos has some financial objectives and tactics to achieve those objectives. One such tactic is avoiding unnecessary investments, modeled in Figure 10.2 as **Avoid Unnecessary Investments**. Many of the activities and gateways in Figure 10.1 are performed solely to realize this tactic. For example, the procurement specialist performs the activity **Analyze Equipment Request** to determine whether the investment can be avoided. Similarly, the procurement manager plays a role avoiding unnecessary investments with the activities **Examine Equipment Request** and **Explain Decision** and the gateway **Approve Request?** Altogether seven activities and gateways in the equipment procurement process realize the tactic of avoiding unnecessary investment.

A third course of action is also realized in the Figure 10.1 process. Mykonos has established the tactic **Find Cheaper Alternatives**. The procurement specialist attempts to find those cheaper alternatives in the activities **Research Equipment Alternatives** and **Prepare Alternative Request** and in the gateway **Better Alternative?** In Figure 10.2 those three model elements all realize **Find Cheaper Alternatives**.

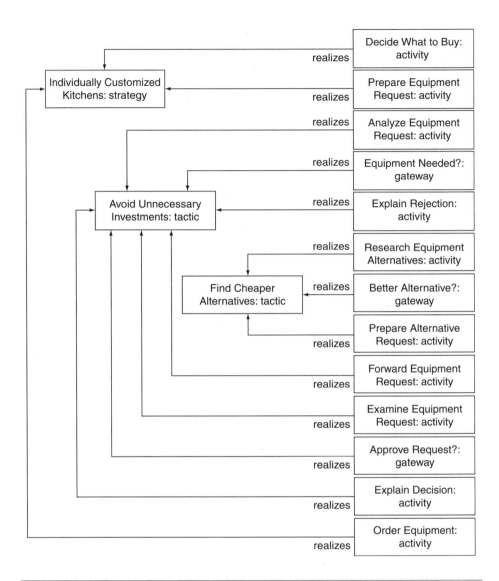

FIGURE 10.2 Motivations for the equipment procurement activities

Business Process Simplification

We have examined the business process model for the procurement process and the motivations behind each of the business process model elements. Now it is time to consider how to improve the business process, using what we know. In particular, now it is time to consider how to simplify the business process. *Business process simplification* is changing a business process, typically removing activities but also sometimes replacing activities with others. Business process simplification is performed for a business reason, either to reduce the cost of the business process, improve the quality, reduce the end-to-end cycle time, or for some other reason.

Much of Chapter 7 was concerned with *model simplification*—techniques to keep models simple to read and understand. Model simplification is an important objective but different from our focus now: business process simplification. When we perform business process simplification, we are not just changing our model of a business process, creating a simpler model to reflect the same business process. Instead we are changing the business process itself, eliminating activities that are currently performed. Chapter 7's focus was about creating a better model. Our focus now is creating a better business.

Often a business process will have some activities and gateways that are not justified by any courses of action. The process includes activities that are performed for no apparent reason, no reason beyond tradition: we have always done it this way. These unnecessary activities might once have had a rationale. Long ago they served a purpose, but the strategies and tactics of the organization changed. Now they are only vestigial organs, remnants of a half-forgotten past. And now they can be removed. Any activity or gateway that realizes no course of action today can be eliminated.

We see no vestigial activities or gateways in the procurement process. Every gateway in Figure 10.1 realizes some course of action, as shown in Figure 10.2. So does every activity. Everything in the Mykonos procurement process has a purpose.

But all three courses of action incur a cost. There are five activities and two gateways in the procurement process to achieve the tactic of avoiding unnecessary investments. Of the 13 model elements in the end-to-end process, more than half are there solely for that purpose. There must be an easier way, and there is. Instead of relying on the procurement specialist and the procurement manager, Mykonos could make the restaurant general manager responsible for avoiding unnecessary investments. The general manager could be measured by his success in managing investments, just as he is managed by his success in revenue, critic reviews, and other metrics.

Figure 10.3 shows the resulting simplified business process. The restaurant general manager decides himself whether the equipment is needed. Once he decides to purchase, the procurement specialist determines whether there are cheaper alternatives and then purchases the equipment. The whole approval and rejection process is gone.

Figure 10.4 shows how the activities and gateways in Figure 10.3 are motivated by Mykonos courses of action. Figure 10.4 has the same strategy and the same tactics as Figure 10.2. The strategy **Individually Customized Kitchens** is realized by the same three activities in Figures 10.2 and 10.4. But **Avoid Unnecessary Investments** is different. Instead of being realized by six activities and two gateways in Figure 10.2, it is realized by a single gateway in Figure 10.4: **Equipment Needed?**

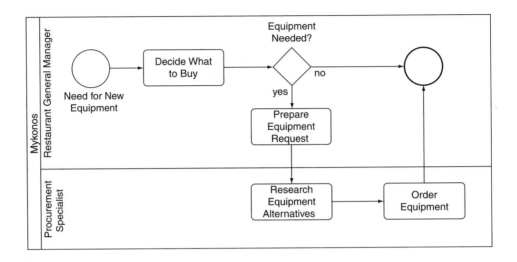

FIGURE 10.3 Equipment procurement process, simplified

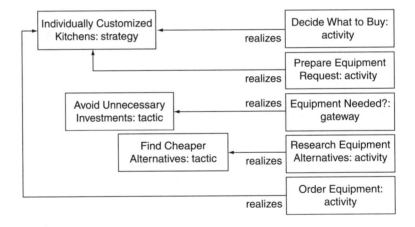

FIGURE 10.4 Motivations for simplified equipment procurement process

Course of Action Valuation

As we saw in Figures 10.1 through 10.4, the careful comparison of a process model with a motivation model can lead to a consideration of changes in the business process. It can also lead to a consideration of changes in strategy. With the model, we know what courses of action are realized by which activities and gateways. We can measure the cost of a course of action by summing the costs of all the activities and gateways that realize that cost. Then the total cost of efforts toward the course of action can be weighed against the benefits. This improvement approach is called *course of action valuation*.

Let's look again at the procurement of equipment. After examining the models in Figures 10.1 and 10.2, Mykonos personnel consider whether the tactic **Find Cheaper Alternative** is useful. Yes, Mykonos saves $100, sometimes $200, by comparison shopping for kitchen equipment when a purchase is made. But much time is spent on the extra activities. Even in the simplified process of Figure 10.3, the activity **Research Equipment Alternatives** takes 3.2 hours of work. The process is also slower. A simulation reveals that the process in Figure 10.3 takes an extra 2.7 business days to complete a purchase after the procurement specialist receives the work. The people performing the procurement specialist tasks are also doing many other more pressing activities in other processes.

Does the value of pursuing this course of action really justify the cost and time to pursue it? Mykonos might be better served by letting the restaurant general manager make the purchase, holding him responsible for the financial results, and performing an occasional audit to guard against corruption. The resulting business process is shown in Figure 10.5 and the connection to motivation elements in Figure 10.6.

Both the process shown in Figure 10.3 and the one shown in Figure 10.5 are significant simplifications over the original process of Figure 10.1. But there are some costs of making the change: the costs of training the general managers on the new process and changing the application that supports today's process. And there are risks as well. The general managers might not make good business decisions about their kitchen equipment. They might be swayed by the allure of owning the best restaurant kitchen and fail to properly consider the costs to Mykonos. Are the benefits worth the cost? Mykonos—like any organization considering a business process simplification—must weigh the risks. The business models inform that weighing.

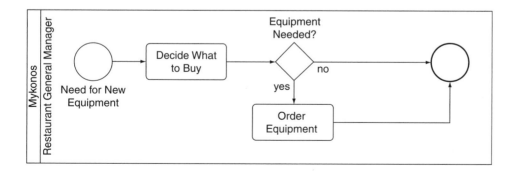

FIGURE 10.5 Equipment procurement process, further simplified

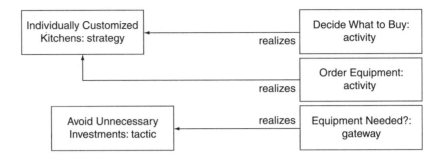

FIGURE 10.6 Motivations for further simplified equipment procurement process

Other Improvement Approaches

Business process simplification is used often; it is an important approach for improvement analysis. Course of action valuation is not used as often. In practice companies are frequently reluctant to examine the costs of their strategies. But course of action valuation is powerful. It exposes expensive strategies—strategies that sound good in theory but in practice are not worth the effort of the business process activities that implement them.

There are also other improvement approaches, other ways of analyzing a business model to discover how to improve a business. Table 10.2 lists eight improvement approaches: both the two already explained and six others. Each approach includes what is meant to be improved, whether the approach is meant to improve the business process, the organization structure, or something else. Each approach attempts to answer a question. For example, business process simplification attempts to answer the question, "Can this business process be simplified and still achieve its purpose?" And each approach includes a summary of the method—how to actually apply the approach.

TRANSFORMATION ANALYSIS

Often businesses make small, measured changes, adding a new activity to an existing process or revising one policy out of hundreds. But sometimes a business will conduct a significant *business transformation*, making a far larger change all at once. The business completely reengineers a business process from beginning to end. Or it conducts a vast reorganization, moving all employees from one organization structure to another. Or a large business has been acquired and after the acquisition it must be integrated into the business that acquired it.

Executing a business transformation is always difficult. The problem is sheer scale. It is simply much harder to make large changes to a business than to make

Table 10.2 Approaches for Improvement Analysis

Improvement Approach	Improve What?	Asking the Question	Using Method
Business process simplification	Business process	Can this business process be simplified and still achieve its purpose?	Examine the motivation of each activity to determine whether it can be eliminated or simplified. Do the same for gateways.
Course of action valuation	Business strategy	Is this course of action worth the effort?	Estimate the cost of realizing each course of action by examining the business activities that realize it. Eliminate any courses of action that are not worth the cost.
Desired action achievement	Business strategy	Are we doing anything to achieve this desired result?	Examine the courses of action that channel effort toward the desired result. Are additional courses of action needed?
Course of action validation	Business strategy	Is this course of action contributing to any desired result?	Examine the courses of action. Are any unnecessary? Is there a course of action that channels effort toward no desired result?
Decision consistency improvement	Decision making	Can this decision be made more consistently?	Examine the business rules that apply to the decision. Does everyone use the same rules? Does everyone understand the rules? Are there situations in which the rules do not apply?
Business rule simplification	Business rules and business policies	Can our business rules and policies be simplified?	Examine each business rule and business policy. Why does the directive exist? What courses of action is it

Continued

Table 10.2 Approaches for Improvement Analysis—*cont'd*

Improvement Approach	Improve What?	Asking the Question	Using Method
			based on? What desired result does it support? Is there a simpler way?
Organizational alignment	Organization structure	Is there an organizational structure that will better achieve our strategies?	Examine each strategy, including whether the strategy determines an organization unit. Should a new organization be created to achieve the strategy? How does the new organization fit with the overall organization structure?
Interaction simplification	Organization structure and interactions	Is there an organizational structure that will simplify the interactions with customers, suppliers, and other outside organizations?	Examine the interactions for duplicates. Can a reorganization reduce the duplication?

small changes. Many transformation efforts fail, and even those that succeed often achieve only some of the original goals.

Transformation analysis is the use of business models to support business transformation. The purpose of transformation analysis is very different from the focus of improvement analysis. Whereas the purpose of improvement analysis is discovering opportunities to improve a business, the purpose of transformation analysis is supporting a transformation effort, supporting an existing plan for dramatic improvement in the business. If improvement analysis is like using models to determine what to improve in a building, then transformation analysis is like using models to perform the actual improvement.

In Chapter 5, we described how several several to-be business processes can be compared to decide which to-be business process should be adopted. Transformation analysis is different. Transformation analysis is not about comparing multiple to-be models and making decisions among them. Instead transformation analysis is about driving to a single to-be that has already been determined. Transformation analysis is not about deciding, it is about executing a decision that has already been made.

Let's consider an example. After completing the improvement analysis of the equipment procurement process (as described earlier in this chapter), Mykonos decides to implement the changes. The as-is equipment procurement process is shown in Figure 10.1. The to-be process is radically simpler, as shown in Figure 10.5. Now your challenge is executing the change, transforming from the as-is process to the to-be.

You start by comparing the as-is process and the to-be, looking for activities that have changed. What activities are performed in both the as-is and the to-be but are performed differently in the to-be? One such changed activity is **Order Equipment**, the final activity in the process and the activity in which the new equipment is actually ordered. The purpose and mechanics of the activity are the same in the to-be as in the as-is, but a different person is performing the activity. In the as-is process, the procurement specialist orders the equipment. In the to-be process, the restaurant general manager orders it. This change in resource performing the activity is significant. The general managers must be trained on how to order equipment, including training on the procurement application that Mykonos uses to support the ordering. The application itself must be changed a bit so that general managers can track their equipment orders. And of course access to the application must be provided for them.

Ideally all these training and software costs would have been considered originally when deciding whether or not to change the process. But when transformation analysis occurs, it is too late for second thoughts. The decision has been made to change the process, and the goal is to execute that process change.

The gateway **Equipment Needed?** changes in a similar way. In the as-is process the procurement specialist decides whether equipment is needed. In the to-be process, the restaurant general manager makes this decision. To effect the change, each general manager must be trained in how to make the decision—how to determine whether the new equipment makes sense economically.

Although the gateway **Equipment Needed?** appears in both the as-is process and the to-be, it encapsulates a somewhat different decision in the to-be. To see why, let's examine the as-is gateways more carefully. There are three decisions in the as-is process. First, the procurement specialist decides whether the equipment is needed, in the gateway **Equipment Needed?** Second, the procurement specialist decides whether there is a better alternative to the requested equipment, in the gateway **Better Alternative?** And finally, the procurement manager decides whether to approve the request, in the gateway **Approve Request?** In the to-be process, there is only a single decision, made in **Equipment Needed?** The second as-is decision is simply eliminated. In the to-be process there is no longer a separate activity to comparison shop. The general manager is responsible for selecting the best equipment. Similarly, the third as-is decision is eliminated and the responsibility rolled into the to-be **Equipment Needed?** gateway. The restaurant general manager does not just decide whether he thinks new equipment is needed. He also commits Mykonos to the purchase.

The to-be **Equipment Needed?** decision replaces both the as-is **Equipment Needed?** and the to-be **Approve Request?** The restaurant general manager will need to be trained in how to consider the financial interests of Mykonos when deciding whether equipment is needed.

Eliminating Activities and Adding Activities

After analyzing the activity and gateway that have changed, you look for activities that are eliminated, ones that exist in the as-is but not the to-be. In transforming equipment procurement, there are many such eliminated activities. In fact, most of the process is eliminated, including the following activities and gateways:

- Prepare Equipment Request
- Analyze Equipment Request
- Research Equipment Alternatives
- Prepare Alternative Request
- Forward Equipment Request
- Examine Equipment Request
- Explain Decision
- Explain Rejection
- Listen to Rejection
- Equipment Needed?
- Better Alternative?
- Approve Request?

Most of these eliminated activities and gateways are performed by procurement specialists. So now we must ask about redundancy. Do we need as many procurement specialists in the new organization? Is this work a significant part of what they do today or a minor distraction from their main role? If it is a significant part of what they do, we need to either reassign the people to new work or to perform a layoff.

The to-be equipment procurement process has no new activities; both activities in Figure 10.5 were already in Figure 10.1. But often when a business process is transformed, new activities are introduced. With new activities come new training, new software support for these activities, and perhaps even hiring new people.

Redesigning the Mykonos equipment procurement process is something of a small transformation. It is a radical rethinking, giving financial responsibility over kitchen equipment investments to the restaurant general managers. But the radicalism is very contained; it only involves a single process, and a rather simple one. Many transformations are larger, involving multiple processes and including strategies, organizations, and business rules. Transformations are often big.

IMPACT ANALYSIS

When a single change is made to a business, many consequences can occur. A new governmental regulation, seemingly simple, can lead to three new policies, a new organization to monitor compliance, and 13 changes to business processes. A small business process improvement can lead to one organization being underutilized and another far too busy.

Before making a change, wise executives try to understand the impacts of the change. What will happen if we make this change? What unintended consequences will result? The attempt to understand the impacts of a proposed change before acting on the change is called *impact analysis*. Impact analysis is looking before leaping.

What is the value of impact analysis? Sometimes the value is avoiding making a bad change, a change that has unforeseen impacts. At other times the change itself is unavoidable. The business must comply with a new regulation. Impact analysis allows the business to understand the consequences before they happen, and prepare for those consequences.

Without models, performing impact analysis is difficult. Businesses are complex, with many organizations, rules, and processes that interrelate in hundreds of ways. Without models, even the most thoughtful and thorough executives will miss some impacts. Furthermore, sometimes executives are mistaken in their understanding of how the business works. Models help avoid the consequences of those mistakes.

Let's reconsider the disease lawsuit task force, described at the beginning of this chapter. As you recall, the task force was chartered to reduce the risk of a lawsuit based on real or imagined ailments resulting from consumption of food at Mykonos restaurants. The task force begins its work by considering the existing Mykonos motivation model. Are there courses of action or desired results that will lead to increased risk of a lawsuit? Figure 10.7 shows part of the motivation model, with two goals and the strategies that channel efforts toward those goals. The goal **Expand Geography** does not increase the risk of a lawsuit. Two of the strategies that channel efforts toward the goal—**Expand to Charlotte** and

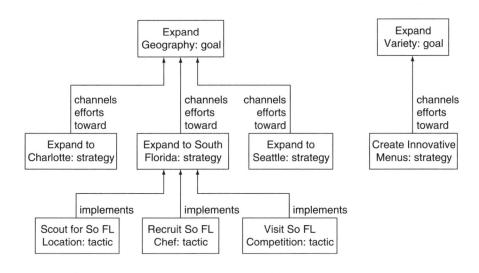

FIGURE 10.7 Part of the Mykonos motivation model

Expand to Seattle—are also safe. But the third strategy is a problem: **Expand to South Florida**. The South Florida courts are known to be sympathetic to tort innovation, and multimillion-dollar awards are common. The task force decides to abandon the strategy of expansion into South Florida.

When **Expand to South Florida** is abandoned, other motivation elements are affected. Figure 10.7 shows how the tactic **Scout for So FL location** implements the strategy **Expand to South Florida**. This tactic is abandoned with the strategy **Expand to South Florida**. It makes no sense to scout for locations when no restaurant will be opened there. Similarly, the tactics **Recruit So FL Chef** and **Visit So FL Competition** also implement the same strategy and are eliminated with it.

Figure 10.7 also shows the goal **Expand Variety**, with the supporting strategy **Create Innovative Menus**. With the new legal environment, creating innovative menus carries a risk. An innovative menu with unusual combinations of ingredients is more likely to attract a lawsuit than a menu of steaks and grilled fish. But the task force does not want to abandon the strategy **Create Innovative Menus** as they abandoned the strategy of expanding to South Florida. Innovative menus are just too important. In this situation the cure is worse than the disease. Instead the task force adopts a new business policy to govern this strategy.

> *Legally Safe Menus: All menus must be reasonably safe from lawsuits.*

The new policy **Legally Safe Menus** is intended to reduce the risk of a lawsuit by creating legally safe menus—menus that are (probably) not going to lead to lawsuits. This policy is the basis for several business rules that check aspects of legal safety. For example, a new business rule is created to ensure that all meat is sufficiently cooked.

> *Meats Sufficiently Cooked: It is obligatory that each menu item is thoroughly cooked if the menu item contains meat.*

As the restaurant lawsuit threat evolves in California and elsewhere, new business rules are created and existing ones are revised to enforce this general policy of keeping menus safe from lawsuits.

How to Perform Impact Analysis

There is no magic in performing impact analysis. In our example the Mykonos disease lawsuit task force simply examines each of the business models to check which are impacted by the new legal risk. That is how impact analysis is performed. The change is considered, and then model elements are examined one by one to see which are affected by the change.

When a model element is affected by a change, the impact can have one of several different results. A new business policy or business rule may be required, as in the previous example in which the new policy **Legally Safe Menus** is created to reduce the risk of lawsuits. A business process activity might be eliminated or modified in other ways. For example, if pagers are to be installed, the host still greets and seats customers but now does so differently because a pager system is used.

Impact analysis takes time. If your business has many models and model diagrams, you must check them all for impact. This checking is not hard work. It is usually easy to determine whether a change under consideration affects a goal or a business process activity. But the work takes some time because every model element must be considered.

ACQUISITION ANALYSIS

Sometimes one company buys another company and the two are combined to form a single, larger company. This purchase is called either a *merger* or an *acquisition*, depending on the legal details of the transaction. For our purposes in this book, the legal distinctions between a merger and an acquisition are not important, and we will use the terms interchangeably. In either case, a decision is made to combine two companies into one.

Prior to an acquisition, the acquirer performs a financial analysis, trying to understand how the acquired company will perform under new ownership. Will sales increase when a vastly larger sales force sells the acquired products? How much? Can costs be cut as redundant operations are combined? How much? This financial analysis is necessary for determining an appropriate financial value for the company to be acquired.

The success or failure of an acquisition often rests not on these financial issues but on the ease or difficulty of *post-merger integration*, the combining of the two companies into one after the acquisition occurs.[1] Can the acquired company be easily integrated into the acquirer? What actions must be taken to perform the integration? How long will the post-merger integration take? This assessment of the size and effort of post-merger integration can be performed using business models. By comparing business models of the two companies, we can identify differences that will lead to integration work.

Let's look at an example. After the acquisition and integration of Cora Group, Mykonos is ready to consider purchasing another restaurant company. You have been asked to evaluate the purchase of Pescado, a restaurant company based in Houston that consists of 11 restaurants. Pescado serves the same market as

---

[1]For some acquisitions, no post-merger integration is performed. The acquired company is kept as a free-standing entity, and the two organizations and their business processes are not combined. But these acquisitions are a small minority. Most acquisitions lead to significant post-merger integration.

Mykonos—business professionals and consumers who are willing to pay $100 for an unusually good dinner for two. But the Pescado restaurants are a bit different. Except for a few vegetarian entrees, the menu is entirely fish and seafood. And everything is alive until a few minutes before it is prepared. When a diner orders sautéed sea bass, the server leads him to the sea bass tank and the diner selects his fish from the 15 sea bass swimming around. His sea bass is then caught, scaled, and prepared.

The tanks are part of the attraction of the Pescado restaurants. Dining there is like eating at an aquarium, with dozens of tanks around the walls. Some of the fish are there only for display, not intended for consumption. Others are on display until they are selected, replaced by fresh live fish the next day or the next week. All restaurants have an element of the entertainment industry, but Pescado is closer to show business than most.

As you perform your analysis of Pescado, you look at the business processes. You begin with the basic Mykonos customer dining process shown in Figure 10.8.[2] The equivalent Pescado process is shown in Figure 10.9. There are three additional activities in the Pescado process that are not performed at Mykonos. The activity **Select Fish from Tanks** is unique to Pescado, as is **Catch Fish** and **Scale and Clean Fish**. There is an entirely new role with its own new swimlane: **Preparer**, the role that performs the catching and the scaling and cleaning. You wonder about the costs of this new role and the additional time these new activities will add to the preparation of the dinners. Is the entertainment worth the cost and time?

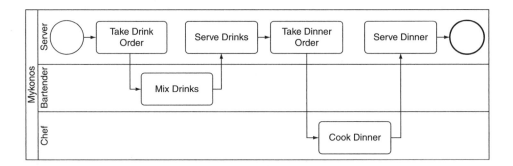

FIGURE 10.8 The Mykonos customer dining process

---

[2]Note that the Figure 10.8 process is the simpler customer dining process originally introduced in Chapter 2, not the more complex process—with subprocesses—from Chapter 5.

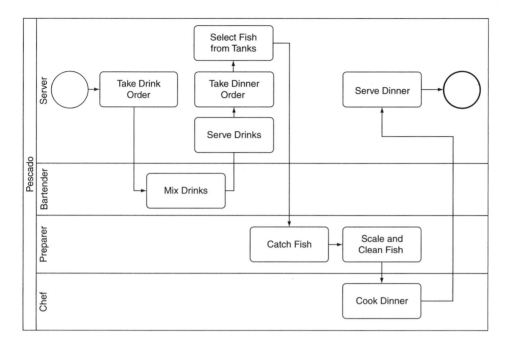

FIGURE 10.9 The Pescado customer dining process

The procurement process for fresh fish is also different. At Mykonos restaurants, the general manager estimates the evening's fish need, and then the chef buys the fish. The very simple process is shown in Figure 10.10.

The same process at Pescado is much more complex. Figure 10.11 shows the process. The fish are purchased alive, and they must be kept alive until they are consumed. A new role is responsible for ordering the fish and caring for them once they are delivered; this person is an **Aquarist**. Figure 10.11 includes a second process as well, also perform by the aquarist. He orders the supplies the fish need, particularly the specialized foods for each fish species, and the aquarium parts and equipment.

After some comparison of the procurement processes, you conclude that the Pescado process and the Mykonos process will never be integrated. The Pescado fish procurement process is just too fundamentally different from the Mykonos fish procurement process: different activities, different timing, even different roles. And the Pescado customer dining process is also very different from the Mykonos one. The processes must be different, and each must be maintained. Given the costs of maintaining separate processes, you start to wonder whether there is really any value in acquiring Pescado.

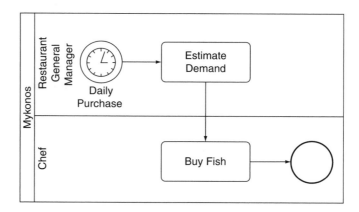

FIGURE 10.10 The Mykonos fish procurement process

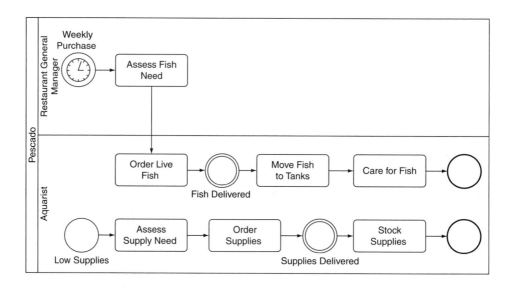

FIGURE 10.11 The Pescado fish procurement process

How to Perform Acquisition Analysis

To perform acquisition analysis, you simply compare models from the acquiring company and the target company. You find differences between the models and consider the impact of those differences. How hard will it be to integrate the business processes? How hard to merge the organizations, given their existing interactions? As with impact analysis, there is no magic.

There are some common obstacles to acquisition analysis. First, it is likely that the target company will not be already modeled. If you are performing the analysis on behalf of the acquiring company, you will have models for your company but not for the target company, the one your company is about to buy. You must model it, creating models for the business processes or organizations you want to compare.

If the target company is already modeled, the models are likely to be of low quality. Today most business models are poorly constructed, with many of the flaws described in Chapter 7. If models already exist, you might need to spend some time improving them: making them consistent, bringing them up to date, and making them easier to understand.

Of the four business modeling disciplines, all are useful for acquisition analysis, for somewhat different reasons. Comparing business process models is quite useful. Often companies perform the same process in different ways. When an acquiring company and a target company use different processes, the processes must either be changed or the differences must be accepted and managed. Either alternative is expensive.

Comparing business organization models is also useful. The two companies are likely organized somewhat differently, perhaps very differently. And their interactions, both internally and with suppliers and customers, will differ. Assessing the extent of the differences is important to considering the costs of post-merger integration.

Comparing business rules can be useful. Business rules are certainly easier to change than other aspects of business architecture. If the target company operates under different business rules than the acquiring company, the rules can be changed. But rules can be easily changed only when the rules are managed separately from the business processes and the business applications. More typically, the rules are hidden deep inside software applications. If so, comparing business rules can only be performed by comparing the details of the applications.

Similarly, differences in business motivation are sometimes significant, and sometimes not so much. If the acquired company is willing to adapt to the goals and strategies of the acquiring company, differences in prior business motivation are not so important. But often there is resistance from the management of the acquired company. They want to continue using the strategies and tactics they know well. This leads to trouble. Understanding differences in motivation models can be important in identifying whether the acquired company is willing and able to change.

> *There are several different techniques for wringing business value from existing business models. Improvement analysis involves finding ways to improve a business. Transformation analysis is analyzing a proposed transformation to determine how to perform it. Impact analysis is considering a*

change and discovering and anticipating the consequences of the change. Acquisition analysis is examining a proposed merger or acquisition to determine the effort of merging the businesses.

The analysis techniques in this chapter are complemented by business simulation—the simulated running of a business model. Chapter 11 describes business simulation.

Business Simulation

Some business models can be simulated. Business process models can be simulated to determine costs, cycle times, and other process results. Business motivation models can be simulated to determine the results of strategies and trends. In either case, simulation is useful for training, persuasion, and analysis. Simulation is also useful for model validation—for finding and fixing errors in a model.

After the successful acquisition of the Cora Group, your management team at Mykonos entrusts you with a new responsibility: improving customer satisfaction across all the Mykonos restaurants. Traditionally Mykonos management has thought about customer satisfaction in terms of the quality of the dishes prepared, and part of your new job is to monitor the quality by traveling around the country and dining at Mykonos restaurants. But you believe that customer satisfaction at restaurants reflects other issues as well— issues that in the past Mykonos central management had ignored. You intend to use your new responsibility to consider customer satisfaction more broadly.

In particular you want to look at customer wait times and the impact of waits on satisfaction. At some of the more popular Mykonos restaurants, patrons wait. They wait for a table to be available. They wait for water, wine, and bread. They wait for the waitstaff to take their orders. They wait for their food, and they wait for their bills. You are concerned that all this waiting makes customers dissatisfied and hurts the success of these restaurants. And you suspect that some simple policy changes could reduce the waits and make the restaurants more successful.

But your focus on waiting is just a hunch, based on your experience of the restaurant business. You are not certain you are right. And even if you were certain, you face big communication and persuasion challenges. The general managers of the individual restaurants have a lot of independence. Each sets the policies for his restaurant. You are not sure how you can convince them to take action and reduce the customer wait times.

You ponder the situation for several weeks while working on other problems. Then you talk to a freelance restaurant consultant—Rhonda Martinez—to seek her advice about this problem. She suggests creating two simulation models. One model is focused on the customer dining process—how customers arrive, are seated, have their orders taken, and so on. The other model has a longer time scale. It is focused on customer satisfaction—how food quality, wait times, and other factors contribute to customer satisfaction and how word of mouth and restaurant reviews affect the view of potential customers and, ultimately, a restaurant's success. She claims that these two models could serve to analyze the problem: to analyze wait times and the effect of wait times on customer satisfaction and restaurant success. Working with the models, she could examine the effect of different policies on wait times. And she claims that the two models could help communicate the results to the many restaurant general managers, ultimately persuading them to change their policies and reduce the wait times.

You have little experience with simulations yourself, beyond playing the simulation game SimCity. But you have worked with Rhonda before, and you have confidence in her work. You decide to try a simulation approach.

WHY SIMULATE?

In Chapter 1 we describe the eight purposes for business models. Model simulation can address three of those eight: training and learning, persuasion and selling, and analysis.

Simulations have long been recognized as useful for *training and learning*. There are hundreds of commercial training games that use simulation. And some mass-market consumer entertainment simulation games are also used for training by universities. For example, the game Capitalism™ has been used in classes at Stanford School of Engineering and Harvard Business School. The use of simulations for training is a mainstream activity today.

But training with a commercial sim is inevitably a compromise; no commercial sim will exactly match the situation you want to teach. Usually there is no commercial sim that even comes close. Fortunately, custom simulations are a good training alternative when no commercial sim fits. A homegrown sim can be created to exactly match your purposes. As we show in this chapter, simulations are not difficult to build.

One of the reasons simulations are so effective for training and learning is that people find playing a simulation enjoyable. Whether homegrown or commercially purchased, simulations are fun.

The use of simulation for training is well-understood and widely appreciated. But simulation can also be a powerful tool for *persuasion*, and this use of simulation is not widely appreciated. In fact, simulations are used so rarely for persuasion that sims are something of a secret sales weapon—an advantage to the people and companies who make use of them.

B. J. Fogg, the director of the Stanford Persuasive Technology Lab, says, "Cause-and-effect simulations can be powerful persuaders. The power comes from the ability to explore cause-and-effect relationships without having to wait a long time to see the results and the ability to convey the effect in vivid and credible ways." [Fogg 2003] Today when people want to persuade, they typically uses verbal techniques, numbers and graphs, or images and video. All these media have limited effectiveness. People dismiss words, ignore numbers, and are sophisticated critics of images and video. But simulations give them the ability to try things out, to experiment and build up their own understanding inside the simulated world. Simulations encourage people to reach their own conclusions through their own trial and error, but faster and more safely than they can in the real world.

As Fogg points out, simulations always come with a point of view. For example, in SimCity it is much easier to build an effective, prosperous metropolitan area if you design an extensive rail system. Will Wright, the creator of SimCity, is apparently a strong proponent of rails instead of roads and designed SimCity to reflect his point of view.

When persuading, you are attempting to communicate a point of view. Often you work against the ingrained biases of your audience. At Mykonos, the general managers of restaurants regard long customer waits as a good thing. The waits are a sign of the popularity of their restaurants and a symbol of their personal success. Convincing them that customer waits undermine their future success is difficult. Powerpoint presentations won't be effective in changing their minds. You want them to try a restaurant simulation with that scenario. They can try to manage a popular restaurant with long lines, and see how poor customer satisfaction, bad restaurant reviews, and general ill-will erode the success, leading ultimately to closure.

Howard Gardner describes seven techniques for changing people's minds: reason, research, resonance, redescriptions, rewards, real-world events, and resistances [Gardner 2004]. When well-designed, a simulation can play to three of these techniques. First, when someone plays a simulation, she becomes engaged. The simulation feels real to her, as though she is really (for example) a mayor of a city. The (simulated) real-world events change her mind. Second, a simulation provides an environment for someone to do (simulated) research by letting her try out experiments and seeing what happens. These experiments are in some ways better than real-world research because they can be performed quickly and without risk. Many alternatives can be tried out that would be expensive or impossible to try in the real world. Finally, a simulation is in its very essence a redescription, a different way to tell a story that can supplement a traditional pitch.

As personal experience, we have used business simulations in the sales pursuit of many large system integration projects. We have sold projects worth a total of several billion US dollars using simulation. Our personal experience is that simulations are strikingly effective in demonstrating a deep understanding of a customer's problems, and convincing them that a proposed solution will solve those problems.

Simulations are also good for *analysis*. Chapter 10 describes several analysis techniques—ways of analyzing a model to reach conclusions about either the model or the business situation being modeled. Simulation can be used as an additional analysis method, a dynamic analysis method to complement the static methods of Chapter 10.

Why do we need another analysis method? For larger models, there are many questions that are too difficult to answer via static analysis. For example, with a small and simple business process model, it might be possible to analyze the cost of the end-to-end process using static analysis without simulation. But most processes are not small and simple. Most have many activities, and the more activities a process has, the more difficult it is to analyze statically. Most processes are complex, with uncertainty, intermittent resource constraints, and cyclic behavior. Complex processes are very difficult to analyze statically. Simulation is required for all but the smallest and simplest business processes.

Motivation models have the same characteristics. Small and simple motivation models can be analyzed statically to determine how the goals, strategies, and influences will lead to results. But most motivation models are neither small nor simple. They have many interacting elements, and they have feedback, time delays, and uncertainty. For these larger and more complex motivation models, simulation is the only effective method of understanding what will happen.

SIMULATING A BUSINESS PROCESS MODEL

Rhonda starts by creating a simulation of the business process, to analyze and understand the causes of the customer waits. She intends to build a general model of restaurant waits that can be adapted to any of the Mykonos restaurants, but she doesn't start by creating something general. Instead she starts by creating a model that replicates the ebb and flow of a single restaurant, Zona.

After some one-on-one modeling sessions with the Zona general manager and some observations of the restaurant in action, Rhonda creates a business process simulation. The simulation shows that each customer party waits 46 minutes on average. This 46 minutes includes all the waits: waiting for a table, waiting for a server to take their order, waiting for their dinner, waiting for their check, and waiting for their change or credit card receipt. The 46 minutes excludes the time spent considering the menu, ordering food and drinks, eating, and settling the bill. Figure 11.1 shows an initial simulation result, a breakdown of the average times spent by customers, organized by activity and presented as a pie chart.

Wait times vary over the course of the week. Mondays and Tuesdays see far fewer customers than Fridays and Saturdays, and far shorter waits. The model has accounted for the typical number of customers on each day and when those customers arrive. The simulation produces wait times by day of the week, as shown in Figure 11.2.

Wait times also vary over the course of a single evening. The wait times are shortest both early and late in the evening and longest in the middle of the evening, when the restaurant is busiest. Figure 11.3 shows a third simulation result: how the wait

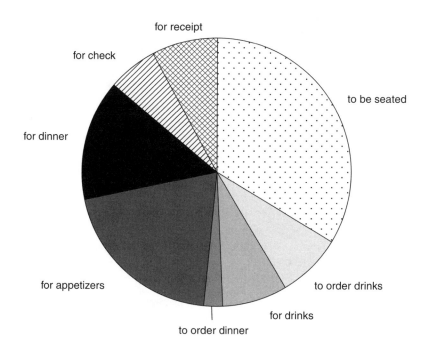

FIGURE 11.1 Average customer wait times, by activity

times vary over the course of a single Friday evening. Here, instead of an average wait time, the simulated waits are expressed as a percentage. Of all the customer parties in the restaurant at 8:30 PM, what percentage are waiting for something: for a table, for dinner, for their check? Similarly, at 8:40 PM, what percentage are waiting?

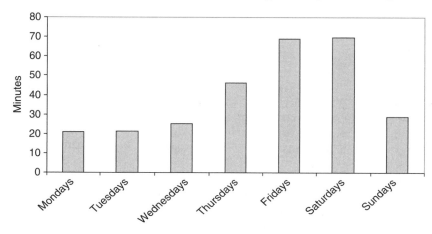

FIGURE 11.2 Average total customer wait times, by day of the week

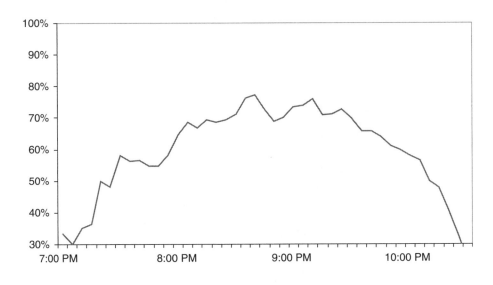

FIGURE 11.3 Percentage of customers waiting on an average Friday evening

The simulation results in Figures 11.1, 11.2, and 11.3 are not intended to create any analytical insights—not yet. So far Rhonda has only replicated the current as-is situation at Zona. The simulation results validate that the model is reasonably accurate, that the model reflects the actual wait dynamics at the Zona restaurant.

Now Rhonda turns to analysis. She starts with a simple experiment. What happens if the staffing is doubled? What happens on Friday nights if there are two hosts available to greet and seat customers instead of one, twice as many servers waiting tables, twice as many chefs cooking meals, and twice as many bartenders mixing drinks? This is clearly an unrealistic experiment—Zona is not going to double their labor costs just to reduce customer wait times. But it is a revealing experiment. Are the customer waits due to staffing resource or due to some other cause?

Figure 11.4 shows one of the results of the experiment—the percentage waiting through the course of a Friday evening. Figure 11.4 is directly comparable to Figure 11.3. The only difference is the staffing of the simulated restaurant. As you can see, there are some declines in wait times, but only modest reductions. At its worst, the Friday night waits with twice the staff are almost 90 percent of the current waits.

Why is the reduction in wait times so modest even when the staff is doubled? Rhonda analyzes the difference by looking at a single simulated party of four in both the as-is model and the (unrealistic) to-be. Figure 11.5 compares the breakdown of wait time for a single party arriving at the peak of Friday evening. On the bottom is the breakdown of waits for the party of four in the as-is model. On the top is the breakdown of waits for the party in the to-be model. The to-be

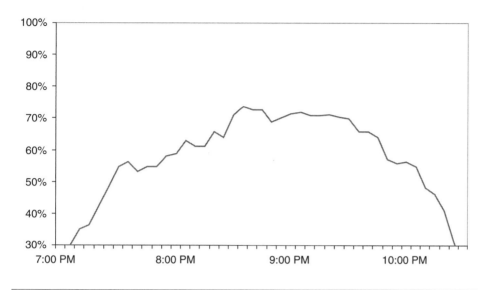

FIGURE 11.4 Percentage of customers waiting on a Friday, with twice the staff

party waits almost as long as the as-is party, but they wait at different points in the process. Instead of waiting for their bill to be prepared or for their server to take their order, their wait is concentrated at two points: waiting for a table and waiting for their dinner. By doubling the staff, we have succeeding only in shifting the wait time.

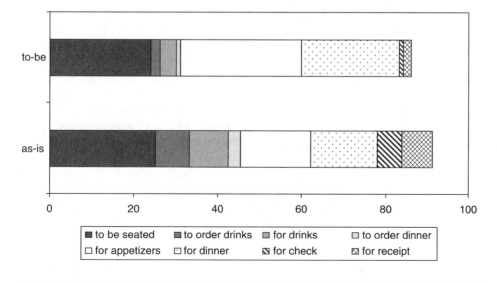

FIGURE 11.5 Friday night wait-time breakdown: as-is vs. to-be

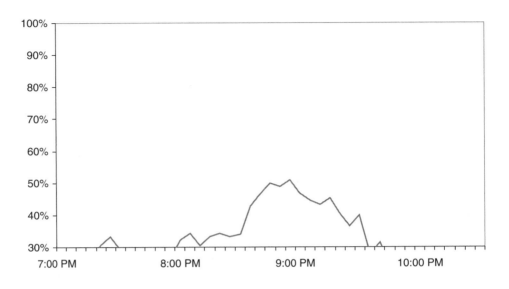

FIGURE 11.6 Percentage of customers waiting on Friday, with twice the staff, twice the tables, and twice the kitchen

Of course, if every table is already occupied, a newly arriving party cannot be seated. They must wait for someone to leave. And when a party orders dinner, the food cannot be prepared if the kitchen capacity is fully taken by other dinners cooking. So Rhonda tries another experiment to test whether the tables and the kitchen capacity are creating the waits. In addition to doubling Zona staff, she doubles the size of the restaurant: the number of tables and the capacity of the kitchen. This is also unrealistic: Mykonos is planning no expansion in the size of Zona.

Figure 11.6 shows the Friday night waits for this double-size Zona. Most of the waits have disappeared. Customers still wait—of course they must still wait for their food to be prepared—but some of the waiting has been eliminated.

Rhonda draws the obvious conclusion from this latest experiment: Zona is just not big enough for the demand on busy nights. Now it is time to try a realistic experiment. Suppose Zona changed their policy and only seated people with reservations on those busy nights. What if they eliminated waiting lists for tables? Rhonda models that policy change experiment. She first returns the model to the normal staffing and the normal size and then alters the process to turn people away who do not have reservations on Fridays and Saturdays. The results are shown in Figure 11.7. People are in fact waiting less. But that reduced wait comes at a cost: Zona is serving fewer people and the bar is serving far fewer drinks to people who are waiting.

Many other experiments are possible. What if Zona limited the size of the waiting list to allow no more than three parties to wait at a time? What if Zona staffed a single additional server on Fridays and Saturdays? What if Zona cross-trained the

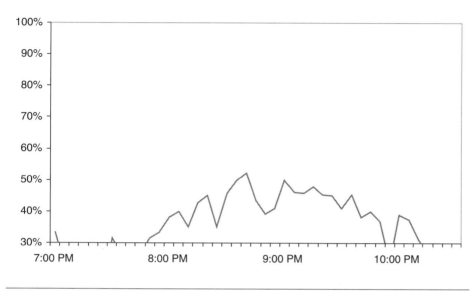

FIGURE 11.7 Percentage of customers waiting on Friday, with a reservations-only policy

servers, so they could perform as hosts if the host was busy seating people? What if Zona only seated smaller parties—those of six people or fewer? All of these simulations could be modeled and the results examined.

You are planning to use the simulation to analyze different policies and improve your own understanding. But the wait times and changes in policy to reduce those wait times are ultimately the responsibility of the general managers of the individual restaurants. You intend to provide this simulation to those restaurant general managers so that they can experiment with various policies for their own restaurants.

Activities, Resources, and Jobs

What does it take to create the kind of business process simulation described in the last few pages? Of course you need a business process simulation engine, a software application that simulates the model. Often such an engine is included as part of a business process modeling tool.

You also need a good business process model, the kind of model described in Chapter 5. And you need to prepare that model to be run in a simulation engine. Preparing a model for simulation requires some additional work beyond what is required to create a static, non-simulated model. But more significantly than the extra work, preparing a process model to be simulated requires additional knowledge.

To create a business process simulation you must understand activities, resources, and jobs and the way these three interact with each other.

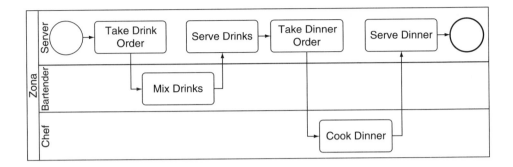

FIGURE 11.8 A process to be simulated

As described in Chapter 5, a business process *activity* is a single step in a larger business process. In our model of customers dining at Zona (shown again in Figure 11.8[1]), **Mix Drinks** is one activity and **Take Dinner Order** is another.

A *resource* is a person who performs the activity. The resource is identified in a business process by the swimlane where the activity is placed. For the activity **Take Dinner Order**, the resource is a **Server**. Note that the resource is an actual (simulated) person, whereas **Server** is a role the person plays. At any one time, many people will be playing the role of servers; seven different servers will be working on a typical Friday night. And over the course of an evening, one person may play multiple roles.

A *job*[2] is something that flows through the process, being worked on by resources and flowing from activity to activity. Examples of jobs include a purchase order and a help desk trouble ticket. In our model of restaurant dining, each job is a customer party. Some jobs represent parties of two diners, some represent parties of four, some represent people dining alone.

The Job Cycle

A job is created at a start event and flows over sequence flows and message flows from activity to activity until an end event is reached. When a job reaches an activity, one of two things can happen. Either a resource is available to work the job or no resource is available and the job must wait until a resource is available, perhaps waiting in a long line of other jobs. Consider the activity **Mix Drinks** in Figure 11.8. The job arrives at this activity after the activity **Take Drink Order** occurs; after the

---

[1] As with Figure 10.8, Figure 11.8 is the simpler customer dining process originally introduced in Chapter 2, not the more complex process—with subprocesses—from Chapter 5.

[2] In much of the BPMN literature, jobs are called *tokens*. This reflects BPMN's theoretical basis in Petri nets. For modeling, we prefer the term *job* instead of *token* because it is a more natural description of a party of restaurant customers, an insurance claim, or whatever is flowing through the process.

party has ordered their drinks, the drinks can be mixed. At this point any bartender can mix the drinks. If a bartender resource is available, the activity can be performed. Otherwise the job must wait until some bartender is available.

Once a bartender is available, he performs this activity—mixing the drinks—until the activity is finished. While he is performing this activity he is not available to do anything else. He can neither mix other drinks nor perform other activities in the model. When he is finished mixing the drinks, the job and the resource separate. The resource is available to do something else—he can mix drinks for someone else or wash glasses or calculate someone's bar tab. Meanwhile the job traverses the sequence flow to the next activity, **Serve Drinks**.

The job cycle is illustrated in Figure 11.9.

a. A job arrives at an activity from the incoming sequence flow.
b. It waits, perhaps behind a line of other jobs, for a resource to be available.
c. Once the appropriate resource is available, the resource works the job.
d. When finished with that activity, the job travels across the outgoing sequence flows to the next activity.

A business process simulation engine performs the job cycle thousands of times, every time a job leaves one activity and travels to another. The jobs—restaurant parties in our example—progress across sequence flows from activity to activity, progressing from **Serve Drinks** to **Take Dinner Order** to **Cook Dinner**. The resources—servers, hosts, and chefs in our example—work jobs when they are at activities.

Collecting Statistics

The simulation engine collects individual statistics as the simulation progresses—statistics about activities, resources, and jobs. These statistics are aggregated into

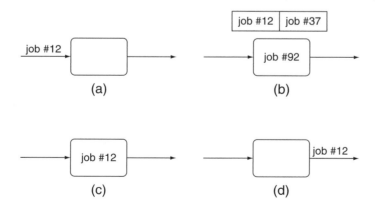

FIGURE 11.9 The job cycle

the simulation results. For example, the results shown in Figures 11.1 through 11.7 are aggregated from thousands of individual statistics.

The engine collects statistics on each activity, each resource, and each job. Activity statistics include how many times each activity was performed, the average duration of each activity, the total cost of each activity, and the other activity statistics shown in Table 11.1. Resource statistics include the utilization of each resource, the total amount of work performed by each resource, and the other resource statistics shown in Table 11.1. Job statistics include the total cycle time of each job, the total touch time of each job, and the other job statistics in Table 11.1.

Statistics are collected for each activity, each resource, and each job, but these individual statistics are rarely examined by themselves. Instead they are

Table 11.1 Statistics Collected by the Simulation

	Statistic	Example
Activity statistics	How many times the activity was performed	**Serve Drinks** was performed 1,291 times over a seven day simulation
	The average duration of the activity	**Serve Drinks** averaged 3.1 minutes
	The total cost incurred performing the activity	**Serve Drinks** incurred a total cost of $912.11
	The total resource hours (i.e., man-hours) of work performed at the activity	**Serve Drinks** represented 73.4 resource hours of work
	The current backlog of jobs at this activity	**Serve Drinks** has a current backlog of one job: one table is waiting for a server to serve them drinks
	The average wait time for jobs waiting at this activity	**Serve Drinks** has an average wait time of 4.2 minutes
Resource statistics	The utilization for this resource	The server **Angela** is 91% utilized; she has spent 91% of her work time actually working on jobs and 9% waiting, on break, or other non-job activity
	The total amount of work performed by this resource	**Angela** has performed 6.3 hours of work
	The total cost of the work performed	**Angela** has performed work that costs $69.21
	The distribution of work across different activities	**Angela** has spent 14% of her time at activity **Take Drink Order**, 11% at activity **Serve Drinks**, etc.

Continued

Table 11.1 Statistics Collected by the Simulation—*cont'd*

	Statistic	Example
Job statistics	The total cycle time of the job, the end-to-end time	**Job-241** has a cycle time of 119 minutes, from the time the party arrived at the restaurant until they left
	The total touch time for the job, how much work was done	**Job-241** has a touch time of 71 minutes
	The total cost incurred by the job	**Job-241** has a total cost of $27.21
	The total wait time for the job	**Job-241** has a total wait time of 53 minutes
	The wait time of the job distributed among the activities	**Job-241** waited at **Seat Party** for 17 minutes, at **Take Drink Order** for 1 minute, etc.
	The touch time of the job distributed among the activities	**Job-241** incurred 2 minutes of work at **Seat Party**, 3 minutes of work at **Take Drink Order**, etc.

aggregated in various ways, producing various averages and distributions. For example, each job keeps track of its end-to-end cycle time as it progresses through the process. When a job reaches an end event and finishes, the simulation combines that newly finished cycle time with others that have already finished and produces an average. It may also keep track of some other cycle time aggregates: how the average changes over the course of the simulation, the standard deviation of the cycle times, and how the cycle time varies with the type of job.

Activity Durations

To be simulated, activities need additional attributes. Duration is one such attribute. When a job arrives at an activity, how long does the resource work on it? Each activity has a **duration** attribute that indicates how long jobs need to be worked. Often that duration is a constant value, such as 10 minutes for every job that is worked by this activity. But duration can also vary, and it can vary in three different ways.

First, the duration can vary depending on the details of the job. For example, the **Take Dinner Order** activity takes much longer for a party of eight than it does a party of two. In fact, the party of eight takes longer for many activities in the customer dining process; not only does the activity **Take Dinner Order** require a longer duration for the party of eight, but so does **Serve Dinner**.

The job that models the party of eight needs to be different from the job that models a party of two. For this simulation, jobs need their own model-custom attribute, **partySize**. A job representing a party of eight will have a party size value of 8, and a job representing a party of two will have a value of 2.

Second, the duration of the activity can vary depending on the details of the resource. A skilled server will serve drinks quicker than a novice because she remembers who ordered which drink. The simulation needs to know that this server is quick, that one is average, and this other one is slow.

For this model, resources need a model-custom attribute, **skillLevel**, to keep track of skill. Values of skill level can then be 1 for an average skill, 0.8 for a quick server, and 1.2 for a slow one.

Suppose we want the duration of **Take Dinner Order** to consider both the skill of the server and the size of the party. How do we combine those elements? We need to encode the duration as a formula, perhaps like the duration in Figure 11.10. The standard duration depends on the party size: 5 minutes for parties of one or two, 6 minutes for parties of three, and so on. That standard duration is multiplied by the skill level of the server—multiplied by 1 for an average server, by 0.8 for a quick server, and by 1.2 for a slow one. (There is no standard technical language for encoding activity durations. In practice each BPMN tool that supports simulation has its own language. In this book we use precise English because our focus is not on the syntax of any language but on what needs to be expressed.)

Third, the duration of the activity can vary randomly. Consider the activity **Cook Dinner**. The duration of **Cook Dinner** might vary from 20 minutes to 45 minutes, depending on what is ordered.[3] Sometimes it takes 22 minutes, sometimes 37 minutes, sometimes 41. As the simulation runs and **Cook Dinner** is executed for different jobs, each job takes a different duration, a random time between 20 and 45 minutes.

When durations vary randomly, modelers often employ a *uniform distribution*. Each duration in a uniform distribution within the range is equally likely; 20 minutes is just as likely as 33 minutes and just as likely as 40 or 45. Uniform distributions are easy for subject matter experts (SMEs) to understand.

Take Dinner Order: activity	
Description	Understand what the diners want to eat while you answer any questions about the menu that arise.
Duration	The skill level of the resource multiplied by the standard duration. The standard duration is 5 minutes for a party size of one or two, 6 minutes for a party of three, 7 minutes for a party of four, 8 minutes for a party of five, 9 minutes for a party of six, 10 minutes for a party of seven, and 11 minutes for a party of eight people.

FIGURE 11.10 An activity duration that depends on the job and resource

---

[3]For a large party, there is a greater chance that someone in the party will order a dinner that takes a long time to prepare. In a higher-fidelity model, the duration of **Cook Dinner** could be made dependent on the size of the party, albeit still random.

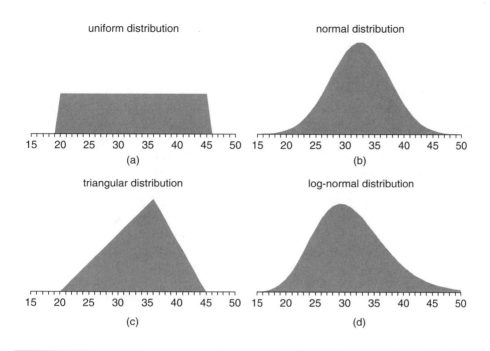

FIGURE 11.11 Some possible distributions of activity duration

It is also possible to use other distributions: a triangular distribution that peaks somewhere in the middle, a standard (bell curve) distribution, or something more sophisticated. Figure 11.11 shows some of the distribution alternatives.

In practice, uniform and triangular distributions are commonly used, and the more complex statistical distributions are much more rare. The statistical distributions (e.g., normal, log-normal, exponential, etc.) often lead to higher model fidelity, but they are usually difficult for SMEs to understand. This is the modeling tradeoff between fidelity and simplicity, a tradeoff we have seen many times in this book.

Work Time and Delay Time

The duration of an activity specifies the work time—the time a person is actually working on a job. But a job can also experience a delay while it is at an activity, time when no one is actually working on the job. A *resource delay* occurs when there is no resource available to work a job. Consider again the job cycle shown in Figure 11.9. At step b, the newly arrived job waits for a resource to be available, perhaps in a queue of other jobs that are also waiting for resources. Step b is not work time, not part of the duration of the activity. Instead step b is resource delay time.

So a job can experience resource delay time while waiting for a person to start working it. A job can also experience resource delay after a person has started working it. The person working the job can become unavailable: she leaves for lunch, she takes a break, she goes home at the end of the day. When the resource working on a job becomes unavailable, the job experiences a resource delay.

In most situations this resource delay is a good approximation to what happens in the world being modeled: the work waits on the person's desk until she returns to it after lunch. But sometimes in the real world, the work will not wait for the person working it. When a server in Zona leaves for the evening, if she has any remaining customers she will transfer those customers to someone else rather than making them wait until she returns the next day! But how does the simulation know that in this situation, customers are to be transferred to another resource? We use the **resourceShift** attribute of the activity: **resourceShift** indicates that the job should be given to another resource if the original one becomes unavailable. If **resourceShift** is false for an activity, a job at that activity can experience a resource delay even when there are available resources—for example, if the resource working the job at the activity leaves for the evening. If **resourceShift** is true for an activity, there will never be a resource delay there as long as at least one resource is available.

A job can also experience a resource delay before work has started. Suppose a job is waiting at the activity **Collect Payment** in our restaurant dining process of Figure 11.8; the dinner has been finished and the party is waiting for their server to settle the bill. Their server is busy with another table, so they wait for her, even though other waitstaff are available. The availability of other waitstaff does not matter; they need their server, the one who served them drinks and dinner and who has their bill. The job waits until that particular resource is available. The activity attribute **consistentResource** is used to indicate this situation—that the resource should be the same as the one used at the prior activity.

In addition to resource delays—waiting for a resource to be available—a job can experience an *intrinsic delay*. An intrinsic delay is a delay that occurs as part of the normal work of the job. Consider the activity **Cook Dinner**, when the chef is preparing food for the diners. There is much work in that activity, of course, but there are also times during the food preparation when the duck is grilling or the onions are sautéing and the chef is not doing anything on this dinner. He is either working on other dinners for other parties, or if the restaurant is empty, he just waits for the duck to be grilled. It might take 40 minutes to prepare the dinner: 25 minutes of work and 15 minutes of intrinsic delay.

When working a single activity, a job can experience both a resource delay and an intrinsic delay. **Cook Dinner** includes an intrinsic delay as part of the nature of preparing food. If many dinner orders arrive at once, the chef might have more work than he can do, and some of the dinners suffer delays—resource delays—until the others are finished. (Or as explained later in the chapter, the chef could be limited by the physical resources of the kitchen—if for example all the grills are occupied.)

Intrinsic delays and resource delays are both delays. In both situations, the job is waiting and no work is being performed. But they are modeled differently. If an activity has an intrinsic delay, its **intrinsicDelay** attribute will indicate the amount of time that the job is delayed. Resource delay is not specified in an activity attribute. Instead it happens when the process is simulated, as a job waits for a resource to work it.

A delay can also occur in a flow, either in a sequence flow between activities in the same pool or in a message flow between pools. For example, when a vineyard supplier to Mykonos submits an invoice for wine, that message flow might be implemented by physical mail, including a three-day delay for the US Postal Service to deliver the letter. For a simulation, a flow delay is like an intrinsic delay in an activity: the job just waits for the specified time and then continues.

Simulating Exclusive Gateways

As you may recall from Chapter 5, a gateway is used to model branching behavior when there are several different sequence flows a job can take and a decision is made about which one (or which ones) to take. Consider the process shown in Figure 11.12, a variation of the dining process of Figure 11.8. Sometimes diners do not order drinks before dinner. The gateway **Order Drinks?** has two outgoing sequence flows: one if the diners order drinks and another if they do not. **Order Drinks?** is an exclusive gateway; either drinks are ordered or they are not.

In the midst of a simulation, when a job arrives at an exclusive gateway, how does the simulation engine decide which way to send the job? Does this job represent a party that is ordering drinks or one that will move straight to ordering

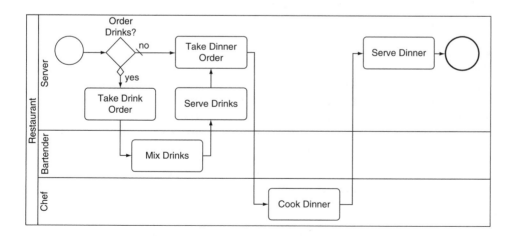

FIGURE 11.12 Simulating an exclusive gateway

dinner? How do we model the exclusive gateway so that the simulation engine knows what to do?

There are three alternative modeling approaches to this question. The simplest approach is for each of the outgoing sequence flows from the gateway to indicate a percentage of jobs. Each sequence flow has a **conditionExpression** attribute indicating whether the sequence flow will be taken. One of the sequence flows is a default; it is the flow taken if none of the others is chosen.

For example, suppose 60 percent of the parties order drinks before dinner and 40 percent do not. The lower sequence flow—connecting **Order Drinks?** to **Take Drink Order**—has a condition expression value of "A random chance of 60%," indicating a 60 percent chance of taking that path. (As with durations of activities, there is no standard language for condition expressions. Each simulation tool supports its own language. We use a precise form of English in this book.) The upper sequence flow—connecting **Order Drinks?** to **Take Dinner Order**—is the default sequence flow. It is taken in the other 40 percent of situations.

A job that arrives at the gateway will have a 60 percent chance of taking the lower path and a 40 percent chance of taking the upper path. Each job is evaluated differently, so in the midst of a simulation run, it is possible for four jobs in succession to beat the odds and all take the upper path. But over the course of hundreds of jobs, the actual results will be close to 60/40.[4]

A second way of modeling how an exclusive gateway determines the outgoing path is to examine an attribute of the job. Suppose that each job in this model had a **beforeDinnerDrink** attribute, indicating whether the party will order drinks before dinner. For some of the jobs this attribute is true and for others it is false. Then for each job, the outgoing sequence flows from **Order Drinks?** will examine the value of this attribute. Those with a value of false will be sent along the upper path, and those with a value of true will be sent on the lower path.

Of course, this just pushes the problem from the sequence flows to the job. How does a job get a value for **beforeDinnerDrink**? In the process shown in Figure 11.12, a natural approach would be to assign this attribute in the original start event when the job is created. Perhaps 60 percent of the parties arriving would be drinkers, and those jobs would be given true values for **beforeDinnerDrink** as they are created. The other 40 percent would be given false values.

There are two advantages of driving a gateway using a job attribute instead of probabilities evaluated on the sequence flow.

1. Job statistics can be analyzed and sorted by the job attribute. For example, do diners who order before-dinner drinks stay longer at the restaurant than

---

[4]Most business process models include this kind of random behavior in gateway branching, activity durations, or resource allocations. To get reliable results, you need to run a simulation long enough to overcome temporary effects. Alternatively, you can run a short simulation multiple times.

those who do not? How much longer? Do they experience more delays or fewer? These questions can be answered by comparing the statistical results of jobs that have a true value for **beforeDinnerDrink** with those that have a false value.

2. Attribute-based scenarios can be created. Suppose a large trade show is expected in town. Trade show participants are known to be more likely to drink (and to drink more) than typical restaurant patrons. A simulation scenario can be run in which for a few days 80 percent of the customers order drinks before dinner. Do longer wait times result? Does the restaurant need to staff more servers, or more bartenders, or both?

There is also a third way to model an exclusive gateway: combining the two approaches and making the gateway split depend on both an attribute of the job and on a random percentage. For example, the larger the party, the more likely someone will want to order a drink before dinner. The gateway sequence flows can be driven by logic that specifies a different percentage for different party sizes. Figure 11.13 shows the **conditionExpression** attribute of the lower outgoing sequence flow from the **Order Drinks?** activity in Figure 11.12.

Simulating Other Gateways

Exclusive gateways are the most commonly used variety of gateway, but other varieties are also used. As you will recall from Chapter 5, a parallel gateway starts parallel work—two or more sequence flows that then progress at the same time, perhaps to be later joined back together by another parallel gateway.

Consider the process shown in Figure 11.14, a refinement of Figure 11.12 that provides more detail on the preparation of food, showing the appetizers, entrées, and desserts. Figure 11.14 is a subprocess, just the preparation and serving of the food, without the messy details of seating the party and settling the bill. (And of course Figure 11.14 is quite simple, e.g., it assumes the party orders desserts.)

no: sequence flow	
conditionType	Expression
conditionExpression	A random chance of :
	30% for a party size of one person
	50% for a party size of two
	60% for a party size of three
	70% for a party size of four
	80% for a party size of five
	85% for a party size of six or more people

FIGURE 11.13 Larger parties are more likely to order drinks

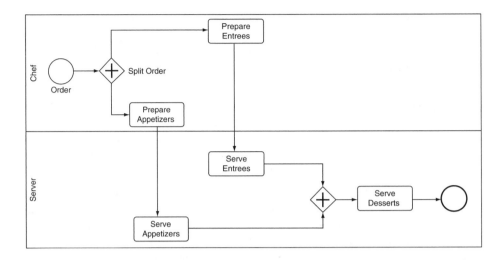

FIGURE 11.14 Using parallel gateways to prepare dinner

The chef starts the preparation of the appetizers and the entrées at the same time. The appetizers can be prepared quickly and are served to the customers when they are ready. The entrées take longer. When this part of the process is simulated, a single job will hit the gateway **Split Order**. The simulation engine splits the single job into two jobs, one traveling the upper sequence flow to **Prepare Entrees** and one traveling the lower sequence flow to **Prepare Appetizers**. Each of the two jobs collects statistics about the work—work time, delay time, etc.—as each progresses along its sequence flow. After the appetizers and entrées are served, the two jobs arrive at the other (unnamed) parallel gateway. At this point they are combined back into a single job, one that carries all the statistics of the two jobs that formed it.

Figure 11.14 assumes that each party orders both appetizers and entrées. An alternative approach is to use an inclusive gateway, as shown in Figure 11.15. In this case, a party can order just appetizers, just entrées, or both appetizers and entrées. During a simulation, the second (unnamed) gateway will do the right thing for each dining party. For a party that is eating both appetizers and entrées, the second gateway will wait for the two jobs to arrive before creating a new job from their combination. For a party that is eating only appetizers, the second gateway will pass the job through, not causing it to wait for anything. The analogous action occurs for the party that is eating only entrées: the second gateway will pass the job through.

The behavior of the first gateway—**Split Order**—is a bit complex. When a job arrives at **Split Order**, sometimes the job needs to travel the upper path, sometimes the lower path, and sometimes it needs to be split so that the two parallel jobs can travel both paths. The logic is controlled by the **conditionExpression** attributes of the two outgoing sequence flows.

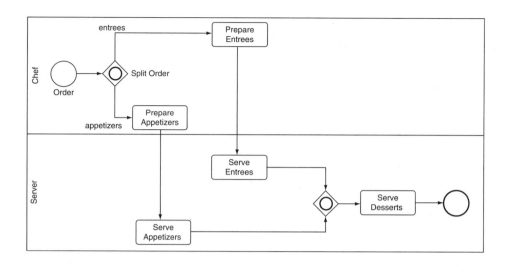

FIGURE 11.15 Using inclusive gateways to prepare dinner

One approach to modeling **Split Order** is to encode the percentage of jobs that take each path. Perhaps 90 percent of parties order entrees, and 60 percent order appetizers, so the upper sequence flow might have a **conditionExpression** value of "A random chance of 90%" and the lower sequence flow one of "A random chance of 60%." Since the two chances are independent, there are four combinations: 54 percent will order both entrees and appetizers, 36 percent will order entrees and no appetizers, 6 percent will order appetizers and no entrees, and 4 percent will order neither appetizers nor entrees.

This last 4 percent—in which neither path is taken—is a problem. An inclusive gateway needs to guarantee that at least one of the outgoing paths is taken or the model is considered invalid. But if condition expressions are used, 4 percent of the jobs will take neither outgoing sequence flow, leading to an invalid model.

Another, better approach that avoids the 4 percent problem is to generate the jobs with a custom attribute **foodOrder** that indicates whether the party orders appetizers, entrees, or both. Then the **conditionExpression** for the two outgoing sequence flows tests the value **foodOrder** of each job. The upper sequence flow tests whether **foodOrder** is either entrees or both, and the lower sequence flow tests whether **foodOrder** is either appetizers or both. Adding model-custom attributes to jobs is a useful technique that solves many modeling problems.

Simulating Start Events

Jobs are created at start events, travel through activities, gateways, and intermediate events, and finally finish their lives at end events. A start event typically creates many jobs, feeding a stream of jobs into a process. Consider again the restaurant dining process shown in Figure 11.12. The start event **Party Arrives** creates a job for each simulated party that arrives at the restaurant.

When does a start event create its jobs? Typically a start event will create some number of jobs every so often. For example, one start event might create two jobs every hour. Every hour of the simulation two new jobs are created. Another start event might create seven jobs every 20 minutes. Yet another start event might create one job every day. The **Party Arrives** start event in Figure 11.12 creates one job every 10 minutes; every 10 minutes a new party arrives at the restaurant to eat.

A start event has a **jobQuantity** attribute to model how many jobs are created at the same time and a **jobInterval** attribute to model the length of time between these times where jobs are created. **Party Arrives** in Figure 11.12 will have a **jobQuantity** value of 1 and a **jobInterval** value of 10 minutes.

But things are a bit more complicated. Zona is not open all the time, only in the evenings. It doesn't make sense for a new job to be created at 3:30 AM. There is another attribute that models the fact that the start event should only create new jobs at certain times of the day: **jobStartDuration**. Zona has a value of "5PM-10PM" for **jobStartDuration**.[5]

Of course Zona sees more customers on a Saturday night than they do on a Monday night. And more people show up between 7:00 PM and 9:00 PM than do before 7:00 PM or after 9:00 PM. As we saw earlier in the chapter, it can be important to model this variation, to see how much worse the waits are on Friday at 8:30 PM than on Monday at 6:30 PM. To model this variation, each start event has not just a single value for **Party Arrives** and **jobStartDuration** but a schedule of values. For the **Party Arrives** start event at Zona, that schedule is shown in Figure 11.16. On Mondays and Tuesdays, there is a steady but slow stream of customers, with one job started every 20 minutes between 6:00 PM and 10:00 PM. On Wednesdays and Sundays, there are more customers, one job started every 12 minutes. On Thursdays there is a job started every 12 minutes between 6:00 PM and 10:00 PM, and there

JobDays	JobQuantity	JobInterval	JobStartDuration
Mondays, Tuesdays	1	20 minutes	6PM–10PM
Wednesdays, Sundays	1	12 minutes	6PM–10PM
Thursdays	1	12 minutes	6PM–10PM
Thursdays	1	20 minutes	7PM–9PM
Fridays, Saturdays	2	12 minutes	6PM–11PM
Fridays, Saturdays	1	8 minutes	7PM–10PM
Fridays, Saturdays	1	15 minutes	7:30PM–9PM
Saturdays, Sundays	1	8 minutes	11AM–3PM

FIGURE 11.16 Start event schedule for **Party Arrives**

---

[5]As usual, modeling tools vary in the syntax of values for these start event attributes. In this book, we use a structured English for readability.

are some additional parties that show up between 7:00 PM and 9:00 PM—an additional job every 20 minutes during those busy hours. On Friday and Saturday evening, there is a base level of jobs started between 6:00 PM and 11:00 PM, two parties every 12 minutes, an additional job every 8 minutes between 7:00 PM and 10:00 PM, and a further additional job every 15 minutes between 7:30 PM and 9:00 PM. Saturdays and Sundays also see Zona open for lunch and so there are jobs that start between 11:00 AM and 3:00 PM.

The schedule in Figure 11.16 shows a party arriving at Zona every 12 minutes on Wednesdays. That regularity is also a simplification. In the real world, parties arrive sporadically. Sometimes 30 minutes passes and no one shows up. Sometimes three or four parties will arrive in a few minutes.

It can be important to capture that variability in your model. When two parties arrive at about the same time, the second party will wait for the host to seat the first party. That wait will never happen in your model if you have modeled parties arriving regularly every 12 minutes.

It is possible to model a variation in arrival times. Instead of a fixed **jobInterval** of 12 minutes, you can include a probability distribution, e.g., a uniform distribution from 1 to 23 minutes, a standard distribution that averages to 12 minutes, or some more complex distribution, such as the duration distributions discussed earlier and shown in Figure 11.11.

The **jobQuantity** can also vary statistically. This variance is convenient when you are modeling a process that has a large number of jobs. For example, in Figure 11.16 there is a line in the schedule for Friday nights that has two jobs starting every 12 minutes between 5:00 and 11:00 PM. Instead of two jobs, you might model that as a uniform distribution of 1 to 3 jobs. One third of the time one party arrives, one third of the time two parties, and one third of the time three parties arrive at the same time.

A schedule in a start event can support high model fidelity; it is possible to get very precise about the load of jobs and the way that load varies from day to day. Of course, there are diminishing returns to that fidelity. Often a start event modeled at a lower-fidelity will deliver as good results as a higher-fidelity approach.

As discussed earlier, the jobs in our restaurant simulation will have a **partySize** attribute, indicating the number of people in the party. The party size for the job influences how long activities take and influences the probabilities within gateways. This model-specific job attribute is set when the job is created at the start event **Party Arrives**. How does this work? The start event has a collection of *assignments*, as shown in Figure 11.17.

To	From
partySize	Uniform distribution from 1 to 8
beforeDinnerDrink	60% true and 40% false

FIGURE 11.17 Assignments for **Party Arrives**

When a job is created at a start event, it is given values for every attribute in the assignments collection. A job created at **Party Arrives** will be given a value for the attribute **partySize** of a number between 1 and 8, and a value for **beforeDinnerDrink**, either true or false. These attribute values will be part of the job, carried with it through all its activities, until the job finishes at an end event.

Simulating End Events

A job finishes when it reaches an end event. As you may recall, each job carries statistical information with it as it travels from activity to activity. (Table 11.1 shows the statistics carried by a job.) When a job finishes, its statistical information is aggregated with the statistical information of the other jobs that have previously finished.

For example, each job carries a *cycle time*—the amount of simulated time since it was created at a start event. For our restaurant dining model, the cycle time will be the amount of time a dining party has been at the restaurant, starting with their arrival at the restaurant. When the job finishes, its cycle time is combined with the cycle times of other jobs that have already finished. Now we can determine the average cycle time: how long diners spend at the restaurant from beginning to end. We can watch for a maximum cycle time: what was the most time some party spent at the restaurant? We can relate cycle time to other information tracked by the job: does cycle time depend on the size of the party?

When you are developing a simulation, you might find that some jobs never finish. Of course some jobs simply haven't finished yet. If you run the simulation longer, they will finish. But sometimes jobs are started but never reach an end event, no matter how long you simulate. This happens when you have errors and mistakes in your model. Certainly in the real world, it would be odd if a restaurant party arrived at Zona on Friday night and never left! Later in this chapter we describe how you can look at job counts at activities to validate your model, to find and correct the errors and mistakes.

Simulating Subprocesses

Not every start event creates jobs. A start event within a subprocess does not create any jobs on its own. Instead it indicates where the subprocess starts. Suppose you were simulating the (rather simple) process of creating a daily specials menu, shown in Figure 11.18. The start event **Start Specials** starts jobs, presumably one job each day. But the start event **Begin Plan** starts no jobs on its own. Instead it shows where jobs that have left the activity **Determine Ingredient Availability** should begin the embedded subprocess **Plan Specials**. For the simulation engine, start events serve these two distinct functions.

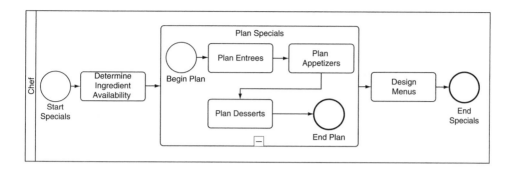

FIGURE 11.18 Simulating start and end events in an embedded process

End events also serve two functions. The end event **End Specials** in Figure 11.18 finishes jobs. Any job that performs the activity **Design Menus** and then encounters **End Specials** will be finished at that point. Its statistics will be aggregated with the statistics of all the other jobs that have already finished. The end event **End Plan** is different. When a job hits that end event, it will finish the subprocess and travel across the sequence flow of the upper process, to **Design Menus**. Just as a start event in a subprocess does not create any jobs, an end event in a subprocess does not finish any. Of course, activity statistics are collected at each activity, including those that have subprocesses. But job statistics are not aggregated when a job hits a subprocess end event, since the job is not yet finished.

Often a subprocess will have neither a start event nor an end event. As explained in Chapter 5, if there is no start event in a subprocess, there is an implicit start event preceding each activity, event, or gateway that lacks an incoming sequence flow. In other words, Figure 11.19 (without start events) simulates just like Figure 11.18 (with start events). When a job finishes with the activity

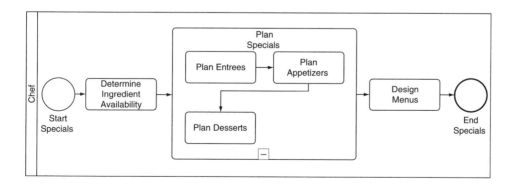

FIGURE 11.19 Simulating an embedded process without start or end events

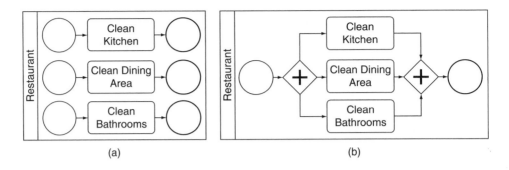

FIGURE 11.20 Two subprocesses that simulate the same start events

Determine Ingredient Availability, it drops down into the subprocess and starts the activity **Plan Entrees**, since that activity has no incoming sequence flow. It is as though there is an implicit start event before **Plan Entrees**, like the start event **Begin Plan** in Figure 11.18. When the job finishes **Plan Entrees**, **Plan Appetizers**, and **Plan Desserts**, it pops back up out of the **Plan Specials** subprocess and begins the activity **Design Menus**. It is as though there is an implicit end event after **Plan Desserts**, like **End Plan** in Figure 11.18.

Some subprocesses have multiple start events. Consider the subprocess with three start events shown in Figure 11.20a. When simulated, an incoming job will split and start the three start events in parallel. It is as though there is a single start event that leads to a parallel gateway; the subprocess in Figure 11.20a simulates exactly the same way as the one in Figure 11.20b.

Resource Schedules

People do not work all the time. Every person has hours he works and hours he does not work. To model realistic working times, resources have schedules. Just as a start event has a schedule for when jobs are created, each resource has a schedule for when he works. The schedule for a server who works at Zona is shown in Figure 11.21. As you can see, he works evenings Wednesday through Saturday as well as Sunday afternoons.

Day	Duration
Wednesdays	4:30PM–11PM
Thursdays	6PM–11PM
Fridays	6PM–12AM
Saturdays	7PM–12AM
Sundays	10:30AM–4PM

FIGURE 11.21 A resource schedule

Resource schedules can be more detailed than shown in Figure 11.21. You can model breaks, holidays, vacations, and other HR detail. But often such detail is not useful. Many good models take a simpler approach. Rather than capture the schedule of each resource—each person—these simpler models just capture the schedule of each role. Figure 11.21 might be the schedule for the **Server** role, for all the servers in the model. This is another example of the tradeoff between the fidelity of more detail and the simplicity of less.

Resource Costs and Other Costs

Resources cost money. Most organizations pay more money for their human resources—their employees and contractors—than for any other expense. When a job simulates through a business process, the job accumulates the cost of each resource that works on the job. If a server spends 5 minutes serving dinner to a party, and the server costs the restaurant $12 per hour in costs, then $1 of costs will accumulate on the job that models that party.

To put the right cost on the job as it is worked by a resource, the modeler must capture the resource's hourly cost. **hourlyCost** is another attribute of the resource. The hourly cost of each resource is captured separately because different people incur different hourly costs. Chefs are paid more than servers, who in turn are paid more than cleaning staff.

Hourly cost is not just the wages (or salaries) received by the employee. It includes the fully loaded cost to the employer of having the employee work: the cost of benefits, employment taxes, training, liability, etc. Sometimes the fully loaded cost for useful work is twice the wages or even more.

Some activities have other costs, in addition to the cost of the resource working the activity. For example, an activity that ships something across the country will incur the cost of the shipping service. This expense for the shipping service is in addition to the expense of the employee performing the shipping activity. The activity expense is captured in an attribute of the activity called **additionalCost**.

Nonhuman Resources and Multiple Resources

In most business process simulations, all the resources represent people. When a resource is working in a simulation, that resource represents a person working in the world. The schedule of a resource is a person's schedule. The people-orientation of resources is not surprising: business process models are people-oriented. They model how people do work. Of course, when people work activities, they are often supported by machines—computers and software, production equipment, and the other artifacts of our technological age. But usually in business process models, we do not explicitly model the support machinery as resources. The availability of the machinery is usually not an issue; it is the availability of the people that constrains the work.

But we have already seen an exception, a situation where the modeling of nonhuman resources is important. In the customer wait model earlier in this chapter, the waits are caused partly by the limited number of tables. Consider again the process shown in Figure 11.12. A job at **Seat Party** will wait if there is no host available to seat the party represented by the job. But the job will also wait at **Seat Party** if there is a host available but no table. The activity **Seat Party** requires two resources, both a human resource—a host—and a nonhuman resource—a table.

An activity has an attribute **resources** that captures the resources required by the activity. Most activities require only a single resource, but **Seat Party** has two resources, and both must be recorded in the **resources** attribute. Note that there is no visual way using swimlanes to show that an activity requires multiple resources.

When a job arrives at an activity that requires two resources, it waits until both resources are available. The job does not grab the resources one at a time; when a job representing an unseated party arrives at the activity **Seat Party** it does not first occupy a host and wait for a table to be ready. Instead the job waits until both resources are available at the same time.

Summary of Business Process Simulation

Business process simulation is used to reveal the costs and times of a business process—either an existing business process or a newly designed business process. To create a business process simulation, you must understand the activities of your business process, the way jobs flow through those activities, and the way resources work those jobs at those activities as they flow through. As a simulation runs, statistics are collected about the jobs, resources, and activities.

To create a business process simulation, Rhonda modeled the business process of dining at Zona. She augmented the static model with several additional attributes. She added durations to the activities, including intrinsic delay times for activities such as preparing an entrée that naturally involves both work (on the part of the chef) and waiting. She annotated activities with the **resourceShift** and **consistentResource** attributes, indicating the way resources can be applied to jobs at activities. She added logic to gateways to indicate which jobs traverse which sequence flow. She added job schedules to the start events. And she modeled resources, including their costs and their schedules.

The result of all this work was a business process simulation that shows how waits occur, what actions and policies result in longer waits, and how waits can be shortened with different actions and policies. You intend to use this simulation to work with the restaurant general managers to show them how their decisions can affect wait times.

But Rhonda wants to go further. She wants to investigate how long waits impact customer satisfaction and how lower satisfaction results in fewer customers and, ultimately, failure. Business process simulations cannot help us with customer satisfaction. We must turn to the other business modeling discipline that supports simulation: business motivation models.

SIMULATING A BUSINESS MOTIVATION MODEL

Business motivation models can be simulated, although the techniques are not as widely understood as those for business process simulation. You may recall from Chapter 3 that actuators can be connected to form a causal loop diagram to show, for example, how a neighborhood becoming known for restaurants (one actuator) will lead to more restaurant customers dining there (another actuator) and in turn lead to even more restaurant owners opening restaurants in the same neighborhood (a third actuator). A simulation can be built from the causal loop diagram, turning the actuators into simulated variables that change over time.

Rhonda builds such a business motivation simulation to explore how wait times affect the views of customers and potential customers. She starts with the causal loop diagram shown in Figure 11.22. As Zona becomes more popular and acquires more customers, word of mouth about the restaurant spreads. More prospective new customers try the restaurant. But as Zona becomes more popular, the customer wait time increases—both the time spent waiting for a table initially and the time spent waiting through the whole dining experience. As wait time increases, the attractiveness of Zona as a restaurant declines. And as Zona becomes less attractive, fewer customers go there; it becomes less popular.

Rhonda sets the initial conditions of the model to reflect the number of customers Zona saw on Friday nights a year earlier. Similarly, she sets the wait times for those modest waits of a year earlier. Then she runs it for four simulated years, producing the results shown in Figure 11.23.

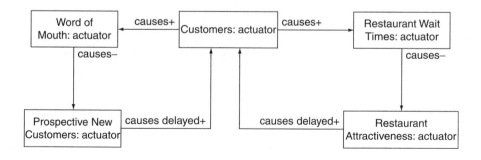

FIGURE 11.22 The basic causal loops of customer waits

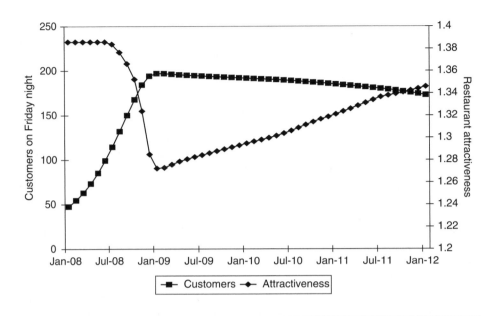

FIGURE 11.23 Simulating the basic causal loops

The simulation starts with 50 customers on a Friday night and with a very modest 30-minute average total wait time. Customers enjoy the good food and the modest waits. Word of mouth spreads. More people are attracted to Zona over the next 12 months, peaking at about 200 people on a Friday night. At that point there are 60-minute waits, and some customers find that those waits make Zona less attractive. Customers are gradually lost, and the wait times gradually decline.

Now Rhonda adds a complication. As more new customers discover Zona, some people start to perceive it as the hot new restaurant. This perception adds to Zona's attractiveness, and more people dine there. The waits increase, but people care less about the long waits; eating at the latest place seems worth it. Of course, once the delays are long enough, people will be deterred from going to Zona, no matter how hot it is. The new causal loop diagram is shown in Figure 11.24.

The resulting simulation behaves differently. Figure 11.25 shows how customers and attractiveness play out over four years. Zona quickly becomes trendy, and Friday night customers approach 250, beyond the capacity of the restaurant. The waits increase to 90 minutes, but the trendiness offsets the impact of the long waits for a while, leading to high attractiveness. Of course, the perception of being the latest hot restaurant doesn't last forever, and after a couple of years Zona loses some of the crowds and returns to being a very good restaurant with a loyal clientele.

But things are not quite so rosy. Rhonda now adds some more actuators to the causal loop diagram, as shown in Figure 11.26. She adds **Former Customers**, the number of people who were once customers of Zona but are customers no

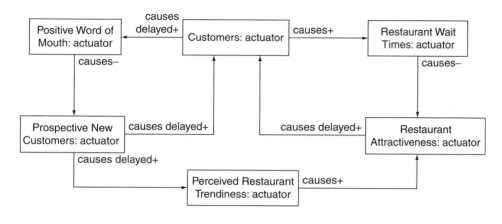

FIGURE 11.24 Including the trendiness of a restaurant in the causal loop structure

longer. Former customers also contribute to word of mouth, but their contribution is negative, not positive. The negative word of mouth serves to discourage people from trying Zona.

Rhonda separates restaurant attractiveness into two related measures of attractiveness. **Restaurant Attr to New Custs** is the degree to which Zona is attractive to new customers and includes the perceived trendiness. But once a customer is

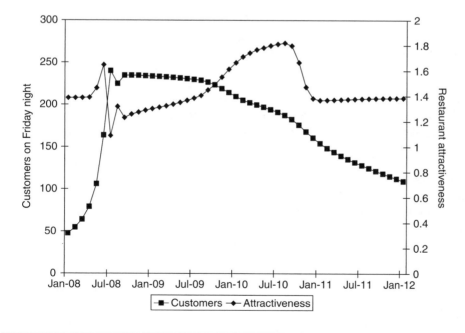

FIGURE 11.25 Simulating the ephemeral effects of trendiness

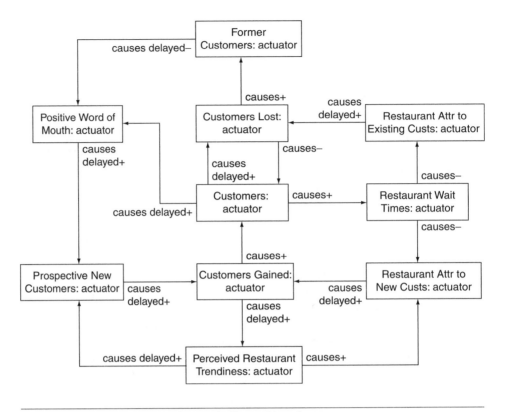

FIGURE 11.26 Simulating the ephemeral effects of trendiness

no longer new, he is less influenced by the trendiness. Now **Restaurant Attr to Existing Custs** is the relevant actuator. Rhonda also refines trendiness a bit, defining **Perceived Restaurant Trendiness** as caused by the number of new customers.

The results of the new model are shown in Figure 11.27. Again the waits spike early as Zona becomes trendy. But now the waits push existing customers away. When the trendiness passes, Zona continues to lose customers as the negative word of mouth from the former customers dominates the positive word of mouth. Zona never recovers.

Rhonda completes the model by adding a user interface so that restaurant managers can try different reservations policies and see the effects play out over time. (User interfaces are described later in this chapter, with Rhonda's user interface shown as Figure 11.38.) If they want to let customers wait, they can see the sad results in Figure 11.27. They can also let their restaurant become a bit popular, then switch to the more restrictive policy of only seating people with reservations. Such a policy forgoes the revenues and some of the trendiness in return for keeping existing customers happier.

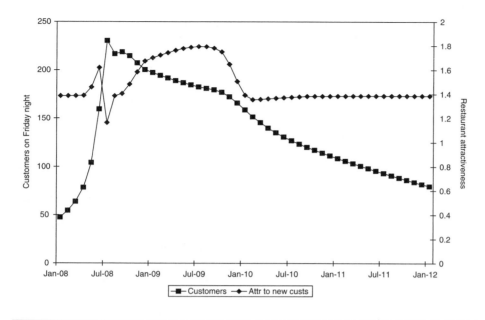

FIGURE 11.27 Simulating the way former customers discourage new customers

Business Motivation Simulation Tools

What does it take to simulate a motivation model? An appropriate simulation engine is required. Business process models are simulated with business process simulation engines, but business motivation models are simulated with a very different kind of engine—an engine suited for simulating strategy. A strategy simulation engine allows you to create a model of actuators influencing one another—like the one shown in Figure 11.26—and then simulate the results, producing a graph over time, like the one in Figure 11.27.

Variables

Creating a business motivation simulation requires more than just acquiring a modeling engine. Your motivation model must be ready for simulation. In particular, you must cast the model elements of your motivation model as *variables*, the key primitive of the motivation simulations.

What is a variable? A variable is some quantity that changes over time as the simulation is run. In the Zona simulation, **Customers** is a variable. The number of customers eating at Zona changes over the course of the simulation, first rising and then falling. **Restaurant Wait Times** is another variable.

Customers and **Restaurant Wait Times** are both *concrete variables*. A concrete variable is a variable that is measurable. You could in principle measure the value of either **Customers** or **Restaurant Wait Times**. You could keep track of the number of different people who eat at Zona at least once every three months to obtain a value for the **Customers** variable. Measuring **Restaurant Wait Times** is somewhat more involved, but with enough stopwatches you could time how long each party waits over the course of a single Friday night, then average those timings to obtain a value for **Restaurant Wait Times**.

Some variables are *abstract,* inherently difficult to measure. For example, it is not clear how you would measure **Perceived Restaurant Trendiness**. You could perhaps poll customers or prospective customers about what restaurant is hot, but your poll would not reflect the fact that some people's opinions on these matters are more influential than others'.

Just because a variable is abstract does not mean it is less important. Some abstract variables are quite powerful; they have great influence on other variables. For example, perceptions of trendiness is a powerful motivator of behavior. Once a restaurant is perceived as the new hot place, many more people hear about it, and many more try it. A Zona model without a variable for trendiness will be less accurate and less valuable than one with trendiness.

Every variable—whether concrete or abstract—is measured in units against a scale. **Customers** is measured in the number of people who eat at Zona at least once over the course of three months. The scale of **Customers** is 0 to 50,000: 0 representing a restaurant empty all the time, and 50,000 far beyond the capacity of the rather small restaurant to serve.

Concrete variables have fairly obvious units and scales, but when you create a more abstract variable you often need to invent appropriate units and scale. For example, in the Zona simulation **Perceived Restaurant Trendiness** has a scale from 0 to 100. 0 is not trendy at all, and 100 is as trendy as it is possible to be, on everyone's lips and in every newspaper article about top restaurants in DC.

Sometimes the appropriate unit of a variable is a rate over time. For example, in Figure 11.26 the actuator **Customers Lost** models how quickly Zona loses its existing customers—how quickly customers of Zona decide to stop patronizing that restaurant. The unit of **Customers Lost** is customers per week: how many customers does Zona lose each week? The scale for **Customers Lost** is 0 to 1,500. On a good week, Zona will lose no customers, and on a very bad week Zona might lose every customer who ventures in.

As you might have guessed, there is a relationship between the actuators in a causal loop diagram and variables in a motivation simulation. Every actuator is a variable. In Figure 11.26, there are 10 actuators, and each is a variable in the simulation; **Former Customers**, **Restaurant Wait Times**, and **Positive Word of Mouth** are all variables.

But there are more than 10 variables in the simulation model. In fact, Figure 11.26 is something of a simplification—accurate enough and shown to present a comprehensible view of the whole but without all the variables needed for simulation. For example, in Figure 11.26, **Customers** and **Restaurant Wait Times** are connected directly by a **causes+** association. But to actually simulate that association, several more variables are needed. One such variable is **Weekly Demand**, as shown in Figure 11.28.

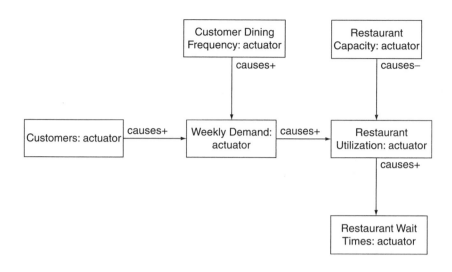

FIGURE 11.28 More detail on the relationship between customers and wait times

Defining Variables with Arithmetic

Sometimes the relationship between variables is expressed in simple arithmetic. For example, in Figure 11.28, the utilization of the restaurant is determined by dividing the weekly demand by the capacity:

$$\text{Restaurant Utilization} = \text{Weekly Demand} / \text{Restaurant Capacity}$$

The capacity is 1,300 customers (per week). When the weekly demand is 650, the utilization is 50 percent—on average, half the tables are occupied and half the tables are open.

The weekly demand is also expressed using simple arithmetic, by multiplying the number of customers by the frequency with which they dine:

$$\text{Weekly Demand} = \text{Customers} * \text{Customer Dining Frequency}$$

Zona's customers frequent the restaurant once every 12 weeks (on average), or at a frequency of 0.083/week. When Zona has 7,800 customers, the weekly demand is 650.

Defining Variables with Tables and Graphs

Often the relationship between variables is too complex to be modeled with simple arithmetic. For example, the relationship between the utilization of the restaurant and the average wait time for customers is not something easily defined by addition, multiplication, and the other primitives of arithmetic. Instead, we model it with a table of values, as shown in Table 11.2. When Zona is 20 percent

Table 11.2 Defining the Average Wait Time Based on the Utilization

Utilization	Wait Time (Minutes)	Utilization	Wait Time (Minutes)	Utilization	Wait Time (Minutes)
0%	30	35%	34	70%	100
5%	30	40%	39	75%	116
10%	30	45%	45	80%	132
15%	30	50%	53	85%	150
20%	30	55%	62	90%	174
25%	30	60%	73	95%	210
30%	31	65%	86	100%	250

utilized, the average wait time is 30 minutes. Customers wait only for their food to be prepared, not for a table, for waitstaff, or for their check. Higher levels of utilizations lead to longer waits. An average utilization of 60 percent for the week implies that Zona is quite busy at the busiest times—8:00 PM on Friday and Saturday nights. This leads to an average wait of 73 minutes. If the utilization is even higher, the waits are longer. A utilization of 90 percent leads to an average wait of 174 minutes, almost three hours.

Of course, at any given time the utilization is likely to be some other value not shown in Table 11.2—not 55 or 60 percent, but 57.23 percent. The simulation engine finds the current value for wait time by interpolating—by creating an estimate of the value based on the two values on either side. The engine notes that 55 percent has a wait time of 62 minutes, that 60 percent has a wait time of 73 minutes, and that 57.23 percent has a wait time of 66.91 minutes, in between 62 and 73.

Some motivation simulation tools allow the modeler to define variable relationships graphically. The modeler has the choice of entering the values in Table 11.2 or drawing the equivalent graph shown in Figure 11.29.[6] Often it is easier to think about the relationship in terms of a graph. Furthermore, most subject matter experts find the graph form easier to understand and validate.

Abstract Variables

Defining a relationship as a table or a graph is particularly useful for variables that are more abstract. For example, consider the attractiveness of Zona to customers. Attractiveness is very much an abstract variable, something we have modeled in

---

[6]Note that the graph shown in Figure 11.29 is fundamentally different from earlier graphs in this chapter. Earlier graphs showed the results of simulations. Figure 11.29 defines a variable in the simulation model itself, a variable used to produce simulation results.

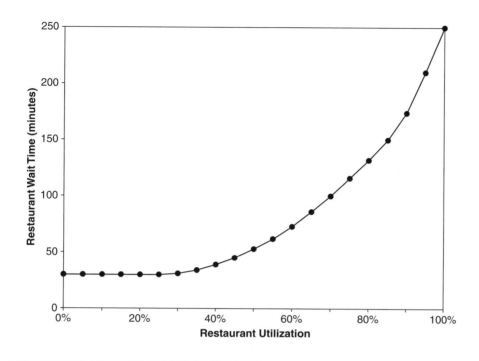

FIGURE 11.29 The relationship between utilization and wait times

the simulation on a 0 to 2 scale, with 2 being the most attractive restaurant in the world, 1.5 being quite attractive, 1 being neither particularly attractive nor particularly unattractive, and 0 being repellant to all customers. Attractiveness depends on the wait times as well as on other factors. But how does the average wait time influence the attractiveness of Zona? Clearly we are not going to create an arithmetic expression that shows how wait time influences attractiveness. But with tables and graphs, creating this relationship is surprisingly easy.

Consider first the causal loop diagram shown in Figure 11.30. The attractiveness of the restaurant to new customers is modeled by the variable **Restaurant Attr to New Custs**. In our model, restaurant attractiveness is determined not only by the wait times but also by the quality of the food and current trendiness of the restaurant. These three variables combine to determine attractiveness.

Each of the three variables could determine attractiveness on its own if the other two were not relevant. If the wait times at Zona were such that customers were not dissuaded, and if Zona were neither a currently trendy restaurant nor last year's tired trend, then the attractiveness of Zona would be completely determined by the food quality: by how well the food delights the palates of the customers. The food quality is itself an abstract variable, with a range from 0 (awful)

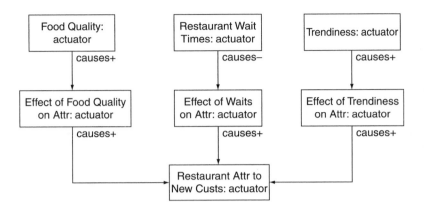

FIGURE 11.30 Determining the attractiveness of a restaurant

to 100 (world class). When the food quality is 0, the attractiveness will be 0, and when the food quality is 100, the attractiveness is 1.5, as shown in Figure 11.31.

Note that Figure 11.31 does not show the relationship between food quality and restaurant attractiveness directly. Rather it shows the relationship between food quality and the *feeder variable* **Effect of Food Quality on Attr**. That feeder

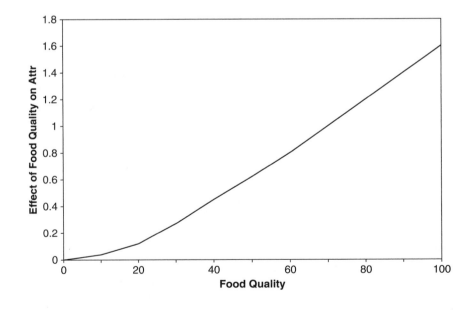

FIGURE 11.31 The effect of food quality on restaurant attractiveness

variable is identical to restaurant attractiveness only if the other two factors have no effect on attractiveness. Mathematically that result is achieved by multiplying the effects for the three feeder variables:

Restaurant Attr to New Custs = Effect of Food Quality on Attr *
Effect of Waits on Attr *
Effect of Trendiness on Attr

If the waits are modest, the waiting time will have no effect on attractiveness. In this situation the feeder variable **Effect of Waits on Attr** will be 1.0. (And of course, multiplying by 1.0 leads to no change.) If the waits are long, the long waits will make Zona less attractive. In this case, **Effect of Waits on Attr** will be some number less than 1.0, and multiplying that number will reduce the attractiveness. Figure 11.32 shows the relationship between wait times and restaurant attractiveness.

Long waits make Zona less attractive, dissuading would-be customers and convincing existing customers to eat elsewhere. For example, an average wait of 70 minutes—not uncommon at a busy restaurant—will lead to **Effect of Waits on Attr** taking a value of 0.83. When this is multiplied by the effect of the food quality and trendiness, the resulting attractiveness value will be 17 percent less than it would be otherwise, without the waits. But short waits in themselves never make

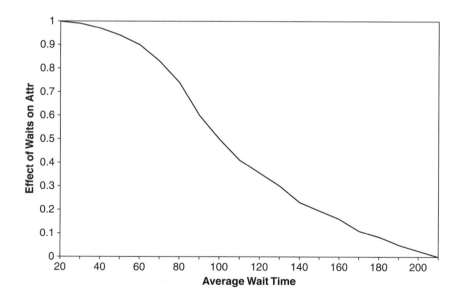

FIGURE 11.32 The effect of wait times on restaurant attractiveness

Zona attractive. A fast-food restaurant might be attractive solely because it is fast, but a fine restaurant like Zona (and all the Mykonos restaurants) do not benefit from speed alone. Only food quality and trendiness can actually make Zona attractive in our model; **Effect of Waits on Attr** never takes a value greater than 1.

The third contributor to attractiveness—**Trendiness**—is also an abstract variable. Restaurant trendiness is measured on a 0 to 100 scale, with 0 being a restaurant that is yet to be discovered by the trend-setters and 100 a restaurant that is their favorite, at least today. Trendiness has its own effect on attractiveness and, like food quality, can contribute to Zona being either more attractive or less so.

Delays

Delays are common in business motivation situations. A corporate goal leads to new strategies, but forming the new strategies takes a while. An influencer occurs and is recognized as a threat, but only after someone within the organization notices it, brings it to the attention of others, and persuades enough people that the threat is real and something worth their consideration.

There are many delays in our restaurant wait simulation. For example, Zona's reputation (modeled in Figure 11.26 as **Positive Word of Mouth**) leads to more prospective customers, people who want to eat at Zona. Some of these prospective customers will enjoy their experience and become Zona customers, eating there more or less regularly. But an increase in prospective customers does not lead to an immediate increase in customers, because the prospective customers do not drop all their other plans and immediately try Zona. Instead they work it into their schedules, they make reservations, they invite their friends or loved ones. It takes some time for a prospective customer to try Zona for the first time.

Figure 11.33 shows the relationship between **Prospective New Customers** and **Customers Gained**, expanded to include the intermediate variable **Samplers** not shown in the more abstract Figure 11.26. An increase in prospective new customers leads to an increase in samplers, people who try the restaurant. The increase happens after a delay as people fit the new restaurant in their plans. Once someone tries the restaurant for the first time, she is no longer a

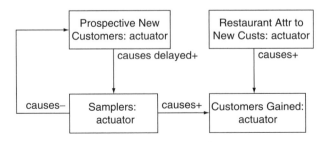

FIGURE 11.33 Prospective new customers try the restaurant for the first time

prospective new customer. So an increase in **Samplers** leads to a decrease in **Prospective New Customers**. Some of the people who sample the new restaurant then become customers, so there is a **causes+** association from **Samplers** to **Customers Gained**.

The **causes delayed+** association from **Prospective New Customers** to **Samplers** is enough detail for the motivation model diagram of Figure 11.33 but not enough detail to actually drive a simulation. Simulation requires more precision. For example, **Samplers** could be defined as being exactly equal to **Prospective New Customers** but delayed by four weeks:

$$\text{Samplers} = \text{Prospective new customers, delayed by 4 weeks}$$

(As usual, we have employed precise English rather than bothering with the syntax of a delay function. In any case, the different simulation tools use different syntaxes for their delay functions, although they all offer this basic delay functionality.)

Figure 11.34 shows the simulation results for **Samplers** and **Prospective New Customers**. To better display the relationship, only a single 12-month period is shown, from July 2008 to July 2009. As you can see, **Samplers** follows the rise and fall of **Prospective New Customers**, after a four-week delay.

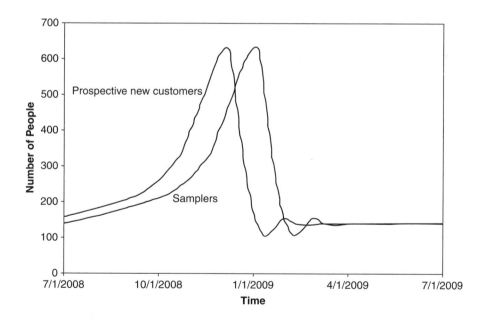

FIGURE 11.34 Samplers follow prospective new customers after a four-week delay

Pipeline Delay and Information Delay

In fact, several different kinds of delay are possible. The delay shown in Figure 11.34 is called a *pipeline delay*. In a pipeline delay the value of the lagging variable (**Samplers**) is exactly equal to the earlier value of the leading variable (**Prospective New Customers**). If there are 150 prospective customers on January 2, then four weeks later, on January 30, there will be 150 samplers trying the restaurant for the first time.

Pipeline delays are a good way to model situations where something needs a fixed amount of time to be prepared. If we were modeling the delay between the decision to offer a new menu and the actual introduction of the menu, a pipeline delay would be a good choice. But the delay between someone wanting to try Zona and that same person actually trying it for the first time is not a fixed delay. Some people plan ahead for 10 or 12 weeks, knowing when they will visit Washington, DC, and making reservations for that visit. Others plan a few weeks ahead, putting Zona on their social calendar. Still others are quite spontaneous, arranging to try Zona the day they hear about it. This diversity in planning behavior is better modeled by a different kind of delay, an *information delay*. With an information delay, some of the effect is almost immediate, some is delayed a bit, some delayed more, and some delayed even more.

The differing delay times can be averaged. For example, if some delay takes 1 day, some takes 2 weeks, and some takes 8 weeks, we might see an average delay of 4 weeks. So every information delay is expressed in terms of the average delay. For example, the relationship between **Prospective New Customers** and **Samples** might exhibit an information delay of 4 weeks:

Samplers = Prospective new customers, with an information delay of 4 weeks

Figure 11.35 shows the results of a four-week information delay. Note that the curve for samplers is smoother than the curve for prospective new customers. It does not reach as high during the peak of trendiness nor dip as low with the long waits. Information delays smooth out the extremes of the leading variable.

Simulating Feedback

In Chapter 3 we introduced causal loop diagrams, and earlier in this chapter we examined several of these diagrams. Within a causal loop diagram are typically one or more causal loops. A *causal loop* is a circular chain of variables affecting one another in turn. One variable affects a second variable, which in turn affects a third variable, and the third variable then affects the first. Or perhaps the loop is longer, with five or seven variables completing the circle.

Causal loops are common in the situations modeled by business motivation simulations. In the simulation of restaurant wait times we are exploring, there are at least 10 distinct causal loops. Using the terms introduced in Chapter 3 some of these loops are reinforcing; these loops drive more and more extreme

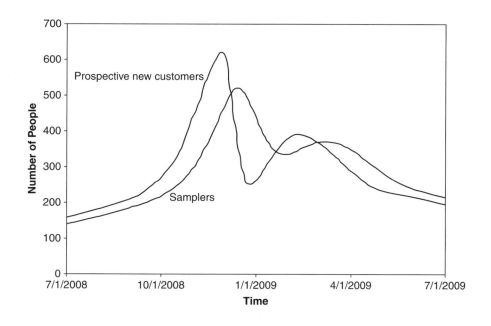

FIGURE 11.35 Sampler follows prospective new customers, after a four-week info delay

behavior. For example, as the restaurant gains customers, more people talk about it. More prospective customers learn about the restaurant through word of mouth from their friends and colleagues. Some of these prospective customers try the restaurant, and some of those samplers like it so much that they become regular customers. This in turn leads to more word of mouth and further prospective customers. The restaurant becomes more and more popular.

Other loops in our restaurant example are balancing; these loops moderate the behavior, returning the situation to some middle ground. For example, as the restaurant earns new customers and it becomes more popular, the utilization grows and the wait times increase. The increasing wait times lead to a decline in the attractiveness and fewer new customers gained. Figure 11.36 shows this balancing causal loop.

Of the nine variables in Figure 11.36, we have already explored six earlier in this chapter.

So we must define only the three remaining variables to completely model this causal loop, the three variables on the left of Figure 11.36: **Enjoyed Proportion**, **Customers Gained**, and **Customers**. Let's start with **Enjoyed Proportion**. When new people sample Zona for the first time, how many enjoy their experience enough to become customers? How many do not enjoy their experience, at least not enough to return? The proportion of people who enjoy their experience is **Enjoyed Proportion**. For a world-class restaurant on a good day, the

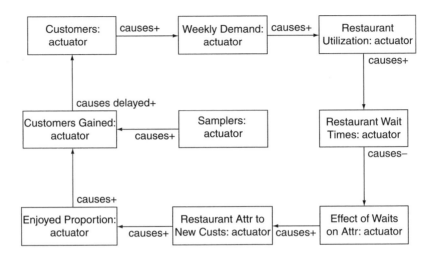

FIGURE 11.36 More customers lead to increased wait times, and then fewer customers

enjoyed proportion might be as high as 0.80; 80 percent of the new samplers like it. For a truly awful restaurant, the enjoyed proportion can be as low as 0.0—no one likes it enough to return.

Figure 11.37 shows how **Enjoyed Proportion** depends on **Restaurant Attr to New Custs**—the attractiveness of the restaurant to new customers. As you will recall, attractiveness varies from 0—not attractive at all—to 2—highly attractive.

The second undefined variable—**Customers Gained**—is quite simple. It is just the number of people who sampled the restaurant this week multiplied by the proportion of those samplers that enjoyed their experience:

$$\text{Customers Gained} = \text{Samplers} * \text{Enjoyed Proportion}$$

Stocks

Only one variable remains from Figure 11.36: **Customers**. The number of regular customers depends on how many regular customers were gained over the last week, on the variable **Customers gained**, as shown in Figure 11.36. **Customers** also depends on how many regular customers were lost in the last week, whether because they moved away, became bored with Zona, or suffered long waits during their latest Zona experience. (For simplicity **Customers Lost** is not shown in Figure 11.36.)

But **Customers** depends on something more than the customers lost and gained over the last week. A newly opened restaurant might gain 100 customers in its first week. In the same week, a long-established restaurant might also gain 100 customers. But they do not end the week with the same number of

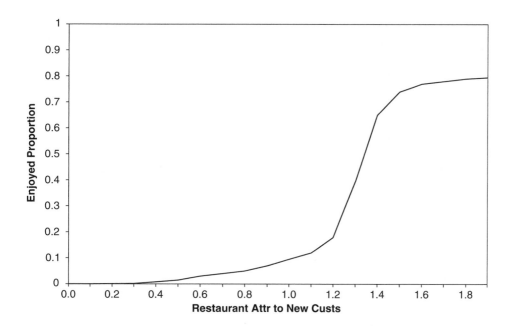

FIGURE 11.37 Restaurant attractiveness determines whether samplers return

customers; the established restaurant already has hundreds of customers from its years of operation. The number of customers depends not only on how many customers are gained and lost that week but also on how many customers the restaurant had at the beginning of the week.

Customers is defined as the previous week's value of **Customers** incremented by the newly arriving customers and decremented by the departing ones:

$$\text{Customers} = \text{Customers in the Previous Week}$$
$$+ \text{ Customers Gained} - \text{Customers Lost}$$

Most variables do not explicitly depend on their previous values. In our model, **Enjoyed Proportion** depends solely on the attractiveness of restaurants to new customers, not on any prior value of **Enjoyed Proportion**. Those variables (such as **Customers**) that are defined in terms of increments and decrements of prior values are called *stocks*.

Our restaurant wait model includes some other stocks. The number of former customers —the number of people who used to eat at Zona but no longer do—is modeled as a stock. **Former Customers** simply accumulates the values of **Customers Lost**:

$$\text{Former Customers} = \text{Former Customers in the Previous Week}$$
$$+ \text{ Customers Lost}$$

Note that we do not draw the relationship between **Customers** and itself in a causal loop diagram. There is no association link from **Customers** back to itself in Figure 11.36.

Stocks are common in business motivation simulations. If we were to model Zona's employees, we would model the skill of the chefs as a stock, with skill falling as new underchefs are hired and rising as chefs gain experience week after week. A model of the menu creation would include customer familiarity with the menu as a stock, rising week after week as the menu stayed the same and falling when changes were made. A model of the finances of Mykonos Corporation would include stocks for debts, capital equipment, and other balance sheet items. Anything that persists over time on its own accord is a candidate for being modeled as a stock.

User-Controlled Variables

In Chapter 2, we described playable simulations that a user can interact with as the simulation runs. A playable simulation does not merely show the user what would happen in a particular situation; a playable simulation turns over the steering wheel so that the user can try his hand at driving. Playable simulations are useful for teaching how to manage a situation and for the related task of persuading someone to take actions they would not otherwise consider.

A playable simulation has a user interface. The user interface allows the user to see what is happening as time progresses and to change some things. For example, Figure 11.38 shows a playable simulation of the restaurant wait model. In Figure 11.38, the user can see the wait times and the customer count and how those values have changed over the past few weeks.

The user can also control things using the user interface in Figure 11.38. He can control whether reservations are taken and whether they are required. He might start 2008 by not taking any reservations, implement a reservations process midway through the year by checking the reservations taken box, and as Zona's popularity increases, start requiring reservations. In other words, he can change things over the course of the simulation.

The user can control the price of dinner, raising prices as Zona gets more popular. And he can spend money on promotion. (For a high-end restaurant like Zona, promotion spending involves sponsoring high-profile charity events rather than coupons or radio advertisements that are typical for fast-food restaurants. But the effect is the same: greater awareness.)

There are two sliders in Figure 11.38, one for setting prices and the other for setting the promotion spending. Each slider controls a variable in the simulation. The price slider controls the variable **Average Price**, measured by the price of the average entrée. Unlike the other variables we have seen so far,

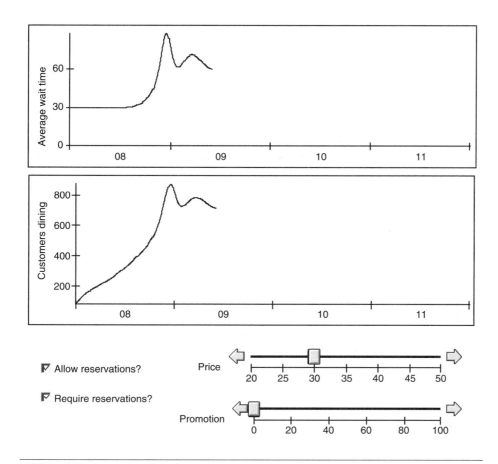

FIGURE 11.38 A user interface to manage restaurant wait times

Average Price is not affected by anything else in the simulation. Rather, it is completely controlled by the user and affects other simulation variables.

The two checkboxes in Figure 11.38 are also connected to variables. The lower checkbox is connected to the variable **Require Reservations?** which takes a value of true when reservations are required and false when they are not. Like **Average Price**, **Require Reservations?** is completely controlled by the user via the user interface. It affects other variables in the simulation model.

More About Simulating Business Motivation

We have just described an introduction to business motivation simulation, providing enough detail for you to build some simulations of strategies and other business motivation situations. When you are ready for more detail, there are many places to turn. Several books describe business motivation simulation. The best of these books (in our opinion) is John Sterman's *Business Dynamics: Systems Thinking and Modeling for a Complex World* [Sterman 2000].

Of course, you need more than knowledge and skills to create a business motivation simulation. You also need a business simulation engine. Though many business modeling packages include a business process simulation engine, none includes a business motivation simulation engine, at least not at the time of this writing. You must acquire your business motivation simulation engine separately.

VALIDATING A SIMULATION

As you will recall from Chapter 7, model verification involves improving the quality of a model by working with subject matter experts to check every model element in a model, and model validation is about improving the quality of a model through simulation. Now it is time to look at how model validation is performed and how simulation can be used to improve model quality.

Consider the business process of IT support: people handling support requests from employees, as shown in Figure 11.39. A phone call is answered by a level 1 technician. He understands the problem and perhaps resolves it on the phone. If he is not able to solve the problem himself, he may escalate it to

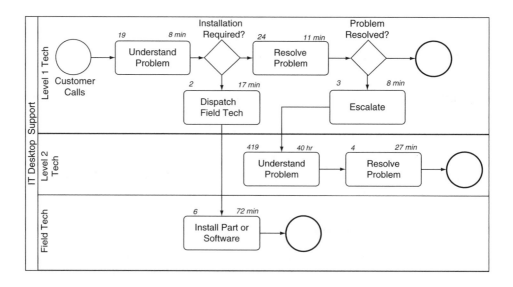

FIGURE 11.39 A tech support process, simulated to validate

a more experienced technician. Alternatively, the problem might be something that can only be solved in person, and the level 1 tech might dispatch a field tech to replace a part or reinstall key software.

The process shown in Figure 11.39 has been simulated for 10 (simulated) days, and some results of the simulation are shown above each activity. On the upper left of each activity are the *activity job counts*: how many tech support jobs are currently working that activity? For example, the activity **Install Part or Software** has an activity count of 6; six tech support problems are currently either being addressed by field techs replacing something, or are waiting for field techs to start working on their problems. On the upper right of each activity are the *average activity times*: For the jobs currently at the activity, how long have they been there, either being worked or waiting? The activity **Install Part** has an average activity time of 72 minutes; the six jobs there have been at that activity for (an average of) 72 minutes each.

Now consider what happens when a problem is escalated from the first level tech support to a more experienced second level. The level 2 tech starts by understanding the problem in the activity **Understand Problem 2**. This activity has an activity count of 419. There are 419 people on the phone, either talking to a level 2 tech or waiting for one to become available. Since there are only eight level 2 techs in total, most customers must be waiting. The activity time is 40 hours—the 419 people have waited an average of 40 hours on the phone at this task.

Figure 11.40 shows a graph of the activity job count for **Understand Problem 2** over the 10 simulated days. The count has accumulated, growing day by day until it has reached 419 jobs on day 10. Clearly something in the model is causing a growing backlog of people waiting at this activity.

This activity job count does not reflect reality. No one has waited 40 hours on the phone for a level 2 tech. Something is wrong with the model and needs to be corrected.[7] There are several model problems that could cause this growing backlog in the simulation. Perhaps too many jobs are being sent to level 2 techs because the decision logic in the gateway **Problem Resolved?** is faulty. Perhaps too much time is being spent by level 2 techs; they actually finish their work in less time than the simulation indicates and so the backlog does not accumulate.

---

[7]Or possibly nothing is wrong with the model and this one run of the simulation is just unusual. Most simulation models rely on randomness to some degree. An activity takes between 1 and 10 minutes, and the actual time for any given job is a random quantity between 1 and 10. A gateway sends 40 percent of the jobs up and 60 percent down, and whether a particular job goes up or down depends on a random chance. Usually business process simulations are not very sensitive to the randomness. If you run the same simulation again, you will get different results, but similar to the first time. And if you run it a third time, the results will be similar to the first and second runs.

But some simulation models are very sensitive to the random quantities used [Law 2006]. And even for a model that is not so sensitive, it is possible—though unlikely—to have a run with radically different results. Reliability analysis of the results of a simulation is important but beyond the scope of this book.

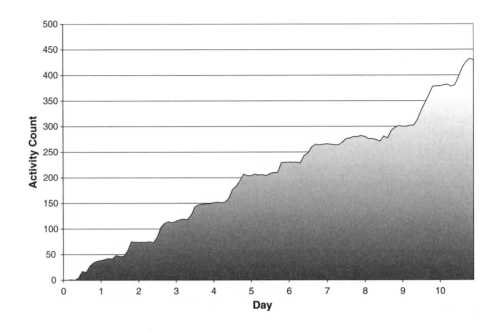

FIGURE 11.40 An ever-increasing activity count

Perhaps there are more level 2 techs in reality than in the simulation. It is even possible that some backlogs do accumulate for level 2 tech support, and after 10 or 20 minutes, the people on the phone give up, hang up, and try to fix the problem themselves.

Whatever the reason for the backlog, the model needs to be corrected to reflect the reality that is occurring. You need to question your subject matter experts to determine what needs to be fixed so that the simulation results provide useful data for your questions. You do not need to ask about the 40-hour backlog—you already know it is not valid. But you can ask questions to investigate sources of this backlog. You can ask whether the simulated activity time spent on **Understand Problem 2** is accurate. You can check the percentage utilization of tech 2s in the simulation and compare that to the subject matter expert's understanding. This process is *model validation*: using the simulation results to drill into the model until you discover the root cause of the problem.

An ever-increasing backlog is one simulation result that is useful for validating a business process model. There are three others that are often used:

- Resource utilization; for example, a resource is 40% utilized in the simulation, but much busier in the real world

- Job cycle time; for example, some jobs take two weeks to process in the end-to-end simulation, but in the real world everything is done within four days
- Job touch time; for example, some jobs are only worked by resources for 20 minutes, but in the real world every job is worked for at least an hour

Business motivation models can also be validated. As with business process validation, you compare simulated results with real-world values. But instead of comparing activity job counts or cycle times, you compare the results produced by motivation simulations: market shares, customers, morale, and so on.

SIMULATION AND STANDARDS

The current version of BPMN at the time of this writing—BPMN 1.1—does not support business process simulation. Many activity attributes described in this chapter and needed for simulation are not part of BPMN: there is no **duration** attribute, no **resourceShift** attribute, no **intrinsicDelay**, and no **consistentResource**. BPMN does not specify modeling support for resources beyond the participant that labels a swimlane, and does not specify modeling support for jobs beyond the ability to set job attributes from an activity.

As discussed earlier in this chapter, start events create simulation jobs according to schedules and quantities specified in the start event itself. The BPMN spec does not include these attributes: there is no **jobQuantity**, **jobInterval**, or **jobStartDuration**. Many tools do support process simulation, in non-standardized ways.

As you may recall from Chapter 5, some start events are timers. A timer models the special case of work starting because it is the right day or time to start. For example, Mykonos central accounting reconciles electronic credit card receipts from the restaurants with the payments from the merchant banks. This process occurs every weekday morning, and the model begins work with a start event, 8:00 AM every weekday.

There is a subtle and important distinction between the timer start events (as described in BPMN) and the simulation of start events as described in this chapter. In BPMN, only some start events are properly modeled as timers. It does not make sense to model the arrival of diners with a timer. They arrive not because they eat at Zona at a certain day and time but instead for their own reasons: some are there for business meetings, others on dates, still others to meet with friends. We use **jobQuantity** and the rest of the simulation-specific attributes as a model approximation of their own logic, not because the process is inherently started by a time occurrence.

BPMN specifies some support for jobs—calling them "tokens" in the specification. An activity (or event or gateway) can assign a value to a modeler-defined attribute of a job as the job passes through the activity (or event or gateway). This support for job attribute assignment is intended primarily for executing a process in a process engine (as described in Chapter 12), but job attribute assignment can also be used for simulating the same process in a simulation engine.

Business Process Simulation Tooling

The good news is that some BPMN-compliant modeling tools do support business process simulation. Of course all these tools support it all differently. The tools available today support simulation to different degrees. For example, we have worked with a commercial tool that supports activities and resources but not jobs. Within this tool there is no way to make a gateway branch depend on the characteristic of the jobs that pass through it, as described earlier in this chapter.

Existing tools also support the same capability in different ways. Every tool that simulates supports capturing the duration of an activity, but there are wide differences in how that duration is modeled.

Standard Support for Business Motivation Simulation

There are a few tools that support business motivation simulation. Each tool is different, with a different modeling language and somewhat different capabilities. As of today, there are no standards for simulating business motivation.

To simulate a business process model, you must first prepare it for simulation. You must provide durations and delays for the activities. You must indicate how jobs are divided at gateways. You must create schedules for jobs that are to be created at start events. And you must model resources, their availability, and their costs.

Once a business process model is prepared, a simulation engine can simulate it, giving you costs, cycle times, touch times, and other statistical results that are difficult to determine with any kind of other static analysis.

Preparation is also required to simulate a business motivation model. The preparation involves defining variables. Most of these variables are dependent on other variables. Some are defined via arithmetic expressions. Some are defined via tables and graphs. Some variables are stocks, and defined by how other variables cause them to change from the values they already have. And some variables are defined by users in real-time, taking a value when a user changes a user interface control.

Once prepared, a motivation model is simulated by a business motivation engine. The result shows market share over time, customers gained or lost, morale changes, or whatever is the topic of the business motivation model.

Chapter 12 describes how to execute a model, and turn it into a software application that a business can use.

Executing a Business Model

12

A business model can be studied, analyzed, and simulated. Some business models can also be executed. When a business model is executed, it becomes software that supports running the business. Instead of being a description of the business, an executed business model becomes part of the business. It is integrated into the business's day-to-day operations.

In the first six chapters of the book we introduced business modeling and the four business modeling disciplines. In the following three chapters we recommended best practices for creating business models. In the two chapters after that we described how to analyze and how to simulate business models. In this final chapter we explore how to translate models into software that runs the business.

Translating models into software is optional. Business models provide value without being translated to software. Business models allow a business to evaluate the impact of a change, analyze a proposed reorganization, or perform a competitive analysis. Business models are valuable in the many different ways that we have explored through this book.

But some organizations reap a further benefit from business models. They *execute* their business models. Executing a business model means translating it into application software and then running that software to benefit the business. By executing a business model, these organizations ensure that their business models are actually used. They avoid one common and tragic fate of business models: sitting on shelves, not used by anyone.

BUSINESS MODELING LIFE CYCLE

The management of business models—from their inception through maintenance and execution—is challenging. If a model is not maintained, it gradually becomes out of sync with the business reality that it models. Ultimately it becomes useless.

When a corporate reorganization occurs, the business organization model must also change. Roles within business processes could change as well. When a new law is enacted and as a result the business forms new policies, the business rule model must change.

When a model is executed, maintenance becomes more important. Now software must be kept in sync with the business model, which must be kept sync with the business reality. When the business model changes, a software developer might need to add a new user interface form, or reconfigure an application. Sometimes a business model must be modified to reflect application changes. One small change to an application might change who should perform an activity.

The *business modeling life cycle* is the process by which business models are created, used, and maintained. Organizations often standardize on a business modeling life cycle to better manage the maintenance of their business models. Figure 12.1 shows a business modeling life cycle.

In the first activity of the life cycle—**Model**—a model is created. The model is created using the disciplines and practices we describe in this book. At the second activity—**Analyze and Simulate**—the model is simulated and analyzed. As a result of the simulation and analysis, the model might be changed. For example, simulated results for cycle time could differ from measured results for cycle time. The simulated results are used to refine the model; hence the sequence flow from **Analyze and Simulate** back to **Model**. Sometimes there are several iterations between these two activities.

The third activity of the life cycle is **Deploy**. When a model is *deployed,* it is converted into a format that allows it to execute as an application. This conversion may involve software development performed by people, or it may be a purely automated process, simply converting the model from a format that cannot be executed to one that can be. We discuss how to deploy business models later in this chapter.

The fourth activity is **Execute and Monitor**. Now the model is executed. If the model had driven application development, the newly created application is now run. If the model had been converted to execute in an engine, that engine

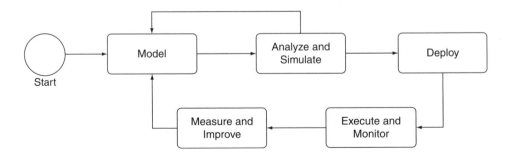

FIGURE 12.1 A business modeling life cycle

is now run. In either case, the executing model is monitored. Data is collected about the model.

The last activity of the life cycle is **Measure and Improve**. The collected data is analyzed and compared with the expected values. The results are then fed back to the modeling effort so that the model can improve.

The life cycle repeats. Measurements lead to model refinements that are then analyzed, simulated, deployed, and executed. The model improves over time. With each cycle the organization learns. The measurements indicate whether something should be changed. Based on the measurements, the organization makes changes to the models or to the business, and then reevaluates the models through additional analysis and simulation. The business environment continuously changes—no matter what we do—and the business modeling life cycle allows an organization to continuously adapt the model to the changing reality.

The business modeling life cycle allows an organization to manage change and continuously improve. There are several benefits to this incremental approach. First, changes to the business are evolutionary instead of revolutionary. Instead of being confronted with a sweeping redesign, employees see smaller, more frequent changes. At each step the employees can adapt more easily. Small course corrections can be taken if needed. Overall, there is less resistance to the change.

Second, the incremental approach leads to better management of the risk. Instead of risking a large failure, the organization can manage many small successes. When one of the incremental changes fails, it is a small setback, not a disaster. The organization can correct course, derive value from what was learned, and continue to the next incremental change.

Third, the organizations can manage the rate of change and associated cost. Instead of a big up-front investment in a large reengineering effort that might not produce the expected results, the organization can make a series of smaller investments in smaller changes. The organization can determine the amount and the rate of change that best fits its economic situation.

FROM MODELS TO SOFTWARE

There are three alternative ways business models can be executed. These three alternatives are shown in Figure 12.2. The first alternative is *manual execution*. When a business model is executed manually, the model is used by people to design software that supports the model. The business model is studied by software developers, and the model helps the developers make decisions about what software to create and how to create it. Business models drive the early stages of software development: the planning and requirements gathering.

An alternative to manual execution is *packaged execution*. For this alternative the end state is not custom software. Instead the end state is a software package, perhaps a third-party commercial package that can be configured in thousands of different ways. The business model is used to select and configure the package.

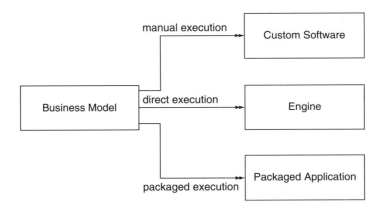

FIGURE 12.2 Three alternatives for executing a business model

A third alternative is *direct execution*. When a business model is executed directly, the model is interpreted by an appropriate engine and run as though it were software itself. A business process model is interpreted by a business process engine. A business rule model is interpreted by a business rules engine. In either case, the business model is not studied by software developers attempting to translate it to software. Instead it is directly executed by an engine to produce the desired behavior.

Next we explore each of these three execution alternatives, starting with manual execution, then packaged execution, and finally direct execution.

MANUAL EXECUTION

When creating a software application, systems analysts or software engineers often start by writing a description of what they are trying to achieve. This description is called a *requirements specification*. The requirements specification details the intent of the application to be built—what it should do to meet the needs of its users. Requirements are important for the success of an application development effort. Without good requirements, application development projects often fail.

One popular approach to capturing application requirements is to write *use cases*. Use cases describe the behavior of an application—not the internal implementation details of how it works but rather what the application does and how it behaves for people who interact with it. Use cases describe the functionality the application provides to the people who use it.

The people who interact with an application in a use case are called *actors*. Use cases describe the actors, what the actors do to the application, and what the application does in response.

Each individual use case describes a single goal or task that an actor is trying to achieve by using the application. The use case describes the steps by which the goal (or task) is achieved: what the actor does, what the system does in response, then what the actor does, and so on. A use case reads like dialogue in a two-character play, with one character talking and then the other, except of course that one character in this play is software instead of human.

Use-Case Descriptions

Let's look at an example. As you may recall from Chapter 5, when a Portia party is waiting for a table they are given a pager to alert them when the table is ready. Sometimes a party decides to leave before they are alerted. They give their pager back to the restaurant host, and he cancels the pager so it can later be provided to another waiting party. One of the use cases of the paging system is **Cancel Pager**, what the host does to notify the system that the pager is no longer in use, and that the party that had the pager is no longer waiting for a table.

Figure 12.3 shows the **Cancel Pager** use case. The use case includes a name, a description summarizing the use case, and the actor who interacts with the system. The use case includes a precondition that must be true before the use case can start: that the host is already logged in. **Cancel Pager** includes the

Name	Cancel Pager
Description	A party returns a pager before their table is ready. This use case usually occurs when the dining party changes their minds, deciding not to wait for a table and leaves the restaurant.
Actor	Restaurant host
Precondition	The host is already logged in.
Trigger	Diner returns a pager before the host sends an alert that a table is available
Basic flow	1. Host has a pager to be canceled. 2. Host enters the pager identifier into the system. 3. System asks whether the pager is to be canceled and the party is no longer waiting for a table. 4. Host verifies that the pager is to be canceled. 5. System records that the party associated with the pager is no longer waiting for a table. 6. System confirms that the pager is canceled. 7. Host returns the pager to the pile of unused pagers.

Alternate paths	2a. Invalid identifier
	    1. System signals error.
	2b. Identifier not associated with waiting party.
	    1. System responds that the pager is not associated with a waiting party.
	4a. Host says that the pager is not to be canceled.
	    1. System responds that the pager is still associated with a waiting party.

FIGURE 12.3 The **Cancel Pager** use case

trigger that causes the use case to happen: the pager being returned. **Cancel Pager** describes the basic flow through the use case when there are no errors or problems, the seven steps from beginning to end. Also described are three alternate paths. Each alternate path describes a single situation that might happen instead of the basic flow, and what results if the situation does happen.

Use Case Diagrams

In addition to use case descriptions like the one in Figure 12.3, use cases are often shown in a *use case diagram* like that of Figure 12.4. A use case diagram shows several use cases from the same application. The actors for the use cases are shown connected to the use cases in which they are involved. Figure 12.4 shows four use cases of the pager system as well as two actors: the host and the dining party. The host is an actor for all four use cases, and the dining party is an actor for one, the **Send Alert** use case.

In the **Assign Pager** use case the host records the name of the dining party and assigns a pager to them. In the **Send Alert** use case the host signals to the dining party that a table is available, and the diner's pager buzzes. This use case includes the dining party as an actor since they see and hear the alert. In the **Return Pager** use case the diners return a pager to the host after it buzzes. In the **Cancel Pager** use case the diners return a pager when they decide not to wait for a table.

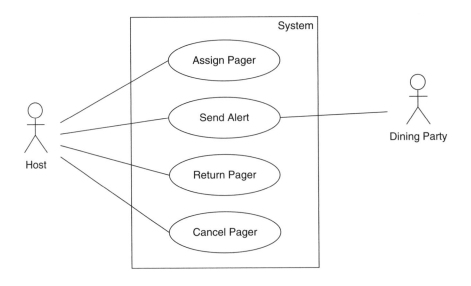

FIGURE 12.4 The use cases of the pager system

Use Cases and Business Modeling

Use cases are models, in many ways like the business models that are described in this book. But use case models are different from business models in one critical way: a use case model is a model used by software developers. It describes the requirements for software, not the details of the business that uses the software. The business models in this book describe the business, not the technology that supports the business.

The business and the software requirements are of course related, and business models can support the development of use cases for a new application. A business motivation model can capture the rationale for a new system implementation. A business process model can capture who is doing work and what activities they perform. The people who are doing the work often become actors in a use case model. Many of the activities in which the work is done are supported by use cases.

In Chapter 5 we considered the to-be business process for Portia after the implementation of a pager system. Now let's turn to the development of the pager technology, work that is accomplished not by Portia but by Memphis Restaurant Technology, a vendor of pager systems with which Mykonos has contracted.

The Portia process is shown again in Figure 12.5. Several of the activities in Figure 12.5 are supported by the pager system. In the activity **Ask Party to Wait**,

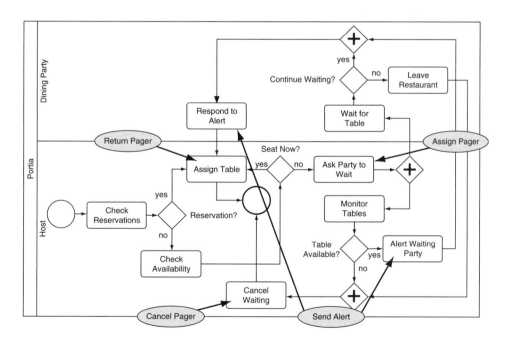

FIGURE 12.5 The use cases that support activities in the Portia seating process

no table is available to the party and the host asks them to wait for a table. At that point the host assigns a pager and gives it to the party. The activity is supported by the use case **Assign Pager**. Later a table becomes available and the host alerts the party in the activity **Alert Waiting Party**. The activity is supported by the use case **Send Alert**. The alerted party responds to the alert in the activity **Respond to Alert**. That activity is also supported by the use case **Send Alert** because their behavior begins only after their pager buzzes. They then present their pager to the host, who collects it and assigns them a table in the activity **Assign Table**. That activity is supported by the use case **Return Pager**. Finally the waiting party may choose to give up on waiting for a table and leave the restaurant. They give their pager to the host, and he cancels it in the activity **Cancel Waiting**, supported by the use case **Cancel Pager**.

Note that a use case can support more than one activity. The use case **Send Alert** supports both the activity **Alert Waiting Party** and the activity **Respond to Alert**. In **Alert Waiting Party** the host starts the pager buzzing, and in **Respond to Alert** the dining party notices the pager buzzing. Both actions are part of the same use case, **Send Alert**.

Figure 12.5 shows the pager system use cases overlaid on the business process activities, showing which use cases support which activities. Figure 12.5 is not intended to be a new kind of diagram. Rather it is a normal business process model with a few use cases overlaid on top and arrows depicting the support associations between use cases and activities. Alternatively, these support associations across model elements in different disciplines can be shown as in Figure 12.6, in the same

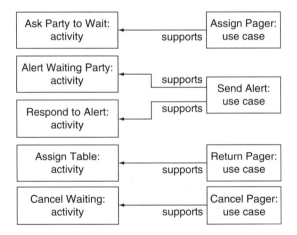

FIGURE 12.6 Another view of the use cases that support activities

way that we have shown the tracelinks between (for example) business rules and gateways in Chapter 6.

Figures 12.5 and 12.6 show which use cases support which business process activities, but they do not show how the use cases are developed. How does Memphis Restaurant Technology decide to create a pager system with these four use cases? Why these four? Why not others?

There is a simple way to decide which use cases to create: walk through the business process. The systems analysts start with a business process model like Figure 12.5 and walk through each activity (and each gateway), asking whether that activity should be supported by an application. Some activities and gateways will not be supported; they will remain manual. For example, **Monitor Tables** is a manual activity. The host simply keeps an eye out for any tables from which a party is leaving. Some activities and gateways are supported by other applications. For example, the gateway **Reservation?** is supported by a reservations system, a different system than the pager system. And some activities need to be supported by the new system under design.

Use case models are a convenient place to trace a business model to models of a software application. Just as we trace activities from business process models to goals and strategies from business motivation models, we can trace use cases to the activities they support.

PACKAGED EXECUTION

Instead of creating new software, many organizations choose to purchase an existing software package that more or less fits their business needs. There are many of these third-party applications available to support a range of common business functions: financial management, human resource management, sales management, and many others. Organizations that purchase a third-party software package can end up paying less and getting more: spending less money than if they develop and maintain the software themselves and getting a world-class application that has benefited from the experience of hundreds of other organizations.

But there is a problem with third-party software packages: they often do not fit the business (as you may recall from the Chapter 1 case study). The business processes supported by a third-party package are different from the business processes performed by the organization that is considering the purchase. For example, Mykonos is planning to purchase a third-party procurement package, and they must consider whether the package fits the Mykonos procurement business process.

The possibility for misfit is broader than just business processes. Third-party packages also make assumptions about organization, and their assumed organization can be different from the actual organization of the purchasing company. Third-party packages make assumptions about business rules and business policies, and their assumed rules and policies can be different from the actual rules and policies. In short, every third-party package comes with an assumed business model and that business model might be very different from what is desired.

The problem of third-party package fit can be addressed in one of three ways: by selection, by conformance, or by configuration. A company purchasing a third-party application package can evaluate the candidate packages based on business model fit. The company only selects a package whose business model closely fits their own. Alternatively, a company can purchase a package and then conform their business to the purchased application. They change their business processes, business rules, and organization to match the software they purchase.

The third alternative is configuration. Most third-party packages can be *configured*; the customer can change the behavior of the package. Typically configuration is performed by setting parameters values or by adding bits of custom software. Sometimes the package software can actually be changed. The work of configuring a third-party application is commonly called *package implementation*. Package implementation is performed by specialists—people who have training and experience in the implementation of that particular package.

All three alternatives benefit from business modeling. When a package is selected, the company's business model is compared to the business models of the candidate packages. Which package supports business processes that most closely match the purchasing company's processes? Which package supports organizations that most closely match? Business rules?

If the company chooses to conform to a purchased package, that conformance is a kind of business transformation that can be driven by business models. The company's existing business processes become the as-is and the business processes supported by the package are the to-be. By modeling both as-is and to-be, the company can better understand what has to change.

Package implementation also benefits from business modeling. The hard and laborious work of deciding how to set configuration parameters is easier when the people implementing the package can refer to models of business processes, business organization, and business rules. Note that there is no magic in this approach. The package implementers use the existing business models as they use other reference materials.

Using business models to select, conform to, or implement a package is called *packaged execution*. Historically, package vendors have been skeptical of packaged execution, skeptical of the usefulness of business modeling in implementing their package. They have tried to convince their customers that their package has all the features needed and that modeling either the customer's business or the business supported by the package is a waste of time.

But now the situation looks different. Many large package implementations have failed, sometimes after organizations spent hundreds of millions of dollars. It is now clear that there is more to package selection than feature lists. It is clear that conformance to a package is often hard and expensive. And it is clear that package implementation is a large and risky activity that benefits from the time savings and risk reduction that business modeling offers.

DIRECT EXECUTION

Instead of developing a custom application or implementing a third-party application, a model can run in a special-purpose engine. Running a model in a special-purpose engine is called *direct execution*. A business process is executed directly as software in a business process engine. The engine interprets the business process activities, the roles that perform the activities, and the logic associated with gateways and flows. A business rules engine interprets the business rules, noting when a rule is violated and informing either other software or people of the violation.

Direct execution has several advantages over both manual execution and packaged execution. Direct execution can be realized much faster. The model becomes working software much quicker when it is directly executed than either when it is translated to custom code or when it is used to implement a package. Software development takes time: requirements are developed using the business model, software is designed, a graphical user interface is developed, the code is written and tested, and finally the code is installed. All this takes months, maybe years. Package implementation also takes time, sometimes as long as software development. By contrast, when a business process is deployed to a business process engine, little new software is written. A graphical user interface sometimes needs to be created to support the process, but the logic to control workflows is built into the engine.

Direct execution supports more agility. When a business process needs to change, the model is changed and redeployed. By contrast, custom-developed software is notoriously difficult to change, often requiring months of analysis, coding, and testing to implement a single business process change. An implemented application package can be fast to change if the desired change happens to be something easy to implement in the package. Other changes are difficult, and some changes are impossible to make.

Direct execution requires less ongoing maintenance. The custom-developed software that results from the manual execution of a model always requires significant maintenance. Bugs are discovered and must be fixed. New operating systems and databases must be supported. New mandates and business policies lead to new use cases. The same forces are also in play for directly executed applications, but each is easier and faster to implement.

But the technology for direct execution is not yet mature. Today there exist special-purpose engines to execute only two of the four business modeling disciplines. Business process models can be executed in a business process engine, and business rules can be more or less executed in a business rules engine, with some caveats as described later in this chapter. But today there are no special-purpose engines to execute business motivation models. One could imagine a business motivation engine that imported a motivation model and tracked progress against the goals and objectives, connecting the motivation model elements to personnel performance planning. Such an engine does not exist today. Similarly, there are no special-purpose engines to execute a business organization model. Even the business process engines—the most mature of the four—have some shortcomings.

EXECUTING BUSINESS RULES

As you may recall from Chapter 6, business rules often are implemented in software applications. Consider again the rule about the acceptance of euros as currency.

> *Euros Allowed:* It is permitted that a cash payment employ European Union currency only if the cash payment is applied to a bill and the amount of the bill is at most 100 U.S. dollars.

Euros Allowed can be implemented in the Mykonos point-of-sale system. When the server collects the cash provided by the customer and records the payment in the point-of-sale (POS) system, she selects the currency in the user interface, selecting euros instead of dollars. The POS system checks the amount of the bill, and if the amount is more than $100, the system rejects the payment with the warning dialog box shown in Figure 12.7. As you can see, the text of the error message is the rule that is violated.

How does it happen that the rule **Euros Allowed** is incorporated as part of the point-of-sale system? Earlier in this chapter we explained how there are three ways a business model can be executed as software: manual execution, packaged execution, or direct execution. For business rules, all three ways are practiced, but the most common of the three is manual construction. Today most business rules are implemented in software by someone reading the rule and writing

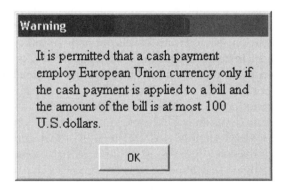

FIGURE 12.7 A warning dialog box from a Mykonos point-of-sale system

application code that implements the rule. Package implementation is common, but most commercial software packages have limited support for business rules. Direct execution of business rules shows promise—and could become the dominant practice in the future—but today it is still a niche activity.

There are some significant shortcomings with the manual execution of business rules. Construction of software is always time consuming and expensive. A business rule must be understood by a software developer and manually translated into code. In our example, the rule **Euros Allowed** must be understood, and code must be developed to check whether the rule applies whether the currency of the payment is euros and the amount is greater than $100. Code must be created for the error dialog box shown in Figure 12.7. All this code must be tested. The whole process takes time and money.

Manual execution also makes the business rules hard to change. Business rules are meant to be changed as the business circumstances change, but changing code to reflect new rules is much more difficult than simply changing rules. In the Euro payment example, suppose the business rule changes to accept Euros only for smaller amounts, those less than $50.

> ***Euros Allowed B:*** It is permitted that a cash payment employ European Union currency only if the cash payment is applied to a bill and the amount of the bill is at most 50 dollars.

This simple change to the business rule has a not-so-simple implementation. First, the code sections that implement the rule must be identified—both the checking and the display of the dialog box on violation. Then both code sections must be changed. The changed code must be tested.

Direct execution of business rules is a better approach. With direct execution, the business rules are managed in a business rules engine. From time to time the application asks the rules engine whether some condition is allowed. For example, the restaurant POS system asks the rules engine whether a bill of $154 is permitted to be paid in Euros. The rules engine replies that such a payment is not permitted and provides the text of the rule that is violated, so the application can present that text in the dialog box of Figure 12.7.

With direct execution, no software developer is involved. There is no translation to software code. Instead the business rules engine works with the business rules as rules. When new rules are added or existing rules changed, the changes have an immediate effect.

Today direct execution of business rules is rare. The rules engines available today—the commercial products and the open source applications—execute *production rules* rather than business rules. Whereas business rules are written in a structured English understandable to businesspeople, production rules are written in a technical rules language that is often difficult for businesspeople to understand without training. For example, the following production rule—written in the open source production rules application JBoss Rules—is (roughly) equivalent to the business rule **Euros Allowed**.

```
rule "Euros allowed"
        agenda-group "payments"
        salience 12
        when
                $p: Payment(type == "cash", currency = "euro", amount > "100")
        then
                retract($p)
                System.out.println("It is permitted that a cash payment employ
        European Union currency only if the cash payment is applied to a bill and the
        amount of the bill is at most 100 U.S. dollars");
        end
```

This production rule states that if a cash payment is made in euros for an amount of more than $100, that payment is to be retracted from the working memory of the rules engine and an error is to be printed. Furthermore, the rule is a member of a group of rules called "payments" and among that group has a salience (priority) of 12. As you can see, this production rule is more similar to code in a programming language than to the business rule **Euros Allowed**.

Many people are confused about business rules and production rules, calling production rules "business rules" and calling production rules engines "business rules" engines. Even some of the vendors of production rules engines have adopted the language of business rules to improve their sales.

But the gap between rules engines and business rules is not so broad, and it is narrowing. There are three alternative ways to close the gap—one that works today and two more promising approaches that are under development. Today, an analyst with the right training can translate a collection of business rules into production rules. This translation work is much simpler and faster than translating business rules into application code.

An alternative way to close the gap is for someone to create a *business rules engine*, an application that directly executes true business rules. At the time of publication, we are aware of no business rules engine, no engine that interprets business rules rather than production rules. But there is great interest in such an engine within the business rules community, and several vendors of production rules engines are considering the support of business rules for future versions of their rules products.

We are also seeing the emergence of another method for direct execution, a method that does not involve rules engines at all. Tools are under development that generate application code from business rules. They translate business rules into Java or .Net code that implements those business rules. This generated code checks for rule violations, and when a violation is detected, it does the right thing.

Direct execution of business rules is still early technology, a bit immature and not yet ready for widespread use, but in the coming years we expect this to change. We expect the technology to become mature, and we expect direct execution of business rules to become a mainstream approach.

EXECUTING BUSINESS PROCESSES

Business processes can be executed in a business process engine. Let's consider a Mykonos example: the Mykonos expense reimbursement process. To support its 143 restaurants around the country, Mykonos has a corporate headquarters. The headquarters is located in Chicago and employs 79 people to manage corporate finances, perform human resources, acquire new companies, and provide services to the individual restaurants. The headquarters employees often travel to other cities to scout for acquisitions and to work with existing restaurants.

When a Mykonos headquarters employee travels from Chicago to Miami (for example) she incurs expenses for air travel, hotels, and so on. She pays for these expenses on her own, and then when she returns to Chicago, she submits an expense report and gets reimbursed.

Figure 12.8 shows the business process for expense reimbursement. An employee submits her expenses, including a description of each expense. She then sends the physical receipts because they are required for tax purposes. To better control expenses and prevent fraud, Mykonos requires a supervisor to approve the submission before finance issues payment to the employee. Once the supervisor receives the submission he reviews all the submission items, looking at the

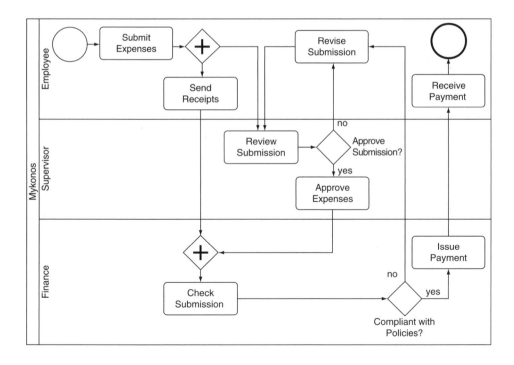

FIGURE 12.8 Expense reimbursement process

descriptions. If everything is in order the supervisor approves the submission. If something is missing or incorrect the supervisor returns the submission to the employee, who must correct and resubmit it. Upon approval, the submission is forwarded to Finance. Finance must receive both the approved submission and the receipts in order to process payment.

The reimbursement process is both manual and riddled with problems. Sometimes the supervisor takes too long and the reimbursement is delayed. Sometimes the supervisor rejects the submission due to insufficient justification for the expense, but the paperwork sits in internal mailboxes and the employee does not find out until weeks have passed. The delays in reimbursement burden the employees who have already paid for travel expenses out of pocket.

Business Process Management Systems

Mykonos decides to execute the expense reimbursement process in an engine. They use a *business process management system*. A business process management system—commonly abbreviated as *BPMS*—is software that combines business process modeling with process execution. A BPMS allows an organization to both model and execute its processes, to ensure that those processes are followed. The BPMS assigns activities to people, tracks whether those activities are completed, and once they are completed, routes the appropriate forms and documents to the next person who is performing the next activity. A BPMS supports both activities that require user interaction and activities that are automated.

Mykonos has acquired a BPMS to execute all its internal corporate processes, not just expense reimbursement but also procurement processes, accounting processes, and human resources processes. For the expense reimbursement process, an expense report is routed from an employee to the appropriate supervisor so that it can be approved. The BPMS ensures that the right activities are performed. Reimbursements cannot be paid until the employee submits both expenses and receipts and until the supervisor approves the expenses. The supervisor must approve or reject a submission within three business days. If he takes longer, the BPMS produces alerts.

Figure 12.9 shows the expense submission entry page, the page presented by the BPMS when the employee is performing the **Submit Expenses** activity. The employee can enter an expense purpose and a dollar amount. Once entered, the new expense is added to a table showing the whole trip. For each expense, the BPMS determines whether a receipt is needed. When the employee completes the entries, she presses the button labeled "Submit Expenses." Then the submission is routed to her supervisor for the next activity, **Review Submission**.

Figure 12.10 shows the page Finance uses when they perform the activity **Check Submission**. Finance can see a submission and the related employee information. They can also see who approved the expenses. There is an (unlabeled) gateway in Figure 12.8 immediately before **Check Submission**. The gateway shows that finance must receive the receipts in order to check the submission. If receipts were received the finance department user can click on

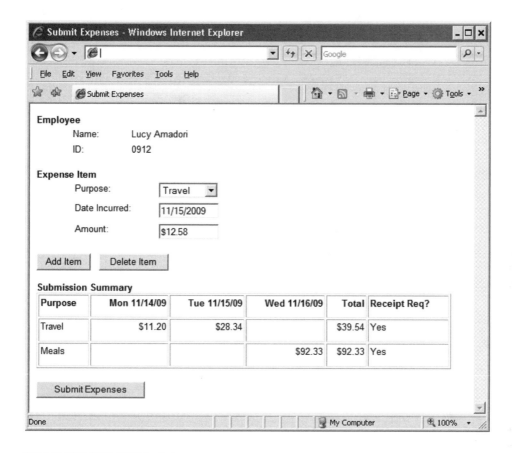

FIGURE 12.9 A page supporting the activity **Submit Expenses**

the checkbox and then press the "Issue Payment" button. This action sends the instructions to the third-party payroll system to issue payment to the employee. If the submission is not compliant with expense policy, Finance can reject the submission, placing it back in the employee's to-do list.

Using a BPMS to manage a process such as the one shown in Figure 12.8 involves several steps. These steps include deploying the business process, creating a user interface to represent the various screens that are needed, and data mapping and integration with other applications and systems.

Deploying a Business Process

A BPMS executes business processes. But the BPMS does not directly execute the visual diagrams created by the modeler, the diagrams like Figure 12.8. Instead a model must be first transformed into an executable format that can be interpreted

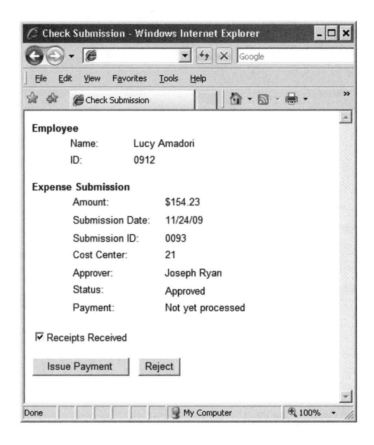

FIGURE 12.10 A page supporting the activity **Check Submission**

by the BPMS engine. This transformation of a model to an executable format is called *deployment*.

When a modeler is ready to deploy a model, the BPMS checks the model for problems that would prevent the model from being executed. For example, if the BPMS finds a business process with no end event, it warns the modeler. Activities are checked to ensure they have both incoming and outgoing sequence flow.

If the model passes the checks, the BPMS translates it into a form that can be interpreted by the BPMS engine. The engine is able to route work from one user to another—for example, to route the expense submission from an employee to his supervisor, and then to finance. The engine is able to present Web pages to different users at appropriate points in the process—pages like those shown in Figures 12.9 and 12.10.

As part of deployment, the modeler indicates which activities are to be deployed. Not every activity is deployed. Some activities are purely manual and not supported by the BPMS. For example, **Send Receipts**—in which the employee sends his receipts in the mail—is a manual process and is never deployed. By contrast, **Submit Expenses**—in which the employee fills in the travel expense form shown in Figure 12.9—is deployed.

One of the advantages of direct execution is agility in supporting change. The business changes, the business models change, and the deployed process needs to change. When change is required, the process is redeployed. The model is rechecked and translated again to the appropriate format, and then the newly changed process can be executed.

Creating a User Interface

Each deployed activity must be supported by a user interface page. For example, **Submit Expenses** is supported by the page shown in Figure 12.9. **Check Submission** is supported by Figure 12.10. Other pages are also needed: one for a supervisor to review expenses and one for Finance to see which submissions are waiting for checks. Someone must create these pages, preferably a user interface designer working with the modeler. Once created, each page must be connected to the activity or activities it supports. A good BPMS provides functionality for creating these pages.

The BPMS also provides some pages out of the box—pages that are useful for any executed process. Figure 12.11 shows one of these pages. In Figure 12.11, the user Joseph Ryan can select from a number of activities that are waiting for his action. He needs to revise his own expense submissions, one submission for a trip to Denver and another expense submission for October expenses not part of any trip. In addition Joseph Ryan supervises others. There are three expense submissions that he needs to review for three different people working for him. The BPMS provides the user interface shown in Figure 12.11 so he can see all the jobs that are waiting for him and he can select one of the jobs to work on next.

Note that the page shown in Figure 12.11 is not associated with any single activity from the executed business process. Instead it is a to-do list that spans all the activities that Joe needs to perform now. If other business processes were implemented in the same BPMS, the list could include jobs from those other processes also waiting for Joe's action.

Data Mapping and Integration

The employee has entered an amount of $12.58 in the amount field of the page shown in Figure 12.9. That value of $12.58 is of course stored in a database, so it can be examined later when the expense submission is reviewed. But which database stores that field? The BPMS has its own database to keep track of information that only the executed process cares about. The BPMS also communicates

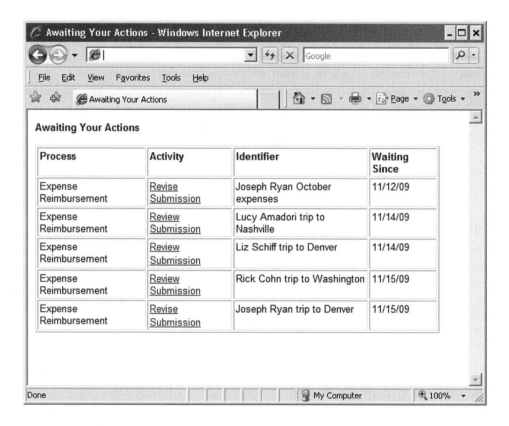

FIGURE 12.11 A page for selecting the next action

with other databases at Mykonos for access to information that is already stored elsewhere.

A typical executed process uses a variety of *data fields*. The expense amount is one data field. The employee name is another data field. Each data field is a bit of information displayed, used, or changed in the executing business process.

Some data fields are private to the business process, used only inside the process and nowhere else. Other data fields include information pulled from external corporate databases. Some data fields even cause those external corporate databases to be changed.

When implementing a business process in a BPMS, the modeler—or a database guru working with the modeler—must identify which data fields connect to external databases and which data fields are private to the process, without any linkage to anything external. This activity of linking business process data fields to external databases is called *data mapping*. Note that data mapping is an integration exercise; to execute the process the BPMS must be integrated with other existing applications that own those databases.

Table 12.1 Mapping Data Fields to External Systems

Field	System
Employee Name	HR system
Employee ID	HR system
Submission ID	(private)
Submission Amount	General ledger
Submission Status	(private)
Supervisor Name	HR system
Cost Center	HR system
Payment status	General ledger
Receipts	(private)

Table 12.1 shows the data mapping for some of the fields in the expense reimbursement process. Some of the fields in Table 12.1 map to existing systems—either the Mykonos HR system or their general ledger. The BPMS pulls some fields from the HR system: the employee's name, ID, and supervisor. The BPMS pulls the cost center from the general ledger to ensure that the expenses will be put in the appropriate categories. The BPMS also pulls the payment status from the general ledger.

Some of the fields in Table 12.1 are private, of concern only to the executing process in the BPMS, not to external databases. For example, the executing process must track the status of a submission, whether it has been approved or rejected. The executing process must also track whether receipts have been received by Finance.

Data mapping can be bidirectional. When a data field is changed, the appropriate external system or systems must be updated to reflect the change. For example, when the submission amount is changed, the general ledger must be updated.

Some data fields cannot be changed by users. For example, no one can change an employee's name or ID, at least not in the expense reimbursement process. Other data fields can be changed. The employee can change the data field for the purpose of an expense by selecting from the pull-down menu in Figure 12.9. She can also change the amount of the expense by typing a new amount. Finance can change the data field indicating whether receipts have been received by checking the checkbox in Figure 12.10.

Data fields are associated with a job, flowing with the job from process activity to process activity. For example, the submission ID is associated with the job. As the submission is routed from **Submit Expenses** to **Review Submission** to **Revise Submission**, the submission retains the same ID.

The value of a data field can affect the flow of a job through the process. Receipts are not needed for expense items of less than $25. If a submission has no expense items that need a receipt, the job need not wait for receipts to be received. It can be approved for payment without any receipts.

Some data fields cannot be viewed by some users. BPMSs usually support the restriction of access to a data field, either for security reasons or for privacy reasons. Furthermore, not every field is shown on every page, even when there are no security or privacy issues. For example, the cost center data field is shown on the **Check Submission** page of Figure 12.10 but not on the **Submit Expenses** page of Figure 12.9. Finance needs this information even if the employee does not. Some data fields are also editable by some users and not others. The user can enter and change amounts for expenses, but her supervisor can only approve or reject. He cannot change the amounts.

Business Process Management

As we have discussed, business processes can be modeled using modeling tools. They can be analyzed. They can be simulated using a simulation engine. And they can be executed in a BPMS. The modeling, analysis, simulation, and execution of business process models is called *business process management*, often abbreviated as *BPM*. BPM is a big-tent term that encompasses a lot of practices involving the modeling of business processes. BPM is not just about executing a business process in a BPMS; it is about the continuous improvement of the process. BPM includes the roles and responsibilities in an organization. It includes the artifacts people use in performing their work. It includes the technology used. BPM is about the ongoing management, control, monitoring, and improvement of the business processes, and ultimately of the business itself.

BUSINESS PROCESS MONITORING

How can we tell if the process we implemented is performing the way we expect? Does it match our simulation? Have we in fact lowered costs? Are we now conforming to the regulation? Most BPMS support the monitoring of an executed process. Since the BPMS is managing the progress of every job, it can measure how the process is performing. The BPMS can measure delays, it can measure the number of jobs in a backlog, and it can measure the efficiency of each activity. The real-time measurement of an executing business process is called *business process monitoring*.

Why is business process monitoring important? Monitoring is important because all models are wrong. The behavior of the executing business process will be different from what we expect and different from what we simulate. For example, a process that we expected to never develop a bottleneck will in fact bottleneck and do so at an activity that surprises us. And even if a process behaves according to our expectations this week, next week will bring new business conditions and new process behavior. So we monitor our processes to learn how they are actually behaving, to adjust them, and to improve them.

Many aspects of a process can be monitored. In practice, it is best to monitor the aspects that are important to the business. For example, for some businesses, customer order fulfillment time is important. For those businesses, we monitor that fulfillment time, how long it takes from when a customer order is received until that order is fulfilled. We monitor how that customer fulfillment time changes, how it rises and falls.

When we monitor a process we track its behavior and maintain relevant statistics. We monitor the sequence flows between the activities, we monitor the time it takes to perform each activity, and we monitor the queues—how many jobs are waiting and where they wait. We also monitor how many times an activity is performed, to track which sequence flows are executed and which are not.

Monitoring is performed in real time. End-of-week reports are not as useful as understanding where a bottleneck is building right now. If you see a bottleneck before it becomes too large, you can intervene—perhaps adding resources—before the problem is visible to customers or to other stakeholders. For example, part of monitoring the Mykonos expense reimbursement process is tracking the **Review Submission** activity. If too many submissions are waiting at this activity, an investigation is necessary. The delay in reviewing expense submissions could be because a supervisor is on vacation and neglected to assign someone else to approve his employees' submissions. It might have happened because a supervisor has too many employees and cannot review all the submissions in a reasonable time. Or it could mean that the supervisor is simply delinquent in his duties.

Business process monitoring is often performed with a dashboard. Figure 12.12 shows two dials from a dashboard for monitoring the expense reimbursement process. A dashboard provides an easy-to-understand visual display of the important measurements within a process.

When we monitor a process we collect data on individual jobs flowing through a process. We also collect aggregate data, averages for all the jobs that flow through. For example, when we monitor the expense reimbursement process we monitor how long on average it takes to process expense submissions,

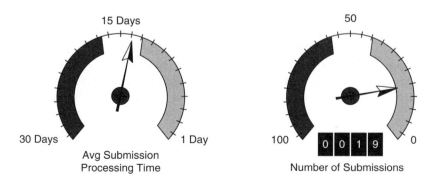

FIGURE 12.12 Dials for monitoring review submission

from the time the expense submission is created to the time the funds are transferred. In addition to the averages, we also monitor and track the individual submissions. How long did submission 3910239 take?

More and more companies today are monitoring their processes, for several reasons. Business process monitoring allows a company to see how it is performing right now. When Mykonos implements business process monitoring, it can understand how its procurement process is performing and where there are bottlenecks in acquiring food and beverages.

Business process monitoring allows companies to see impending problems and address them now, before they get worse. For example, Zona is crowded every weekend, and delays are growing. Is it time to implement reservations-only seating on the weekends?

Business process monitoring is useful in investigating the impact of a change. When a process is tweaked, the effects can be monitored in real time to determine whether the change had a positive or negative effect. Did the implementation of reservations-only seating cut the customer wait-time as expected?

Simplifying the Business Process for Monitoring

Let's consider an example of a business process monitoring of the same Mykonos expense submission process. At any time, Finance would like to know the number of unpaid expense submissions, the total dollar amount of those expense submissions, and how long it takes to reimburse employees. Finance would also like to understand the reasons for any delays in the process. Are employees paid late because of supervisor approval delays or because of delays in the third-party payroll processing?

Figure 12.13 shows the expense reimbursement process. Note that this is the same business process as shown earlier in Figure 12.8, but Figure 12.13 is much

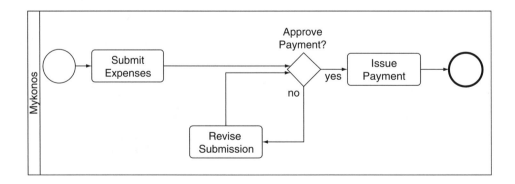

FIGURE 12.13 The expense reimbursement process, simplified for monitoring

simpler. Many of the activities in Figure 12.8 are not present in Figure 12.13. Figure 12.13 omits the activity **Review Submission** because Mykonos does not care about monitoring that activity separately. The new gateway **Approve Payment?** incorperates both **Approve Submission?** and **Complaint with Policies**. Figure 12.13 also omits the activities related to the submission of receipts and the checking of those receipts, since those are manual activities.

Business processes are complex, showing us every activity that is performed to make the business process work. We only monitor a subset of those activities, so for monitoring, the business process model is always simpler. Typically we only include the most important sequence flows through the process, and we include only the activities that are needed to determine whether the business process is performing well. For monitoring, less is more.

Events

Business process monitoring monitors *events*. An event is simply something that happens, something that is noticeable by a system and noticed more or less when it happens. Our BPMS implementation can notice when expenses are submitted, so one event in expense reimbursement is **Expense Submission**. Other events include **Expense Approval**, **Expense Rejection**, **Expense Revision**, and **Expense Payment**. Together these five events allow us to monitor everything important in the expense reimbursement process.

Figure 12.14 shows how the five events relate to the simplified business process model used for monitoring. Each event occurs on one of the sequence flows.

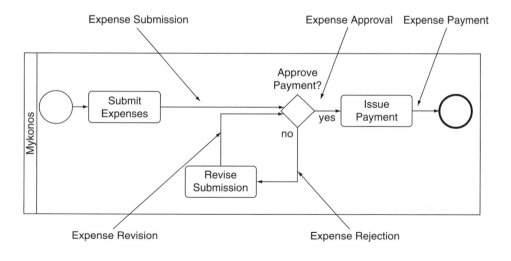

FIGURE 12.14 The events of expense reimbursement

When we see an **Expense Rejection** event for some job, we know that the job has traveled on the sequence flow from **Approve Payment?** to **Revise Submission** and is now waiting for the employee to make revisions. Some time later, we will see an **Expense Revision** event for that job, and then we know the job is once again at **Approve Payment?** waiting again for a supervisor to decide whether to approve or reject it.

Events connect the execution of an activity to the monitoring of that execution. The BPMS knows when **Submit Expenses** is executed. At the moment the employee presses the "Submit Expenses" button (shown in Figure 12.9), the BPMS creates an **Expense Submission** event for the job that has just been submitted. Similarly, at the moment the supervisor presses the button approving the expense submission, the BPMS creates an **Expense Approval** event for that job. To monitor the process, only the events need be monitored.

Dashboards

As a process is monitored, its state needs to be presented in a meaningful way to a variety of stakeholders. The presentation is typically performed using a *dashboard*. A dashboard is a one-page graphical display that shows the status of changing data. Most dashboards are web-based, so the users need not install any special software. Dashboards typically use graphical elements such as meters, gauges, and graphs to provide easy-to-understand status for measurements of interest. As the underlying situation changes, the graphical elements update, so the users of the dashboard always see the current situation.

Different stakeholders have different dashboard needs. The Mykonos COO would like to gauge whether managers are approving expenses and if there are any delays. He would like to track patterns and to address potential problems. The CFO would like to see the total outstanding amounts for reimbursements and how that changes from day to day. He would like to track expense amounts and predict the impact on the balance sheet and income statements.

Figure 12.15 shows the dashboard that the Mykonos COO uses to track performance of the expense reimbursement process. This dashboard shows the same process as Figure 12.13. The process is annotated with counts of the jobs that have passed through each sequence flow. By examining the process, the COO can determine that expense submissions are not bottlenecked at approval, but rather at **Revise Submission** and at **Process Payment**. The dashboard also shows the average processing time for an expense reimbursement and the number of outstanding submissions.

Each organization decides what measurements it wants to track and display, and at what level alerts should be raised. At Mykonos a backlog of 50 submissions waiting for approval is significant enough that the dial is red. For a company of 1,000 employees, a backlog of 50 would be trivial and the dial would be green.

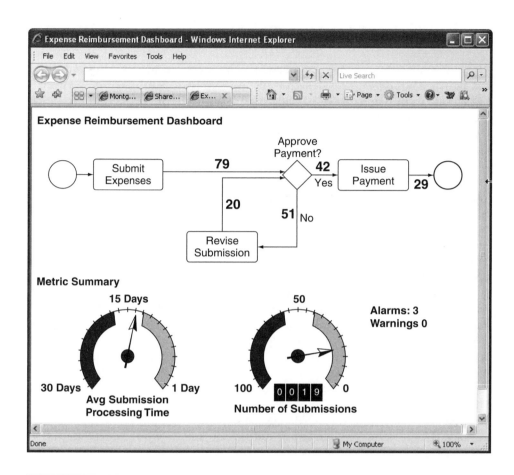

FIGURE 12.15 Expense reimbursement dashboard

Some dashboards support drill-downs so that the user can see the details of a particular job. For example, the COO might want to drill down to check on individual expense submission and see which activities have been performed and which are pending. He might want to check durations, seeing how long each activity took for that expense submission. He might want to see alerts, understanding where too many expense submissions have backlogged. This detailed information allows him to identify potential problems and address them.

To create good dashboards, you must understand the audience. What level of granularity is appropriate? Do they want to see bar charts or tables or dials? Do they want to see the current situation as it compares to normal conditions? Do they want to receive alerts when data is outside of the normal? Do they want to drill down into the underlying jobs?

BUSINESS ACTIVITY MONITORING

For monitoring the expense reimbursement process we harvested events from the BPMS. The BPMS provides the events **Expense Submission**, **Expense Approval**, **Expense Rejection**, and **Expense Payment**. But the fifth type of event—**Expense Payment**—cannot come from the BPMS. The payments are actually made by a third-party payment service and the BPMS is not aware when those payments are made. We want to monitor the whole process—end to end— so we must find a way to generate events from the payment service.

This situation is common. Although a BPMS attempts to manage a process from end to end, some parts of the process are either supported by or entirely performed by third-party applications that the BPMS does not control. Most BPMS include some software for integrating to freestanding applications, for generating events so that we can notice when a job is performed outside the control of a BPMS. This software is called a *business activity monitoring* system, often abbreviated as *BAM*.

BAM notices when an existing system does something, creates an event when that something occurs, and ties events from multiple systems to show a single picture of the business process. Typically this involves some light system integration work. For example, in the expense reimbursement process, Mykonos invokes an application provided by the third-party payment service to direct the service to issue payment. The application reads in a file extracted from the accounting system that includes the ID of the expense and the amount to be paid. The application writes this information to a log file once the third party is directed to issue the payment. To implement business process monitoring on expense reimbursement, we monitor the log file and create the event **Expense Payment** to match the expense. Now our business process monitoring can notice when a payment is made.

Each legacy application is different. Some applications provide an application program interface, making it easy to notice events. Other applications are harder. Sometimes events can only be noticed by monitoring log files.

BAM complements BPMS, creating events for applications and services not orchestrated by the BPMS. But BAM can also be implemented as a poor man's alternative to a BPMS, an alternative that offers some but not all the BPMS functionality. Most business processes today are supported by a collection of legacy applications. A BAM system can monitor an existing process in the way that it is currently executed, using those legacy applications. No changes need to be made except minor changes to notice events.

A BPMS implementation is a much more radical step than a BAM implementation by itself. A BPMS implementation changes the way people work. They must now use the BPMS implementation of their process to perform their work, using (for example) the page shown previously in Figures 12.9 to submit an expense report rather than the Excel spreadsheet they used previously. A BAM implementation is a less intrusive approach. After a BAM implementation, the process is performed exactly the same way, with the same legacy systems. The only difference is that the process can now be monitored.

Sometimes BAM is performed as a first step toward a BPMS implementation. The process is modeled, BAM is implemented, and now the process is visible for the first time. The areas for improvement are clear; insight is gained. A BPMS implementation uses this newfound insight.

Implications for Modeling and Execution

A business process model can provide a great deal of business value. Even more value can be achieved when the same process is executed within a BPMS or at least monitored by BAM. In either case, the business can see exactly what is happening. If the process is executed, the business can easily change the process, responding to changing conditions.

Today, most business processes are neither executed in a BPMS nor monitored with BAM. These technologies are still young, and their penetration is still small, in part due to simple awareness. Most business managers are not aware of the value they could achieve with model execution. The lack of awareness is due to the technical maturity of the technology. Today there is little interoperability among the BPMS tools. Processes often must communicate, but it is difficult to make a process implemented in one BPMS tool communicate with another process implemented in another tool. As a result, organizations are not able to achieve the promised value. As standards are adopted, we expect more organizations to directly execute their process models.

Direct process execution requires skills beyond modeling. Some software development, database, and integration skills are also required. Typically a team must be assembled to collect all the skills. Training is often also needed.

Process Improvement

In Chapter 10, we discussed improvement analysis and business process improvement. Business process monitoring is useful for analyzing the performance of processes and identifying areas for improvement. For example, Mykonos might have predicted that the expense reimbursement process would average two days' cycle time—two days from the expense submission to payment. In practice, the cycle time averages more than 16 days. There appears to be significant room for improvement.

By analyzing the measurements we collect, we can understand why the process takes longer than we predicted. We use this understanding to improve both the process and our model of the process, as shown earlier in the business modeling life cycle of Figure 12.1. We cycle through, making changes to our original models. When our business environment is not changing quickly, each cycle leads to more modest changes and our process performance improves. Of course, sometimes the business environment changes quickly, and our cycles are instead focused on adapting to the changing circumstances.

THE FUTURE OF BUSINESS MODELING

How can we expect the practice of business modeling to change over the next 10 years? Predicting the future is always a risky endeavor. Many unexpected things can happen. But the trends are certainly clear. Business modeling has become increasingly used over the last 10 years, and increasingly accepted. We expect that trend to continue. We expect business modeling to go mainstream over the next 10. Ten years from now almost all companies and almost all government agencies will use business models for the purposes we have described in this book.

In the coming years, we expect tooling to improve. In particular we expect that tools will become multidisciplinary, supporting all four business modeling disciplines. Today most modeling tools support only a single modeling discipline. The tools that support business process modeling have weak or no support for business motivation modeling. The tools that support business rule modeling only handle business rules. But as we have shown in this book, business modeling is not four separate practices. Rather it is a coherent whole, one practice with four disciplines. Ten years from now, we expect all the popular tools will support all four disciplines.

With the tooling support for multiple disciplines, we also expect the profession of modeling to change as well. Today the people who create business process models do not create models from the other three disciplines. The people who practice business rule modeling only create business rules. Today the tribes are separate. But business modeling is fundamentally a single profession, with many common best practices that span all four disciplines. Ten years from now, we expect business modelers will know and use all four disciplines.

We expect model simulation to go mainstream as well. Model simulation is a niche activity today. In our experience, fewer than 5 percent of all business process models are simulated today, and certainly fewer than 1 percent of all business motivation models are simulated. But simulation is becoming more popular, and we expect that trend to continue. Ten years from now, we expect most business process models and most business motivation models will be simulated. Companies and government agencies will routinely create business simulations to analyze new situations and to persuade their stakeholders and clients to undertake the right course of action.

Direct execution is poised to go mainstream as well. Direct execution promises the best approach for business model execution because the models can be easily changed to support changes to the business. As the tooling matures and direct execution becomes more widely understood, it will become the most common method of executing a business model. Ten years from now we expect direct execution to be the usual manner of executing a business model, with manual execution and packaged execution only practiced occasionally, in exceptional situations.

All this growth and mainstreaming makes today an exciting time for business modelers. There is much new opportunity for people who understand business modeling, and there are many new uses of business modeling for modelers to explore. But of course there are risks. As we have explained throughout this book, business modeling should never be practiced for its own sake. Business models should only be built and used when their use is justified by the economics. Only by keeping an eye on the practical value of your business model can you ensure that you build a model that is more valuable than the effort it takes to create it.

Business models can be executed. A business model can be executed manually, used as requirements for software development. A business model can be executed directly, run as software in an engine. Or a business model can be used to configure a packaged application. Direct execution is in many ways the most promising way to execute a business model, but it has limitations. Today, only business process models and business rule models can be executed directly.

A business process model can be directly executed in a BPMS. A BPMS supports the routing of business process jobs from activity to activity, from the person performing one activity to the person performing the next and from one user interface page to the next. But a BPMS implementation can be a radical step for an organization. A BAM implementation is a more conservative approach, monitoring a process as it is currently, supported by several legacy applications.

Bibliography

[Avery 2001] Avery, Christopher M., *Teamwork Is an Individual Skill: Getting Your Work Done When Sharing Responsibility*, 2001, Berrett-Koehler Publishers, San Francisco.

[Bartlett 1904] Bartlett, John, *Familiar Quotations: A Collection of Passages, Phrases, and Proverbs Traced to Their Sources in Ancient and Modern Literature*, 1904, University Press, Cambridge.

[Beck 1999] Beck, Kent, *Extreme Programming Explained: Embrace Change,* 1999, Addison-Wesley Professional, Boston.

[Brown 1998] Brown, William J., Malveau, Raphael C., McCormick, Hays W. III, and Mowbray, Thomas J., *AntiPatterns: Refactoring Software, Architectures, and Projects in Crisis*, 1998, John Wiley & Sons, New York.

[Cockburn 2001] Cockburn, Alistair, *Agile Software Development*, 2001, Addison-Wesley Professional, Boston.

[Conklin 2006] Conklin, Jeff, *Dialogue Mapping: Building Shared Understanding of Wicked Problems*, 2006, John Wiley & Sons, Chichester, UK.

[Date 2000] Date, C. J., *What, Not How: The Business Rules Approach to Application Development*, 2000, Addison-Wesley, Boston.

[DePamphilis 2003] DePamphilis, Donald M., *Mergers, Acquisitions, and Other Restructuring Activities: An Integrated Approach to Process, Tools, Cases, and Solutions*, 2003, Academic Press, San Diego.

[Eriksson 2000] Eriksson, Hans-Erik and Penker, Magnus, *Business Modeling with UML: Business Patterns at Work*, 2000, John Wiley & Sons, New York.

[Fogg 2003] Fogg, B. J., *Persuasive Technology: Using Computers to Change What We Think and Do*, 2003, Morgan Kaufmann, San Francisco.

[Fowler 1999] Fowler, Martin, *Refactoring: Improving the Design of Existing Code*, 1999, Addison-Wesley, Boston.

[Fowler 2003] Fowler, Martin, *Patterns of Enterprise Application Architecture*, 2003, Addison Wesley; Boston.

[Gardner 2004] Gardner, Howard, *Changing Minds: The Art and Science of Changing Our Own and Other People's Minds*, 2004, Harvard Business School Press, Cambridge.

[Halpin 2001] Halpin, Terry, *Information Modeling and Relational Databases: From Conceptual Design to Logical Design*, 2001, Morgan Kaufmann Publishers, San Francisco.

[Harmon 2003] Harmon, Paul, *Business Process Change: A Manager's Guide to Improving, Redesigning, and Automating Processes*, 2003, Morgan Kaufmann Publishers; San Francisco.

[Havey 2005] Havey, Michael, *Essential Business Process Modeling*, 2005, O'Reilly, Sebastopol, CA.

[Larman 2003] Larman, Craig, *Agile and Iterative Development: A Manager's Guide*, 2003, Addison-Wesley Professional, Boston.

[Law 2006] Law, Averill, *Simulation Modeling and Analysis, 4th edition,* 2006, McGraw-Hill, New York.

[Mayer 1997] Mayer, Martin *The Bankers: The Next Generation*, 1997, Truman Talley Books, New York.

[Miller 1956] Miller, George A., "The Magical Number Seven, Plus or Minus Two: Some Limits on Our Capacity for Processing Information," 1956, *Psychological Review*, 63, 81-97.

[Mintzberg 1998] Mintzberg, Henry, Lampel, Joseph, and Ahlstrand, Bruce, *Strategy Safari: A Guided Tour Through the Wilds of Strategic Management*, 1998, Free Press, New York.

[Moore 1991] Moore, Geoffrey A., *Crossing the Chasm*, Harper Collins, New York.

[Morgan 2002] Morgan, Tony, *Business Rules and Information Systems: Aligning IT with Business Goals*, 2002, Addison-Wesley, Boston.

[Norman 2004] Norman, Donald A., *Emotional Design: Why We Love (or Hate) Everyday Things*, 2004, Basic Books, New York.

[OMG] Object Management Group, *Business Process Definition Metamodel (BPDM)* working draft, www.omg.org/BPDM/1.0/Beta1/PDF, Needham, MA.

[OMG 2007] Object Management Group, *Business Motivation Model (BMM)*, www.omg.org/docs/dtc/07-08-03.pdf, 2007, Needham, MA.

[OMG 2008] Object Management Group, *Semantics of Business Vocabulary and Rules (SBVR) 1.0*, www.omg.org/spec/SBVR/1.0/PDF, 2008, Needham, MA.

[OMG 2008b] Object Management Group, *Business Process Modeling Notation*, V1.1, 2008, www.omg.org/spec/BPMN/1.1/PDF, Needham, MA.

[Ould 2005] Ould, Martyn A., *Business Process Management: A Rigorous Approach*, 2005, British Computer Society, Swindon, UK.

[Ross 2003] Ross, Ronald G., *Principles of the Business Rule Approach*, 2003, Addison-Wesley, Boston.

[Ross, 2005] Ross, Ronald G., *Business Rules Concepts: Getting to the Point of Knowledge*, 2nd edition, 2005, Business Rules Solutions, Houston.

[Rummler and Brache 1995] Rummler, Geary A., and Brache, Alan P., *Improving Performance*, 1995, John Wiley & Sons, San Francisco.

[Schwartz 1994] Schwartz, Roger M., *The Skilled Facilitator: Practical Wisdom for Developing Effective Groups*, 1994, Jossey-Bass Publishers, San Francisco.

[Senge 1990] Senge, Peter, *The Fifth Discipline: The Art and Practice of the Learning Organization*, 1990, Doubleday, New York.

[Sharp 2001] Sharp, Alec, and McDermott, Patrick, *Workflow Modeling: Tools for Process Improvement and Application Development*, 2001, Artech House, Boston.

[Sterman 2000] Sterman, John, *Business Dynamics: Systems Thinking and Modeling for a Complex World*, 2000, Irwin Professional Publishing, New York.

[Tolstoy 2000] Tolstoy, Leo, translated by Pevear, Richard, and Volokhonsky, Larissa, *Anna Karenina*, 2000, Penguin, New York.

[van der Aalst 2002] van der Aalst, Wil, and van Hee, Kees, *Workflow Management: Models, Methods, and Systems*, 2002, MIT Press, Cambridge.

[Welborn 2006] Welborn, Ralph, and Kasten, Vincent, *Business Processes.... Where Business and Technology Meet: Get It Done!* 2006, John Wiley & Sons, New Jersey.

A

Activity, 105, 177–179
  attributes, 107–108
  resource, 107
Acquisition analysis, 285–289
Actuators, 64–65
Aesthetics, 27, 30–31
Application program interfaces (API),
    31, 372
As-is and to-be processess, 126–128.
    see also Business process models
Associations, 93–95
  part of, 46, 80, 84
  influences, 92–93
  interacts with, 88–92
  reports to, 84–86
Attractive business process
    model, 28

B

Best practices
  descriptions, 47
  impossibility statements, 154
  interactions, 92
  necessity statements, 153
  obligation statements, 148
  organization models, 95–97
  overly large and complex, 63
  picking business rules forms, 155
  prohibitive statements, 150
  restricted permissive statement, 151
  restricted possibility statement, 155
  solely software activities, 108
Black Box, 125–126
Bulldog, 252

Business continuity workshop,
    227–228
Business motivations and processes,
    128–129
Business transformations, 5–6
Business activity monitoring (BAM),
    372–374
  and execution, 373
  process improvement, 373–374
Business modeling, xi, 2
  ascend, 2–4
  attractive models, appeal of, 27–29
  business transformations and, 5–6
  deployment engine, 36
  enterprise architecture, 38–40
  fundamentals
    accounting, 24–25
    classic business model, 21–22
    fidelity of, 19–20
    validity of, 20–21
  generating business value, ways of,
      10–16
  IDEF family of languages, 26
  income statement, 23
  lifecycle of, 345–347
  managing change and, 6–7
  maturity and, 24–25
  motivation models with, 27
  organizational
    changes, 6–7
    complexity, 7–10
    dynamic and detail complexity,
        9–10
  project scope, 12
    conception phase, 219